Sarah Barnwell Elliott

Jerry

A novel

Sarah Barnwell Elliott

Jerry
A novel

ISBN/EAN: 9783742892393

Manufactured in Europe, USA, Canada, Australia, Japa

Cover: Foto ©Thomas Meinert / pixelio.de

Manufactured and distributed by brebook publishing software
(www.brebook.com)

Sarah Barnwell Elliott

Jerry

JERRY

A NOVEL

BY

SARAH BARNWELL ELLIOTT

"In the awful mystery of human life, it is a consolation sometimes to believe that our mistakes, perhaps even our sins, are permitted to be instruments of our education for immortality."

NEW YORK

HENRY HOLT AND COMPANY

1891

PART FIRST.

" 'You know very well that every human being has his tree of life, or his flower of life, just as each is arranged. They look like other plants, but their hearts beat. Children's hearts can beat too. Think of this. Perhaps you may recognize the beating of your child's heart.' And then they went into the great hot-house of Death, where flowers and trees were growing, and marvelously intertwined. There stood the fine hyacinths under glass bells, some quite fresh, others somewhat sickly. There stood gallant palm-trees, oaks, and plantains, and parsley, and blooming thyme. Each tree and flower had its name; each was a human life. There were great trees thrust into little pots, so that they stood quite crowded, and were nearly bursting the pots; there was also many a little weakly flower in rich earth, with moss around it, cared for and tended. But the sorrowful mother bent over all the smallest plants, and heard the human heart beating in each, and out of millions she recognized that of her child.

" 'That is it!' she cried, and stretched out her hands over a little crocus flower, which hung down quite sick and pale."

JERRY.

CHAPTER I.

> " Alone, and empty-handed in this world
> Where loves and hopes lie thick as Heaven's stars."

HE sat in the doorway with his elbows on his knees, and his chin in his dirty little hands. His yellow face was expressionless almost; and his thin, straight lips looked as if they could never have smiled or laughed as a child's lips should. A tired face with all the lines set as in the countenance of an old person; a stolid face that gave small sign of heart, or mind, or soul.

Motionless he sat with the spring sun sending a thousand flickering lights about him, and cutting his shadow sharp and black on the block of light in the doorway.

Behind him, a clay-daubed log-house; before him, a barren, rain-gullied yard,—a broken rail-fence, and a few poor apple-trees that seemed ashamed of the meager blossoms they could show. A rickety grindstone stood at the corner of the house where the mud chimney jutted out,—an axe stuck in a log near the wood-pile,—one lean, straight-tailed hog rooted in a corner of the fence.

In all his life the child had never looked on any other scene,—had never lost sight of the smoke from that poor chimney. Now he rose slowly, pulling up his ragged trowsers.

"I'm agoin'," he said at last, looking straight before him, "it aint no use; I can't git to see you no mo', and you telled me as it wornt much, for you wuz agoin' to the 'Golding Gates,' not much fur," and putting his hands in his pockets, he walked away slowly down a well-worn path to where a spring made a still, clear pool in the gray rocks. He paused here a moment to drink out of a sun-bleached gourd that lay on a ledge, then passed beyond to where in a corner of the fence there was a grave. Some rails had been laid about the off-side of this grave; but only to an insignificant height this extra fence had reached, as if the strength that built it were not equal to the task.

The child stood and looked; his expression did not change; no special feeling seemed to stir within him; but at last the straight lips parted, and he spoke to the grave as he had spoken to himself up at the house. "I'm agoin', Mammy," he said, "it aint no use; Dad he beats me, an' Minervy Ann Salter's done come to live, an' las' night her beat me too; it aint no use. I aint took much rails," he went on, "an' mebbe Dad'll lettum stay; mebbe he'll furgit you're down here if I kivver you good; mebbe he'll furgit," and without haste or excitement he climbed over the outer fence to reach a brush-heap which was there.

"I'll kivver you good," he repeated, and dropped the brush piece by piece over the fence on to the grave; then beyond he picked a long branch of blackberry blossoms.

Gravely he scanned from end to end the blooming brier; he recrossed the fence, and stood once more by the grave; again the sharp little voice broke the stillness. "You wuz powerful proud of blossoms, Mammy," he said, "an' I'll lay 'em thar; but I'm agoin'; I can't git to see you, but dad can't nuther, can't beat you no mo'; an' mebbe," nodding his head slowly, "mebbe he'll furgit them rails."

His task was done, and he stood slouching like an old man; his shoulders rounded forward; his hands in his pockets, and his bare feet drawn close together.

The poor grave had become a brush-heap, with the long spray of snowy blossoms on the top; and the stolen rails were covered.

"Mebbe he'll furgit them rails," and he turned away toward the house,

Straight up the path to the house, and in at the door; there he paused and looked about him. In one corner a bed; in another the pile of straw where the child slept,—the broad, broken fireplace where stones served for andirons,—the cracked dutch-oven,—the frying-pan, and battered coffee-pot,—the few tin plates and cups—the splint-bottomed chairs—the string of red peppers over the chimney; all these things that had been always about his little life, he was about to leave. He drew his dirty shirt-sleeve across his nose, pausing in the act as his eyes in their survey reached a dark corner of the house; he walked over to the spot. A faded, blue homespun apron hung there; he eyed it gravely, then touched it softly.

"It's your'n, Mammy," he whispered, "it aint Minervy Ann Salter's; her aint never so much as teched it,—it's been a-hangin' thar ever sense dad knocked youuns over; dad aint agoin' to 'member it," and while he spoke he drew himself up by the uneven logs until he reached the peg where the apron hung. Once more on the floor with his prize in his hands, he looked it over with a gleam of recognition in his eyes as if every smirch upon it had some association for him; then rolled it up with clumsy carefulness, wrapping some straw about it to make it fast.

"It aint Minervy Ann Salter's," he said decisively, "it's Mammy's, sure*ly*," and he turned and left the house.

A road passed by the old rail-fence, turning down

the hillside ; a rough, red clay road where the winter's ruts had hardened into shape under the spring sun ; with here and there a well-worn stump garnishing its ugly length, or the rounded shoulder of some mighty buried cliff making a few smooth steps. On either side the woods crept up so close that the roots of the trees were travel-worn, and much bark was missing from the trunks at the usual height of the wheel-hubs. A lonely, desolate road lying like a long red gash cut on the face of the world as God had left it,—the only mark that man had made.

The child paused as he climbed the fence, paused astride the top rail, and hitched the strings that answered for braces a little higher on his shoulders, then turned the straw-wrapped bundle over slowly in his hands.

"It aint no use," he repeated once again, as if at the last some memory laid faint hold upon him, "it aint no use, mammy," he whispered, "an' I've done kivvered youuns good,—rale good," almost pleadingly, "good as I could." One moment more he paused, then climbed down to the rough road, and turned away resolutely from all the landmarks of his little life. If he realized at all the step he was about to take,—if he had any fear of the world or the treatment he would meet with there,—if he felt any sorrow for the ties he was breaking, he gave no sign more than the pause as he crossed the fence. What had roused him now seemed more than he could bear, and so he went away.

The road grew more and more rough as it descended the hills ; the rocks more frequent and more scarred and scraped by brake-locked wheels ; the trees were taller and bent in more various directions as they had to find more unequal rootage among the rocks. Tall, shining poplars ; broad-leaved chestnuts ; slim, gaunt oaks that had no room to spread, and from tree to tree rank vines—wild grapes and briars that made an impassable barrier on either side.

Straight on the child walked; not picking his way, nor avoiding rock, nor root, nor mudhole; straight on, neither fast nor slow, looking neither to the right nor to the left. His little bundle close under one arm; his hands in his pockets; his hat crammed well down on his head, so that his colorless hair, creeping through a hole in the crown, could scarcely be distinguished from the equally colorless felt.

Down, down the road wound, with sometimes a level sweep—sometimes a slight rise that showed it was not taking the most direct route toward the valley: still, it made toward the valley: the ruts deepening into gullies,—the woods becoming more and more dense,—the rocks changing from yellow to a pale gray,—the clay shading to a more sanguinary hue that prophetically stained the feet of the child e'er the first day of his wandering was done. The noonday sun looked straight down on the rough road and the human mite that followed it, then slowly sank down the western sky: the shadows blackened in the woods; the rocks and the stems of the trees took on weird shapes; the wind rose and fell, dying far away up the hillside.

The child walked on: the shadows and the gathering darkness did not seem to disturb him: on between the black woods, with the narrow strip of sky above him turning slowly from blue to violet, where presently the watchful stars would shine and flicker in their places.

The road broadened, and a fence stood sharply defined against the sky; a section of fence that seemed to run along the brow of a hill.

The child paused, then went on more slowly: where was he, and who lived here?

Gradually the road rose until it reached the fence, then both dipped abruptly, and before him, in a little basin-like hollow, a light shone.

He stopped again, as if for consideration, then approached cautiously, over the fence and through a field where the belted dead trees stood up like gaunt specters against the sky.

Nearer and nearer the child crept, pausing every few moments to make observations, until he was so near that the fire, shining all over the one room of the house, showed him quite plainly the faces gathered about it, and striking out through the open door made a broad path of light across the field.

"I aint never sawn them folks," he said softly to himself, "them aint never been up our way." Again he looked to make quite sure, when suddenly there came the sharp bark of a dog that dashed out at him, and a woman following quickly made retreat hopeless.

"Who's thar!" she called out; then to the dog, "Hold yer mouth, Buck, consarn yer!" and a troop of children coming to the front, the boy was discovered. He stood quite still, a black shadow in the stream of light, his hands in his pockets,—the little bundle close under one arm, and his yellow face, all drawn and haggard from hunger and fatigue, turned up to meet the eyes of the woman.

"Mussy me!" she said, kicking the small dog aside, and taking a snuff-stick from her mouth, "whar's you come from?"

"No whars," the child answered, looking furtively in the direction of the fence as if bent on retreat.

"No whars," the woman repeated, setting her arms akimbo, and again kicking the small dog over, "that's a rale likely tale; whar's youuns' mar?"

The child paused a moment as if thinking, then said slowly:

"I dunno."

"Yer dunno?" raising her voice; "I 'llow thet's a peart look-out fer sense: well, where's youuns' par?"

"Over yon," pointing to the hills that loomed above them.

"Thet's more like now," a little satisfaction coming into her voice; "an' whar mout you be agoin'?"

"Over yon," pointing to the west, where the yellow light still lingered in the far, day-faithful horizon.

"Thet's rale sensible," sarcastically; "I reckon you've about telled all youuns knows, aint yer?"

"I reckon," humbly.

"Jest so; I reckon yer have, ceppen youuns' name; is you got any of thet?"

"Jerry."

"Jerry," the woman repeated, and looking him over from head to foot, laid her hand on his shoulder; not roughly, yet a shiver ran over the child's thin little body, and his tired eyes flickered in their upward look.

"Lord-er-mussy, chile!" and she gave him a little shake, "thar aint no use a-trimlin' an' a-jumpin', I aint agoin' to knock you;—looks like you is usen to beatin'."

"I is," stolidly.

"An' I 'llows thet you is runned away," putting her head on one side with a knowing look, "aint thet so?"

There was a pause, then a quick gasp as the child's voice, grown suddenly sharper, broke the silence. "Does you know Minervy Ann Salter?" fearfully.

"No."

A sigh of relief came from the boy.

"Her's a great, big woman," he said meditatively, "an' her knocked me deef an' bline, her did, an' I runned away."

"Well, I never! jest alisten, Delithy," to a younger woman who had joined the group.

"I hearn," Delithy answered, taking out a piece of straight comb that held up the knot of sandy hair on the back of her head, to comb it straight back from each side the ragged part, and screw it up again, "I hearn; but aint her no kin to youuns?"

"Minervy Ann?" the boy asked with some scorn, "no!"

Then inside the house a baby began to cry, and the women turned simultaneously.

"I reckon you kin come in, Jerry," the elder woman said, and the child followed her.

Tired and stiff and hungry, the fire, and the smell of something that was cooking on the hearth, made the lines of the child's face relax, and sent a gleam of light into his hopeless eyes. All that long spring day he had walked without a stop for rest, and nothing had passed his lips since he drank from the still pool near the brush-heaped grave. Now he squatted at the corner of the wide chimney and watched intently the coarse corn bread that was baking in a spider over the coals.

"Youuns looks powerful hungry," Delithy remarked, when the baby being hushed and the children settled in a convenient staring distance of the new-comer, silence reigned,—"how long sence youuns had wittles?"

"I aint had a bite sence mornin'," not moving his eyes from the bread.

"An' been a-runnin' all day?"

"I were feared to run," he said, "I were feared I'd give out."

"Well, I reckon you jest would."

"Kin I have a *leetle* bite?" the boy went on, pointing to the bread, but not moving his eyes from it; "I'll chop wood for it."

Delithy moved her snuff-stick thoughtfully across her big white teeth, eyeing the boy the while.

"An' I'll tote water," was added by the sharp little voice to the pitiful bargain; he was so hungry.

"Youuns seem usen to work," Delithy remarked.

"I reckon I is," thoughtfully, "kin I have it?"

"It's Jake's bread," she answered slowly, watching the boy intently as with a dull satisfaction in his longing that was with her a form of humor.

"Well, Jake aint a-comin' this night," the elder woman put in, returning from where she had deposited the baby on the bed, "an' I reckon Louwisy Dyer is able to give a bite of bread 'thout tradin'; I 'low 'twont hurt, though, to tote a leetle water," stooping over the bread. "Youuns is sure 'bout it?"

"I is," and for the first time that day the little bundle dropped from under the boy's arm, and both hands were stretched out, "jest sure,"—then further utterance was stopped by the bread.

"Fur all the world like a hongry dorg," Delithy said, after some thought, "I never seen ther like," and again she combed and put in place her sandy locks.

Then in a tin-cup the elder woman gave Jerry some cold coffee, and told him where in the loft he could sleep on some fodder.

And the child crept away up the ladder, and quickly fell asleep with his bundle safe inside of his shirt.

"'Cause it might git lost in ther fodder," he said.

CHAPTER II.

> "But the child's sob in the silence curses deeper
> Than the strong man in his wrath."

"THAR'S Jake an' a man alonger him."

Toiling up from the spring with two buckets of water, Jerry heard the words and stopped. The midday meal was over, and still Jerry had not gone away from this first resting-place; dinner and breakfast had been added to his obligations; but it was not this so much that held him, as that he was weary,—weary of his little life,—weary from the tramp of the day before, and loath, moreover, to leave the unwonted kindness of these pitying women. And now he was bringing water for Delithy's washing. "A man alonger him," the words rang in his ears: who was it? Fear made him cautious, and leaving the buckets he crept on his hands and knees to where he could see this man.

Across the field between the dead trees, blackly silhouetted against the golden glory of the western sky, he saw them coming; two long, thin, slouching mountaineers, walking with the uneven regularity of men who followed the plow. He cowered, trembled, shrank, with his face bleaching to a deathly gray; his eyes grew wide and bright with terror,—his chin dropped, he seemed as one paralyzed.

"Dad!" he whispered, then all was still.

Nearer they came across the dreary field: Delithy paused over her tub; the elder woman stood in the doorway; the children gazed open-mouthed; and through a bunch of maple bushes whose young spring leaves glowed red in the sun-light, two glittering, fear-charmed eyes were watching.

Then Jake's voice:

"Hardy, gals, hardy; I'm back."

"I reckon I'se got eyes, Jake Dyer," the elder woman answered, "an' yeers too, fur all yer holler like I'm deef."

"Aint youuns deef, Louwisy?" jocularly, "don't say!"

"No, I aint deef," then to the stranger, "good evenin'."

"Mister Bill Wilkerson," Jake went on, "I makes yer knowed to Mis Louwisy Dyer, my old woman: an' Mis Louwisy Dyer, I make yer knowed to Mister Bill Wilkerson; likewise Miss Delithy Suggs," and Jake bowed with a flourish.

Delithy nodding, said, "Evenin'," to her new acquaintance; then she added with calm and complacent certainty:

"Youuns is drunk, Jake Dyer."

"No, I aint drunk nuther," Jake retorted, but with no sign of anger, "an' Mister Wilkerson aint drunk nuther; but he's done lost hisn's boy, he has."

The women looked at each other, and the children looked at the women.

"Weuns went to meetin' yisterday," Mr. Wilkenson began, "an' w'en weuns come home Jerry, my boy, he were a-missin'; an' he must a come this road, fur t'other road 'ud tuck him to meetin'."

"An' no folks over thar sawn him," Jake put in, "an' as Mister Wilkerson were made knowed to me by Preacher Dunner, I tole him to come alonger me an' hunt fur thet boy."

Still the women did not speak, and the children gazed stolidly in their faces, until Wilkerson, looking from one to the other, said:

"Have youuns sawn him?"

"Yes, weuns *have* sawn him," Delithy answered sharply, returning vigorously to her washing, "he tuck a bite here last night; but he's plum gone now, he is."

"Thet's so," Louwisy added with earnestness, and the children stared in silence.

"Well, thet jest beats me!" Wilkerson said slowly, pushing his hat a little further back on his head, "I never hearn ther like; he's jest a-spilin' fur a beatin', Jerry is."

"I 'llowed from ther looks of him as he were a-spilin' fur wittles," and Delithy, shaking the suds from her hands, took up a bucket and went toward the spring, leaving her parting shot to do what work it could.

Only a little way down the steep path, then she stopped, for on either side stood two buckets full of water.

"Pore creetur!" she muttered, looking about her hastily as she poured the water out, "he couldn't tuck much mo' beatin'," and hiding the buckets in the bushes, fearing that Wilkerson might search, she went on her way.

Straight on through the black night the child walked; down, down, and the early dawn found him in the valley, with the grim, flat-topped old Cumberland mountains lying behind him like huge sleeping creatures, showing black against the eastern sky. All night long he walked; from the time when Jake's voice broke the spell that held him still behind the maple bushes.

He had not paused for brake nor brier, until by a long detour he reached the road; then once more he had followed it without deviation, over rocks and stumps, and unseen gullies; often falling; often his terror had bidden him run, but while never stopping, he never ran. Sore and bruised, and weak with hunger, he still pushed on, with always the thought that his father might come on him in the darkness without warning; in the gray dawn of the growing day he had looked back to the lessening hills, while the new thought came to him:

"Dad mout git a nag an' ketch me yit!"

The fields that had shown green and fresh about him as the darkness lifted ; the rail-fences that had loomed like long rows of skeleton ribs, jagged and twisting on either side the road--endless fences that seemed to wind and crawl for ever by him as he walked—were with him still ; and still the road lay straight and red as blood before him, until the color had grown into his eyes, staining wherever he looked.

He was afraid, deadly afraid of stopping ; but at last he had been obliged to pause at a house and beg for food, and in her way the woman had been kind to him.

"Youuns misewell stop an' rest," she had said, looking him over almost contemptuously; "nobody ain't a-runnin' atter sicher splinter as you nohow ; an' I 'llow 'twouldn't be no satisfaxion a-knockin' you nuther."

But Jerry had resisted with patient persistence. "Gimme in my han's," he pleaded, "an' I kin eat while I'm a-walkin' ;" then he had added persuasively, "an' when I gits a chence, I'll come back an' chop youuns' wood, I will."

The woman had looked keenly into the wistful eyes before she parted with the bread ; but then she had given it all.

"I b'lieve youuns is honest," she had said, "I b'lieve it sure ; but yer'll never git no chence ceppen to lay down an' be planted afore many days."

The child took the bread with a look of wonder growing in his eyes that were fastened on the woman's face.

"Planted ?" he had repeated slowly as to himself, "planted !" and he had turned away without another word ; had walked slowly but steadily down the long red road, and as he munched the hard corn-bread had said over and over again to himself, "Planted—planted."

This had been hours ago in the early morning, and now in the noonday brightness the child, still plodding on his way, had but the one thought—"Thet's what Dad done to youuns, Mammy; you said yer were agoin' over yander to ther 'Golding Gates,' not much fur, you said; an' thet's what Dad done, he planted youuns so yer couldn't go." On and on through the gathering heat he walked, with this one thought repeating itself over and over again in his mind,—"thet's what Dad done,"—at last it was too strong for him, and he stopped in his going; for a new fact had come home to him. He stood quite still for a moment while his little face blanched, and a look of longing—untold, bitter longing, came into his eyes as he turned them to the fading hills.

"An' I hepped 'im!" he cried aloud to the empty fields and sky,—"I hepped 'im, I piled ther bresh thar! Oh, Mammy, I never knowed—I never knowed!" and down on the hard red road he cast himself, sobbing as if his heart would break. And always the burden of his cry, "I never knowed, Mammy, I never knowed!"

Presently the sobs died away, and lying there dull with grief, the sound of a horse's hoofs struck on his ear. For one second he listened too terrified to move, then sprang up: it was a man on horseback, and coming from the direction of the mountains! One frightened glance,—one instant's blindness, then down the road he sped as fast as his feet could carry him,—straight on and on like a hunted animal fleeing for its life.

Would the fences never end—would the road lie between those level fields forever—was the man coming any faster—would he catch him? A terrified look over his shoulder: the horse was trotting smartly; there was no hope, and a voice hailed him—"Stop!"

He tried so hard to run a little faster, but it was no use, his breath seemed to fail, and once more he fell prone in the dust. One moment, then the horse stopped beside him, and a voice broke on his ear—

"Git up."

But he could neither speak nor move, he could not even distinguish if it were his father's voice.

"What ails yer?" and he was lifted by the arm after a kindly fashion, and above him he saw a rough old face that was unknown to him.

"What *air* youuns skeered about?"

Jerry's voice came back to him now with a long, sobbing breath.

"I were feared," he faltered, "feared youuns'd ketch me."

"An' I *have*," the old man answered simply, "but I aint agoin' to hurt yer: whar air yer agoin' to?"

"Over yon," pointing as always to the west.

"Well, yer'll never git thar if yer try runnin'," the old man went on with clear common sense, "but git up, an' I'll tote youuns a piece."

The child looked up: the poor little face was smeared now with tears and dust in addition to its usual yellowness, but in the eyes was the same wistful look that had made Delithy put his father off the track; that had made the woman feed him that morning, and that now made the rough old countryman lift him on the raw-boned horse that waited so patiently for his double load.

"Tuck a good grip," the old man said kindly, as he settled himself in the saddle, "youuns kin hold on good, I'm solid; but you looks powerful weakly an' small to be so fur off?" he went on interrogatively, "you're about five miles from anywhars: what mout be youuns' name?"

"Jerry," the child answered from where he leaned against the broad back of the brown jeans coat.

"Jeremiah, I reckon," the old man went on in a superior tone.

"Mammy usen to call me 'Miah,'" came with a little catch in the voice, "but I'se mostly called Jerry."

"Jest so, but it stan's to reason as youuns' name is Jeremiah: now what mout be ther balance of youuns' name?" in a still more persuasive voice.

"Does you know Minervy Ann Salter?" came irrelevantly from the child.

"I can't say as I rickerlec' any sicher name," was answered.

"Well, my name is Wilkerson, sense you dunno Minervy Ann."

"Jeremiah Wilkerson," the old man repeated, "is thar any mo' to it?"

"I dunno rightly," Jerry answered, "but Dad 'llowed thar were a P. in it som'ers."

"A P.; well, I reckon it were Jeremiah P. Wilkerson; thet sounds right peart."

"It do so," and the little voice had a ring of pride and pleasure in it, "I reckon thet were it, Jeremiah P. Wilkerson, it soun's rayly purty."

"An' youuns' par, what were hisn's name?" the old man went on, pleased with his success, his husky voice jolting out in time to the jog-trot of the horse.

"Bill," and at the awful name the child gave a frightened look behind; "can't weuns git on a *leetle* faster?" he asked anxiously, "I'm feared."

"Feared?" his new friend repeated, pulling the horse to a sudden stop, "thet's cur'us sure!"

"I'm feared of Dad," Jerry explained hastily, "I'm feared he'll git me agin; an' if youuns ain't agoin' no further, I'll 'light an' walk," trying to look round the broad back that obscured his view of everything.

The man thought a moment in silence, then again urged his beast into the slow trot that seemed its normal pace.

"I'm agoin' further, Jeremiah, an' I'll have a leetle talkin' alonger youuns," was answered meditatively, then with much condescension—"I'm a preacher, Jeremiah; I'm Preacher Babbit, I am," pausing that this announcement might have full effect; "an' I'll not be far from ther mark if I say you is a-runnin' away; now aint yer?" pausing, "aint you a-runnin' off from youuns' dear par, William Wilkerson, an' youuns' pore mar; aint yer?"

There was a moment's silence after this unexpected attack; then with a new hard tone in his voice the child answered:

"Mammy ain't thar no mo', an' Minervy Ann Salter's done come thar to live, an' her knocked me deef an' bline, an' I runned away."

"I reckon youuns' par done married agin, Jeremiah; ain't thet so?" coaxingly.

"I dunno," came sullenly, "but I hates 'em, I do."

"No, Jeremiah," and Preacher Babbit cleared his throat, and stroked the fringe of beard under his chin in a way that would have shown a less ignorant person than Jerry that a lecture was coming—"ther Holy Scripter says as leetle boys mustn't hate their pars," he began slowly, "an' you mustn't nuther; thar's nothin' good as comes of leetle boys hatin' their pars, an' you mustn't do it, Jeremiah. Now, I'm agoin' to hold a meetin' down these ways to-morrer, an' mebbe youuns dear par'll come, and he'll furgive you, an' tuck you home again: ther par in ther Testy*ment* did: now, Jeremiah, jest think of thet!" and Preacher Babbit made a well-meant effort to turn his face over his fat shoulder so as to bestow a look of encouragement on his little companion.

But Jerry had no thought for him, instead was looking eagerly from one side of the road to the other. They had come a long distance in the slow jog-trot, and now were in the woods again, with the evening closing in on them. Everything was in Jerry's favor, and in an instant he had slipped off the horse's tail, and lay sprawling in the road; but only for a second he lay there, then was up and off, speeding blindly through the thick woods. In vain the worthy preacher called; the child would not hear: a dreadful suggestion had been made to him; a prayer-meeting was to held, and his father might be there. No thought of distance came to reassure him; no thought at all was with him, only the dread conviction that his father would be at the meeting; for his father always went to meetings.

No persuasions could call him back to that dreadful possibility. He fled until the old man's voice faded from his hearing, then he sat down to rest; but not for long, and through the night he wandered as he had done the night before. Once he lay down, but in the stillness his terror increased, and with it the dull pain that had been with him ever since the woman's unconsciously cruel words had forced their way into his mind, and with them the pitiful conviction that he had aided his father in the deed that had shut his only friend away from him. Living in the heart of the Cumberland Mountains, whose heights he had never before left, his ignorance was dense, and to him things were strangely mingled and perverted. The thought that he might go back and pull away the brush he had piled over his mother, and so undo his share in the work that had imprisoned her, had not yet occurred to him. He was not accustomed to thinking, and, until lately, little accustomed to feeling anything save hunger, and cold, and blows. But now a great awakening was on him; a great loneliness held him; a great loneliness that had been with him ever since the one soul that loved him had been put away from him in a mysterious manner that he had not understood until now; and now the awful conviction was with him that he had helped to shut his mother up in the earth.

So he could not stop to rest, for he would begin to cry again, and crying made him feel so sick and weak. Very, very tired he was when at last the day dawned, and he found himself in a long, straight clearing that extended as far as he could see: a clearing like a roadway, only up and down the center were beams of wood, and across them long shining pieces of iron. He stopped and looked at it; it must be some kind of road; but a new kind he had never before seen.

He climbed the slight embankment on which it was,

and stood looking wonderingly up and down; then with his back to the rising sun, he followed slowly this new kind of road. He was weak and tired, and the stepping from beam to beam confused him so much, that it took all his attention to step just the right distance, and not to fall. Carefully he made his way until something caused him to look up, when he found himself in a straggling line of small houses.

He paused and turned about, for the moment forgetting all his ills in the wonder called forth.

"Lotser folks must live here," he muttered, "an' I knows dad aint never seen it, 'cause I aint never hearn him tell nuthin' 'bout it, I never did sure!" and with his hands in his pockets he stood regarding the houses about him. Presently he saw a curl of smoke come from a chimney, and watched a woman as she slowly opened a door, then a window; then he went nearer, for he was too hungry to pause for consideration.

Slowly he approached the house that he had just seen opened, and leaning against the open door said stolidly:

"I'm honggry."

The woman turned quickly, and her eyes opened wide as they rested on the ragged, starved specimen of humanity confronting her.

"Mussy, but you're a rough 'un!" she said, scanning Jerry without seeming to heed his words until he repeated slowly:

"I'm honggry, gimme a bite of sumpen?"

"Most folks works fur their wittles," was the ungracious reply.

"I kin work too," the child persisted, "but I'm plum wore out now, I is," and he sat down slowly on the step. The widow Perkins paused before further words of harshness to watch the child's movements, which had been made assured by the kindly treatment he had met with in his wanderings through the unopened regions from which he had come: and while she watched, the thought came to her, suppose he was one of a gang of tramps sent ahead to "spy out the land," —suppose if she refused him what he asked, he should bring the whole company down on her, a lone widow! She had read of such things in the papers. And she stared at the child with a growing anxiety in her eyes as she asked quickly:

"Will you git away if I give you some wittles?"

Jerry looked up slowly.

"Don't you warnt me to tote no water for youuns when I gits rested?" he asked innocently.

The woman's silly fears having once taken hold of her, grew with every word the child uttered: he was surely a "spyer," and she must persuade him to go away.

"You're too little," she said kindly, "I couldn't abear to see you workin'."

Jerry listened in wonder: yesterday a woman had fed him; but she had expected him to work for her in the future, so he thought; but this woman was a new experience, and would not let him work at all.

"Here's bread an' meat, child, an' some good hot coffee," she went on, handing him a plate and cup, "an' when you're through, I'll give you more to take along." Jerry looked up at her with his wistful eyes full of wonder; but he had no words. His life had been one strictly of command and obedience, and he had no vocabulary of thanks. He listened without comment to the kind words that came from the woman's lips as he ate and drank, and when he had finished took in silence the fresh supply of food that was given him wrapped in a greasy paper.

It was very strange, this kindness, and emboldened him, and he laid his dirty little hand on the woman's frock as she stood near him.

"Kin I lay down awhile?" he asked.

"Lord, honey," and the woman's voice was actually tremulous from uneasiness,, "I aint got any place fitten to sleep in," going on more hastily as if to cover the clumsy lie, "but if you'll go 'long the track apiece, there's a car of straw where you kin rest jest as easy. now you go 'long an' try it," and she walked out of the house in her anxiety to point him in the right direction.

But Jerry's ignorance foiled her: he did not know what a car was, so could not understand her words nor her actions, except that she wanted him to go on, and he was too tired; he listened patiently, however, until she paused to see the effects of her advice,—then—

"I wanter drink of water," was all that came slowly from the child's almost colorless lips; and the woman's heart sank. Was, this stupidity, or was it cunning to make time until the rest of the party should come up? Whatever it was, she answered amiably, though with more haste,—

"Yes, honey, jest you wait, an' I'll git you some," and she hurried into the house.

Jerry waited; he could not understand this person, but she gave him what he most needed, and he was content to obey her. Presently she returned, looking anxiously up and down the road, and in her hands a tin dipper full of water, and a black bottle tightly corked.

"Drink this, honey," handing him the dipper, "an' here's some more in the bottle; 'twon't be much load to carry," encouragingly, "an' I'll take you to the car myself; none of the neighbors is up yet," glancing keenly at the nearest houses, "an' nobody 'll see you git in the car," and as she talked she walked quickly down the railway to where on a side-track a box-car was being loaded with loose hay. Left unlocked at this little country station, there was no difficulty in pushing the doors far enough apart for Jerry to creep in; then the woman handed in the bottle of water and package of food, and pulled the doors close as she had found them. One anxious look about to see if she were observed, as well as to see if the tramps she feared were at hand, then this sagacious woman returned to her house congratulating herself on her shrewdness. The hay was fragrant and soft, and Jerry, not at all comprehending why he was there, but perfectly contented with his quarters, waded and clambered to a far corner, where, putting safely to one side his food and bottle, he made for himself a little nest, and curling up was soon in a dreamless sleep.

Securely hidden from all the world, his immediate wants provided for, the sleep that came to him was almost the sleep of death. So through all the noise and bustle of the approaching train; through the new unknown motion to which he was shortly subjected, he slept; and not until far into the day did he rouse from the lethargy that had overpowered him.

Slowly he opened his eyes and looked about him: there was the loosely packed hay shivering from base to apex—his bottle and bread jolting straight up and down, and his own sensations beyond any words of his to describe.

He was terrified; he called aloud; he tried to stand, then gladly sank again into the hay. What was the matter—such noise—such furious motion? He was now afraid to move, and for a long time lay quite still, but at last hunger overcame him, and he opened his bundle. There was the bread the woman had given him, and the meat he had regarded with such satisfaction; he touched it, as if under the strange circumstances he doubted his senses; but it was as real as it looked; he tasted it, then ate heartily, putting away the fragments carefully,—a lesson he had learned as a dog learns to hide a bone. He felt better after this, and drinking some water from his bottle resumed his place Thoughtfully he regarded the roof of the car, then pulled more hay down about him.

"When it gits through runnin' away and busts," he muttered, "I misewell fall soff," and burying himself still more deeply, once more forgot all things in sleep.

On through miles of level fields—through hills and forests, and swamps,—away from every thing and soul he had ever known,— on and on until the sun set and the new moon rose thin and fair, looking down on the far-off brush-heaped grave,—on slow Delithy telling for the twentieth time how that she had "fooled thet Wilkerson man,"—upon the kindly woman in the valley, wondering over his fate,—upon old Preacher Babbit preachir.g from the "Prodigal son," and using the little waif to point a moral,—upon the widow Perkins still waiting for the tramps.

On hurried the battered old car where the little boy lay sleeping. On into a world he had never dreamed of,—into a world where he would have to work, and fight, and suffer more intricately, more bitterly perhaps, and perchance with less reward than if he had followed to its end his life among the lonely hills.

On the train rushed toward the west, while the moon set, and the night blackened : then in the early dawn a sudden stop.

CHAPTER III.

" On to days of strangest wonder—
Was it Providence or Fate ! "

THE grating, creaking doors were pushed back, and the faces of men appeared in the opening.

Jerry looked out cautiously from his lair : he was afraid, for ever since the sudden stoppage he had heard strange sounds outside. Rumblings as of wheels over rocks ; strange cries and calls ; awful shrieks and whoops that made him put his fingers in his ears and cower lower in the hay, and above all clanging as of a hundred cow-bells rung at once !

Where was he,—what was it all ?

So now when the doors were rolled back, he peeped forth cautiously to make observations. The hay was being taken out, and he could see the heads of horses ; then beyond he saw men swarming in every direction ; and vehicles rushing about, nor were any of them like the vehicles of his mountain home ; and going in and out among this crowd of men and wheels were great black things with black smoke coming from them,— huge things, rolling back and forth on the same kind of road he had found down in the woods.

He stood there looking out on all this seeming confusion, a gaunt, wonder-stricken specter, not heeding the calls of the men who, catching sight of him, had for the moment ceased from their work.

" Say, sonny, is you deef ? " and one of the men, springing into the car, laid a hand on the child's shoulder. Jerry did not start ; but looked up slowly, dumb with fear and wonder.

" Be jabers, he's er idgit ! " said a great Irishman, twitching one rag-fringed leg of the boy's trousers.

"Where's you come from?" the first man asked, shaking him slightly.

"I dunno," slowly.

"That's wholesome; where's you goin', then?"

"I dunno."

"Sure enough!" laughing, "do you think you'll have a safe trip?" and again came the pitiful answer:

"I dunno."

"P'raps you can tell us how you feel?"

"I feels feared, an' I feels honggry," looking from one to the other.

"Pore laytle divil; pitch 'im oot, Dick; sure he's had a fray ride," and the big Irishman pulled the child toward the door.

He did not resist, except for the one second he paused to feel if his little bundle was safe inside his shirt; then he yielded himself to the man's strong grasp, and was put down in the muddy street.

"Git away, now," but the child did not move: all about him was the rush of a great railway terminus bewildering him and terrifying him; he did not dare to move.

"Put him on the sidewalk, Pat, he'll get killed tryin' to cross." So the Irishman half lifted, half dragged the boy to the pavement, then left him.

It was early, but numbers of people were abroad; work-people hurrying with baskets to their day's toil, and to Jerry crouching in a doorway not ten steps from where the man left him, they flitted like figures in a dream. He had no thoughts, he had no words for his fears: he was seated on something immovable, he was leaning against something solid; it did not matter that the street, and people, and houses seemed for some time to sway and jolt as he had been doing for hours in the car; everything was so strange that nothing could surprise him any more: not even a big man with shining buttons on his coat, who pushed him with a stick and told him to get up. He only felt sorry to move because he was weak and hungry: other than this he had no sensations, and was too dazed to ask any questions when the man, taking him by the arm, led him down the street.

He was very weary, and was glad when at last they stopped in front of what seemed to him a hole in a big rock. Inside a number of people were gathered,—people that looked sick, and ragged, and dirty; and who laughed when he dropped on a bench against the wall. His chief sensation was still weariness, and he nearly fell asleep in the corner where he had been put; only rousing when after long waiting he was led into another room, where he saw more men with shining buttons, and one sitting high up above the others.

Here he was put in a little pen with a low fence all around it, and the man who had brought him said something he could not understand; and the man seated high up looked at him very hard, then asked his name.

"Jerry," he answered, and the familiar sound seemed to bring him out of the dream he was in; the very twang of his own voice, so different from the voices about him, made things seem more real, and he looked around him more intelligently.

"What other name have you?" the man went on: there was a pause, then the child looked up asking:

"Does youuns know Minervy Ann Salter?" There was a smile even in the well-ordered police room, and the man answered:

"No."

"Well, then, my name is Jerry Wilkerson," slowly, "an' Preacher Babbit, he says as he 'llows I's named Jeremiah P. Wilkerson," with great stress on the P. "Jeremiah P. Wilkerson," the official repeated, then went on:

"Where have you come from, Jeremiah?"

A puzzled look came over the child's face.

"I dunno," he answered slowly, "but it's over yander whar ther sun gits up; it's a fur way, an' powerful lonesome."

"What is the name of the place?"

Jerry shook his head.

"It ain't got no name as I knows on," he said.

"How far is it from here?"

"I dunno."

"How did you come?"

Jerry paused a moment; he could answer this, for he could recall with pain and weariness every change in his mode of traveling.

"I walked a piece," he began with slow literalness, "an' I runned a piece 'cause I were feared; an' I comed a piece on Preacher Babbit's nag, an' I drapped off 'cause he were agoin' to sen' me back; an' I loped a piece to a cur'us kinder road; an' a woman give me sumpen to eat, an' shet me in a box of strawer, an' when I woked up agin," looking up almost excitedly, "it were a-gittin' along ther all-gracious-beatenest kind er way! An' I were feared agin: an' ther fellers tuck me out an' sot me down in ther road whar all sorter tricks was lopin' round, an' smokin', an' hollerin'; then him," pointing to his captor, "come an' got me, an' brunged me here."

The sharp little voice ceased; the hard faces about the room looked a little softer, perhaps, and the next question did not have such a business-like ring to it:

"Why did you leave your home?"

The child's face changed, and all his sorrow and remorse came back to him while he answered with a look of pitiful despair in his eyes:

"Mammy were gone, an' Minervy Ann Salter come thar to live, an' her knocked me deef an' bline, an' I runned away."

"Where had your mother gone?"

"I dunno."

There was a pause, as if the officials were nonplussed; there was no law providing for a case like this,—no refuge for such wanderers: he did not deserve punishment; he was not an orphan: and the officer asked:

"Where are you going when you leave this place?"

"Whar ther sun sots," was the quiet answer.

"Have you friends there?" smiling.

"Mammy said she were agoin' thar, her did, an' she 'llowed 'twornt much fur to ther 'Golding Gates'."

The men looked at each other.

"San Francisco?" one hazarded.

The child shook his head.

"I dunno; but her p'inted whar the sun sots, her did, an' I'm agoin' thar."

"Are you going on to-day?"

"I 'llowed I'd rest awhile," was answered simply.

"Where will you rest?"

"I 'llowed youuns 'd lemme rest right here; an' I'm honggry," looking up as a dog might.

"Poor little creature," and the chief officer put some money on the table, "let '63' take him in the yard and feed him; his case shall be attended to later,"—then to the child, "Jeremiah, you must wait until I see you again."

"Jest so, I'll wait sure," nodding reassuringly; then he followed "63" out into the dingy yard. Here he was fed, then placed on a bench with orders not to move until "63" should come back.

"Kin I lay down?" he asked wearily.

"Yes, but don't you go away from this bench; do you hear?"

"I do," and the child lay down while the man went away with the empty plate and cup. Soundly he slept until the sun crept round the high buildings and shone on him, a poor ragged little mite.

Two men stood looking down on him as he rested; one his captor, policeman 63; the other, the official who had provided food for him.

"I have a brother who runs a boat on the river," "63" was saying, "I reckon he can find him work to do."

"If your brother will take him, it will be better

than turning him adrift on the street," the officer answered, "poor little devil; waken him."

So Jerry was roused, and once more coming back to the bewildering world, he looked about him slowly, fastening his eyes at last on "63."

"I aint got off ther bench onest," he said, remembering the last order given him.

"All right," the man answered, "but I want you to come with me now."

"Whar?"

"I am going to take you to my brother."

The child got up, paused to feel for the little bundle inside his shirt, then putting his hands deep in his pockets, he turned to the officer.

"Youuns aint a-comin'?" he said familiarly, with perfect unconsciousness of the distance between them.

"No."

"Well, far'well," holding out a dirty hand that looked as small and thin as a bird's claw.

"Good-by," and the officer shook the little hand quite heartily, "take care of yourself, Jeremiah."

"All right," then returning his hand to his pocket he followed his guide out of the court-yard.

Down the broad, busy streets, now swarming with the full rush of daily traffic; choked with vehicles of every kind; the pavement thronged with passengers; the shops with buyers; Jerry looked and wondered, but asked no questions. Without any understanding of what he saw about him, he accepted the bewilderment, and with, the stoical inertness of his class, he followed his guide in silence; slouching along, his hands in his pockets, his hat drawn well down to his ears, and his eyes grown keen and thoughtful during his few days of travel, wandering over the scene about him. Suddenly his guide stopped.

"Hello, Sam!" he called, and a huge, rough-coated man turned at his call.

"Hello, George!" was answered, then the two men drew together, and turning aside from the stream of pedestrians talked earnestly for a few moments, at last pulling Jerry forward.

"Here's your boss, Jerry," "63" said; then to the man called "Sam"—"don't you think you could find work for him on the boat?"

Sam looked the limp boy over from head to heels.

"Work?" he repeated slowly, "he looks more like a candidate for planting," and he laughed a little fat, chuckling laugh.

"Planting!" and the child's face changed suddenly,—"planting" a word that until lately had meant nothing save in connection with potatoes and corn; but that now had come to mean the putting out of sight of people! Now they spoke of "planting" him. His heart sank within him; how could he get away?

A troubled, keen look came into his eyes as he measured the man introduced to him as his "boss,"—he was very big, the child thought, and as his hopes of escape seemed to lessen from this survey, his fears increased and, combined with his weariness, came near overpowering him, and he leaned against "63."

"He looks awful weakly," Sam went on, "but as you ask it, George, I'll give him a trip; there aint nothin' mean about me," rubbing his fat chin; then to the child,—"What kin you do?"

"Chop wood, an' tote water," was answered slowly.

"An' leanin' against George; that's hopeful," laughing.

"I kin," the child repeated, "when I gits rested."

"You're sure now?" the "boss" went on, "an' when I gives you a hatchet you wont cut my boat to pieces? I'm most afraid of you, I am."

But Jerry had had no training in the matter of jokes, and for answer drew his sleeve across his forehead where the perspiration of fear had come in great drops when the man spoke of "planting,"—of dealing with him as his mother had been dealt with.

A little tremulous motion passed over him, and for the first time the idea came to him distinctly that he should go back and take the brush off, and so undo his part of the evil deed; and with this thought the longing that his mother should hear him say over and over again; as he was whispering now while the men talked—"I never knowed—I never knowed!"

Then, the conference being over, the captain laid his fat hand on Jerry's shoulder:

"Come along now, Samson," he said, "an' we'll chop that cord of wood," and as in the morning that now seemed so far away, the child was half-led, half-carried down the street.

Narrower and dirtier the street grew, and the appearance of the people changed; then at the beginning of the wharf that projected into the water, the captain gave Jerry over to a rougher, larger man, and with a farewell joke about leaving the wood until the next day, he turned and went back into the town. Down the hollow-sounding plank wharf until they reached a rusty looking steamboat that in its earliest youth could never have been of the better class of vessels, and that now looked cracked and frail enough. In and out among barrels and bales, the child followed his third guide until they reached the gang-plank; then he stopped. The swift, swirling water that was suddenly revealed to him seemed on every hand, and he realized that only a floor was between him and this new thing. He shrank back, cowering away from the big man.

"I'm feared—I'm feared!" he cried aloud, "lemme go—lemme go!"

For a moment the man paused, looking down in astonishment on the frightened child; but only for a moment, then with an oath he lifted him, and, striding across the plank, dropped him on a pile of rope and bagging that was near at hand.

Very still the child lay, not making an effort to change in any way the position into which he had fallen; and the realization of his absolute helplessness rushed over him with dreadful force. Who would lift him again across that narrow plank; and he shivered now to think of the water slipping by so silently, so swiftly! He was afraid to look at it, yet longed with a strange fascination to see it once more; and where had it all come from?

"An' I can't never get back no mo' to tuck thet bresh off," he whispered to himself; for the feeling that had come to him so gradually had at last taken hold of him with great force, until now it had reached the point of remorse.

"An' ther blossoms air done dried up by now," he went on, "an' mammy'll 'llow them's bresh too," the little whisper died away, and he put his hands over his face.

The sun had set and the darkness was falling fast when the captain returned; and Jerry crouched closer to the ropes and bagging as he passed. He had a great fear of this man, and thought with longing of all the people who had helped him on his way; even of old Preacher Babbit who threatened to take him home again; but this man was bigger even than "Minervy Ann Salter," and he was entirely in his power.

"Mebby he'll furgit me," he whispered, as he heard the loud voice giving orders in the distance; wondering the while what the increased noise meant, when suddenly a sound broke on his ear that he knew was a bell simply from the family resemblance it bore to the cow-bells of his native region. After that, a strange scream like some he had heard that morning; again it came, and with it a great sigh and shudder, and the frail structure that held him from the water shivered from end to end.

For a moment he crouched closer to the floor; then as the second scream and shudder seemed to make certain the feared destruction, he sprang to his feet with a pitiful little cry.

Terrified as only an ignorant child can be terrified, he clung to the guards and looked to where the gang-plank had been; in his desperation he would have dared that journey back to land.

Alas, the plank was gone, and between him and the city, now sparkling with myriad lights, there lay a broad expanse of water repeating indefinitely every flickering gleam. They were moving.

"Like ther box of strawer!" he said fearfully to himself, then stood quite still, looking down steadfastly into the water,—magnetized, fascinated, he watched it.

"Slippin' away like snakes," he whispered, as if afraid the water might hear him, and hearing might crawl up to where he stood. "I hates it—I hates it!" he said, unconsciously raising his voice. Then a heavy hand fell on his shoulder, and the captain's rough voice asking:

"What's that you hate?"

"Ther water," catching his breath with a gasp.

"Why?"

"'Cause it favors snakes," the child answered hurriedly. "'Cause it sorter crawls away an' don't make no soun'," then more slowly—"thar's sich a lot, I'm feared."

"Come away, then. Have you had anything to eat?"

"No."

"Are you hungry?"

"I is," still clinging to the guard.

"Come this way, then," turning away; but the child did not move. "Come along, I say," and the captain's big voice grew louder.

"I'm feared to leggo," and the thin face looked up fearfully.

"You fool! come to me."

Two terrors. The child chose the least, and letting go his hold on the side of the boat, he walked unsteadily to his master, seizing his coat anxiously.

"Now are you dead?"

"I'll 'llow I'm nigh to it," looking furtively at the

open space left for the gang-plank, through which a broad expanse of water was visible; "it creeps an' crawls, an' I hates it," and he turned his face away.

The captain laughed; but he was merciful enough not to take his coat from between the clinging hands until they had reached the dingy, ill-smelling cabin where the men ate; here he gave the child into the care of the cook, with orders for him to be fed and given a place to sleep.

So all night long the boat shivered and strained against the mighty current of the great river; and the child slept uneasily, waking often with a shudder, as he remembered the black water slipping by so near him.

CHAPTER IV.

> " Patient children—think what pain
> Makes a young child patient,—ponder !
> Wronged too commonly to strain
> After right, or wish or wonder."

JERRY'S hope that the captain would forget him was doomed to disappointment, and with the earliest dawn he was wakened from his troubled sleep and put to work, coiling rope, separating into different piles the almost innumerable boxes and bags of supplies that were to be put off at various way landings. So the long day passed; and Jerry worked with his face turned away from the water ; looking at everything, even the awful captain, rather than at the dark sliding stream.

" It trimmels 'cause it can't abear to tech the water," he said, pausing with a rope in his hand. The man working near him looked at the child curiously.

"What trembles ? " he asked.

" It," Jerry answered, striking the side of the boat; "jest youuns feel how it trimmels," looking up as the boat shivered under the thud of the engine; " it can't abear to tech ther water 'cause it favors snakes."

The man laughed.

" You'd better not let the boys know as you're skeart of water," he said ; " they'll devil the life outer you."

" I'm feared sure," the child repeated; and the captain lounging by heard him.

" Ha, ha ! " he laughed, " the boys must larn you better'n that, Samson; nobody kin run on this craft that is a coward: we'll dip you a few times when we git in order and have nothin' to do," and he laughed again until he shook; "it'll help your lily-white skin, Samson."

The child made no answer save to bend lower over his work. To be put in that water,—to feel it slipping by him, feeling like snakes! His straight, sunburned hair almost stood on end. Anything would be better than this, even his father and Minervy Ann Salter. And when his fellow-worker would be at some far-off task, he would creep to the side of the boat and watch with fascination this latest enemy. He must get away—he must even dare to cross the plank alone.

"How long 'fore youuns has time?" he asked at last.

"To dip you?" and the man laughed; "by mornin', I reckon, an' you kin bet your life they'll duck you good; the boys won't like nothin' better."

"Ther mornin'?" the child repeated, "after weuns git done sleepin' to-night?"

"That's it," and the man chuckled to himself as he thought of the fun.

Poor Jerry watched at every landing for his opportunity: he would watch the gang-plank swing into place, but his courage failed time after time, for to the fear of the precarious crossing was added the fear that seeing him on the plank would tempt the men to dip him. He determined to wait until night, and watched with sickening dread the growing order on the boat.

At last the day was done, and Jerry felt safer, and made up his mind to get off at the first landing after nightfall. If he fell in the water,—if they should catch him and bring him back,—these were possibilities too dreadful to be entertained for a moment.

Slowly the twilight ended and the darkness came: supper was over; preparations were being made for a stoppage, and in the hurry Jerry was forgotten and unnoticed as he crouched in the shadow near the gangway.

The night was inky black, with a light rain falling that was scarcely to be felt at first, but that nevertheless promised a thorough wetting. A dreary night to run away in; but Jerry was desperate, and waited in the shadow with his hat pressed well down, and his bundle safe inside his shirt.

Close up under the high bluff the boat swung; the bell clanging, the whistle screaming, and every other noise that could be made, breaking the cloud-weighted stillness of the night. Boxes and barrels and bales were put on and off with all the marvelous celerity of trained handlers; and still the child saw no chance, for lights flickered everywhere. At last there came a moment's cessation of the noise: was the plank to swing into place again as he had seen it do so many times that day, and he be carried on?

There was a tremulous sigh, a stifled gasp, then a little shadow sped across the wavering plank: one second in the glare of the lanterns, the next buried in the black shadow of the bluff. No one called after him—no one seemed to have seen him—and in and out between the piles of landed cargo he crawled, surely but slowly making his way to the impenetrable darkness outside the circle of barrels and boxes.

At last he came to where a little way up the bank a clump of bushes grew, and above them a small tree that had toppled over with the caving in of the bluff: carefully he crawled up, glad to find a place where he could rest and hide until the boat went away.

"They'll furgit me 'till mornin'," he thought, then watched the moving lights, and listened to the noises that sounded so preternaturally clear and far in the black stillness. The rain whispered softly, and mingled with it came the low licking of the river, eating hungrily into the shore.

Gradually it attracted Jerry's attention, and he listened anxiously: it seemed so near that if he put his foot down the creeping coldness would wrap it round. He drew his feet up under him, and listened intently, until all other sounds passed from his hearing entirely, and only the hungry gnawing of the river was with him.

The boat swung out into the stream, and away on her journey: the boxes and barrels were carried slowly up the bank; all life and light faded away; the rain patiently filtered through the foliage of the little tree and through the child's few garments where he crouched listening to the voice of his enemy.

"Ef I drap to sleep it mout ketch me," he muttered, and he took a closer hold on the slim stem against which he leaned. This made him feel more safe, and as he moved, some more sand sliding down against his back, the thought came to him that a great deal might roll down and "kivver him like his mammy!"

And with this thought his remorse for the help he had given his father came back upon him; the present was forgotten, and his voice broke the stillness of the night. "I'll go back," he said, as if taking an oath, "go back if Dad knocks me over onest a minute—I will, sure." When the morning dawned he would turn his face, not his back, to the rising sun, and it would surely guide him home.

"An' I'll tuck all ther bresh an' ther dirt off, Mammy"—talking softly to himself, his heart feeling lighter for the resolve—"an' weuns kin run away agin; an' weuns kin talk, and Dad wont be roun' to cuss us," so the one love of his life would come back to him.

Poor love that had been so surreptitiously given; had been able only to show itself in such humble ways: the secret soothing after a beating,—a little coffee hidden that he might drink it when his father was out of the way,—a bundle of dry leaves pushed under the straw he slept on to make his resting-place a little softer. So he remembered his mother. He could not understand her going from him, but he could remember how it had happened: remembered how his mother stood still and watching while his father beat him,—remembered how he would not cry out because she had warned him not to, even when in his drunken fury his father raised him to dash him against the chimney! He remembered the breathless, silent, upward swing—then the sharp cry as his mother's arms wrapped close about him, and the blow that followed. He covered his face as the sound of the dull thud came back to him; and after that the strange stillness there was about the house when he waked again and found himself on his pile of straw, and on the bed his mother lying, and the old woman, their only neighbor, watching her. He talked to her that afternoon, and heard her speak then of the "Golden Gates"; and his father crouching over the fire heard too, and did not curse her. That night he fell asleep lying there close by her side; and in the morning she was there still, but though he called and spoke to her until his father and the old woman turned him out of the house, she never answered. He had understood nothing that followed until he had learned wisdom from the woman in the valley. Now that he understood all that had happened, he would go back; would begin his return journey when daylight came, and it would not take him long: he could soon get back again and pull the brush off.

Slower and slower the thoughts came; the ugly little head drooped against the tree; the loose sand settled more warmly about him; the rain, the wind, the gnawing of the water faded from his hearing, and he slept as soundly as the dead woman on the hillside.

Slept while the clouds floated away, and in the dawn his pitiful eyes watched the sun rise—eyes that grew wide with despair.

At his feet the mighty, impassable river, and beyond the other shore the sun rose.

CHAPTER V.

> "What use in hope?
> What use!
> In waiting long with empty hands held high—
> In watching patiently the clouded sky—
> What use—you soon will die?"

WE yearn and strive, and long, and grieve, and hold up praying hands. Then stand and watch with death-like serenity, may be, while our hopes, our beliefs, our loves, all of them dyed to the most prismatic loveliness by the light gone from our eyes—the strength from our youth—the blood from our hearts, fade from us as certainly as the day fades down the western sky. Fade from us entirely, until we are glad when they—

> "Put the death-weights on our eyes
> To seal them safe from tears."

The ragged tops of the great mountains behind him—the broken cliffs falling down a hundred feet below him—and far off beyond this wild desert of rock—in the gold and purple glory of the dying day—the distant valley lying like a dream.

And where were the "Golding Gates?"

Jerry crouched on the dizzy pinnacle of barren rock only a step away from the narrow foot-track he had so persistently climbed. Ever since the day before he had been toiling up and up the grim mountains, sure that at last he had reached his goal. The path wound up and up along the dizzy cliffs; through tiny clefts; through yawning defiles; avoiding and rounding the higher peaks until now on the western side, with the apex of the mighty ridge left behind, it touched with one curve this crowning height of its course ere it turned to descend.

He crouched there with the September wind striking sharply through his thin clothing—his face looking drawn and blank—his hands clasped close.

Where were the "Golding Gates?"

When the river had intervened between him and his resolve on that May morning that seemed so long ago, the child had resumed his old course toward the west,—toward the "Golding Gates"; but with as little hope of seeing them, as there was hope left in his heart that he would again see his mother.

Still, as evening after evening he watched the western sky, the "gates" seemed to grow into absolute certainties that some day he would touch. Sometimes through rain mists he watched the glorious flame-lights shoot up to lay warm hands upon the homeless clouds: sometimes across the hot dry prairies,—trackless, wild, deserted,—the sun fell suddenly like a fiery ball: sometimes it sank in clear amber depths that seemed to vibrate and throb in tremulous pulsations. It had grown into his life and his heart, this hope for the "gates" his mother had been so sure were near, and for weeks as he made his way toward these mountains,—pausing to work for his food,—pausing until some merciful hand would wash and patch his clothes,—begging a lift from some kindly emigrant,—for all these weeks, ever since these mountains came in sight, he had made sure that behind this last barrier he would find the gates.

And now with this last disappointment his strength seemed to leave him, and he shivered and crouched close to the rocks as the wind struck him.

"Youuns 'llowed 'twornt much fur, Mammy," he whispered, looking out wonderingly, hopelessly to the fading distance, "An' I've done come, an' come fur a long time, an' it don't seems like I gits to nowhars," a moment longer he looked out across the grand scene, then he covered his face with his hands.

"Oh, Mammy, Mammy!" he wailed, "I aint got no place--I aint got nobody—oh, Mammy, Mammy!" and the frail, uncared-for, unlovely little creature was shaken with a storm of sobs.

Somehow in the months he had wandered the knowledge of his loneliness had come to him. He had worked sometimes for people in very different spheres from the one he lived in, and he had seen mothers and children together in ways not practiced in his own class; and watching he had learned that people belonged to each other, and with this knowledge came the other, that he belonged to no one. Still, the "Golding Gates" opened as a vision before him: always inextricably mixed in his mind with the sunsets; always looking warm and shining; they had become home, and mother, and love to him; he ceased to feel lonely when he thought of them, and what work he had to do was done more briskly because of this vision in his mind. Somehow they would welcome him and make him happy when he reached them, for his mother had said she would not be tired, nor sick, nor hungry any more when she got there. Now he crouched, unheeding all the desolate grandeur spread before him: one wild spring would have ended all, but he did not know that; he did not know what death meant; he could not understand how and why he stood where he was; he simply accepted facts, and only reasoned enough to avoid pain and hunger.

But at last he realized his loneliness; his "Golding Gates," his hope by day and his dream by night, had been taken away from him, and his life was left unto him desolate.

He crept slowly from off the great boulder, and once more on the path passed downward wearily; climbing, slipping, letting himself down from rock to rock, he made his way mechanically. There was nothing to make him him hasten now,—nothing ahead of him to make him heedless of the toil: he did not think any more of following the sunset, for this last revelation,—

this last long view across the valley, had somehow made him feel that his mother had been mistaken. He had seen so far from the top of that rock: it would take him until the blackberries blossomed again before he could go as far as he had seen; and now he felt so weak and sick he could not do it.

Heavily, unthinkingly he moved, guided by an instinct that made him go further down where he might find some fellow-creature. He knew that nobody lived among these barren rocks; a woman on the other side had told him so; she had warned him that he would get lost, or starve to death, or fall from some high place and be killed, or some "wild critter 'd kill him jest to git what small pickin's thar was on his bones; they gits mighty hungry, the varmints do." But Jerry was not to be dissuaded from crossing the mountains; his Mammy had said he would find the "Golding Gates," and his own eyes had seen the sun sink behind these very mountains for many weeks,—of course the "Gates" were behind them too.

From every meal he had saved some scrap as store to help him over the mountains: he had not told his hopes; he had used no contrary arguments, not even when the wild beasts were represented as ferocious enough to eat such a lean morsel as he was. He sat in stolid silence, filling with his hoarded treasures of broken food a small cotton bag some kind person had given him in which to carry his bread and meat.

And early in the dawn he had started on his well nigh desperate undertaking: had climbed all day as far as his strength would allow: had slept in a crevice of the rocks at night, pushing aside his fears by thought of the "Golding Gates" he would reach on the morrow. And when the morrow came, tired and hungry,—for his little store of food had not satisfied him,—he still pushed on higher and higher, when every step made him feel more surely the biting wind. Up and up, not scanning much in front of him,—not looking much beyond the next step he must take—

the next rock he must climb; going on in perfect faith that when the sun set he would be safe and happy inside the "gates"; and far down in his heart there was a feeling that somehow his Mammy would be there, and he could tell her all about that "bresh."

And crouching in the cutting wind he saw only a barren wilderness of rocks, and far off across infinite distance the sun fading grandly down the western sky. No nearer now than when from among his own hills he watched it die.

No nearer love and rest now than then, but only more lonely for his last hope gone.

In those dim days of ignorance he had piled that grave with brush to hide the rails that were to keep it safe; now in his wisdom it seemed to him that he had only aided a most evil design. Then he had set out in undoubting faith to find a happy land where there would be rest and plenty: now when his hand reached for the hard-won prize, it faded from his grasp.

Down into the gathering shadows he went; further and further still: an endless distance it seemed to him when at last he came to a little grass, and lying down, for he was very weary, he looked back to where so high above him the light lingered. His head felt heavy and hurt him, and his body seemed torn by a hundred little creeping pains. He lay quite still, wondering in a dull, vague way what ailed him. He was hungry and weak, and must reach some place that night where he could be warmed and fed.

"If I could git to feel a good fire," he said "I 'llow I'd be better."

Slowly he rose and stumbled on; his head seemed to grow more heavy, and a deadly chill mingled with his many pains.

Down, still down the path led, but it was broader now, and more worn, as if constantly used.

"Mebbe I'll git to som'ers atter a while," pausing

as for a moment the whole mountain side seemed to waver and tremble.

He covered his eyes.

"It's me as is a-shakin'," fearfully, "an' I aint got no place: if I could jest git to feel a fire, jest fur a minnit: Oh, Mammy, Mammy!" then all faded from him, and he sank down on the roadside. At last he was worn out; for with his hope his little strength had failed him, and lying limp and haggard among the gray rocks, he looked as if the "Gates" had at last opened for him, and the weary, ignorant little soul had crept in among the paradise flowers.

CHAPTER VI.

"Is your wisdom very wise,—
On this narrow earth?
Very happy, very worth
That I should stay to learn?
Are these air-corrupting sighs
Fashioned by unlearned breath?
Do the students' lamps that burn
All night, illumine death?"

"WHERE did you find him, Joe!"

"I were a-comin' down Blake's trail, an' I sawn him a-lyin' thar liker dead critter, I did," and Joe poked the fire, "an' I says, says I, Joe Gilliam, yon's dead; but when I got nigher I sorter changed, an' I poked him, says I, 'Sonny,' says I; an' he riz right up lookin' wild like; says 'ee 'Mammy, I aint got no place,—Mammy, I aint got nobody!' I were tuck all to pieces, Doctor; says I 'Sonny, you shell hev a place,' says I, an' I brunged him here, I did," and again the man pushed the fire, going on more slowly—"I aint got nobody nuther, Doctor; but I 'llowed thet as I hes a leetle place I'd keep him fur comp'ny like; an' 'cause he talks like my own home folks."

The man addressed as "doctor" stood looking down into the fire.

"If we can keep him, Joe," he said.

"He's powerful bony," Joe admitted, "looks like he'd been starved fur a long time; an' he never had nothin' alonger him ceppen this leetle passel," taking a small, dirty, newspaper-wrapped bundle from a crevice in the wall, "seems like it's strawer inside," turning it over slowly.

The doctor took the bundle, looked at it for a moment, then replaced it in the wall.

"An' he's been a-cryin' jest like he's hollerin' now ever sence yisterday mornin'," Joe went on seriously; "fust I 'llowed as I could fotch him roun', but 'twornt no use, you bet."

"Poor little creature," and the doctor turned again to the bed where Jerry lay in a consuming fever, turning his head from side to side with the never-ceasing cry—"I never knowed, Mammy,—I never knowed." The voice was sinking lower each hour from weakness, and the doctor had to bend down now to hear him—"I never knowed—I never knowed," the pitiful cry went on.

Then the doctor whispered—

"I know that."

There was a pause in the monotonous movement of the head; the wild eyes fastened on his face, and the little hand crept up to touch him.

"An' ther blossoms?" the weak voice went on.

"Beautiful?" was answered.

"What?" uneasily.

"Pretty," the doctor repeated.

"They was, sure; an' youuns was powerful proud er blossoms, Mammy."

"Yes."

"An' I never knowed—I never knowed."

"Yes."

"An' I never knowed," more slowly as the eyes closed and the hands fell limp on the quilt,—"I never knowed."

The doctor's finger was on the fluttering pulse.

"He is going to sleep, Joe," he said; "but you must watch him if you want him."

"I will," Joe answered. "An' I dunno, doctor, but he's got a grip on me, he has; I reckon his talkin' done it."

"And give him whiskey and milk all night."

"Jest so."

"And I will come up again in the morning." Then the doctor stooped under the low doorway, and mounting his horse, rode off.

Patiently Joe watched, and when the night fell he rose from his place in the chimney-corner to close and bolt the stout wooden shutter that guarded the window, and to bar securely the door. He shut the door very carefully, trying it again and again; then reaching down a long, lean rifle he proceeded to load and cap it, then put it against the wall near his chair, full cocked.

"Youuns is dange'ous, Tom," he said, as if the rifle understood, and patted it gently; then, as by a preconcerted signal, there emerged from one corner a huge, hideous yellow dog, stump-tailed, bow-legged, but with a breadth of chest and a jaw that promised a hopeless grip.

"Youuns is honggry, is you, Pete?" going to the corner and lifting most carefully the leaves that made his bed, "I'll feed you, jest hev a leetle patience,"—then he peered about the low rafters with a torch flickering and flaring in his hand. "It's better to know fur sure," he said as he put down the torch and proceeded to feed the evil-looking dog. "Eatin' means a good grip, Pete," giving him a rough caress; then once more taking up the rifle, he looked carefully to its condition.

So the night swept on, the moon sending but few rays to touch the low log house so far back under the rocks. The man dozed in his chair—the sleeping boy looked dead—the fire flickered weirdly, and the dog breathed loud in the corner. Slowly the dawn crept over the mountains, and with the first ray of light the man roused himself with a start, reaching his hand to his rifle before his eyes were well opened, and listening intently. He could hear nothing but the breathing of the dog—was the child dead? He crossed over to the bed, and bent his ear to the thin lips; but the breath came regularly, and raising him for the whisky, he laid him down again and covered him as gently as a woman might.

Soon the fire blazed, and the breakfast for the man

and the dog was under way; then he made the same survey he had made the night before, of the dog's bed and the rafters, before he opened either the window or the door.

He was a middle-aged man, with close-cut gray hair, keen gray eyes, deep set under bushy eye-brows, and filled with an eager light. He was short, squarely built, with long, powerful arms, and shoulders rounded forward as from years of stooping. Canvas trousers, high, heavy boots, and a red flannel shirt that opening at the throat showed a neck like a bull-dog's.

His movements were slow and silent, and his long arms seemed to reach from place to place like the legs of a great spider. The meal that he cooked was simple enough, and after carefully giving the dog much the larger part, he ate slowly and earnestly.

Away off from under the shadow of the cliffs the sun was shining brightly now, and standing in the doorway one could see far below where the long shafts of light struck down, losing themselves among the black pines, and beyond sweeping like a tender hand over the barren, brown rocks.

Joe only looked down the trail, he did not watch the sunlight; he did not heed any of the beauty about him; he was listening intently, with his arms folded, and his hat drawn down to shield his keen eyes.

"I can't spar' another day," he said, stepping out a little distance to get a better view down the path. "I aint done a good stroke for three days an' mo'," walking restlessly back. "I 'llowed he'd come afore now." Then going within he gave the child the milk ordered, looking steadfastly at it the while.

"I aint tasted no milk in a-many a year," he said slowly; "poor leetle Nan wanted a cow powerful," and he drew a long breath that in the civilized world would have answered for a sigh, then he turned to the child.

Mechanically the milk was taken ; the heavy eyelids did not rise, the parched, cracked lips seemed scarcely to close on the cup, and once more on the hard pillow, the narrow, yellow face looked beyond the reach of human help.

"Pore leetle varmint, he's hed a rale rough time sure," and Joe lifted the toil-worn, bony hand and laid it back on the coverlid as gently as if his great strength were trained to the handling of little things ; then he returned to his watch in the doorway.

Slowly the doctor came : the way was long ; the path was narrow and steep, and on every hand were pictures that could have detained him all day.

Slowly but surely, and Joe's brow cleared as the first sharp ring of the horse's hoof on the rocks struck his ear : very far away, but in the death-like stillness of the rocky wilderness the sounds came very distinctly, with every now and then the rattle of a loosened stone rolling down to some unknown depth.

"Et laist," Joe muttered, and went forward to meet his guest.

"Is he alive ?" was the first question.

"He is ; but looks morer like dead," then Joe took the horse to tie it, and the doctor stooped under the doorway.

He put his hand on the child's pulse, then lifted the eyelids to look into the eyes.

"Has he been quiet all night ?" to Joe.

"Jest the way yer sees him."

"Well, I will wait until he wakens," and the doctor put a small tin bucket on the table, "it is the milk, Joe, and you had better put it in a jug in the spring."

But Joe did not move ; he stood looking at the doctor doubtfully.

"How long will he be a-sleepin' ?" he asked.

"I do not know," placing a chair in the doorway ; "why ?"

"I wanter go to my work."

"Your work?" slowly, not turning his eyes from the scene outside the door; "what is it, Joe?"

A keener light came into Joe's eyes, and he cast a furtive glance at the rafters, and toward the dog's corner.

"I works over in Eureky; I's been a-doin' it ever sence before youuns come to Durdens."

"That will take you until night."

"If I works it will: but I'll jest tell 'em I'm a-comin', thet's all I wanter do"; then after a moment's pause, "do you reckon he'll sleep thet long?"

"You may go; but leave me something to eat."

"I aint got nothin' fitten, doctor," with real regret in his voice, "I aint never onest thought 'bout thet."

"Any meal?"

"Lord, yes, an' bacon, too; but thet's all."

"That will do; but remember, I do not wish to be on the road after dark."

"All right," then Joe paused, again looking doubtfully at the doctor, "and Pete?" he asked slowly, "will you give him a bite?"

"Yes."

"Thenkey, doctor," with a grunt of satisfaction, and in an incredibly short space of time the horse was unsaddled and tethered; the milk in an earthenware jug in the spring, and Joe on his way down the mountain-side, with a long swinging stride that soon took him out of sight.

Very still the man in the doorway sat, looking out with a far-reaching look that seemed to be searching time rather than space. Perfectly still, with his arms folded, his head bent, and his broad-brimmed hat drawn down to shade his eyes. The sunlight crept nearer,—a bright snake glided slowly past among the rocks,—a lizard basked on the logs of the house,—the hideous dog came out and sniffed about the figure sitting so still, and a busy spider span its web across the corner of the doorway.

Quite still until a little sound reached him,—a long

sigh with a sobbing catch in it. He rose quickly, and laying aside his hat bent over the child: another sobbing sigh, then the eyes opened slowly,—looking up without a question in them,—without a hope, only so weary.

Then the little whisper—

"I never knowed."

"Yes," the doctor answered, "but you must drink this for me," and he raised the child gently.

Again the unchildish eyes opened and looked into the man's eyes above them.

"Mammy 'llowed 'twor'nt much fur; but I'm done give out sure," and the weak whisper died away.

"I know that," the doctor answered; "but drink this."

The child obeyed, looking steadfastly into the face above him:

"I kin chop wood fur youuns," with a little gasp, "an' tote water when I gits rested, I kin."

"Very well, but you must rest now," and he turned over the hard pillow before he laid the child down again.

Suddenly there was a movement, and the little wasted creature looked like a hunted animal: "Whar's it!" the weak voice breaking with a cry, "hes youuns tooken it? Oh, gimme, gimme, gimme!" and he clutched the doctor's arm, "oh, gimme! it can't do you no good."

"What is it?" kindly.

"My bundle, my leetle bundle," and the words finished with a pitiful wail.

For a moment the doctor was puzzled, then he remembered the bundle Joe had shown him the day before, and stepped to the side of the fire-place.

"Is this it?" holding up the shabby little package.

It was as if a beam of light had swept across the child's face.

"Thet's it," lifting his hands with sudden energy to

clutch it, hiding it under his pillow,—"it aint nothin' to do no good," he explained, looking up deprecatingly, "it aint wittles; it aint nothin' youuns wants," pressing the pillow down as securely as he could, "it aint nothin'," still more pleadingly.

"Very well," the doctor answered, drawing the covering up a little higher, "you shall keep it, you need not be afraid; but go to sleep now," then he turned away to his place in the doorway, while the child, with his hand on the bundle under his pillow, went to sleep. So the day passed; the doctor moved only when it was absolutely necessary to wait on the child—to cook his dinner, or to water his horse; he sat like one resting after a great strain; every muscle seemed relaxed, and a supreme weariness that seemed other than the weariness of body, possessed him. No word, no sign escaped him until toward the afternoon he walked out to the trail and stood looking down.

"If God will ever forgive me," he said slowly, then for one instant he covered his face with his hands. Suddenly the sound of a falling stone caught his attention; he looked up quickly, and with his hands in his pockets stood waiting for Joe.

"I aint much late, is I, doctor?" coming up slightly blown.

"Not much."

"An' the boy?"

"Better; but I will come again to-morrow; give him the whisky and milk all night, and do not take away his bundle, he has it under his pillow."

"All right," and Joe took the saddle from where it had hung all day, while the doctor went to look at his patient once more.

"Poor little devil," and he laid his hand on the forehead of the sleeping child, "what have I saved you for, and will you thank me when all is done?"

"All right, doctor" Joe called, and taking the tin bucket, the doctor turned away.

"Every hour, Joe, whisky or milk," he repeated, "and leave the bundle where it is."

Then the doctor rode away down the mountain; and his face changed as he went. All the gentleness faded from it, and the lines about the mouth grew set and stern,—his every-day face that no one realized was a mask.

CHAPTER VII.

"The steadfast silence that holds peace for wrong
Or love,—that keeps the smile on quivering lips;
That holds the tears back from the brave, sad eyes;
That with a steady hand doth sod the grave
Of all its hopes, so none may know a grave
Is there!"

A LONG, low, unpainted, weather-beaten frame house standing a little back from the road that at this point turned, and became the one street of Durden's. A house without the very smallest attempt at beauty,—that fulfilled but one end—a shelter.

The main shed, extending straight down from the apex of the roof, takes under its protection a broad piazza, in whose shadowy depths the doors and windows of the house open.

The windows are glazed, which is a luxury in the town of Durden's; but the doors and blinds are simply battened, like the rest of the houses.

Three chimneys come from the roof, one from either end and one from the middle; wonderfully square and ugly; but softened to the view on this cool September day by slender plumes of smoke. A thin rail extends round the piazza save where a clear space is left for the steps, at the corner of which stands a hitching-post for horses. The reddish-brown soil of the yard is baked to the consistency of brick, rising and falling in mimic ravines and hills as the rain is pleased to wash it. No sign of a fence,—no sign of paint or whitewash anywhere,—no vestige of any attempt at flower, or shrub, or grass;—an ugly, barren, neglected place.

In a high-backed, splint-bottomed rocking-chair,

with his feet on the hand-rail that goes about the piazza, a boy sits reading; delicately made, and fair, and with a finish in his dress and bearing that shows familiarity with localities very different from Durden's. Indeed, he looks entirely out of place in this rough environment, and seems perfectly to realize the unfitness of things.

Evidently he is very tired; but only of himself and his book, for no work can ever have soiled his white hands, nor hardened his delicate muscles; yet he yawns and stretches very wearily, clasping his hands behind his head.

"A beastly hole," he muttered. "I shall be cross-eyed if I read any more," but yet, for lack of other interest he takes up his book again. The shapely head bends forward, the long lashes shade the girlish cheeks where a little flush has come from the exertion of the last yawn, and the boy is beautiful. No other word would describe him; indeed one would not be tempted to fit any other adjective to him.

And the doctor, riding up and tying his horse, thinks how different this face is from the other he left up on the mountain-side.

The boy rises.

"At last!" he says, coming forward, "I thought you might possibly spend the night."

"Scarcely; I waited only to watch the case."

"And how is the case?" yawning again.

"Progressing favorably."

"Unlike your humble servant," turning to follow the doctor indoors.

The doctor paused to hang up his saddle-bags and hat, then turned to look at the boy.

"You look in good case," he said.

"'My face is my fortune,'" looking up with a smile that made this same face brilliant, "but really, I am nearly dead of loneliness: and at noon a letter from Mamma; a letter a month old, but telling of the most enchanting things; really, you know!" with an earnest, regretful look in his beautiful eyes.

The doctor listened quietly, watching the boy's face that seemed to charm him against his will.

"It is very unfortunate," he said gravely, then went into a fire-lighted room where a table was laid for two, and a servant in waiting.

"Dinner at once," he said, "and a fire in the study;" then sitting down in the great arm-chair he turned to the boy who stood near a window. "Is there any news, Paul?" he asked.

"Nothing, except no end of balls, and lunches, and lovely art exhibitions, and operas, and concerts, and everything that can make a fellow long to go home; and I go everywhere with Mamma, don't you know: I wish you knew her," the boy added slowly.

"Yes," and the doctor leaned his head back as if this precocious child worried him.

"Yes," Paul went on, drawing a letter from his pocket,—"and she sends you a message."

The creamy paper rustled in the boy's hands; a faint perfume floated on the air, and the words came softly—"'I miss you more than I can say, and long for you with a longing that I hope you may never realize. Would it not be possible to persuade your guardian to come home with you some time this winter, so that I can see you?'" pausing and looking steadfastly at the doctor; but there was no movement, and he read on—"'Thank him for me for all his care of you: I know he will do whatever is best for you, and in the highest sense of the word make a man of you,'"—the boy stopped, folding the letter slowly.

"Thank you," came coldly from the doctor, and he passed his hands wearily over his eyes.

"*Did* you ever know her?" the boy asked hesitatingly, after a moment's silence.

"Yes."

Then the dinner and lights came in, and the conversation ceased.

The meal was rather silent, and afterward the evening in the book-lined study seemed rather cold and still. The lessons went on without much heart, dragging heavily; with cold patience on the doctor's part; with undisguised weariness on the boy's part, until the tasks were done.

"Now I will fly back with delight to my novel of which I was so weary," and the boy rose and stretched himself; "to think I should be thankful to my lessons for anything," he went on, "to think that I should fall so low that one dullness is a boon because it makes the next dullness seem less dull."

"I am reading," the doctor said, not looking up.

"I beg pardon," hurriedly, and the boy, with the color burning in his cheeks, subsided with his book into an arm-chair.

But he did not read; instead, he watched furtively the man before him, wondering what was the point of his life. Why did he live in this lonely fashion away off in these wilds; why study so diligently; why spend his time and his money on the poor creatures, the scum of the country who gathered out in this region? Like to-day, spending hours over one little waif who was no earthly use to any one. Was he altogether right in his mind? He must be, Paul concluded, for he remembered quite distinctly his father's dying words about him,—'I give him Paul as unconditionally as such a thing can be done, and charge him to be all to him that he would be to his own son.' Paul remembered it all quite distinctly, and the last talk his father had given him. After that the long months when his mother pleaded not to give him up,—the lawyer's protest, and the letters from this guardian that had made his mother so ill: then his journey to this far western region, his reception, and wonder at his surroundings. It was very strange; and with all his precocious, shallow knowledge of the world, he could make nothing of these facts that met him on every hand.

Now he found that there had been some acquaintance between his mother and his guardian : a new piece of knowledge that deserved much thought. Why not ask about this new puzzle? Why not, indeed ! After that last snub he would rather put his hand in the fire than say a word. No really harsh word had ever been said to him by this man, yet Paul would sooner have attempted to strike him, than positively to disregard one wish of his. He shirked his duty sometimes when in a particularly rebellious frame of mind, and when his guardian was not at hand to look him over after a cool, calm way he had. Sometimes he longed to see him angry, to hear him curse and swear and storm as he had heard other men do ; he thought it would be almost refreshing. This intense calm,—this controlled stillness that nothing seemed to disturb, was frightfully monotonous, and the man must surely be devoid of feeling. And yet he helped all the poor and sick, and got no pay for it : certainly a strange man.

And this strange man sat in the brilliant circle of lamplight reading on and on ; turning page after page as if nothing existed for him save that book. All day long he had been resting with no eye to scan his features,—no keen curiosity to probe his self-control : —all day he had been resting with only the wild creatures about him.

So they sat until the word came of a miner who had fallen and injured himself; then the doctor closed his book and ordered his horse, and telling the boy not to wait for him, rode away in the darkness to spend the hours of the night among the lowest of mankind,—watching the death-struggles of the strong,—the misery and desolation of the weak.

Aye, what did life seem to him ;—what use in all its toil and striving ;—what comfort for all its sorrow and suffering ?

As well as he could he eased the agony of body,

and comforted the heart,—for he knelt and prayed for the passing soul,—this strange man whose life had no visible point.

And riding homeward in the wild dawn he whispered once again . .

"If God will ever forgive me!"

CHAPTER VIII.

"And with no language but a cry."

JERRY sat in the low doorway very much as he had done on the spring morning before he left his home, with the sun shining all about him, finding out all the hollows in his small face, and showing the grave eyes grown larger and more wistful. His hopes had all failed him; the only object he had ever had was seemingly an illusion; a blankness had come to him that was strange and unaccountable, and he realized thoroughly but one thing—that he was sorry he had ever wakened from his sleep on the trail. He felt more lonely now that there was nothing to remind him of his past save his little bundle. His clothes were all new and warm; Joe had brought them from Eureka, whatever or wherever that might be. Red flannel shirts and thick trousers, and a thing Jerry had never known before in his short life,—a pair of boots! In his recollection his father had possessed one pair; but further than that he did not know boots. Now he sat in the sunshine, thinking as far as his half-awakened faculties could think. Heretofore his life had been but a dull routine, never reaching beyond the old rail-fence, of helping his mother with the scant crop, or picking berries that his father took away to "peddle,"—which meant to Jerry that his father would return with a small store of provisions, but always whisky. So his life had passed in ignorance and silence, with pain and hunger for variety. With his mother's disappearance came the first change and excitement. She had talked to him of the "Golding Gates," and then for the first time he had heard that there were such things as peace and plenty. After that his journey—the excitement—the failure—the long sleep and slow awakening to kindness and rest, and this strange blankness for which he could not account, for he knew his life was more full than ever before.

He sat in the sunshine, slowly revolving the reasons of things as far as he knew them, and gradually coming to the conclusion that he had missed the "Gates," because he had not his mother with him, and added to this was the hopelessness of ever being able to return and undo the evil done to his mother. He leaned against the door-post sorrowfully. "I can't never git back," he muttered, "Joe 'llows as he dunno how I made out to git here ; cause he 'llows I muster come from whar he come from, 'cause I talks like all his'ns folks : an' ther big water,—I'm fearder that, sure!" He would not continue his wanderings, for he had no hope now, and one place was as good as another. Joe never beat him—Joe gave him food and clothes. There was nothing for it but to stay where he was ; mind the house by day while Joe was gone ; cut wood down among the pines, and have the supper cooked when Joe came home : this was the routine. "If I only hed Mammy," he would whisper in the long, silent days, turning his bundle over in his hands. But when Joe came home at night the fire was always burning, the supper ready, and the little face watching for him. And Joe felt he had done a good thing in taking in the little waif.

"He's sumpen ter say 'hardy' to when I gits home of evenin's," he said to the doctor as if to excuse his weakness ; and long before there was any hope of seeing his house, Joe would look up the trail to try to catch a glimpse of the open door and the little figure showing black against the firelight.

And when supper was dispatched, and the house closed for the night, it was something pleasant to feel that if he put down his pipe and asked a question there was a voice to answer him.

He often wondered over the child, and occasionally put a question to him; but the doctor had said to wait until the child was quite strong before he took his mind back to the things that had caused his illness. So Joe waited until one night, when the crisis was reached unintentionally.

Joe had sat silent for a long time, when, putting down his pipe and looking solemnly into the fire, he said:

"To-morrer pore 'Lije Milton is agoin' to be buried, Jerry, an' you kin go alonger me if you hes a mind thet way. 'Lije an' hisn woman come from home, too."

Jerry, squatting by the fire, was silent for several minutes, then looked up slowly.

"Buried?" he said.

Joe looked at the child in astonishment.

"Well I reckon thet's what I said; buried," he repeated.

"What's thet?" very simply.

"My soul, boy!" in absolute wonder, "why, pore 'Lije is dead, dead as a cole stone, an' weuns is agoin' to bury him. Aint you never been to a buryin'?"

"I dunno," hesitatingly.

"Aint you never seen nothin' die?"

"I dunno," with a tone of humility added to the ignorance.

"Aint you never broke a chicken's neck?"

"No, but I hev sawn it done," somewhat of confidence coming again into his voice.

"Well, when its neck's broke, an' it's a-lyin' thar rale still—"

"But it don't," Jerry interrupted quickly, "it hops around powerful, it do, jest all over ever'thing."

"Thet's true," Joe acknowledged, seeing the weakness of his simile, but at a loss for a better, until after a little thought he looked up slowly, "but it do git rale quiet afterwards."

"Thet's so," Jerry allowed in his turn.

"An' cole, an' stiff," Joe went on, with superiority growing in his voice.

"It do," looking up.

"Well, then it's dead: it can't crow no mo', an' if it's a hen it can't cluck no mo' to its chickens; it can't eat ner nothin', an' it's dead," solemnly.

Jerry made no response, his little mind was far too busy, was groping too earnestly for him to make any sound; and Joe went on:

"An' thet's what's come to pore 'Lije Miller; he's dead, plum dead: he can't eat, ner talk, ner do nothin'; he jest lies thar stiff an' cole, an' youuns kin call him furever! Pore Mis. Miller were jest a-howlin', but 'Lije never knowed it."

"An' what's buryin'?" Jerry asked again in the silence that followed Joe's words.

Again Joe looked the child over from head to heels, as a naturalist would scan a totally new and unexpected development in some well-known species. This ignorance was something entirely beyond his experience,—any extreme being beyond him,—and he scarcely knew how to account for it; but with exemplary patience he tried to make it clear to the child.

"When folkses is dead," he began slowly, "we digs a hole an' puts 'em in, an' kivvers 'em good."

The child's eyes grew wider as he listened, and he fastened them on the speaker with an intensity that made Joe halt a little in his speech.

"They're 'bleeged to do it," he explained hastily, as if the child had condemned the practice.

"An' puts rails 'round it, an' bresh on top?" the little, anxious voice questioned.

Joe was puzzled for a moment, but he answered bravely, nevertheless:

"Sometimes they do when critters air roun'; they purtects 'em thet away."

"An' can't theyuns never git up no mo'?" with his pitiful eyes still on the man's face.

Joe shook his head.

"Not fur a long spell," he said, "an' I aint rale sartain sure 'bout thet: but some preachers b'lieves it, an' calls it the 'jedgment day,' an' says as all folks as is dead gits up then: gits up a-singin' an' a-shoutin' to march to the 'Promis'-lan',' whar thar aint no mo' sickness, ner nothin' bad. My Nancy Ann's gone,—gone in at the 'Pearly Gates'!"

"'Golding Gates'," the child interrupted eagerly, "the 'Golding Gates,' Mammy 'llowed she were agoin' thar, her did."

Joe looked at the child earnestly.

"Is youun's mammy dead?" he asked, too curious to remember the doctor's injunctions.

Jerry shook his head.

"I dunno," he answered, and all the light died out of his eyes, "I dunno; I dunno nothin'!" covering his face with his hands. "Mammy's goned away, an' I piled bresh on her, I did," the burden of his remorse breaking out in a wail, "an' some blossoms; but I never knowed—I never knowed!" rocking back and forth with the pitiful refrain coming almost hysterically from his lips,—"I never knowed, I never knowed!"

Joe was startled, for he remembered the days when this cry never faltered until the voice was too weak to cry. Was the child becoming ill again? And in his anxiety he remembered the doctor's quieting words.

"It's all right, Jerry," he said gently, "you done all right: ax the doctor when you sees him, he knows."

The pitiful cry died away and the rocking ceased as Joe went on:

"If youuns Par buried her—"

"The woman in the valley named it 'plantin'' of her," the child put in wearily.

"Well," Joe granted, "some folks do name it plantin', but I don't 'llow as I like it; it soun's like weuns wus taters or corn, so I says buried, I do: an' if youuns' Par buried youuns' Mar, her muster been dead, sure; an' if you piled rails an' bresh roun' her, you done jest right; you purtected her, you did."

Jerry leaned against the chimney, silent; his remorse was being stilled, but his hopelessness was increasing with every word Joe uttered. He would never see his mother again unless what Joe only half believed should turn out true;—the "Jedgment day," when all the dead should rise; and he looked up asking:

"An' when'll it come?"

"What?" in some anxiety lest his stock of learning should be exhausted.

"The day when all the folks gits up?"

"Thar aint no man as knows," Joe answered with reassured solemnity, "the doctor told my Nancy Ann as nobody knowed; he said the horn 'ud blow an' all 'ud rise: but some folks don't b'lieve it; pore 'Lije Milton never b'lieved it, 'cause he 'llowed he'd ruther never git up no mo'; he 'llowed he'd done lived in a mine as is a hole in the groun', and he'd jest as lieve stay thar;" then rousing as from a meditation he turned to the child, "but you done right, Jerry, an' youuns pore Mar is a-restin' mighty easy, I reckon, an' you kin rest easy too," with which grain of comfort the child went away to his bed in the corner; and Joe, feeling troubled about him, determined to tell the doctor of his perplexity, and ask his advice. He had done his best, but he was dimly conscious that his knowledge had run short under the child's questioning, and any further probings from this quarter would put him where he would have nothing to say. Besides, he was in some doubt as to the soundness of the child's mind; such dense ignorance puzzled sorely his own half-knowledge. He could not comprehend this extreme any more than he could realize the other, and he felt obliged to appeal to a higher power.

He would ask the doctor the next day, for of course the doctor would be at 'Lije's funeral.

CHAPTER IX.

"Death endeth all :
And then ?
The tears are dried—The dim hope fled,
Love lieth still, and cold, and dead—
Death endeth all :
And then ?

A DIM, gray day with the clouds drifting so low that they hid the tops of the mountains, and hung far down the sides like ragged curtains. No rain was falling, and the wind was still save now and then it rose in sudden gusts that tore the clouds to pieces.

Joe and Jerry set out on their way at an early hour, as the distance was not short, and the occasion one that demanded the respect of long and solemn waiting, especially from Joe, who had the honor of having come from the same county in Tennessee as 'Lije Milton. Many in the colony had come from neighboring States and counties, but Joe alone had come from the same place.

They had beaten their clothes clear of dust; had greased their boots, and scrubbed their faces and heads until the skin shone, and the hair lay as sleek as wax. But it was a great day in Durden's and one that required these rites and ceremonies. 'Lije Milton was a miner of high degree; indeed, a mine owner, and not only this, but one who had dared to go so far as to doubt the doctor's doctrine of a hereafter : one who had actually argued this point with the doctor, but who still loved the doctor, and had more than once declared his intention of knocking down any one who agreed with him in his opinions against the doctor. He could not second the doctor in his views, but no one else should dare to take such a stand while " 'Lije Milton hed a fist ! "

And 'Lije was held in most profound respect : he had killed a "grisly" with a jack-knife,—he had knocked down a mule with his fist,—he had discovered the new mine,—he had scalped more Indians than any one else had ever seen,—he had been to more places, even to the end of the old mine where everybody knew he would have to meet old Durden's ghost that lived there in peace and plenty.

All these things 'Lije had done: and all these things Joe poured into Jerry's ears, adding a full description of the awful terror of the black depths in "Durden's mine," where 'Lije had met and conquered the wandering spirit of the ancient possessor.

" Thar's water in thar thet never quits a-drappin'," Joe went on, "an' 'Lije kep' on a-hearin' it, an' a-hearin' it 'tell it jest wore him plum out, an' he 'llowed he'd go in thar an see 'bout it, an' he did," pausing solemnly, "you bet he did; an' he were gone two days, he were ; an' I tells you, Jerry," drawing a long breath that seemed to catch a little, "'Lije wornt never the same man sence; never, sure's youuns is born," stopping to put a fresh piece of tobacco in his mouth, "an' he never tole nobody what it was he sawn in thar, ceppen thet he hearn things a-cryin', an' the water allers a-drappin': but he 'llowed as ole Durden'd never pester him no mo' ; an' now 'Lije is gone, an' aint no better man 'an old Durden."

"Were ole Durden buried ?" Jerry asked, his mind occupied with these rites he did not understand.

Joe shook his head.

"I aint plum sure," he said, "fur ole Durden were dead an' gone 'fore ever I come out to this place ; but I hearn as he never wus ! He tumbled off some rale deep hole in the mine, an' nobody never knowed rightly whar it were ; but nobody couldn't git no mo' men to work in Durden's mine." Then more meditatively, "I aint never worked none in thar, but they do say as thar's mo' gole in Durden's mine 'an any man kin dig, they do."

"Gole?" the child asked.

Joe turned back in the narrow path to look down on him.

"My Lord! boy, aint you got nary idee?" he said, "aint you never seed no gole?"

Jerry shook his head, leaning humbly against an adjacent rock.

"I dunno nothin'," he answered wearily.

"Aint you never seed no money?"

And again Jerry shook his head. Joe was in despair almost; the child surely must be wrong in his mind.

"Well, Jerry," compassionately, "I mus' 'llow as you is a most onknowin' creetur: well, jest listen; money jest means ever' blessed thing an' creetur," taking his hands out of his pockets to emphasize his words,—"money means mules, an' powder, an' shot, an' a house, an' ever' kinder truck; money means wittles, an' clothes, an' boots, an' hats; money means you is too good to do nothin'; money means terbacky, an' segyars, an' whisky,—"

"Dad hed whisky all the time," the boy interrupted quickly.

"Then youuns Par hed money," Joe finished conclusively, "an' money air made outer gole, an' gole air yaller an' shines; an' gole jest lays roun' loose in Durden's mine!"

"An' gole makes the 'Golding Gates'?" the child queried deprecatingly as Joe was about to proceed on his way.

"You bet it do," he answered, "'cause the preachers says thar's riches thar as never fails,—never!" and again turning from the child he walked on.

Down, down, down to the funeral of this hero who had passed by the shining treasures of Durden's mine in order to do battle with Durden's ghost; but who had, nevertheless, come back a changed man.

Jerry listened and wondered, if the confusion of ideas in his mind could be called wonder. His pure and simple conception of the "Golding Gates" had become inextricably mixed with his father and the money that bought whisky! *Could* it be the same gold?

His judgment wavered for a time; but before he reached 'Lije Milton's it had settled to the conviction that the gold that bought whisky, and so represented his father and all his misery, could not be the same thing that made the entrance to the wonderful land of which his mother had told him,—the land where he must meet her. "Mammy'd never go no whars as thar wus whisky," he whispered to himself,—"never, sure's I'm alive." Still this conclusion did not change the mystery: did some people like beatings and hunger, and so go to a place where all was gold, and so all was whisky? 'Lije Milton was right; leave the gold, if gold meant whisky.

Yet there was something strange about it all; Joe seemed to set great store by gold, but not by whisky, for he never got drunk.

And Jerry was at a loss.

"I'll ax the doctor," he said softly to himself,—"Joe says as he kin jest tell about ever'thing—I'll ax him," and he followed silently down the steep way.

The clouds came lower and lower over the rough land that was torn and rent in every direction by hands hungry for gold,—the rough, red land so dark and unlovely; with no exquisite coloring; no beautiful fresh greenness; no gorgeous autumn staining,—poor, hard, rock-broken land.

But humanity did not seem to miss the soft loveliness that had spread about their paths in the far East; they did not ever think of the wind that sobbed among the black pines and crept down the lonely gorges as the same wind that swept across the green hills far away beyond the Mississippi. A little child listened to it because it sounded "like Mammy a-singin' "; but that was all.

The people had come only for gold, and what use in listening to the wind, even if it did come from their old homes. All was equal out here in the West, and money was made more easily. In the East it had been long toil and little pay; riches and luxury were all about them to be envied and longed for, but not to be won by them. What folly to listen to the wind,—what folly to think of their old homes where their fathers had been content; the old men and women making their living so hardly,—the old graves where so many had laid them down in weariness and hope. It had done very well for the old who had been content to see others above them; but in this new West things were very different.

The wind was whispering very low to-day—and Jerry listened almost unconsciously: in his own home the clouds and wind came down just as they did here, and he felt less lonely when they closed about him, as he followed Joe in puzzled silence.

At last 'Lije Milton's house was reached: a frame house with an upper story, which, being the only one in Durden's, had caused much talk at the time of building. But 'Lije's wife, who had come out later than he, had made him build this addition which his friends had criticised quietly. Criticised because they were friends,—and quietly because 'Lije was not over scrupulous about either words or blows.

There were curtains at the glazed windows, and a fence about the front yard, which last was more than even the doctor's house could boast: more than this, there was a horse-rack in front of the gate for the convenience of any one stopping either at 'Lije's, or at any other house in the settlement.

Inside, all was in solemn order: a large fire burned in the broad fireplace of the best room; on the walls were frightful prints; a gorgeously painted clock ticked on the mantel-piece, flanked by two brilliant china vases; the bedstead in the corner boasted a feather-bed, a rare and costly thing in Durden's, and was covered by a patchwork quilt that would have defied any rainbow to a contest of colors. A rug of fringed woolen rags was on the floor in front of the hearth, and on the backs of the three cane-seated rocking-chairs were tidies of wonderful workmanship. Rows of medicine bottles stood on a table in one corner to show that no money had been spared in 'Lije's illness; and around this gorgeous apartment,—for it was gorgeous and luxurious for Durden's, and Mrs. Milton saw with much pride that all were awed by it,—were placed benches and chairs for the accommodation of friends. They were pretty well filled now, and had been so for hours, by rows of women and children, with their long bonnets either pushed back from their heads, or held in their hands.

Near the fire, rocking slowly in the largest of the rocking-chairs, backed by the gaudiest tidy, sat the widow. Her straight, sandy hair was screwed into a tight knot at the back of her head; her dress made of curtain chintz was gorgeous in palm leaves a foot long, buttoned in front with large white china buttons, also a rare article in Durden's.

"'Lije never grudged her nothin', you bet!" and all the women moved their heads mournfully. "'Lije never grudged nothin', thet was sure," they said, then looked to where, on two rough carpenters' benches, rested the painted deal coffin, and in it all that remained of the hero of Durden's.

A powerfully made giant, now lying in unwonted quiet and unnatural neatness, arrayed in a suit of "sto' clothes" that proved more than anything the great wealth and importance of the man, and the calm disregard his widow had for money. "Thar aint nothin' mean 'bout me," she had said, "an' 'Lije *shell* be buried in the best clothes thar is in Durden's, an' them is his own sto' clothes," and all the settlement agreed with her, and looked with much just pride into the eyes of the people who had come over from Eureka to the funeral.

Outside a group of men stood about the door and lounged against the fence; and inside, through an open door another group of men could be seen in the kitchen, where refreshments were being served by two or three women.

All had been in and out more than once, for it was not often that corn-bread and bacon, and whisky and coffee were to be had without stint, and had with the choice either of "long" or "short sweetenin'"! But "there warnt nothin' mean 'bout Mis. Milton."

No one went in as if they specially needed or desired the food and drink, but with an air of accommodation, as if they took it only to please their hostess and their dead friend.

So it all was when Joe and Jerry arrived: it took a little time to make their way through the group in the front yard, for every one had some word to say to Joe about the boy. Gossip and news spread even in that wild country, and everybody knew that Joe Gilliam had found a boy and had taken him in; but more than this Joe scarcely knew himself. That the boy's name was Jerry,—that his mother was dead,—that he had run away from home and would have died in the attempt but for Joe,—was all that Joe knew, except that the boy was hopelessly ignorant,—might be considered even a little off in his mind. But Joe let none of this appear in his talk.

"Is thet your boy, Joe?" they asked.

"Thet's ther boy," looking down on Jerry, standing beside him with his hands in his pockets.

"Where'd ye' find him?"

"A-comin' down Blake's trail."

"He looks mighty skimpy."

"He do," Joe acknowledged; then a silence fell, during which all the group was occupied in looking Jerry well over, and no sound could be heard save the chewing and spitting of tobacco. This was the way of their kind, and Jerry, seeming to understand it, was silent under the scrutiny. Then Joe turned away toward the house, and Jerry followed him.

"Tuck off youuns hat," Joe whispered as they entered, and the child obeyed.

All around the room his eyes wandered ; over the rows of ugly, work-worn, stolid-looking women,—wearing on their faces and in their eyes a sort of unquestioning stoicism. They knew all that life could possibly hold for them ; they had solved, as far as they could hope to solve or as far as they had realized them, all the mysteries of their days : they knew no higher desire than the bare necessities of food and clothing ; their hopes were bounded by their actual wants ;—their sorrows, their joys, their pains and pleasures were borne without any outcry ; nothing but their fatalistic stoicism possessed any intensity for them, and from that they were seldom shaken.

A birth, a death, a beating came naturally into the day's work, and passed by with little comment.

Jerry looked about him now without any understanding of what this gathering meant. Lije Milton was dead, Joe had told him, and they had come to see him buried, or planted, whichever name one preferred using : and Jerry had come to see, and to judge and condemn, or exonerate his father : to satisfy himself as to his own action in piling the brush on his mother's grave, and then in deserting her. It was a thing of momentous importance to him, for either it would settle forever on his life the burden of remorse and pain ; or it would prove to him that the burying of his mother was an absolute necessity, so leaving him no hope but the day of Resurrection, which Joe seemed to hold as very questionable.

It never occurred to him that the burying of his mother, right or wrong, would have deprived her of life, and so have exonerated him from all ill-doing : he felt only that either his father had buried her to keep her from running away to the "Golding Gates," or that she was really dead, and there was nothing in the future but the "Jedgment day."

Next to the long white box which Joe was now approaching, Jerry was the center of attraction, for all were curious to see Joe Gilliam's boy.

Fortunately for Jerry the curiosity of this class was not demonstrative: a fact satisfied them, and Jerry standing among them proved all the story they had heard, and the passing whisper that "Joe ain't found much," ended the matter.

But Jerry realized nothing after his first look around the room, save that Joe was standing, hat in hand, gazing into a long box that seemed strangely like one he had seen before. His patient eyes grew more wistful, and a look of pain and wonder came in them as he watched Joe.

He was afraid to go nearer, afraid of the certainty that would be his if he looked in that box. Almost it seemed as if he would again see his mother as he had seen her last, before his father had nailed the box up to put it in the ground. He trembled from head to foot as he stood looking up with eyes fixed steadfastly on Joe's.

"Yon's afraid," one woman said to another, and the all-important widow, hearing the words, looked at the child.

"You kin look in," she said, "'Lije aint a-goin' to hurt you: he never b'lieved he'd git up no mo,' an' I don't b'lieve it nuther— " obstinately.

Jerry only half comprehended the words as he stood watching Joe, and had no thought that they were addressed to him; but Joe fully realized not only all that was being said, but all that was being thought; and beyond this, the awful breach of funeral etiquette of which Jerry was now guilty. Not to stand and look mournfully at the poor lump of clay clothed in the mocking emblems of daily life—not to stand and think how "he'd falled away in his sickness," and how he looked "rale nateral,"—not to make a close inspection of the defenseless fellow-creature so as to be able to describe and criticise for the benefit of less fortunate friends; was to show a decided lack of breeding, and mortally to offend all surviving relatives.

And Joe, not in the least comprehending Jerry's trembling terror, drew the child forward; drew him forward until the questioning eyes could not but look down to the dead for their answer. The gaunt, grayish-yellow face—and the great toil-worn hands crossed in unearthly quiet. There was no sound, no movement from the child; he stood and looked while his heart seemed to sink within him, and the daylight seemed to fade from about him. His disconnected wonders were drawing together—his weary questions were finding answers.

He had done no wrong, had aided in no ill against his mother: he had been right to lay the rails about her, and to pile the brush there; and his running away was not leaving her.

White and still he stood, losing his ignorance—losing his fair hope of the "Golding Gates,"—and with a loneliness sweeping about him even as the clouds swept down and clung about the mountain-side,—a loneliness that grew and grew as the ceremonies of the day went on.

Every blow that drove the nails home in the coffin-lid seemed to echo back through all his useless journey, to his poor home among the far-off hills! Every dull thud of the clods as they fell from the busy spades, seemed to choke him,—to fill him with a stifling, breathless horror,—to separate him still more hopelessly from the only love his days had known.

What it was the doctor read,—what it was the hoarse voices sang,—what it meant when all stood bareheaded while the doctor looked up to the dull gray sky, the child could not comprehend: it was to him like a dream, and over and over he whispered—"I aint got nobody, Mammy,—I aint got nobody."

All the way home he plodded silently after Joe: no words passed, only the whisper soft as a breath:

"I aint got nobody, Mammy, I aint got nobody."

And when his scarcely touched supper was over, he wrapped himself in his blanket with his little bundle held close in his arms. Somehow he was less lonely while he could hold it close, could know and remember that his mother had worn that very apron, and had hung it on the very peg from which he had taken it. This was a comfort to him, for amid all the changes and wonders of the life he had lived of late, he seemed to be losing hold of the stolid facts that hitherto had filled his days. Things seemed strange and unreal to him, and the poor faded apron was something tangible that proved to him that his past had been more than a dream.

CHAPTER X.

" The fair pure soul of a little child,
Opened wide to the light of day—
Looking away to the far Paradise,
Forgetting its roots are in clay."

"MORNIN', doctor."

"Well, Joe."

"I'm done brunged him, doctor."

"Very well; where do you go from here?"

Joe turned his hat over in his hands once or twice, and threw his weight from one foot to the other before he answered with a jerk:

"Eureky."

"You work there steadily, do you?" gravely.

"Not percisely," giving his hat another turn, "but I makes a livin' fur me an' Jerry."

The doctor took his pipe from his mouth and blew out a wreath of smoke.

"What is your work?" he asked.

There was a pause, then Joe answered slowly:

"It's hones' work, doctor, I promise you thet."

"The same work your wife used to cry about?" the doctor went on.

For one moment Joe stood irresolute, then he turned from the study-door where he had been waiting.

"Jerry's out har," he said, and walked away down the hall.

"Very well," the doctor called after him, "send him in."

Coming from the glare of the daylight into the comparative gloom of the study, where the windows looked like holes cut in walls of books, Jerry was blinded for a moment; but in a little while it seemed more natural to him, for the somber books seemed to shade the sunshine down to the likeness of the light up under the rocks where Joe's little house stood.

A bright fire burned, for the season was late autumn, and in front of it, in a long, low-hung smoking-chair, rested the doctor.

Hat in hand, Jerry paused just inside the door and looked about him.

Books were unknown to him, and the walls might just as well have been lined with stones for aught he knew. He did not look at them with wonder, even, nor at anything except the doctor looming like a shadow in the clouds of tobacco-smoke.

This man was a power to Jerry; a hero, a magician who could cure every kind of sickness; who knew everything; who could "bury folks," which was to Jerry the most mysterious of all his attributes.

So Jerry paused and looked at him with a deep, wondering interest, and some awe.

"Shut the door, Jerry," the doctor said, "and come here."

Slowly the door swung on its hinges, closing with an uncertain grating of the lock that betokened much hesitation, then the clumsy boots tramped heavily across the floor. Close up he came and stood looking down with much gravity on the doctor, who returned his look with corresponding interest.

"How are you?" he said.

"I'm well as common," Jerry answered.

"And Joe is good to you?"

"I 'llow he's rale good, I do," with a little more heartiness creeping into his voice, "he gin me boots, he did," looking down to where his trousers were carefully stuffed into the coarse, rough tops.

"Well, sit there by the fire," the doctor went on, pointing to a stool near the hearth, "and tell me all about it; I hear that you went to 'Lije Milton's funeral."

"Buryin'," Jerry corrected, taking his seat quietly, "Joe he names it a buryin', he do."

"Well, a burying if you like: Joe said you had never been to one, before," the doctor went on encouragingly; Joe had implored him to talk to Jerry on these subjects, as from Joe's conversation with him Jerry did not seem quite right in his mind: so the doctor, watching the child carefully, put his question.

"I 'llowed I never hed been to nary a-one," looking steadfastly at the doctor, "'cause I never knowed what it were 'tell I sawn it; but when I sawn it I knowed it," shaking his head like an old man, and turning his eyes from the doctor to fix them sadly on the fire.

"And did you hear the words I read, Jerry?"

The child shook his head.

"I reckon I hearn," he answered slowly, "but I never knowed 'em—I aint never hearn none like 'em."

"Can you read?"

A blank look came over the child's face,—

"I dunno," he answered without looking up.

"Could your father read? or your mother?"

"Mebbe," was answered doubtfully, "but I never hearn nothin' 'bout it; an' I dunno nothin' nohow," putting his elbows on his knees and his chin down in his hands. So much that was bewildering had come to him, that he felt weary and despairing when made to realize, however kindly, his ignorance. "I gits rale tired a-steddyin' 'bout things as I hears Joe a-talkin' 'bout," he went on, "I jest sets an' sets, an' keeps on a-steddyin' 'tell I'm plum wore out, I is."

"Tell me some of the things you do not understand," the doctor suggested, becoming more interested in the boy, about whom there was an air of such unspeakable loneliness;—whose place in the world's general plan seemed to have been forgotten. No one owned him; no one cared especially for him; and having been instrumental in restoring the boy to life, the doctor felt in some sort bound to try to help him: and now the child looked at him gravely, asking—

"Do gole makes money as buys whisky?"

"Yes."

"An' do gole make the 'Golding Gates'?"

"The 'Golden Gates'?" slowly.

"Thet's what I said," earnestly, "the 'Golding Gates'; thet's whar Mammy 'lowed she were a-goin', her did," solemnly, "an' her pinted straight out the winder to whar the sun were a-setting, her did."

"And they buried her?"

"They did, sure," then with a little catch in his voice,—"an' I piled bresh on her, I did," looking up wistfully.

"Well?"

"An' I were feared as she couldn't never git up no mo', 'cause of the bresh," speaking more rapidly as he touched the cause of his agony, "an' I hearn a woman a-sayin'as her were planted, an' I 'llowed as Dad hed kivvered her in so her couldn't run away to the 'Golding Gates'—an' I 'llowed I hed he'pped him, I did, but I never knowed—I never knowed!" putting his hands over his face.

"But you did right, Jerry," the doctor said; "the brush will protect the grave from washing."

"An' it kivvered the rails, it did," looking up anxiously, "I 'llowed as 'twornt a-tuckin' nothin' jist to lift a few rails from the fence; Dad'll never know; but 'twornt a-tuckin' nothin'. Mammy tole me never to tuck nothin' as wornt mine, her did."

"And would not your father have given you the rails?" the doctor asked, more to draw the child out than to decide on the wickedness of stealing the rails.

Jerry shook his head.

"Dad never sot no store by Mammy, never, sure's youuns is born," turning his eyes once more to the fire, "Dad were a-goin' to bust my head agin the chimbly, an' Mammy ketched his'n arm, her did," his face lighting up and his eyes flashing—"an' Dad knocked her agin the wall, he did, an' chunked me a-topper her! it was in the mornin', an' the nex' mornin' thar were a-buryin'; an' then Minervy Ann Salter comed to live, her did," breathlessly, "an' her knocked me deef an' bline," pausing, "an' I runned away," with a fall in his voice and a change in his whole manner: the running away had been such an utter failure.

The doctor sat silent while the wretched story dawned on him: would it be merciful to open the child's eyes to all the story—merciful to make him understand all its bearings?

"But Mammy he'pped to split them rails, her did," the child went on slowly, "an' I only tuck a few, only a few; an' I kivvered 'em good so Dad couldn't seen 'em; 'cause if he tuck 'em away ole Molly,—thet's the sow," in an explanatory tone, "ole Molly'd a-rooted it sure, jist sure," meditatively, "fur ole Molly were the meanes' hog a-livin': I 'llow Minervy Ann Salter's done kilt her by now, I reckon her hes," drawing his shirt-sleeve across his nose; "pore ole Molly, her were pisen mean, sure, but her b'longed to Mammy, an' I'd like powerful to see her onest more, I would,—I aint got nobody," putting his face down on his arms that were crossed on his knees—"I aint got nobody—" with a little cry that struck home to his companion's heart.

"And I too have nobody, Jerry," the doctor said.

The child looked up slowly.

"Not nary a soul?" he asked.

The doctor shook his head.

"My mother died when I was a little baby," he said.

"An' youuns' daddy?" interestedly.

"He married again."

"An' she beat youuns?"

"No, but she did not like me, and I lived with my uncle."

"An' you never runned away?"

"No, but after I was a man my uncle died, and I came out here."

"What fur?" gravely.

"There are people here; people who get sick, and lonely, and tired, and I can help them; I can make them well, and help them to be good so that they can go in at the 'Golden Gate' when they die."

"Does you b'lieve thar's a 'Golding Gates'?" wonderingly; for his own belief in it had seemed to fade from him in the presence of death and the grave as he had lately realized them.

"Yes."

"An' youuns mammy is thar?" softly.

"Yes,"

"An' my mammy?"

"Yes."

There was a moment's silence; then the thin little face was raised again.

"I comed a fur ways an' I aint never sawn it."

"And I have never seen it, but I know it is there."

"Whar?"

"On the other side the grave."

"The grave?"

"Yes, where we will be buried."

"Like 'Lije Milton?"

"Yes."

The child turned away again to the fire that danced and flickered up the chimney, as if he saw some vision in the flames: and the doctor, thinking his own thoughts, almost forgot the child.

"But 'Lije Milton never b'lieved as he'd git up agin," came at last, rousing the doctor from his dream, "and Joe says as 'Lije'd jest as lieve stay in thet thar hole furiver, an' hisn woman tole me them same words, her did."

"Maybe he would," the doctor answered, "but that does not mean that he is going to stay there: you may be willing to sit by that fire forever, but that does not mean that you are going to do it."

"Thet's true as mornin'," the child said slowly, "I'd jest as lieve stay har, but I aint agoin' to: an' 'Lije will hev to git up?"

"Yes."

"When?"

"I do not know."

"Joe 'llows as it's named the 'Jedgment day,'" deprecatingly.

"Some people call it so," the doctor answered.

"An' what does you call it?"

"I call it going home," watching a wreath of smoke as it floated away slowly.

"To youuns' mammy?" the boy asked.

"Yes," and the doctor drew his hand across his eyes. How persistently the child clung to the one love of his life: and he pictured to himself what a poor, draggled creature this mother had been, yet how divinely the child's love wrapped her in its beauty. Her life had been given for his;—and some day he would know this. Then with a sigh the doctor roused himself.

"You must learn to read, Jerry," he said.

"Read?"

"Yes, like this," taking a book from a table near him, and opening it, "you see these little marks?"

"I do."

"Well they are words, and a great many of these words put together make a book; a book like one of these," pointing to the shelves.

The child looked about him in wonder; on every side were rows and rows of these things called 'books,' what were they—what did they mean?

"And you must learn so that you can take one of these and know what is in it."

"What fur?" gravely.

"So that you will know everything without asking any questions," the doctor answered, "and there is a book that will tell you about the Judgment day, and about the home where your mother has gone, and about what you must do to get to your mother."

The solemn eyes opened wide, and the boy came close to this friend who would do so much for him.

"Show me it?" almost breathlessly.

The doctor took up a small Bible that lay near, and put it in the boy's hands.

"That will tell you all about it, when you learn to read it."

The child went back to the hearth, but not to the stool; the crowding emotions drove all unnaturalness from his mind, and he squatted down after his own fashion. He turned the book over and over tenderly, from time to time wiping his hands on his trousers; over and over, then he opened it—nothing but little black marks and dots—nothing he could know or understand; it was disappointing, and he shut it up again.

"It'll tell me the way to go?" he asked wonderingly.

"Yes."

"To tuck me right straight to mammy?"

"Yes."

"An' when I gits thar kin I tell her 'bout thet bresh?"

"Yes."

"An' 'bout ther big water I were feared on?"

"You can tell her everything, Jerry, but it will not be any use, for she knows it all now; she is always watching you, and is always near you; you can not see her, but she is always with you."

"My Mammy!" looking quickly over his shoulder, with a sort of terror gathering in his eyes—"tell me agin, doctor, I 'llow I don't rightly on'erstan' youuns," dropping on his knees and creeping to the doctor's side.

"It will take a long time for you to understand, Jerry," looking pityingly down into the anxious eyes, "but you must believe what I say; believe that your mother is near you, watching you; and when you are good she is happy, and when you are bad she is sorry."

The child looked all about him where he knelt with the book clasped in his hands, and a whisper crept through the silence—

"Mammy!"

A mystery more strange than all others had come to him which there was no hope of solving; this, however, made no difference,—the doctor said he was to believe it, and his lonely heart had grasped it and was hugging it close. And the doctor watching him saw the little hand reach out with an uncertain, longing gesture;—if only he could touch his mother!

And all the way home the happy thought went with him that his mother walked beside him. Almost he heard her footsteps and would pause to listen.

CHAPTER XI.

> "And with small, childish hands we are turning around
> The apple of life which another has found."

"I CLEAN furgot," Jerry said slowly.

He was squatting on the hearth, looking into the fire, with the book the doctor had given him held close in his hands. "I clean furgot 'bout the gole, Joe."

"Folks mostly 'members gole," Joe answered, packing his pipe carefully. "An' I 'llowed as you never knowed nothin' 'bout it, you'd ax the doctor."

"Aint you got no gole as you kin lemme see?" the boy asked.

Joe stirred diligently in the fire until he found a coal to suit him, then picking it up deftly with his hard fingers, he dropped it on his pipe.

"Mebbe I hes," he answered slowly, running his hand deep into his trouser pockets. "Mebbe I hes one piece as you kin see," and he drew out a five-dollar piece, old and dingy.

"Look at thet," he said with some pride, "jest turn it over an' feel of it."

Jerry turned it over obediently, but no exclamation of admiration escaped him, no word of any kind, and a look of disappointment clouded his face.

"It aint much purty," he said at last, holding it at a little distance, "it ain't much yaller, nor much shiny, it aint."

"It's ole," Joe granted, "an' heapser folks is hed thet."

"What fur?" looking up simply.

"What fur! Lord, boy, sure ernough you dunno

nothin'! What fur? Great-day-in-the-mornin'!" bringing his fist down heavily on the table, "why, fur ever'thing,—jest ever' blessed thing!"

Again Jerry turned his eyes on the money that to him meant so little—good for everything.

"Good to git me to Mammy?" he asked at last.

"You bet," Joe answered hastily, "fur if you hev ernough, you aint agoin' to cuss, ner sw'ar, ner steal, ner hev a-hankerin' atter other folks' truck; an' if you don't do noner thet, you kin git anywhars."

"Mammy never hed none," thoughtfully.

"An' her never went no whars," Joe struck in conclusively.

"Her went to the 'Golding Gates,'" slowly, "'cause the doctor says so," the doctor being overwhelming evidence.

Joe rubbed his hand all over his ragged hair: what could he say; his own knowledge embraced only barren facts and unproved beliefs.

"The doctor 'llows as she hev gone to the 'Golding Gates,'" the child repeated.

"An' I 'llows it," Joe answered, "an' I 'llows as my Nancy Ann—leetle Nan, I calls her mostly,—hev gone thar too."

"An' her never hed no gole," simply.

"Not rayly much," Joe answered hastily, "but jest you rub thet gole in the ashes," he went on, changing the subject, "an' you'll see jest how it shines an' shines 'tell it gits right in a feller's eye, it does." Then more meditatively, "It seems like a eye don't rayly count, it gits holt of a feller all roun', it do."

And Jerry stooping, rubbed diligently first one side of the coin, then the other, in the warm soft ashes until the gold shone and glittered.

"It do shine," he said at last, turning it over in his palm, "folks oughter keep it a-shinin'."

"Folks hes too much to 'tend to, they hes," Joe answered, blowing clouds of smoke out in his satisfaction over having convinced Jerry of at least the beauty of gold; "they'll tuck thet to the sto'," Joe went on instructively, "an' Dan Burk 'll give 'em a lotter truck; fur all he's pisen cheatin'!" again striking the table. "When I come har he never hed nary a thing, an' his'n woman tuck in what pore little washin' she could git, her did; an' now—God-er-mussy!—thar aint nothin' good ernough fur her—nothin'; an' my pore leetle Nan air dead!"

Jerry sat silent, turning the gold over in his hands: he did not understand all of Joe's words, but being accustomed to this mistiness of comprehension, he said nothing.

There was a long silence, then Joe knocked the ashes from his pipe.

"An' the doctor wants ter see me?" he said.

"He do," Jerry answered; "he wants to see you 'bout sumpen, I dunno rightly what; but he says, says he, 'Jerry, tell Joe I wanter see him right pertickler,' says 'ee, an' I says, says I, 'Doctor, I will.'"

"Thet's cl'ar," Joe said slowly, "an I'll go to-morrer, I will"; then to the boy, "gimme the gole, boy, it's to buy wittles, it is."

And Jerry delivered up the money he had made to shine, the money he did not as yet know the meaning of, but that, nevertheless, had a mysterious fascination for him.

He had turned it over many times, had looked at it with a longing desire to know its full value and meaning: he should have asked the doctor about it, and must surely remember to do it the next time he saw him. He would go and see him again very shortly, for there was growing up in his heart an absorbing adoration of this man—this man who had first made him well, and had now made him happy. Had told him his mother was near him always—had given him a book to tell him the sure way to reach her.

"I loves him, I do," he said to himself, and Joe hearing the indistinct whisper roused from his revery.

"What's thet youuns says?" he asked.

Jerry looked up—

"I says as I loves the doctor," he answered gravely.

"I 'llow I do too," and again Joe rubbed his stubbly hair, "he's a rale gentleman, he is, ceppen he's mos' too hones'."

"I wonder!" Jerry said slowly.

"It's so," Joe went on, "the doctor jist helps all the mean,—pisenes' mean trash thet comes to Durden's, an' he never axes a center pay, he don't."

"What's pay?" and Jerry pushed the fire that had fallen a little apart.

"Well," and Joe's tone was well-nigh hopeless, "if youuns aint the all-beatenes' boy I hev ever saw! aint you never done a job afore you leff home?"

"I hepped Mammy hoe the crap," Jerry answered, "an' I hepped her split rails, I did, an' I 'llowed I could tuck a few to lay roun' her, I did."

Joe was in despair almost; only one thought the child seemed to have—his mother, and the grave he had heaped with brush—how could anything be explained to him? And into Joe's half-developed mind crept the thought that whatever Jerry took hold of he would never let go—never. While the child's strangely simple question found him always without an answer, and about things he had thought himself in full knowledge of.

"Pay means to gie a feller pay when he works fur youuns," Joe began; "an' the docter works on all the trash as gits sick, an' they never gie him a cent."

"Did you pay him fur a-workin' on me?" the child asked.

Joe shook his head.

"He 'llowed as you didn't rightly b'long to me nohow—an' he wouldn't tuck no pay: an' when Nancy Ann an' my leetle baby died he never tuck no pay nuther, 'cause he 'llowed as I were too pore, he did; but I'll pay him yit, you bet!" slapping his pocket that jingled as if there were more gold pieces there like the one he had shown Jerry, "I'll pay him 'cause I loves him, I do."

"An' what kin I do?" the child asked slowly, "I dunno nothin' ceppen to hoe, an' chop wood, an' to tote water."

"You kin larn," Joe answered comfortingly; "when I were a little chap I never knowed nothin' nuther, but I larned: jist keep youuns' eyes open, an' youuns' yeers open, an' you'll larn a heap, you bet."

"An' I'll larn to read the book," Jerry added, taking his Bible from the floor where he had laid it while he rubbed the money, "an' I'll read it to you, Joe, 'bout how you mus' git to Nancy Ann," he went on simply.

"I'm 'bleeged, Jerry," Joe answered, taking Jerry's offer as it was meant, "but I don't sot much store by larnin," gravely, "but I reckon it'll take all you kin git to git you along: folks as aint got much natteral sense needs a heaper larnin', they do."

"An' I'll try to git it," humbly, "an' I'll ax the doctor 'bout gole, I will."

"An' I'll go to see him in the mornin', I will," and Joe began to bar the door and the window, and Jerry crept away to his blankets in the corner, and Pete to his leaves; and when all was still Joe made his usual rounds, and leaned his loaded rifle by the bedside.

CHAPTER XII.

"'Nevertheless,' continues he, 'I, too, acknowledge the all but omnipotence of early culture and nurture; whereby we have either a doddered dwarf-bush, or a high towering, wide-shading tree; either a sick yellow cabbage, or an edible, luxuriant green one.'"

AFTER Joe had been to see the doctor, Jerry had been told that he was to go there every day that he might learn to read and write. There was no school in Durden's, and Eureka was too far for Jerry to walk there every day; so the doctor had agreed to teach Jerry, and the money Joe would have had to pay the school-master in Eureka, he was to give to some poor people in Durden's,—families the doctor knew to be worthy of help.

"So I'm a-payin' fur you, Jerry, and you mus' try to larn," Joe had said; and Jerry, with a very humble and dejected mind, had promised to make every effort in his power. The feeling that he had to learn because he had not enough natural sense was dispiriting; but it was some comfort to know that the doctor had learned all these things, and if he had begun life with a deficiency of mind, Jerry felt there was hope. And he said mildly in answer to Joe:

"The doctor jest knows ever'thing, Joe, an' I 'llow he hed to larn 'em; I reckon he had mighty leetle sense when he started."

Joe shook his head.

"I dunno," he answered honestly, in spite of the point Jerry so unconsciously had made, "I dunno 'bout hisn sense; but if larnin' kin do thet much fur any pusson, then I says larn, I do."

"I will," Jerry had said earnestly, and had trudged away down the mountain-side with determination in every step. It was all a great mystery to Jerry, and somehow since he had learned what books were, and that they knew everything, he felt somewhat afraid of them, and looked at the study as an educated child would look on a haunted house. He dreaded the room, but overcame his fears sufficiently to stay there alone for hours when the doctor would leave him to go on his round of visits. He would endure everything in order to learn : his motives were simple, but because of their simplicity were strong ; first, the doctor had said he must learn ; and second, Joe was paying precious gold for his learning. But beyond all this there was the longing to read the books that would tell him everything, and show him the way to his mother ; and with these motives behind him he plodded patiently along the road to knowledge close at his master's heels. And the doctor had asked himself if he were wise in the course he had begun with Jerry : would not his own ignorant, narrow groove in life be happier for him ?

Maybe ; but it was right to lift, be it ever so little, every immortal soul. He had made a vow once to help in some way every life that came in contact with his own—more than this, to seek out lives and strive to raise them : a step might not be altogether clean, yet people could mount by it. He would raise the boy as high as was possible ; would give him as much education as he would take—this would be doing only his duty. The life of this poor little waif was as lonely as his own, and what was marvelous for his class—feeling the loneliness. Usually if they had enough to eat and clothes to cover them, this was sufficient ; but this child, living in comparative comfort, knew there was something he missed, and was hunting for it vaguely—blindly. Only a spark of soul, maybe, but he would keep it alive, and perhaps light a life that would be a beacon to many.

And the possibilities that he was setting up a " will-o-the-wisp "—could he overlook them ? How many chances of inheritance were there against this boy—what lay behind in his blood? Still, he would try; for the child was surely above the average; already he had shown thought and gratitude: standing looking up in the doctor's face, with his hands in his pockets, he had asked gravely:

"Do gole keep a feller from cussin'?"

The doctor took his pipe from between his lips the better to see the sharp little face.

"Joe 'llows as gole keeps a feller from cussin'," the child went on, "and from stealin', and a-hankerin' atter other folk's truck; do it?"

And the doctor answered slowly:

"Sometimes it does, Jerry," smoothing his mustache over his lips that were smiling.

"An' gole gits aheaper truck?"

"Yes."

"An' pays you fur a-workin' on pore folks, an' sick folks, an' pisen mean folks?" eagerly.

"Yes."

"An' I can't pay you," wistfully, "but I kin chop wood, an' hoe, an' tote water, I kin."

"It does not make any difference, Jerry," was answered gravely, "I was glad to make you well."

Then there was a silence while the boy from where he stood looked pityingly on the man.

"An' nary a pusson he'ps youuns," slowly, "'cause you is big an' strong, an' knows ever'thing," the child went on as if to himself, "an' I can't do nothin',—nothin' ceppen sot a heaper store by you; an' I do,—fore God, I do; jest you say, an' I'll do it sure, jest sure! Farwell!" and then the door was shut, and down the hall the heavy boots had tramped out of hearing; and the lonely man had listened and known that into his life a true love and gratitude had come—like a sweet, fresh rain falling wastefully on fire-hardened clay. True, still all that duty could do should be done for the child.

And Paul, coming in and finding Jerry's slate full

of poor little efforts at writing, propped on the table so that the fullest light fell on it, and knowing whose it must be, pondered on the meaning of this man's strange life. What was the point of this new freak that made a man like his guardian spend hours on this wretched little creature. He had better be a clergyman at once. And was this what his mother meant by being a man? Was this the hope entertained for him? A feeling that was hatred almost, came over him; and he swore a silent, angry oath that no such hope should be fulfilled.

But he had a curiosity to see this boy,—and one day he waited for him—one day when the doctor was out. It was a crisp, cold day, with a thin covering of snow rounding all the sharp outlines about the country, and making the pine woods look like fairy-land. Very cold in the early daylight when Joe went away to his work; and Jerry as he put things to rights, whistled a straight sort of tune he had heard Joe whistle as he sat idle on Sundays—whistled on and on in calm contentment, not knowing that the day would mark a turning-point in his life; life was a good thing as it came to him now.

His work was soon done, and shutting up the house securely, he tucked his trousers deeper into his boots, tied his hat down over his ears with a woolen scarf, and put on a coat of Joe's which, if rather large, was warm.

A queer figure he made trudging across the white country, his long coat flapping against his heels, and occasionally sweeping the snow off some drift higher than the rest, and his sharply-cut yellow face looking out from the folds of his scarf. But the hollows in his face had filled out,—the angles had rounded down, and the expression had changed in a way that was remarkable. His eyes were wistful still, but there had crept into them a keen, thoughtful look that asked a question with every glance.

Still whistling the straight tune, he steadily overcame the obstacles of the steep, slippery path; then out across the sweep of the valley where the wind seemed to gather up its scattered forces and attack one on all sides, keen, bitter, merciless.

But the boy did not pause; steadily on against wind and snow until the road that formed the one street of Durden's was reached, then he slackened his pace, and even with this pause was almost breathless when he reached the doctor's house. Still the end was accomplished, and up the steps and down the hall he went, and in at the study door in perfect peace with himself.

Always reverent in his demeanor toward the study, yet this time he paused longer in his closing of the study door: a new presence was there, a person that in all his visits Jerry had never before seen. Fair and tall, but still a boy; certainly a boy, for his trousers were stuffed into his boots—but such boots! A round fur cap was set on one side of his fair head—a fur-lined cloak, held in place by a glittering clasp, was thrown back over his shoulders, and his hands, small and white, were stretched out to the roaring blaze.

Jerry paused inside the door and looked at this new person without any hesitation or expression of embarrassment; the same honest observation that would have been called forth by any unknown wonder, now came to the front in honor of Paul; for it was he who occupied Jerry's eyes and thoughts.

"Well," Paul said slowly, giving the new-comer a stare quite as unmitigated as Jerry's own, "is your name Jerry?"

"It are," gravely, coming toward the fire.

"It are, are it?" Paul went on with a mockery in his tone that was not lost on Jerry—"you must love lessons to come on such a day as this."

"I do," Jerry returned, beginning to divest himself of coat and hat, "an' I loves the doctor too."

"That is really wonderful,—and your coat," slapping his legs with a riding-whip he held, "who made that?"

"I dunno," turning the clumsy garment over with recollection only of the great comfort he found therein, for what were cut and fit to Jerry? "Joe he gin it to me, an' its rale warm, it are."

"Rayly?" and Paul threw his hat on a neighboring chair, and his cloak on top of it, "Well, the doctor are gone out, he are," he went on.

"Doctor's mostly out when I gits har," Jerry answered calmly, but not without some appreciation of the sarcasm contained in Paul's English; for he was beginning to realize the great gulf that separated his language from that of his master, "an' I allers waits fur him, an' I steddys my book tell he comes."

"You don't say!" Paul went on, showing himself master of the vernacular, "an' when he comes do he say youun's is a good boy?"

Jerry shook his head quietly enough, but the color stole up slowly into his dark face—

"He says, says he, 'Does youuns knows yer lessing, Jerry'?" steadily—"an' I says, says I, 'I'm a-steddyin'," taking his place on the accustomed stool, "an' then," with an expression of despair in his eyes that quite amuses Paul, "I tries to say it, an' I'm thet flustered I can't do nothin'."

Paul laughed with real amusement in his tones this time, and asked his next question with an honest desire for information.

"And the doctor looks like a meat-axe, don't he?"

"A meat-axe!" indignantly, "no, he don't nuther; he says, says he, 'Jerry, try agin,' ceppen the doctor he says 'agen,' he do."

"The mischief!" and Paul poked the fire viciously; "when I miss," he went on, "he's as mad as the devil, and does everything but fling the book at my head."

Jerry looked his companion over from head to foot, a look of scorn almost.

"I jest don't b'lieve thet," he said quietly, "I jest don't b'lieve it."

The quick color sprang into Paul's girlish cheeks—"The devil!" he cried angrily, looking down on Jerry where he sat in his favorite position with his elbows on his knees and his chin in his hands—"I'll beat the life out of you."

Jerry shook his head.

"No, you won't, nuther!" a new light of defiance shining in his eyes, "and you jest better not try it."

Paul laughed lightly, already half ashamed of threatening such an enemy.

"You need not be so uppish!" he said, with great contempt, "do you suppose I would touch such a dirty little beggar as you are? You are a fool!"

The color deepened in Jerry's face, and slowly he rose from his place as the full meaning of Paul's words reached his mind.

"I aint no beggar," and he drew his slim figure to its full height, "an' I aint dirty; an' you kin jest take thet for youuns' lyin' words," and before Paul could move to defend himself—could in any way realize what was coming, Jerry's rough hand struck him fairly in the mouth.

But that was all Jerry did, for in a second Paul's soft, plaited riding whip was wrapping itself round Jerry's back and shoulders in quick, stinging blows—blinding, bitter blows that fell with bewildering rapidity!

It lasted only for a moment,—then the smaller boy's arms, hardened by toil, were wrapped tightly about Paul's body, and Jerry strong with rage and hatred bore him relentlessly back, heedless of all obstacles, until Paul's spurs caught and he crashed down among the chairs and stools, and in an instant, before he could at all realize what was being done, Jerry was sitting on top of him.

"Now jest dar' to say ther doctor's a meat-axe!" he cried, emphasizing his words by tapping his finger on the end of Paul's nose, "an' jest dar' to say thet I'se a beggar an' dirty—jest you dar' to say it, an' I'll jest gouge youuns' eyes plum out," giving Paul's nose a little tweak.

"I will kill you!" Paul cried in a fury, trying in vain to free his arms from where Jerry pinned them with his knees, "damn you! let me get up—I'll tell the doctor—I'll have you put in jail—I'll kill you!"

"When you gits up," Jerry answered quietly, his success having restored his temper—"but I'se agoin' to set right har atopper you tell the doctor comes, I is; ef you 'llows thet I'm agoin' to let you git up an' beat me agin, you is got the wrong pig by the leg sure; I aint agoin' to stir, I aint."

"Let me get up, I say," and Paul's voice sounded constrained, for a dreadful thought had come to him—suppose the servants should find him in this horrible position! and his pride put its flag at half-mast:—"I will not touch you, I promise,"—then one step lower—"I will pay you, Jerry, just let me get up?" pleadingly—"and I will never say a word about it."

"An' you'll take back what you cussed me?" gravely.

"Yes."

"An' 'bout the doctor?"

"Yes."

"Well, I don't much keer," patronizingly, "git up," and Jerry sprang nimbly from off his fallen enemy, "but don't youuns never furgit this dirty beggar," with stinging sarcasm, "an' thet trick of ketchin' a feller roun' the legs is a rale good un, you bet; a boy 'cross the mounting tole me thet; its been a long time, but I aint never furgitted it, an' to-day it come in rale handy," but Paul had gone in silent, unspeakable rage, slamming the door after him.

What a black disgrace! How could he ever revenge it—how could a gentleman retaliate on this little vagabond—this vagabond he had waited to see? "But I'll pay him off if it takes my whole life," and locking the door of his room, he cast himself down on his bed and cried like a girl.

And in the study Jerry was putting the chairs straight, and shaking his head in a threatening way as he swept the hearth. He was too much excited to study, and at the same time very much pleased by the realization of his newly discovered strength.

"I gits it a-cuttin' wood," he said, feeling his arms, "an' I'll git some mo' cause it come in rale handy," then he sat down with his elbows on his knees and his chin in his hands, gazing into the fire.

What kind of person was this boy he had whipped—who was he, and where did he come from, and what made him so fine?

He talked like the doctor, and his hands and his voice were like a child's—what was it that made them so different? they were both boys.

"An' he looked at me like I was a dorg, he did," the color coming into his face again, "but I punched hisn's nose good, I did; but he's rale purty—rayly purty," thoughtfully, as Paul's fair face came up before him. Still, he shook his head as he said—"It's rale purty, but thar's a leak sommers," and he could not like it.

CHAPTER XIII.

> "The true gods sigh for the cost and the pain—
> For the reed that grows never more again—
> As a reed with the reeds of the river."

AND the doctor, coming in with an open letter in his hand, sat down as if worn with a weariness deeper than that of body, and closed his eyes with but one glance in the direction of the boy. Jerry sat quite still.

What ailed the doctor? and anxiously watching him all thought of Paul and the recent fray passed from his mind.

Was the doctor sick—was he going to die like 'Lije Milton? and a great terror came over the child. To die like 'Lije Milton:—the doctor die—then the wider question, must everybody die? It had never occurred to him before, this idea, and who would bury the last one?

But the doctor, who saved every one; what would become of all the people if he should die?

Maybe he was dead now! And the boy was afraid to move, while his heart was rising up within him, swelling with this great imaginary pain.

"I'll jest die too," and in his preoccupation he said the words aloud, rousing the doctor, who opened his eyes with a sigh.

"What is it, Jerry?" he asked.

"I were feared you were dead," was answered hesitatingly, "an' I 'llowed I'd die too."

"Not just yet for either of us," and the doctor held out his hand for the book. Then suddenly it came to Jerry's mind that he did not know his lesson, and he began to feel anxious about the affair with Paul—what would the doctor say?

"I don't reckon I knows it," he began, not for one moment doubting that confession was a necessity.

"Well."

"Well," slowly, "thar were a feller in here when I come—a rale purty feller," gravely, "an' he says, says 'ee, 'Does you love lessings?' says I, 'I do;' says 'ee, 'What do the doctor do when you don't knows 'un?'—says I, 'He says, Jerry, try agin,'—says 'ee 'The doctor looks at me liker meat-axe,' says'ee, 'an' mos' chucks the book at my head,'—says I, 'I don't b'lieve it," his face beginning to color with the recent excitement; "then I furgits rightly what comed next, 'cause I were so mad; but he cussed me a dirty beggar, he did," his fists involuntarily doubling themselves, "an' I ups an' knocks him in the mouth, I did, an' he licked me liker dorg!"

"What?" and the doctor sat up straight in his chair as the long story climaxed so astonishingly.

"Don't git skeered," and Jerry put his hand reassuringly on the doctor's shoulder, "I never hurted him much; I jest tripped him up an' sot on him, I did, an' I punched hisn's nose till he asked me please to git up, he did; but I never hurted him much."

The doctor was smiling now, a smile that broke over his face as the sunlight breaks through a cloud, and lighted up and transfigured every line of it, making it look as it must have done in his youth when all the untried, beautiful years and days lay before him where to choose; then his face became grave once more and the lines about his lips hardened as the thought came to him—"Would Paul tell him of this difficulty?" he thought not, Paul told him nothing.

"I do not suppose that you did hurt him," he began coldly, "but I do not like it, and you must not fight in my house: as long as you are here, Jerry, you must behave like a gentleman."

"What's thet?" quietly.

Again a smile flitted across the doctor's lips; the boy was so unconscious, and he answered—

"I am a gentleman."

Jerry stood and looked at him with a curious wonder growing in his eyes.

"An' you 'llow as I kin be like youuns?" drawing a long breath; "nary time, an' it's no use a-tryin' it; you kin jest as easy make a hick'ry stick outer sourwood, jest as easy," then more slowly, "but I'd like to," and his patient eyes looked wistfully at his friend.

"We must try, Jerry," and the doctor laid his hand kindly on the boy.

"I will," the narrow face lighting up in its earnestness. "I'll jest do ever blessed thing you says, I will," and a new future, a grand, overwhelming possibility, opened before the child.

To be like the doctor: a thought that had only dimly dawned on him when the question came up of his learning to read; that had never been a defined thought, but only a glimmer of light that for one instant had shone and faded. And now it had been put before him not only as a possibility, but as an expectation and an end set for him by the exemplar himself!

Jerry drew a long breath as he stood there trying to realize this great thing: stood there rough and untrained, ignorant and a pauper, and set this end before himself. Heretofore he had been one of many who only lived from day to day; to whom life is an accident that for some is smooth, and for some, rough: now he had begun another journey with an end that seemed far more impossible to him than the "Golden Gates," had seemed. To try to be something, to try to rise, presented a far more vague and intangible outline to him than the effort to reach some place had done. A realization of this future was impossible, and he came back to the original suggestion as to something he conld take hold of. He knew the doctor; every day he saw him, touched him, spoke to him; and he could grasp this first proposition of trying to be like him.

"An' I will," he said, speaking aloud as if he were alone, "I will if it kills me."

And that night when the bitter wind howled up and down the mountains, driving the snow until it banked high against Joe's little house; and Joe in front of the roaring fire smoked, and told of dark danger in the heavy snows,—Jerry sitting there scarcely heard, for he was looking at his future in the flames, and wondering. And in the midst of the most thrilling of the stories he got up from where he squatted on the hearth, and drew a chair forward.

Joe paused.

"I 'llows as youuns aint a-listenin'," he said in a rather injured tone.

"Yes, I is," and Jerry seated himself in the chair gravely, "but I 'llows as I'd ruther hev a cheer; the doctor don't never sit on the flo'; leastways, I aint never sawn him a-doin' it."

"The Lord hev mussy!" and for many minutes Joe sat silent, regarding his small companion with doubtful looks. "Air youuns crazy, Jeremiah P. Wilkerson?" he said at last, "jest plum crazy?"

Jerry shook his head.

"The doctor 'llows as I mus' be a gentleman," he answered, "jest like him ezackly; an' I will," nodding his head complacently, "I will if it kills me!"

"An' the doctor 'llows to give youuns a good buryin'?" Joe asked with solemn sarcasm.

"I never axed him," Jerry answered literally; and as he hitched his heavy boot-heels on the rung of the chair, a mild sense of self-approval swept over him that was like a breath of summer air; and he did not know that Joe's story remained unfinished, the narrator smoking slowly and in silence, only now and then glancing at his preoccupied companion.

"Thet boy air a cur'us one, sure," Joe's thoughts ran, "a reg'lar nubbin."

CHAPTER XIV.

"As to the assertion that *no* amount of evidence could establish the supernatural, we ask in amazement, 'On what is the supernatural based? Does it rest on anything higher than the idle habit of mind induced by the observation of constant recurrences?'"

THE fight with Paul was a great event in Jerry's life, and Joe chuckled over it with much satisfaction, being proud of Jerry's "sperret."

"An' the wuss youuns air, Jerry, the wusser hisn's lickin' air," he had said more than once; but this triumph was soon overshadowed by an occurrence of solemn portent.

It was going to be a bitter winter; everybody said so, and Joe had stopped work some time before to make preparation for it. Jerry worked with him heartily enough; coming home from the beloved lessons an hour earlier that he might help Joe bring the wood up from the gorges where the pines grew best: helping him build a sheltered pen for the three pigs that were to be kept and killed as needed: helping him make a bin to keep the meal dry, and a box in which to pack salt beef.

Jerry rather liked it; there was a sense of plenty and comfort about the preparations which he had never experienced before. All winter there would be enough to eat, and enough to wear, and wood to warm them. All this his father could have done, the boy thought, but he never had, and the winters had been black times of terror to him and his mother.

But he said nothing to Joe about this; drew no comparisons; for already he was imbibing some idea of keeping faith since once the doctor had said to him—"You should remember you are speaking of your father"—and the boy had felt his face grow very hot: he did not realize why, but since then he had not talked about his home nor his old life. Indeed, he abhorred the thought of it, for gradually there was growing on him the knowledge of the fact that his mother had died for him. Sometimes he would sit up quite still in the night with his little bundle held close in his arms, and try not to long to kill his father, try not to curse him and the great brutal woman who was now his wife. For, living with the doctor day after day, he was gathering to himself a more clear and distinct understanding of right and wrong, and of the vast difference existing between the doctor and the people about him; he was making every effort to imitate and follow him in all things, and his love for this man was boundless. But growing up with this adoring love he bore for his hero, there was a deep grievance and bitterness: it was the doctor's love for Paul that Jerry had learned to watch for and suffer from; for Jerry hated Paul. The slow, cool scorn with which Paul looked at him;—the manner in which he stood aside to let Jerry pass, as if the danger of touching him was to be avoided—the way in which he vacated the library whenever Jerry entered, was too much to be endured without breeding a hatred deep and lasting. But if Jerry had known it, Paul had also a great pain: if only it would not be beneath him to whip this little cur—this wretched little pauper who had dared to fight and overcome him; and beyond was always the dreadful doubt—"Did the doctor know?"

So the bitter feeling grew between the boys, and Jerry's wonder as to the connection between Paul and the doctor became one of the chief problems of his life—for he could not touch Paul if the doctor "sot much sto'" by him.

He would have liked to have asked the doctor about it, but the same feeling that now made him keep quiet about his own affairs made him hesitate about asking questions. So he only watched that he might learn with certainty what the feeling was between these two. And the watching made him heavy-hearted; for there was something in each that he could not understand nor copy, and they could talk of things of which he knew nothing; yet Paul was only a boy.

But there was always a brisk change when Jerry went back to the little house under the rocks. Joe was always there before him now, working busily and whistling the one straight, endless tune they had in common.

Each day the journeys for wood were made, until the piles grew so high that Jerry thought they would last forever. But Joe knew better, and worked day by day while Jerry was in the settlement, and after Jerry came home, far into the late evening. At last the stacks had grown high enough even for Joe, and as the covered pen was ready, Joe proposed that they should go for the pigs before another fall of snow.

"It'll be a heavy one when it do come," he said, looking at the clouds that were gathering; clouds of deathlike, ghastly white, "an' the devil couldn't drive them pigs up these rocks then."

So Jerry came home earlier than usual, and they set off.

"Jim Martin lives nigh ole Durden's mine," Joe said, "an' you kin jest tuck a leetle spy in the hole, Jerry."

Jerry's eyes opened very wide.

"I'm feared," he answered, forgetting in his excitement that the doctor had told him to say 'afraid.'

"Most folks is," and Joe shook his head mysteriously, "but I 'llows as it can't hurt you jest to peek in fur a minnit."

"An' the water?" Jerry asked in a low tone.

"I 'llow it's a-drappin yit," Joe answered, "an' it'll keep on a-drappin' tell the Jedg*ment* day; it soun's powerful creepy, it do."

To see "ole Durden's mine!" Jerry felt his hair

rise up, and all his veins tingle; to look in, and maybe to see the gold glittering on the walls and floor, as he thought it must,—to hear that water dropping all day and all night, never ceasing, never forming into a pool or stream that any human eye had seen. An indefinable trembling came over him as he tramped down the path behind Joe, and he longed for yet feared the termination of the afternoon.

"Thar's Jim Martin's," and Joe pointed to where a thin curl of smoke floated up slowly from among the rocks.

"Jim's house is piled thar plum aginst the rocks, it are, jest fur orl the worl' liker dirt-dauber's hole; but my Nancy Ann 'llowed she never wanted no rock wall to ourn house."

"I keep a-hear*ing* someth*ing*," Jerry interrupted, laying great stress on the final g, which he found much difficulty in pronouncing, "someth*ing* a-roar*ing*."

"It's a stream as comes down the mounting nigh the mine," Joe answered, "an' it falls over the rocks jest as purty!"

"A falls," Jerry suggested, feeling quite sure he had said the correct thing.

"Falls," Joe repeated, "the doctor names it thet too," he went on, "so I 'llows as youuns is correc'—a falls; an' you kin see it from up thar, from a rock as is jest ezackly over the hole of Durden's mine," stepping a little aside from the path to where one rock rose higher than the rest.

Jerry followed eagerly; a short, sharp climb, then he heard a slow, astonished exclamation from Joe.

"Great-day-in-the-mornin'!"

The boy leaned forward; and there, a little below the level of the peak on which they stood, lying on a thin, flat slab of rock that projected far out from the dizzy cliff, was the doctor.

"Well, Joe," looking up to where they stood above him.

"Evenin', doctor," Joe answered; "weuns is agoin'

to Jim Martin's atter them hogs, an' I 'llowed I'd show Jerry the water."

"And it is very beautiful," the doctor said, turning his eyes again on the somber gloom of the scene below them.

On all sides the grim, barren rocks darkening down into the deep gorge where the crowding pines dimmed the shadows to blackness: and from the far cliff where the light lingered longest, down from rock to rock the silver water falling and crying aloud—holding up "white pleading hands—" down into the black gorge and out to lose its life in the hot, dry plains.

"I reckon it's sorry to come down," the child said with a sigh; and the doctor turned and looked at the wistful face lifted to the far heights. Had the boy read his thoughts—the thoughts that came to him like voices from his own life as he lay there watching the water that forever was falling like one in a dream—forever that weary cry!

"An' Durden's mine is down thar," and Joe holding by a broken rock leaned over and pointed to where below them the shadow deepened to the semblance of a black hole. His voice broke harshly on the silence, and the boy sighed once more and looked into the eyes of the man below him. He could not tell what he saw there, but it was the same thing that made him sigh.

"An' the rock youuns is on, Doctor, is mighty thin," Joe went on as he stepped back to where Jerry stood.

"It has held me many times," the doctor answered slowly; then they turned and left him.

To Joe it was the place where the "water came down an' looked rale purty"—to Jerry it was a place that made him afraid—made him feel as he had done when at last he had stood on the greatest height he could reach, and saw the sun setting across the plain; a feeling that made him walk in silence after Joe, and scarcely heed the talk of Durden's mine. Yes, he would go and look, what matter if he *were* dragged in to perish there; it would be better than this feeling he could not understand. The doctor understood, for the doctor looked into his eyes sometimes, and even in his blind ignorance Jerry could see and know the unuttered longing.

"He's lonesome too," he whispered to himself, and followed silently down to where the black hole yawned.

Darker and rougher the gorge grew—the path narrowed to the merest thread of a track—then there came a level space covered with piles of *débris* from the mine, and through the broad cutting in the pines that once had been the road could be seen the village of Durden's, that had grown from the few miners' huts that at first had congregated around "Durden's find"; and near by, the stream that fell so far, fretted and fumed in the artificial channel which the old miners had cut for it.

"They says thet the water runned right in har," Joe explained as they stood in front of the mine, "an' ole Durden got the fust gole outer the water; atter thet he foun' it in the rock, he did, an' he jest sot to work an' dug a ditch over yon for the water, an' dug in the cave fur the gole."

Then he led the boy nearer and nearer, picking his way carefully over the rocks and rotting logs that were strewn about the opening of the deserted mine, down into a sort of basin, where they paused and looked up to the slab far above them on which the doctor lay; and it looked so high and thin, such a precarious resting place!

A few steps further, and the blackness of darkness gathered about them.

"Listen!" Joe whispered, pausing.

There was the sharp rattle of the stone they had dislodged that rolled somewhere into the darkness; then through the silence came the drip of far-off water—slow—heavy, regular, save that now and then there came a double sound as though too much had gathered for one drop—a quick, irregular sound like the catch in a sob or a sigh.

The boy stood very still ; the silence and the darkness seemed to grow about him and the sound of the dropping water seemed to rise and swell, then to fade and die like some creature crying ! He was awe-stricken—he was afraid to stir—even to raise his hand to touch Joe who stood so near ! Like one in a nightmare who could not move nor cry !

Great drops of sweat gathered on his temples—he trembled like a leaf in the wind ! was there anything back there in the darkness ?—anything coming toward him—anything ?—that drawn, white face he had seen in the coffin ! The dead eyes were open and staring at him—something touched him !

A wild cry broke from his lips, and turning he fled up the rugged opening—falling, scrambling, breathless, until he lay sobbing under the ghastly white light from the snow-clouds ; hiding his eyes and crying with sharp, quick gasps.

"Great-day-in-the-mornin' !" and Joe stood over the trembling child in much wonder "I jest teched you, an' sicher holler I never hearn—what ails you, anyhow ?" trying to raise the boy, "thar warn't nothin' to skeer you."

"I seen him—I seen him !" Jerry answered between his sobs—"I seen 'Lije Milton !"

Joe sat down on a rock overcome.

"'Lije Milton ?" he repeated slowly—"an' Lije never b'lieved as he'd git up agin !"

No doubts of the fact crossed his mind ; no question as to how or why ; that Jerry had seen 'Lije Milton was a simple fact which proved to his mind that the dead hero did not sleep in peace and quiet.

Gradually the sobs died away, and Jerry lifted himself as one exhausted.

"Less us go," he said, "less git away from this place," and Joe followed obediently.

Jerry, somehow, was taking rank above him, and this last revelation raised him into something of a hero.

All the slow way home they were silent, except for

the orders and cries to the hogs that were inclined to wander in their going. Neither at supper was there any conversation, and it was not until Joe had smoked one pipe, and had fairly started on another, that he broke the silence.

"It were surely cur'us, Jerry," he began, gravely, "thet I've been agoin' there a heaper times, an' never sawn ner hearn nothin' ceppen the water a-drappin'—naryer thing ceppen thet, an' thar's sumpen in it sure—jest sure," looking solemnly at his companion, who, in a chair opposite, gazed steadily into the fire, "thar's sumpen in it," he repeated, "fur it stan's to reason thet 'Lije wouldn't hev come fur nothin' : thar's somethin' onlucky 'bout thet place fur youuns, Jerry, thet's what it means," decisively, "an' you hed jest better keep clar of thet hole."

"I will," Jerry answered, drawing his sleeve across his nose, "I'll never go nighst it agin, you bet—I mean again," he corrected himself.

"Agin or again," Joe repeated, "don't make no diffrunce to me; I aint pertickler 'bout sich leetle trash as thet, but don't you go anigh Durden's; mebbe thar's a heaper gole thar, but it aint fur youuns," pushing the fire into a brighter blaze, "an' I feels a kinder all-overish when I 'members how youuns screeched when I jest barly teched you; sposen you gits yer leetle book an' read a spell," throwing another log on the mass of coals, "it'll be sorter cheerfuller to read 'bout the leetle boy as got the fly in hisn's eyes," then more slowly, "but it beats me how he done it."

"The doctor said it was the words he wanted to larn me," Jerry answered, as he took his book down from a shelf, "I spec it aint—it is not for rayly true." Joe's English was demoralizing, and Jerry puzzled sorely over his words, speaking slowly and correcting himself when he remembered. And Joe was very lenient, treating these efforts as signs of the weakness of Jerry's intellect.

"Jest please yerself 'bout words, Jerry," he said kindly; "I don't rayly hev no feelin' agin one word or ernether; it's orl one to me, jest so I kin on'erstan' youuns; now jest pole erlong 'but thet boy an' hisn's fly."

So Jerry found the place and read slowly and earnestly, holding the book to catch the firelight. And Joe listened with much satisfaction, a look of pride growing in his eyes as he watched the child; and when the page was turned Jerry paused, as he always did, to show Joe the picture.

"It's jest as naytral," bending his gray head over the poor woodcut, "thar's the leetle boy, an' thar's hisn's fly—a rale big 'un—an' it's flewed away, it hes."

"'The fly is out of my eye,'" Jerry read in a sort of recitative.

"It jest is," Joe commented, "an' thet's what I said, it flewed away."

It was more cheerful, the reading, and their spirits rose in a measure; but when bed-time came, Jerry, by Joe's advice, brought his blankets and spread them close by Joe's bed; and once or twice in the night Joe got up to put more wood on the fire, and waked the boy to tell him to "quit a-cryin' so pitterful."

The darkness and the sobs together were more than Joe could bear, and the next morning it was determined that Jerry should ask the doctor about his vision in the mine.

Jerry's heart was very heavy as he trudged away to the doctor's, for with the feeling that his mother was always near him—the feeling that had given him so much comfort—there was mingling now the mystery of the dead who walked the earth because they were not easy in their graves. Joe believed it firmly; and yesterday, had he not seen 'Lije Milton with his own eyes? And was his mother wandering like this?

She had died for him.

"If she had let Dad bust my head agin the chimbly her'd a-been a-livin' right now," and he drove his hands deeper into the cavernous pockets of his coat,—Joe's coat that Paul had laughed at. His heart was heavy, yet with it there was a feeling of importance that sustained him; 'Lije Milton had come to warn him! And he held himself a little more erect.

The fire burned brightly in the study, and the doctor was there when Jerry entered.

"Well, Jerry," he said, then returned to the book he was reading, so that the questions which hung on Jerry's tongue had to be put away until the lessons, which were done mechanically that day, were over.

"We shall have some heavy snows," the doctor said when they had finished, "and you may not be able to come every day, Jerry, so I have arranged copies and lessons which you can do at home on the days when the weather is too bad."

"Yes, sir, and I'm very—" pausing doubtfully—"much obliged to you," the doctor suggested gravely.

"Much obliged to you," Jerry repeated, then added quickly, "I rayly—rayly are!" as if the copied words did not satisfy him, nor express his gratitude.

The doctor smiled, then asked kindly:

"Did you get your hogs home safely?"

"Yes, sir; and, doctor," feeling that the time for his revelation had come, "I went into Durden's mine," his eyes growing wide as he spoke.

"Well."

The boy paused; with the doctor listening, the story seemed, somehow, to lose all importance.

"It is the truth, doctor," then in the excitement that came over him, he returned to his own special English: "Yes, sir, sure as I stan' afore you, I sawn 'Lije Milton—I did, an' Joe 'llows as he come to tell me thet the gole in Durden's mine aint fur me."

"Did you expect to buy Durden's mine?" the doctor asked quietly.

Jerry shook his head.

"No, sir."

"Then why should 'Lije Milton come back to tell you that you must not have it?"

Jerry looked doubtful.

"Joe said so."

"Well, Joe is mistaken: nobody can work Durden's mine unless they first buy it, and it will take a great deal of money to do that."

"Is Durden's mine full of gole?" the boy asked.

"I do not know," the doctor answered, "I have never examined it, but they say the new mine is much better."

"An' I never sawn 'Lije?"

"I do not think you did, Jerry," and the doctor smiled kindly on him.

"Well, farwell," looking up longingly into the face above him, "mebbe I can't git back to-morrow."

"Good-by, Jerry," holding out his hand.

The boy took it reverently, and looked at it almost adoringly; then for an instant his hold on it tightened and he raised his eyes—

"You goes to thet rock a-heaper times?" he asked.

"The rock over Durden's?" with some curiosity in his tone.

"Yes, sir."

"Very nearly every day," waiting for what the child would say next.

There was a pause, then still holding the doctor's hand Jerry drew a little nearer.

"Joe says it's awful thin," pleadingly, "an' you'll fall, please, doctor?"

The doctor shook his head.

"You and Joe need not be anxious," he said, "that rock will outlast me."

Jerry turned to the door—

"Farwell," he repeated, "but I'm afraid fur you," then the door was shut, and the sound of his footsteps died away before the doctor moved.

It had been so long since any one had cared—since

wistful eyes had watched for good or ill to him—so long!

Far back in the years there had been eyes whose faithfulness and love had never faltered ; eyes that looked at him now from out the shadows when the day darkened—from out the fire—from out his books! Eyes he had turned away from—eyes

> " that looked into his eyes with smile
> That said ' be strong,' yet covered anxious tears the while! "

So long ! And now these humble eyes looked up and pleaded for his safety—watched lest ill should come to him—loved him,—believed in him.

Poor little waif : poor little ignorant heart still half asleep ; was it kind to shake it free of dreams—to make it open its eyes to the broad, blinding light of knowledge—the merciless light that spared nothing ?

The fresh shadowy dawn wherein he now lived, was it not better ?

CHAPTER XV.

> "Like dry and flimsy autumn leaves that blow
> From all far distances, until by chance
> They meet and rest within some sheltered spot :
> So lives oft come together, and so rest,
> Until some wilder wind sends them apart
> To longer wanderings on the 'lonely road.'"

THE day Jerry came home from the doctor's with his bundle of books and copies was the last of the open weather, and the winter closed in with cruel coldness.

For days the snow fell: the world lay motionless: no sound of wind, no movement, a death-like stillness while the snow-banks grew higher and higher—the pine branches drooped and cracked sharply under the growing weight—and in the long, bitter nights the beams and logs of the house groaned and strained—shuddering as with a sudden blow from an unseen hand.

The wild creatures roamed and cried through the dark hours, coming nearer to man, growing fiercer and bolder in their hungry need. Each day as the door was opened, a path had to be cleared through the snow before Joe could do anything toward the day's work. Then in the long hours when Joe was gone, Jerry lived a lonely life in the dark house with window and door barred, and only the fire and Pete for light and company. Joe taught him how to load and use the rifle, and charged him not to hesitate to fire on man or beast.

He fed the hogs with the rifle close at hand, and watched with a nervous fascination the great tracks that day by day came about the house; and sometimes he heard the creeping footsteps and wild cries as he sat spelling over his lessons by the firelight.

A dreary life, until one day Joe brought home a window-frame fitted with glass, and screwed it in the window.

"You kin see now, Jerry," he said, "an' kin read youuns' leetle books," and the boy looked up very thankfully.

After that he worked diligently, sending his papers to the doctor when Joe happened to pass that way, and in return receiving words of commendation, and freshly arranged work. And in the long evenings he explained to his friend the processes by which he worked, and showed him all his papers, until over Joe's manner there came a change. He treated the boy so tenderly,—listened to his words and explanations so proudly, and when Jerry read aloud sat silent and admiring. Out among his friends he spoke of Jerry as "my boy"—and made allusions to the future when Jerry should stand with the best.

He bought the boy a cot; toiling up the slippery trail with it on his back; and Jerry's eyes opened wide with delight and wonder. Then he brought a new book from the doctor, and made a little shelf for Jerry to keep his books and papers on. And Jerry, grown white and a little thin from his winter's captivity, looked gravely out of the window, and wondered what all this attention from Joe meant.

He was growing very silent as the days went by, and was learning to brood in the enforced loneliness of his life.

From Joe he had heard all that he knew of Paul and his connection with the doctor; that Paul was the son of a friend who in dying had given him to the doctor, though some people thought that Paul was enough like the doctor to be his own: that Paul was very rich, and one day would own most of the mine in Eureka; and the reason Jerry had seen so little of him during his earlier visits to the doctor, was that Paul was daily in

Eureka learning from the engineer all about the mine and mining.

"He'll hev a heaper gole sure," Joe had said thoughtfully,—"but I 'llows thet thar's some as'll hev as much." And Jerry had listened with a dull pain at his heart.

The doctor loved Paul—the doctor worked for Paul's interests; and Paul, a rich man, would pass Jerry by like the dust in the road.

It was a bitter thought to Jerry.

It was not often during the long winter that the boy could go to the doctor; but each time he came home with a clearer and more mortifying knowledge of his own deficiencies, and of the distance that lay between even Paul and himself—while the doctor seemed hopelessly far. But with this knowledge there came ever a firmer determination to overcome all.

He worked eagerly—carefully—unceasingly; doing his sums,—writing his copies over and over, and reading his few books until he knew them very thoroughly. He saved and spelled out every scrap of newspaper that came into his hands, storing in his mind a strange medley of words and ideas; while through and over all was the memory of the doctor's words that had taken root and were bearing fruit in the boy's ways and tones—the suggestion that some day Jerry could be as the doctor was. He thought of it by day, and dreamed of it by night, building wonderful castles in the air. He would be a gentleman some day, and have books all around his room; he would have clothes such as Paul had, and walk and talk as Paul did—only he would be stronger, and love his lessons, which Paul did not. But one thing hurt him—one thing was a great disappointment to him—he could never touch Paul again, because Paul belonged to the doctor. And not only did Paul possess the doctor's love, but was protected by it from any revenge in Jerry's power. He could never touch Paul again, even though he had a feeling that Paul did not love the doctor—had not Paul called the doctor a "meat-axe"?

"But I whipped him for that," the boy would say to himself, and feel startled at the sound of his own voice coming back to him from the empty room. Each day he tried to read in the Bible the doctor had given him, but could make very little of it as yet: the words were strange and different from the words in his books, and he was often at a loss to understand them. But here Joe occasionally was able to give him unexpected help; telling him roughly and vaguely some of the stories brought to his mind by the names Jerry spelled out.

"Adam he were the fust man as ever growed," he said, "an' Eve were the fust woman, an' she were made outer Adam's bones, she were; an' youuns kin read an' see as thet's the livin' truth: an' the critters an' the yarbs were made fust to gie Adam sumpen to eat."

"But the 'Golding Gates,'" Jerry asked, "it don't tell about that."

Joe shook his head doubtfully.

"I don't ezackly onderstan' 'bout thet," he said, "but I allers hearn thet the Bible telled all about it: I knowed a preacher onest as telled me a heaper tales, an' he 'llowed thet they comed from the Bible: an' the doctor he tole my leetle Nan 'bout the good place, an' he read it out the book thet thar wornt no mo' sufferin' thar, ner no mo' cryin'. Lord! I'll never forgit how he sot thar an' read the book 'tell I'd jest as lieve a-died alonger Nancy-Ann," looking meditatively into the fire.

And Jerry, never thinking of turning to any but the first part of the book, plodded on as faithfully, as trustfully as he had journeyed toward the setting sun because his mother had pointed there for the "golden gates": he worked his way through verse after verse, with full intention of reading the whole book because the doctor had given it to him as his guide to his mother.

And gazing into the fire, or out of the window, he would dream and wonder without ceasing—longing for the snow to be over and the spring to come. He grew to love old Pete, and was sorry when the hogs were killed one after another, even though they lived like princes in consequence of it, having plenty of meat, and plenty of grease for their bread.

Jerry had never lived so well in his life, and he appreciated all his comforts, but not as he would have done a year ago; for he wanted now something more than food and clothes. In that little time he had been educated up to unappeasable wants, and the beautiful, happy time when he could be satisfied, was forever past.

The time when with childish eyes we look no further than from hour to hour; touching mysteries and wonders as the butterflies touch the flowers; glad for the sunshine; hearing music in the rain; sleeping, and dreaming golden dreams through the dark hours, until Want comes to us held in the arms of Knowledge—want that creeps into our hearts and voices—looks longingly from our eyes—walks with us all our days, until death stills our longing with a friendly hand upon our hearts.

And Joe watched and wondered: was it "books an' larnin'" made the boy so quiet; made him grow so tall, and slim, and white; and stand looking so long and so silently out of the window?

The boy was changing in every way, and between the two a different relationship was being formed. Jerry had risen to a great height in Joe's estimation, and gradually all his pride and love had centered on the boy. "My boy" he called him, and had a growing ambition concerning him. He had not for one moment forgotten the fight between Jerry and Paul, and each visit he paid to the doctor, in carrying back Jerry's papers, he would look at Paul and smile in a way to rouse all Paul's ire.

"Jerry's rale well," he would say, "an' gittin' rale strong."

And Paul would try to answer unconcernedly, but once or twice he found the doctor's eyes fixed on him with a criticising look in them that was anything but calming: and the boy took Joe into his list of hates.

"I can not see what you find to interest you in that stupid man and boy," he said to the doctor one day.

"Neither of them are stupid," the doctor answered, not lifting his eyes from his book, "and the boy is above the average in intellect: he is learning rapidly."

"And what good will his learning do him?" scornfully.

"The same good your learning will do you, possibly more."

"More good!" haughtily "I have a name and a fortune to support."

"And Jerry has both to make," then the doctor returned to his book.

Paul did not feel that he could say anything more just then; but the conversation rankled in his mind.

That Jerry should be put on an equality with him was an insult hard to bear—but that Jerry should dare to found a name and fortune was a still more bitter thought. He would brood and brood over the thought—sometimes ending with an oath—sometimes with a laugh: Jerry should work in his mine yet!

But he told the doctor none of this.

So the winter had its day; a long, merciless day that seemed to have no end.

And many folded tired hands for aye—and many would have found their graves a warm refuge. Hard and earnestly the doctor worked among the hovels in Durden's and Eureka; helping in money and words, and skill. No weather stopped him—no hardship seemed to turn him aside; and often Joe would come home and tell many things he had heard of the doctor's devotion to the people—a devotion he could not understand. And Jerry minding the house and the hogs up on the mountain; and Paul cursing his loneliness down on the plain—both wondered, and tried to find some reason for this strange and uncalled-for sacrifice of time, and comfort, and money; but it was a riddle neither of them could read as yet.

Only "eyes that have wept see clear"—see clear and far into the lives, and hopes, and sufferings of their fellows—only eyes that have wept have this second-sight.

PART SECOND.

"Get leave to work
In this world,—'tis the best you get at all:
For God in cursing, gives us better gifts
Than men in benediction. God says, 'Sweat
For foreheads,' men say 'crowns'; and so we are crowned,—
Ay, gashed by some tormenting circle of steel
Which snaps with a secret spring. Get work; get work;
Be sure 'tis better than what you work to get."

CHAPTER I.

> "There is no caste in blood,
> Which runneth of one hue, nor caste in tears
> Which trickled salt with all."

A RUMOR had come to Eureka,—a rumor that Eureka was to have a railway, and the town was wild with excitement.

So many years had rolled by without one ripple to mark their going, that this sudden waking up seemed to bewilder the people. So many quiet years wherein Jerry up on the mountain-side, and Paul in the valley, had grown and developed "each after his kind." Paul, absorbed in himself—Jerry, clinging close to the aim set before him in his childhood, absorbed in dreams grown out of his study of his idealized master, the doctor. Through all these years he had followed without question in any direction the doctor had indicated; had plodded eagerly through anything the doctor would teach him. But though a dreamer, his education had opened his eyes to many things that he would gladly have ignored. He now recognized his own class very distinctly; he realized the rank from which he had sprung, and looking on them he saw the haggard, stolid drudges—the weary, dirty, ignorant women—and his mother had been such as these?

He hated his class because they were so low, and he hated himself for the feeling; he hated social grades and the "accident of birth," and history was to him a black record of injustice, and suffering, and wrong; a narration of how the strong crowded down the weak, and that only because they were weak.

And at last his dreams took shape, and to himself

he seemed to come down out of the clouds. The doctor's life-work had been to raise humanity—his own life-work should be to raise his class.

Wrong must be righted; and in this wide western land, where all had equal chances, all should rise.

The Master of Mankind had come down to earth to lift up all humanity—aye—and had been murdered by a mob! Even so; but His teachings had lived, and through eighteen hundred years had worked and leavened the world; and now the time had come for reform!

And what higher task could a man set for himself? surely he would be a reformer.

But with the patronizing patience of youth he determined to begin humbly: he would show that he was not a wild theorizer; he would be practical at the start, and possible all through. And he asked the doctor's advice about opening a free school in Durden's, for he had decided that education must be the first step in reform.

But the doctor shook his head.

"Make them pay you, Jerry," he said, "if it is only ten cents a month; putting a money value on it is the only way to make them appreciate it."

"But many of them are too poor to pay," the young man answered slowly.

"None are too poor to buy tobacco and whisky," quietly; "besides, you are old enough now to think of making your own living."

Jerry looked up quickly with the blood rising slowly in his face, as the doctor went on:

"Joe is old now, and he has done a great deal for you."

"I could not help it," Jerry answered eagerly, "I was too young to know, when he first took me in, and since then he has never allowed me to work; my education has been his pride."

"Very true, and it all has been quite right until now; but now," and as of old the doctor tramped up and down the room with his spurs rattling at his heels, "now it will be good for you to work; you will be helped mentally and morally by working for yourself. I think the school is a good plan; but I advise you to take the school already established in Eureka, and make reasonable charges; the schoolmaster is old now, and never has been of any practical value."

"And what will he have to live on without his school?" Jerry asked.

"He has land; land that will bring him in a little fortune before long," thoughtfully, "besides he has money put away: I will speak to him if you like, so that you can secure the school-house and his influence."

Jerry looked doubtful: his intentions about the great work he had chosen, had been so different. He had pictured to himself a beginning where all would be gratitude and good feeling: where he would tell the people what he purposed doing for them, and begin by being a hero!

Now, the opening scene was all changed; and he put in a position to sue for patronage.

He had never spoken to the doctor of this great purpose, and now, somehow, the disclosure seemed impossible, for there was no escape from the doctor's reasoning: it was undeniably right that he should support himself; a thing that had not occurred to him in his dreams.

And yet, how could he say to the people—"I am doing this entirely for your good—but you must pay me for it"? How could a man professing to work on a high moral plane, push cash payments?

And he answered slowly:

"Let me think of it, doctor?"

"Of course."

And Jerry walked home slowly.

This conversation had taken place a year before the railway excitement had touched the little towns of Durden's and Eureka, and for that length of time

Jerry had been schoolmaster in Eureka after the doctor's plan.

It had made Joe very proud, and it was music in his ears when he heard the people say—" Mr. Wilkerson "; and when he saw Jerry making out his monthly bills, or signing receipts as " J. P. Wilkerson," his heart would throb with delight. But the height of his joy was reached when the Eureka *Star* published a flourishing notice of the " talented young schoolmaster, Professor Jeremiah P. Wilkerson."

Fully realizing the absurdity of the position, the amusement of the doctor, and the sneers of Paul, Jerry found this notice hard to bear ; but his cup seemed to overflow when he found that in his pride Joe had taken the notice to Paul as a triumph for Jerry !

No scoffing remarks from Paul—no labored explanation even, would have made the old man understand the amusing side of the notice or the little worth of it ; and though feeling just as Jerry knew he would feel, the doctor said such kind things to Joe that he returned home greatly elated, and with two pins fixed the bit of newspaper to the wall where he could see it always without any trouble.

But the year had seemed a lifetime to Jerry.—He had had to unlearn so much—to bear so much—to be disappointed in so much ; for outside of books he had no knowledge.

His whole life, since Joe had taken him in, had been spent between the little house under the cliffs and the quiet of the doctor's study ; and this year of practical work among the people had been a revelation to him.

Among the delusions which had been dispelled was the one that Joe worked in Eureka. Not that Joe had ever said that he worked in Eureka, but somehow the belief had grown up with Jerry, until now he discovered that a mistake had been made somewhere. To his astonishment he found that few people in Eureka knew Joe Gilliam—that fewer still knew where he worked, and no one seemed to have asked what his work was.

All this came to Jerry by accident, for it did not occur to him to ask any questions about Joe: but when later on he found that even in Durden's everybody believed that Joe worked in Eureka, he felt as if walking in a mist full of strange surmises concerning the old man, and in his musing his thoughts took curious shapes; for why should there be any mystery? Back through all the years his thoughts had gone and had found many things that could not be accounted for.

Why had the house been so carefully guarded? What was there in it to tempt a thief? And working nowhere that Jerry could hear of, how did Joe make his money? For Joe surely had money. But even this was a revelation to Jerry; for until he had gone to Eureka and had seen the way in which Joe's class lived, it had never occurred to him to question Joe's mode of life. It had been so different from the doctor's, where Jerry often lunched or dined, that it had seemed to him coarse and rough; but one insight into a Eureka house, and his eyes were instantly opened to the fact of Joe's superior mode of life; and at once he faced the mystery of the source of Joe's money.

So through these puzzles that were almost troubles, and many others, the year had waxed and waned and worn away as years will do if only one is patient enough. And Jerry had rearranged all his plans and ideas; had patiently readjusted all his theories as to poverty and want, placing them on a new basis that he deemed firm and practical, and that he was sure would stand all tests.

But suddenly, like the swift, unaccountable changes in a dream, the greatest excitement ever known in that region had laid hold on Durden's and Eureka: the deepest and widest excitement that could touch any small, unimportant place—a railway was coming! As surely as the sun shone and the wind blew, a railway was coming, and hundreds of people with it. Eureka was to be made a great city; the value of land was to reach an unheard-of figure, and all the inhabitants would bloom into millionaires!

How the report had come, or whence it had come, no one knew; but it was there among them like fire on the prairies. Nothing could quench the talk it roused, nor the hopes that flared and flamed in every direction.

Money was coming to all without one stroke of work being done: Fortune was walking calmly across the hot, dry plains—across mountains and rivers—steadily on to the town of Eureka, her chosen, favorite child.

The days and the years had passed very quietly until the talk of a railway had waked up the community, and intoxicated it with the thought of wealth. The people gathered on the corners with an eager, hungry look growing on their usually stolid faces; stopped each other on the street to discuss this all-absorbing possibility; wild with delight; shouting and drinking; betting their all as to where the railway would enter the town, what land would be the most valuable, and who had the best chances for the future.

It seemed to ring all the changes on the different characters; the parsimonious became absolutely stingy, holding their money with an eager grasp as the possibility of getting more seemed to come nearer to them; the avaricious became greedy for it; the reckless threw it away more wildly. The very children and women caught the infection, fighting among themselves, and drawing their husbands and sons into the horrid drunken frays that seemed to occur in every house and shop.

"I never hearn the like," and Joe paused in his eating and put down his knife and fork, "Eureky is jest a-bilin' over."

"It will be a great thing for Eureka," Jerry answered, then went on more slowly as if trying to understand his own words—"and people talk of buying the land in every direction."

"What fur?"

"To make money," and Jerry's voice and expression were very grave.

Joe looked anxiously into the young face opposite him.

"Does youuns want some?" he said doubtfully. Jerry looked up quickly.

"Do I want land?" he asked; "thank you, Joe, I have no need for land, and I think it a wrong thing to speculate in."

Joe took up his knife and fork to go on with his supper, while a puzzled look came over his face. With each year that had passed Jerry had become a greater mystery to him, until now he had no real hope of ever understanding him again. "His boy" had developed entirely out of his reach and knowledge, and Joe could only admire.

But this last enunciation was to Joe the strangest of all Jerry's sayings—that to speculate in land was a sin. Was this a remnant of Jerry's youthful weak-mindedness that education had failed to correct? And from this time Joe watched Jerry with careful curiosity—watched while Jerry strove in vain to right himself and hold his place amid all this wild excitement.

It seemed marvelous to Jerry how in the twinkling of an eye all about him was changed, and he had to stand and see not only his dreams and his theories swept away, but the long year's hard work annihilated, while this intoxicating greed for gain absorbed the people in its whirling vortex.

Jerry had read a great deal about money and money's power; had thought that he had some knowledge on the subject, and so thinking had built for himself a bulwark of calm indifference to this thing that so swayed the world; indeed, he had determined to live entirely above it.

But now as he watched he began dimly to realize that the cumulative, crushing, almost crazing influence of money was an awful thing,—a thing to be afraid of. He looked and listened appalled and astonished, and his hopes for his class seemed futile. How useless to try to make anything of these creatures so far down in the scale of humanity ; so hungry for this power that was in itself so unworthy, and of which they could make only the lowest uses.

How he despised them, and how he hated the knowledge that he had been born one of them.

Nor had he any opportunity to take counsel and comfort from the doctor, for his time was fully occupied by the school, and by the long conversations he was now called upon to hold with his patrons, the parents of his scholars.

Their confidence in Jerry first arose from his having been called "Professor" by the *Star*, and now they thought they could get no better views than his as to the land speculators who were already creeping into the towns. So they asked, and Jerry answered unhesitatingly against these strangers, and tried to show the people the dark sin that was hidden at the core of the fair-seeming schemes these land-speculators set forth to tempt them.

To speculate in land was a crime, he told them, and the Government was responsible for it ; the Government should hold all land and rent it ; should not throw out God's gifts which should be dispensed fairly, to be scrambled for by the crowd. Of course the weak would go to the wall—the weak who had every right to life save the strength to hold it.

In answer, the plausible first speculators insisted, that the land, *having* been thrown out for a general scramble, would all be grasped by "sharpers," unless they, with command of ready money, should be allowed to buy it, in order to hold it for the poor people who would come with the railway : this was all they wanted to do, and would promise to sell it fairly, with only enough margin allowed to pay themselves for their trouble and expense.

Their trouble !

And Jerry enlarged on this phase of the question with a sarcastic strength that won him scholar after scholar, and made the people hold their land against all temptations.

He was earnestly true in his opinions, and put them forth with the strength that truth begets. He saw many visions of the multitudes that were to come : visions of poor people seeking new homes and new openings in which to begin new lives.

They had always lived up five pairs of stairs, he thought, with only enough land at the base to bear the weight of the five stories ; but was this all the land the livers in the tenements were entitled to? Scarcely enough land to bury them in unless they were buried five layers deep?—packed away like sardines in a box ?

Their lives spent in horrible want and misery ; with no right to God's sweet air and sunshine that is so freely given. Looking out with hungry, hollow eyes ; hunting in noisome garbage piles and gutters for dirty refuse. Naked—skulking—starving until almost they gnawed their useless hands that could find no work ; while the broad, breezy fields were tilled by steam.

It was surely a black sin.

And in the depths of the fire Jerry saw visions of model farms spreading far across the plains ; fair homes where the scum from all the cities—from all the world, would settle and become honest citizens.

All they needed was room for expansion ; room to be thirfty, and moral, and religious ; room to breathe in, and looking up to realize their God—realize Him not as a careless " First Cause " who let the creatures of his hand multiply until they overflowed his world and crushed and crowded each other down to death and hell ! Not so, but as the merciful Father who made room enough for all, and did not send disease and misery as the cures for the mistake of over-population!

Jerry's heart was on fire with the time-old wrongs of humanity, and his tongue was ready.

Shortly the *Star* caught up his views and polysyllabled them until they were scarcely to be recognized: but Joe's heart swelled with pride.

"It were rayly liker preacher," he said over and over to himself, and listened eagerly to all that reached him about Jerry; and in himself he began to realize a most notable character; one who had rescued from poverty and obscurity a great light!

Jerry was the "coming man"—a man bound to rise; a man with all the glory of no ancestry,—of ignorance and a log-cabin about his early years.

And Joe gathered the papers secretly, and paid Dan Burk to read them to him; for he was afraid to ask Jerry. So Dan read the fiery columns to Joe, and declared himself willing to extend Joe's credit to an indefinite extent; congratulated him on his boy, and prophesied that some day Jerry would be President!

And Joe went home and made the fire, and ground the coffee for supper, and in the midst stopped his work and put it all aside, covering his face with his hands.

"I oughter a-done this for youuns, Nan," he whispered, "I oughter a-done it!" then went away and hid among the rocks, that Jerry might not find, when he came home, that Joe had done his work for him. Nan had always done her own work—and crouching down among the rocks he looked back at the little house saying: "Surely it's God's truth that dead folks come back—surely it's God's truth."

Meanwhile in Eureka the talk ran high. Day by day the reports and surmises grew more wild and numerous: land values were run up to an imaginary price that no fortune could compass—then a sudden stop!

The people were breathless and puzzled—the speculators, who had come with such laudable desires to spare everybody trouble, and to save land for the poor who would certainly flock to this new opening, were bewildered !

"Somebody" had bought up all the public lands ! It was declared that within a radius of twenty miles all the Government lands were gone !

There was a pause of deathlike stillness ; then a howl of rage and curses went up against this mysterious person who was to reap this immense fortune. People, and speculators, and adventurers made common cause against this crafty "Unknown"; and all small jealousies and animosities were merged in one great anger against this person who had over-reached them.

And Jerry, boiling with indignation, denounced the "Unknown" openly and without stint : the soulless creature who had done this wicked thing ; had speculated on the necessities of the hungry hordes that would surely follow the road.

His visions were all swept away ; for the land about Eureka was all gone ; bought up to be held until the crowd should flow a living stream across the mountains to this "promised land," only to find the sharpers before them !

It was a black crime, but a crime legalized by the Government ; and God would surely curse such a Government and Nation.

CHAPTER II.

> "Drink to lofty hopes that cool—
> Visions of a perfect state;
> Drink we last the public fool,
> Frantic love and frantic hate."

HIGHER and higher the excitement ran: who was this mysterious buyer?

The newspaper was sarcastic, then angry, then bitter; Jerry's articles grew longer and more darkly withering; but all to no purpose, the Unknown did not reveal himself.

Nearer and nearer the fateful railway came: built only from the nearest town, it seemed to come with magical rapidity. It had worked its way now to one of the lowest passes in the mountains, and before long all doubt as to where it would come into Eureka would be over.

And as time went on public opinion slowly but surely came to the one verdict, that this unknown person had bought his land in the right place: the town of Eureka would spread all over his domain, if he would allow it.

Higher and hotter the talk rose, and reports flew hither and thither. Then one morning,—one cloudy, cold spring morning,—a morning Jerry never forgot; whose piercing dampness often touched him; whose cloudy heaviness often weighed him down in after-days,—a notice appeared in the *Star*—a notice short and terse, offering high wages to workmen to lay off in lots this great tract of land; and the doctor's name was signed to it.

Jerry's heart seemed to stand still; and a silence seemed to fall over the town.

The doctor. The hero, the friend, the trusted benefactor of the town.

Jerry turned away silently from the man who had shown him the notice; he wanted to be alone, for he felt as if some hand had wounded him sorely.

His hero doing this thing, speculating in what was man's inalienable right, Land; the dust from which God made him.

Had not the doctor often discussed with him the sin of speculating in land? More than this, had they not extended their discussions to the finer point of the injustice that lay at the foundation of large estates; and had not the doctor disapproved to a great extent of it all? How, then, must this action be read.

Was he doing it for Paul Henley?

Jerry's face darkened: this thought seemed to hurt him more than all the possible sufferings of the immigrants who were expected; and that this was so, made him ashamed. Yet, was it possible that the doctor loved Paul to this extent—that beautiful, delicate, useless creature.

Jerry clenched his fists.

Was Paul made of different flesh and blood that he could not guide a plow; could not dig; could not eat common food, nor wear common clothes? Had God made him of finer stuff; so fine that his guardian was driven to wrong-doing in order to provide for him?

For twenty-four hours the country side made no sign, no sound; then whispers crept about; angry, malignant whispers, that intensified as the day went on.

All these years that the doctor had been among them, they said, pretending to devote his time and money to the bettering of his fellow-creatures, he had been making his plans for this grand stroke of business. In his long rides about the country under cover of visiting the poor and sick, he had been searching the land for gold ; been working hard in his own interests, and in the interests of his adopted son, Paul Henley.

They declared that he had been for years in secret communication with this railway company, and had known all along how things would turn out. That he had bribed the Government to let him have the land for next to nothing ; had bribed the railway company to come in over his land, and to put the shops and station on his land.

More than this, he had bought up gold-land at the same low price, deceiving the government. The realization of the awful wickedness of these reported actions and motives seemed to dart like a flash through the usually stolid minds of the people ; and within a day after reading the doctor's call for workmen, they made up their minds that no hand in either town would be lifted to work for him.

And listening, and thinking, Jerry found that a public benefactor had no right to look after his own interests ; he saw that once to begin a course of self-sacrifice is to be bound to it for ever ; the world watches closely and never permits a retrogression, not the deviation of a hair's breadth from the prescribed path.

Prove your nose patient, and you prove it a poor thing meant for the grindstone. Unselfish natures prefer being imposed on, says the world, and benefactors have no right to be anything but benefactors.

Meanwhile, Jerry felt like one walking in a dream ; and after the first shock, after his mind had re-established itself ; all the talk, even the printed notice, seemed absolutely preposterous and impossible.

And all through the long day, during which he received many visits from his patrons, it was very clearly realized by him that not only all Eureka, but all Durden's, had declared against the doctor, and were ready to cry him down, and as far as possible to ruin him.

Jerry could scarcely believe the situation, and more

than once during his many interviews with the people, he asked them if it were possible, even with this provocation, for them to condemn this man who had spent years in their service; who had been their friend in every phase of life; who had set no limit to the time nor the money spent for them.

And the answer came sharply—if the doctor had not pretended; if from the first he had declared his intentions, they would not have blamed him; but he had won their confidence by false pretenses so that he could cheat them, and this they could not forgive.

Jerry's repeated assurances that the doctor had bought the land for some good purpose, and not as a speculation, were not heeded, for all the facts of the case, as far as the people could see them, were against the doctor. The buying of the land was one fact; the notice in the *Star* was another fact; Jerry's ignorance of the transaction was a third fact; and the fourth fact, which every one knew, was that for years the doctor had been buying up the interests in the Eureka mines in the name of Paul Henley.

All this evidence could not be disputed, and Jerry could only retreat on the declaration that, after all, there was no real reason why the doctor should not buy the land; no real reason why the people should blame him for his course; no reason save that he had given them so much that they felt they had a claim on all.

He determined after much hesitation that he would go to the doctor and ask him for some explanation; and yet, how could he do such a thing? what right had he to question any act of this man? how dare he look beyond his word and teaching?

Besides, the doctor knew all that had been said about this transaction before he revealed his name, and if he had cared for the opinion of the people, he would have printed his explanation along with his call for workmen; and if he had cared for Jerry, he would have given him long ago some hint that would have stopped his pen, and so would have been left unsaid many hard things which had irritated the people against the unknown buyer.

And with this last unavoidable conclusion, Jerry faced a truth that he had long realized, but from which he had turned away—the truth that the doctor had never loved him. For years, ever since he had realized that the doctor was in every particular different from those about him, Jerry had watched him carefully, and by means of the deep love he bore him had learned that the doctor's life was one long struggle to lose himself in anything that would absorb him. Through all disguises Jerry had seen this motive in all that the doctor did for the people about him; and when he turned to his own case Jerry still saw this motive. The discovery hurt him, for always the thought followed, "I am a work that keeps him from remembering—I am a duty that satisfies his conscience; only this I am to him." It was through his love that Jerry had felt in the doctor's nature the lack of this same love: found that the doctor had another theory than the one he held as to honest love and honest hate: the doctor never flinched from his duty to all the world, nor to any segment of it that came within his reach, but he did not love it.

And bitterly it had come home to Jerry that all the adoration he had without question lavished on this his Ideal, had fallen unheeded, if not unseen. This knowledge had not come to him all at once, but gradually, like the shadows that follow the morning sunlight—all is still bright, but when you look attentively the shadow is where the sunlight was.

The doctor was a mystery that with all his love Jerry could not solve. He was learning new lessons about him now, but his heart was growing heavy with the new wisdom.

For years Jerry had realized in some measure the doctor's suffering, and had pitied him. Too often he had seen him sit for hours and never turn a page—too often had seen the mask drop from his face and a deadly weariness take possession of it—too often had found him lying face down on the rock over Durden's Mine—too often he had seen these and other signs not to know that his past needed sympathy. All this had made him love this man with a pitying love that was pain : but now the new wisdom that hurt him took the form of the question—"Was the doctor greedy for gain—was it possible that this pitiful weakness touched his idol ? "

That there must have been sin in his past to cause all the suffering in his present, Jerry never doubted, but he had made sure always that they had been the sins of a noble nature ; but avarice—could his idol fall so low as that ?

CHAPTER III.

> "Necessity, whose sightless strength forever
> Evil with evil, good with good must wind
> In bands of union which no power may sever:
> They must bring forth their kind, and be divided never."

JOE listened silently to Jerry's report, first of the notice, then of the determination of the people not to work for the doctor; and finally of all the evil things they said of him.

Then he laid down his pipe and leaned forward with a hand on either knee.

"I've been a-tellin' him ever sence I knowed him," he began in a slow, conclusive voice, "as he were a-helpin' orl the p'isenest mean trash in the country, an' I says, says I, 'Doctor, the least leetle wind'll blow trash in folks' faces,' says I," then with a long-drawn breath—"Cuss their measly hides!" and he took up his pipe again.

"Of course it is all right for the doctor," Jerry said as if convincing himself, "all right for him to do as he has done."

"To speckylate in lan'?" and Joe paused once more in his smoking; "I'llowed as youuns jist 'spised sich doin's; the papers says you do, an' Dan Burk 'llows thet you do, an' as youuns is got the rights on it."

Jerry pushed his hair from his forehead nervously. "I mean that the doctor will do it in the right way," he answered anxiously, "the doctor will not speculate; he has bought the land for some good purpose."

"To gie it away?" Joe suggested sarcastically, "pay fur the lan'—pay to lay it out, an' gie it away?"

He shook his head. "The doctor's mighty easy fooled, but he's got mo' sense ner thet."

"He may put the lots at a very low rent," then Jerry left the fire and went out into the darkness. He did not want to talk about this matter yet, for in his own mind he had come to no conclusion. Up and down he walked on the level bit of path that the doctor had trodden so slowly, when years before he spent the day at Joe's house to watch that the life came back to Jerry's poor little body.

Up and down in the darkness, trying not to judge his hero, his friend, his exemplar and help to all that was good and true; putting away forcibly all thought of self, and of the position the doctor had allowed him to take; pausing in his walk where the doctor had paused to say—"If God will ever forgive me!" that short, pathetic prayer that told so much and yet so little—just there Jerry paused and said—"He can not do wrong!'" then he went in again to where Joe still smoked by the fire.

"It must be all right, Joe," he said, sitting down slowly.

"I aint never blamed him yit," Joe answered; then more patronizingly than he had spoken to Jerry in years, he went on—

"I aint got much larnin', Jerry, but I'se knowed a heaper folks sence I kin 'member, an' one thing I jest will say, thet no man aint a-goin' to gie away liker fool fur moren twenty yeer, an' orl of a suddint turn roun' an' cheat folks fur money as he don't need; I I don't b'lieve it no moren I'd b'lieve a p'inter dorg as tole me he couldn't smeller mink. It's no use a-talkin' to me thet away," and he knocked the ashes out of his pipe with unusual vehemence, packing it again as if protesting against the need of any justification of the doctor—"An' youuns, Jerry," he went on more quietly, "as knows the doctor bettern mos' folks; you kin stan' by him better," then more slowly—"If I didn't hev sicher sighter work on han' darned if I wouldn't lay out the lan' fur him my-seff!"

Jerry did not answer, for Joe's mention of his work made him think for the moment of the mystery in which he lived between these two unknown lives.

"Pore doctor," Joe said at last, bringing Jerry back from his musings, "aint thar no way of you a-heppin' him, Jerry?"

Jerry shook his head.

"I will go and see," he answered, "but if he had wanted my help he would have told me long ago, and have stopped my writing," the words were said unintentionally, and Jerry was angry with himself for having exposed this sore place, especially to Joe, whom he felt, somehow, would be glad to widen a little the distance between himself and the doctor. Joe blew out a cloud of smoke.

"You dunno the doctor yit," he said, with a little grunt that might have been a stifled chuckle—"he never blazes no road behind him, he don't, an' he aint a-goin' to persuade you not to bust yer brains out agin a tree, if so be you hes a mind to do it; an' he never 'splains nothin', ner axes nothin'."

Jerry listened and had no answer; rather, his heart grew cold within him as Joe went on, because of the confirming truth in the old man's words—

"An' he'll gie you cloze, an' wittles, an' firewood; he'll gie you as much as a house, but you mus' sot thet house right fur over yander, right fur, 'cause he don't want no pusson's shed j'ined onter hisn's, you bet: he gies away liker fool; but, Lord! he don't want nothin' a-trailin' atter him: but orl the same, I 'llowed as you mout he'p him." They were hard things that Joe had told, but they were true; he knew they were hard too, but it was not in his humanity to refrain from this little exposition of the man who had for years supplanted him in the life of "his boy,"—he had taken the second place very quietly, but he felt a little triumphant just now.

And the next afternoon when Jerry made time for his visit to the doctor by giving a half-holiday, he remembered all these hard sayings of Joe's, and would allow to himself only that he was going to explain his own action, and to warn the doctor of the feeling that was out among the people. Several leading men had been to see Jerry during the morning, and from them he had gained his view of the state of the community.

All were angry and indignant, and very impatient to make known to their late friend this new feeling which had developed toward him. That morning an angry notice had appeared "declining to work for the doctor at any price—no one would lift a finger for the man who had deliberately cheated the town out of all it had hoped to make by the railway,"—and the notice was signed "The citizens of Eureka and Durden's."

Jerry had read it angrily, for he knew that the baffled speculators were at the bottom of it. These slow thinking, shiftless natives—as in his heart he called his own class—would never have had the energy nor the sense to make a combined move: they might be keen at a bargain, but they had to be taught to think,—taught that sin was hidden in land speculations. And he became more angry with them; naturally, but unreasonably so; when he remembered that he had taught them the chief lesson on this point.

His object and his work had been true and right; but like most honest men who long to be benefactors, he had done too much; or perhaps his pupils had pushed his theory too far.

He had denounced the Government for selling its land, and the people saw the reason in this; he had denounced the people who had bought this land as a speculation to the detriment of their fellow-creatures, and the people followed him here also; but he had not thought of providing for the contingency of an honest man buying this land for honest purposes.

"And who would have dreamed of such a thing!" he said to himself with unconscious sarcasm and in much bitterness of spirit when he found out who the mysterious buyer was, and that the people had applied all his teachings to him. "Who would have believed such a thing!" and the people showed their faith in his judgment by refusing to believe it.

Hurriedly and angrily he tramped along the road; he wanted to have a long talk with the doctor, and the time spent in reaching his destination provoked him. After much argument with himself he had determined to explain to the doctor the position he had taken, and why he had taken it. It had been a hard decision to reach after Joe's words, but he felt that he could not be silent now, and so be identified with the people's notice: but beyond all these motives he had a hope that the doctor would let in some light on his own action, and he longed for this light with a great and loving desire.

Alas, he reached his destination to find the doctor indefinitely absent, and a note as his only alternative. And the writing of that note was the hardest thing he had ever tried to do. If he still believed in the doctor, as he assured himself that he did, what had he to say? Say that his articles in the newspaper did not point to the doctor—say he was sorry for the doctor—say he hoped that he would be just about the land, or say that he knew he would? If he believed in the doctor any of this would be worse than folly—if he did not believe in him?

And he laughed a little bitterly at himself because he wanted to say all these things, at the same time asserting violently that he believed in this friend of his life!

He pondered long, then left only a few lines to say that he had seen the refusal of the people to work for the doctor, and had come over to put himself at the doctor's service. He made no comment, only the simple offer, then went his way slowly feeling himself in a more complicated position than before.

He could not retract his own opinions—he could

not explain the doctor's position, nor could he publish the fact that he had offered his services to his benefactor and so take a decided stand by him, for this would seem like parading his gratitude,—he could only stand still, and probably be misjudged by both sides: and this was hard.

All the way home he turned the matter over and over in his mind, but could see no way to better things: he must wait, and if the doctor sent any answer to his note, abide by that.

"Well," was Joe's greeting when later he came in and found Jerry standing by the fire with a troubled look on his face, "well, is you an' Paul agoin' to start to work to-morrer?"

Jerry turned away.

"The doctor was out," he answered shortly, putting the supper on the table, "and I had to leave a note."

"An' Jim Martin," Joe went on, drawing up his chair; "Jim Martin he come along a-steppin' as jest as swonger, and a new feller alonger him; says I 'Hardy, Jim, whar's the railroad a-comin',' says I; says 'ee, 'Joe Gilliam,' says 'ee, 'we are cheated,' says 'ee, 'an' the road aint going to do no good'; 'why, Jim,' says I, 'I hearn as you done mader pile anyhow,' says I; 'Lord, Joe,' says 'ee, 'who on airth telled you sicher spin as thet,' says 'ee; says I, Jim, 'I hearn it,' says I, 'I hearn as youuns buyed orl the spar' lan', 'cause you done saved orl the money the doctor's been a-givin' you ever sence he come,'—whoopee!" and Joe laughed as Jerry had never seen him laugh before. "You oughter seen him, Jerry; he looked like he'd been a-settin' oner nester ants, he did;" then more slowly, "It's jest what I'se been a-tellin' the doctor, a-he'ppin' orl the trash in the country, an' notter man to he'p him now."

"I hope he will let me do something," Jerry said, but his hope was very small, and died the next morning when he found on his desk in the schoolhouse a sealed note from the doctor thanking him for his offer, but saying he had telegraphed for workmen; which fact Jerry was not to mention. Very short the note was, but it was some comfort to know that the doctor trusted him to this extent even. This was his first feeling, then the news in the note made him thoughtful. Telegraphed for workmen; and Jerry pondered over this fact as, lighting a match, he burned the note.

That was where the doctor had gone the day before: he must have ridden day and night to have reached even the nearest post-station, and must have sent a man on from there with his message; and what would Eureka say? and what would Durden's say?

The doctor had education, talent, money; of course he would triumph in the end; but what would he have to go through with and contend against before that end came?

And was it right?

Jerry broke the pencil he was sharpening.

He taught very vigorously that week, so that the children made tremendous strides in learning, and the one small tree behind the schoohouse was denuded of almost all the hopeful branches it had put out during this eventful spring. This outward vigor was the sign of the growing excitement and anxiety in Jerry's mind. Looking back he could not understand how Eureka, kept so long in the background, had come so suddenly to the front. Durden's story was common enough. The mine had been discovered by a poor man, who had come from a poor community in the Eastern States; the rush of people consequent on this discovery had come from the same part of the country; they brought no capital, and the scheme failed. This was the reason given by the doctor. The story Jerry heard from old Joe made the failure seem unaccountable; the mine was a good mine, Joe said, but haunted.

That a superstition should so sway people was strange. it was true that the people who had come were simple, uneducated, agricultural people, not ambitious, and contented with very little. Still, it was strange that they should not dig for the gold that Joe said "lay all about in Durden's Mine." And here again the doctor said that though he had never made an examination, he was sure that the Eureka mine was much better than Durden's. Whatever was the cause, Durden's had failed; then the old story followed, when the people could not get home again and had spread themselves on the plain, and returned to their old habit of planting small "patches."

The discovery of the Eureka mine was the next event; the doctor, who had arrived about that time, united with 'Lije Milton in buying up the interests; they had worked patiently and cautiously, and had been repaid.

All this Jerry could easily understand; but who was it that had *now* made the fact known that the land was full of gold—so full of gold as to bring a railway there? Who had had influence enough to persuade capitalists to run such a risk; capitalists having sufficient power to force the stock up until now, before its destination was reached even, many fortunes had been made by the road. Who could have managed this?

The question had come in the wake of a natural sequence of thought and reasoning, and the answer stared Jerry in the face. Only one man could have done it—one man who had bought all the available land near the town—one man who held most of the interests in the Eureka mine!

True, not an acre of private land had been touched, nor had any such offer been made—only the public lands had been taken. Not a pocket in Eureka had been injured by this gigantic speculation; not a soul in either town could say they had lost a penny, or had missed a penny they would have made—but those who were coming?

"For some good purpose he has done it," Jerry

said; "I know it—I know it!" And still he was not sure.

For two weeks—the longest Jerry had ever spent—the towns remained in a quiescent state. The excitement about the land speculation was starving for lack of new developments; the railway excitement had grown old, and the people watched anxiously to see what would come next.

Nearer the railway came; it was known how that many stations along the road had required only a week's time in which to make towns of themselves; and yet Eureka and Durden's had not stirred! Indeed, they could not stir; no one could speculate or make any money further than would come to them from their private lots; and had they not been told that to sit still and hold this land would make them rich?

The people were in a rage, and the speculators in despair; while the quiet prairie, and the grim, untouched mountain-side where gold was said to lie in lumps, seemed to mock them!

How easily they had been outwitted! and many curses, that were not more than half smothered, followed Paul and the doctor whenever they rode through the town. Once more Jerry went to see the doctor, and once more missed him; and a nod as the doctor cantered by the schoolhouse was all that Jerry had seen of him. Was he angry? Jerry wondered; did he suspect him of being disloyal? The blood mounted in the young man's face, and he remembered Joe's words that the doctor neither gave nor asked explanations—he could not ask one.

Meanwhile, the speculators worked quietly among the people, and as the railway neared the town and the excitement increased, they offered higher prices for the land. And in the town there were men who had combined all the teachings given them, making a theory of their own. Thus they stopped work, because in any case selling their land would make them rich ; and they did not sell because only to hold the land would make them rich also.

And they waited in vain !

Day by day they scrambled for food while they watched with eager eyes for the promised money to pour into their laps ; and the eager eyes grew hollow and hungry. They had defied the doctor, and so could not ask work of Paul Henley or the Eureka engineer ; and not having planted gardens, they were starving.

At last one desperate woman struck the keynote of the position, and for many, solved the question. She chose a time when her husband was drunk, then sought the Land Agent ; the amount he offered seemed fabulous, and the bargain was closed. The drunken husband made "his mark" before the drunken magistrate, and the land passed into the hands of the Agent. Sober, the man made the best of it and of a shrewish wife, and other men sold their lots and houses.

Suddenly the town waked up : the one lodging-house was filled with these homeless creatures ; and their old homes assumed a wonderful appearance. They were whitewashed, houses and fences ; the lots were plowed and laid off to look like thrifty gardens,—seed were actually planted, late as it was !

The former owners began to regret ; and Jerry looked on angrily.

Then one day, as the bright May sun blazed triumphantly over the broad plains, a wagon-train turned slowly into the town.

And all Eureka turned out at the doors, even Jerry and his school came out to look ; and they said "immigrants." But this was no common party ; there was a director to it who evidently knew his business : he stopped his train in front of the schoolhouse and asked his way to the chief engineer of the mine.

Eureka was watching, and saw Engineer Mills come out of his door and point to an empty house near by ;

then the party turned in that direction, and disappeared from all curious eyes.

Now indeed, all Eureka was roused; very slowly, it is true; but roused before the next day dawned to the fact that these men were workmen—and had come to do the doctor's bidding!

The town was in a stir. Knots of people, men and women, gathered on the corners and in the shops; and Jerry felt anxious. He went about a little to sound the people, and found the sentiment divided.

The two shopkeepers of the two villages, Dave Morris and Dan Burke, who were leaders, were amiable; for this influx meant trade; and Titcomb, the editor, was amiable also; but the laborers were furious, for this meant that they had been ignored, and that their revenge had failed!

And Jerry began the afternoon session with much trouble on his mind.

How long that day was to Jerry he could not express, but in the evening when his work was done, he found a new feeling abroad. The shopkeepers had joined the mob; for these workmen did not mean trade; they had brought their own supplies—everything, and more, that a colony would need. Curses were spoken out loud, now that the leaders had turned, and nobody seemed surprised—nobody defended the absent man who had been their friend for all these long years.

Jerry questioned bitterly should he be silent, or should he speak and try to check these things that as yet had not been said exactly in his hearing; for the people still respected his connection with the doctor: but he turned away silent, his words would have no effect now, and if he spoke what could he say? and he made his way slowly out of the town.

Joe listened with the greatest delight to the news of the new workmen, and of their having brought everything with them that they could need.

"Fur onest the doctor hes hed sense," he said

slowly, "an' fur onest these durned fools will see thet money an' larnin' kin beat 'em orl holler! I'm rale glad, I am; an' I'm glad the doctor buyed the lan' an' started out fur hisn's seff—ceppen if it's fur Paul," he added slowly.

Jerry kicked the fire viciously, and Joe went on:

"But I can't, to save me, see the sin of speckylatin' in lan'," he said, "I works fur another feller, an' I makes my money; an' I tucks thet money an' I buys lan', an' if I kin fin' a feller fool ernough to gimme twicest as much as I paid fur the lan', thar aint no sin in thet; less it's a sin to be a fool."

"And there are a hundred people nearly starving," Jerry began wearily, "because they have no land to plant; and you living in plenty, have it all held back for the money it will bring: money you do not need—I call that sin."

"I 'llows as I worked fur the money," Joe retorted, "'Merricky's a free country, an' if I gits 'long faster ner another feller,—thet aint no sin."

"But it's a sin to grind the other down to starvation point that you may make more than you can possibly want," Jerry went on, but without any enthusiasm in his voice: he was so weary of his own arguments; and his teachings had brought him so little satisfaction. He actually felt a cowardly wish growing on him that he had never said a word on the land question, but had allowed all to take their chances.

"An' if I dunno nothin' 'bout t'other feller," Joe went on slowly, "ceppen what I reads 'bout him, or gits Dan Burke to read 'bout in the paper; fur sartain youuns's don't spec me to write him a letter an' say—'Come out har, an' tuck somer my lan' fur nothin'?"

"That is the very question," Jerry retorted; "if Government holds the land, then every man is free to rent only so much as he can plant, and everybody will be provided for."

"An' if I gits me a steam-plow, as I hearn tell 'bout by somer these new fellers," Joe suggested, watching Jerry's face keenly—"I kin jest plant the whole perrairy, I kin, jester hummin'; an' I 'llow thet wont leave much fur 'tother feller?"

"Very well," Jerry admitted, "and you make an enormous crop of corn, and the price goes down; the people who have no land, have no taxes to pay, so can afford to buy your cheap corn: every year doing this, your prairie wont pay for itself; for provisions produced in such quantities will be too cheap."

Joe looked on him with an expression that was as near contempt as he could bestow on Jerry. "I aint no fool, Jerry Wilkerson," he said, "to plant one thing orl the time 'tell folks throws it way," emphasizing his words with his pipe, "I'd plant 'taters!—'taters, sir, as can't be feed fur mules an' hosses; then the corn'll run up high ernough, I reckon."

"Perhaps," Jerry answered slowly, looking down another vista of consequences that Joe's words had brought to his mind—the advances in labor-saving machinery. The effect that this would have on all the problems of the day, and especially on this land problem, was a question that needed an answer; and the answer needed much thought.

"Perhaps," he said, then looked up angrily; "you say America is a free country, Joe, but because she is free, is that a reason why she should be without a conscience? Because I am out of prison is that any reason why I should steal and murder?"

Joe looked up in astonishment.

"Is youuns gone plum crazy?" he said at last, "I never spoke no word 'bout stealin' ner murderin', Jerry."

"No, but because you are free to make money and to buy land, is that any reason that you should for the love of gold crowd others out until they die of starvation?"

Joe shook his head slowly.

"If I hed a-been thet mean, Jerry, the buzzards woulder hed youuns longger-go—you bet!"

The argument was useless, and Jerry turned away.

"God will surely bless you, Joe, for what you have done for me," he said; then went outside into the darkness that he might think.

CHAPTER IV.

"Come near me! I do weave
A chain I can not break—"

HOW long we live before we realize that life is the one breath we breathe the while we say "I live"—before we are content to draw from every day its fullest uses and benefits unglorified by dreams of to-morrow—before we learn that whatever effort we may make to touch another life, it can but end in a longing that is never satisfied.

Each soul lives and dies alone.

Day by day we knit bonds that bind until the blood flows, but do not join—we tremble for the life of this one, or the love of that one—we feel our hearts die because this life has passed away from our grasp, or that love has failed us in our need—all this we do, fighting through our little day, and when the end comes we must let go, and journey out along the "lonely road" without a footstep timing ours, or a hand clasped in our own.

And now when difficulties began to gather about him, Jerry found that by some strange chance he stood alone. Not only alone, but opposed to the one man who could have helped him: whose views he would have sworn that he not only knew, but held. And when under the test of this crisis the degradation of his class was fully revealed to him—its greed, and its ingratitude,—and he realized the immeasurable task he had set for himself in the raising of this class—he acknowledged to himself without reservation, that he had been a fool, and began to look for some way out of the dilemma. Indeed, under the cool shadow of reaction he was tempted to trample under foot all high resolves, and to laugh to scorn all enthusiasm.

But no time was left him in which to beat a retreat, for the next morning he found a crowd collected in front of the school-house; men, and women, and boys.

He stopped for a moment; were they waiting for him—waiting to compel him to face this issue? On a nearer view, however, he found that they were watching the house where the doctor's workmen lodged.

Would there be a difficulty, he wondered; and his step grew slower, for he would not lift a hand against the doctor.

At last he mounted the little platform; for with all his tardiness of gait he reached it at last, and the crowd seeing him coming turned from where they watched for the workmen and gathered about the little porch. There were murmurings and cursings from among them, and as Jerry put the key in the lock a man stretched over and laid his hand on the latch.

"I don't mean no harm, Mr. Wilkerson," he said, "but we want to ask a few questions before you goes in."

Jerry looked about him slowly on the upturned faces, then putting his hands in his pockets stood still and waiting. There was silence for a few seconds, while Jerry's thoughts flashed backward over all he had written and said to these people, knowing that every word was about to be brought home to him now, to force him to take sides: his blood boiled at the thought; but he would not take the initiative: at last a middle-aged man stepped to the front.

"Mr. Wilkerson," he began, taking a piece of tobacco from his mouth, and carefully putting it in his pocket, "had the doctor any right to buy so much lan'?"

"Yes," Jerry answered, "as much land as he had money to pay for."

"An' take it from aller us?"

"Did you intend to buy?" sarcastically.

"Well, yes," slowly.

"Well, it seems to me that you have had time enough," Jerry answered; "the prairie has been before you all your lives, why did you not take it in and work it? All these years you have been free to search the hills for gold; why have you not done it?"

"'Cause it wasn't any use tell the railroad come," the man answered.

"You have known for months that the railroad was coming," Jerry went on.

"Well, an' if we did, we never had no money to plunk down all at onest fur the lan'," and an angrier tone crept into the man's voice, for he felt in a confused way that this was not the Wilkerson of the newspaper. And truly, Jerry was questioning from under the reaction that had come, and the man answering from his life-long views, and not from Jerry's new teachings, which were not enough his to be used. But Jerry, rejoicing in the slowness of the man, which kept him from saying, "You told us not to buy it," cried out: "Nonsense! tell the truth; say that all the money you could have saved you have put in whisky; and now when a great opportunity has come, a great opportunity to make fortunes, you have no money put away that you can invest. This is the truth, and you know it!" becoming more excited as he went on, "and all that you have to find fault with to-day is that another man has looked ahead, and has provided himself with money that he can double—double and treble if he will; aye, he can possess this whole country!"

"God made the lan' for all," was called out angrily from the crowd, "an' you said so yerself."

"And why have you been too lazy to take it?" Jerry retorted; "did you expect the Almighty to fence it in for you, and write your names on the fences? is this what you expected? You could have bought this land for fifty cents an acre; but fifty cents would buy three drinks of whisky, and you wanted the whisky, and the land would keep."

"An' so it would," was called out.

"And so it did," Jerry cried sharply, "kept until two months ago. I am not going back from anything I have written in your paper: I said there that it was wrong to speculate in land—as wrong as to speculate in water, or air, or sunshine, if such a thing could be, for all these things are necessary to life, and are meant alike for all! Speculating in land is in my eyes a sin, and I consider it every man's duty to warn every other man against a thing that seems wrong, and so I warned you. You had no money to invest, for, as I have said, you have saved nothing; but if you had had bags of gold, I should have done my best to keep you from speculating in land,"—and there came a little catch in his voice as he remembered his desertion of his higher principles at the beginning of his speech; and yet, these people were so low!

"But now," he went on, his excitement increasing unreasonably as he realized that already he had taken the position of champion to these low creatures. And as this realization became more clear to him, his words became more harsh—"But now you are not troubled because you think the doctor has done a wicked thing in buying this land; you are troubled only that he has done a thing you were unable to do! You are angry because this man who has been your friend for all these years,—who has given you time, and money, and help in every way,—you are angry because he has now the opportunity to better himself. You let any smooth-tongued villain turn you against him,—you refused to work for him,—you take all my words and apply them to him, for whom, God knows, they were never meant!

"My words were meant to warn you against the miserable land-sharpers, not meant for this man, too high and too noble to be for one moment doubted! The doctor has bought in a great tract of land; we do not know yet what he will do with it; but I say, and I mean every word that I utter, that if he had bought the United States, I would be sure that it was for some good purpose,—I would be sure that it was for the benefit of the many, and not for his own benefit,"—and as Jerry spoke his own full confidence came back to him, and with it a great shame that he had for one moment doubted this man.

"Now," he went on, while his voice grew raspingly clear,—"if any man has anything to say against the doctor, let him remember that he has Jerry Wilkerson to fight," and taking out one pistol he laid it on the low, flat rail that went round the little porch, and put his hand on the second, that was still in his belt.

The crowd swayed a little, and backed away from the evil-looking weapon, and from the shining eyes of the young man, looking very dangerous as he stood in the level rays of the morning sun, holding his fast-cooling audience at a dreadful disadvantage. It was no rare thing in Eureka for men to be shot on much less provocation than this, and the day was not yet far spent enough for any excitement to have culminated, or for the men to have recovered from the drinking of the past night: their nerves were still tremulous, and they moved away from the platform.

"We never meant no harm to you, Mr. Wilkerson," they said, "but all the same it's durned hard lines!"

Then the door of the next house opened, and the workmen came out in a solid body; and Paul Henley was with them. They stopped a moment on the steps as if awaiting some advance from the mob gathered at the school-house; and in that moment the doctor rode up.

He stopped between the two crowds and looked about him: on the one side Paul, and the clean, respectable workmen; on the other the wretched mob,—dirty, thriftless, malignant,—people he had worked for but had not bettered; and in the midst, standing high on the platform, with the sun shining full on the pistol he had placed in front of him, Jerry, the one whom for so many years he had carefully trained and taught!

Only for a second the doctor paused, then nodded to Jerry, and rode on to the workmen.

He knew that the feeling of the community was all against him—he knew that at any moment a bullet might find him; but that was nothing. He had held his life with a loose grasp for so many years, that he scarcely remembered to heed any danger that threatened it. If one weighed possible results always, or always feared death, life became only a burden, he said; so that life or death meant very little to him, and he stood in the morning sunlight a ready mark for any man who thought himself wronged or defrauded.

Not long he talked to the men; then Paul's horse was brought, and the party moved off quietly, steadily, almost like drilled men, and every one completely armed, as could be seen plainly.

The crowd about the school-house was very still; they were deeply impressed by these orderly, strong-looking new-comers; nor had they forgotten Jerry's words, nor the menacing pistol that still glittered under their eyes.

It was not safe to trouble Mr. Wilkerson, they thought, for in no position had he shown any fear. In their eyes he had defied and bitterly criticised the doctor, whatever he might affirm to the contrary; and now he had not only defied and criticised them, but had abused and threatened them also: had stood there one to many, and had not flinched.

But besides all these considerations for keeping quiet, they were also interested in watching a reporter, who stood in the shade scribbling busily.

There was much of deep mystery to them in this man, and it was something far beyond their comprehension that any man should spend his time in writing down everything that was done in the town, and take the trouble to send it away to be put in a newspaper!

And so intent did they become in watching him, that they did not know when Jerry went into the school-house; and realized no more than he did that this retreat was a great boon to the reporter.

"The school-master finding the mob unwilling to make any assault, retired into the school-house."

So the reporter wrote while the dirty crowd watched him; and Jerry, hurt and angry, tried to find peace in his room.

"But it is thought that Eureka will soon see exciting times"—the reporter went on; and Jerry, thinking these same thoughts, but wholly unconscious of his position as a mob leader, determined to wait after school, and warn the doctor: for the doctor could not know, as well as he did, all that was threatened against him.

CHAPTER V.

> " So, one standing strong in the prime of his years,
> With his life in his grasp, looketh back through dim tears
> To the days of his youth :
> To the fair dewy dawn of his fresh young life—
> E'er his soul had been stained by the hardening strife
> Through which he had won."

JERRY waited very patiently on the school-house steps, with his warning on his lips. Sat there alone, watching the evening light that drifted slowly across the plains ; while behind him the mountains loomed black and gloomy, with the patient shadows huddling together about their feet waiting until their hour should come to possess the land. Before him stretched the road that formed the one street of Eureka, where in front of the wretched shop the men squatted in groups and rows, chewing, and holding what might be termed " silent converse " with each other ; while the women sat in the doorways of the miserable shanties, and up and down the road the children and hogs disported themselves indiscriminately. A wretched, squalid scene ; and made more so by the contrast with the few houses which the speculators had been able to buy and repair, and which shone out here and there like the " whited sepulchres " they were. A hopeless scene ; yet all about it was the exquisite glow of the evening light ; a cloud of light that reached to the black hollows of the mountains. God had not forgotten these creatures, and the place was not so wretched that his glory could not rest there ? So Jerry thought,—but also,— " they heed no light nor beauty, what use to strive with them and destroy one's self for their benefit? "

Alas! All the "warmed over" enthusiasm of the morning had deserted him, and he covered his face with his hands. He would not think of these people; instead, he would think what he should say to the doctor; he tried faithfully, but in spite of all his efforts could only think,—"What will the doctor say to me?"

His conscience was clear, and the doctor, if he thought about it at all, must know this; and the old answer that came to all his reasoning on this matter, came once more,—"the only thing to be explained was the doctor's course toward him"—and there had been many opportunities for this if the doctor had willed it.

Still, he would wait and warn the doctor: it was all he could do, and however painful the interview might prove, he would do this service; a service the doctor would scarcely value because he did not realize the extent of the danger that threatened not only himself, but his workmen.

So Jerry waited, and, in spite of all his reasoning, hoped that his warning might clear away the cloud that had come between them.

All was very still save the idle clatter of the children in the street, and the occasional calling of one woman to another:—all was very still, when as the sun vanished the fine, clear tone of a horn sounded through the evening, and Eureka stopped to listen! Clear and sharp, almost imperative, yet sweet; a tone Eureka had never heard before!

Once more it sounded, while Jerry watched the shadows stealing slowly from their dens in the mountains; then the usual noises of the time and place resumed their sway. But it was not long, for they ceased again when the doctor's workmen came walking down the street, and behind them the doctor riding slowly.

"He has sent Paul home for fear of danger," Jerry thought, and the loneliness about his life seemed to enlarge and to join hands with the creeping shadows on whose edge he stood, waiting to warn this man he loved so well. Quietly the men moved, seeming to pay no heed to the sights and sounds about them; talking among themselves, and to their leader who had a horn slung about his shoulder. They did not look like common workmen, now that he saw them more nearly, and he wondered what was their station in life.

He waited patiently while the doctor gave directions, and talked with the men, then as he turned to ride away raised his voice—

"Doctor!"

"Well, Jerry"—how sweet the name sounded on his lips!

"I wish to tell you, sir, that there is more danger in the threatenings of these people than you may suspect,"—his words came quickly enough at first, then more slowly as the doctor watched him with a look as if only politeness made him listen—"they mean some of the things they say."

"I have no doubt of it," was answered quietly.

"And you will be careful, Doctor?" almost pleadingly.

"I am never very rash, Jerry," drawing his hat on more securely, preparing to start, "but I am very much obliged to you for your warning; good evening"—then Jerry stepped back and said no farewell, because he could not.

However much we may think ourselves prepared for a great sorrow, or a great pain, when the blow falls there is in it always a keener cruelty than we expected. There seems to be always some additional refinement of the agony that we had not looked for, and that makes us say—"If it had been done without this, I could have borne it." No matter how widely we may have spread our lines of defense in order that the poor heart hiding in the center might be somewhat protected, the blow when it falls seems to break through every guard. For who can measure the force of a stroke which another is to deal us?

And so, though for a long time Jerry had been conscious of the fact that he represented to the doctor only a part of his duty, he now found to his hurt that all along he had had in his heart an unrecognized hope that he was something more. A hope that he knew only when he looked on its dead face as the doctor rode away. Mechanically he took up his dinner-bucket and books, and began his homeward journey. He could not realize all at once what had happened to him—he was not sure that anything had happened. Only he seemed again to be the lonely little child, cast loose from all his moorings. Had he read the doctor's actions aright, and did they say—"You are old enough to take your own path,—my duty by you is done"?

For years he had listened to and learned from this man: for years he had looked up to him and been guided by his counsels,—had made him his ideal and hero,—had loved him with that strongest love that man gives to man,—and now all was done. Either by the vile insinuations of enemies, or by idle reports,—by a simple misunderstanding, or through indifference,—this man he thought so strong had been turned from him.

His life seemed shattered; for he was young and trustful still, and had grown up to this love and influence as the flowers grow up to the sun. He had had no great sorrows since his childhood to take the edge from his feelings,—no betrayals to loosen his faith in mankind; on the contrary, all had so fallen out in his life as to make him trust implicitly and love unquestioningly, and this revelation of the mutability of all he clung to was very bitter. He had been taught the most liberal views; had been encouraged to tell fearlessly his opinions; had been told that the truth must be spoken at all costs, and adhered to: had learned from watching the highest life that had come within his experience, that all lives are lost that are not lived for others. And now on his first essaying to champion the right; to teach what he thought were the highest, purest principles—his teacher and exemplar turned from him!

He could not understand it nor realize it all at once, and had no feeling save a great sorrow that was deepening down into a corroding bitterness.

He hated himself for being so sorely smitten by the loss of this friend who could so easily cast him aside: and he determined that no eye should see his sorrow or realize his humiliation.

He did his evening's work quietly, almost mechanically: told Joe, whose keen old eyes watched him questioningly, of the gathering at the school-house; of his speech; of the fact that he feared a real difficulty, and had warned the doctor. Told even of the horn that had sounded so "thin and clear" to call the workmen home.

He seemed to hear it now, sounding through the beautiful tinted air,—sounding all to rest,—sounding the last hour of his love and trust!

It seemed as if he would hear those high, clear tones through all the coming years!

And he hastily opened a paper Joe had bought from Dan Burk,—a large, important paper from the far-away outside world. He paused a moment, for facing him, in huge type,—heading the telegraphic column, was his own name!

"*J. P. Wilkerson—*" then on the next line—"*Great and continued excitement in Eureka! Townspeople in Arms! Mass Meetings held by Wilkerson*, the schoolmaster, and leading man of the town! Dark threats against the imported workmen! *Notwithstanding* his immense interests, which may be seriously involved, Mr. Paul Henley and his guardian, supported by Engineer Mills of the Eureka mines, keep a firm front! Grand article from the Eureka *Star* written by Wilkerson! Base ingratitude of the latter's position!"

Then followed a garbled version of one of Jerry's articles.

Steadily he read it all through while Joe watched him,—steadily to the end; then he laid the paper down without a word, and sat quite still, looking into the fire.

So this was what was being said of him; this vile caricature was what had turned the doctor from him. It could not be possible; it was so absurd that even in the midst of his anger it made him laugh almost. The people *were* armed, but that was a custom; who would think of going unarmed in that wild country? And there *were* threats against the workmen; but the enormous falseness of his position as ungrateful and a mob-leader, was manifest—must be manifest to the doctor. Then his face grew darker: Paul held up as a model of manly firmness—Paul, who on every occasion quietly stood behind the doctor!

"Notwithstanding his immense interests"—ah, that was the keynote! Paul owned all that vast tract of land; Paul would be master of immense wealth—this was the keynote; this was what made people call him manly, and brave, and calm! Money bought all these golden opinions,—money threw a halo around his boyhood's enemy—ah, the power of this pitiful gold!

For a long time they sat silent: Joe smoking slowly and Jerry gazing into the fire with the bitterest of bitter thoughts surging through his brain, and a mass of hatred and anger gathering in his heart that would suffice to wreck his life.

At last Paul had gotten the better of him. It made no difference that he had followed with unfaltering zeal every suggestion that the doctor had ever made to him; it made no difference that he had studied and worked beyond his strength sometimes; it made no difference that he had admired and loved so faithfully: all this made no difference, Paul had won the day.

There was some freemasonry among these well-born people; a birth-mark that made them understand each other ; a class brotherhood that made them stand by each other. He was one of the "common herd" and must stand back : a duty had been done by him ; a life-long obligation laid on him that held him fast—bound him hand and foot. They could push him to one side and go on their way ; but forever he must watch that no act of his crossed their paths or wishes.

He hated himself—he hated his position,—almost he hated Joe because he had not left him to die on the roadside !

"Well," Joe said, as he carefully picked out a suitable coal to light his pipe, "how does it suit youuns ?"

"It is all a stupid lie," Jerry answered with deliberate slowness, as if afraid to say too much.

"Dan Burk says it's orl true," Joe went on, "an' thet orl the country jest swars by youuns," rubbing his hands with much satisfaction, "an' he says as you could make the people do anything you likes."

Jerry sat silent : he was sore and hurt, and did not wish Joe to see how much he had been humiliated.

"An' it beats me," Joe went on, "why you don't jest tuck the people an' make things go youuns' way: I'd jest tuck aholt of Durden's an' play the devil alonger Eureky an' thet Paul Henley," then with a chuckle—"Dan allers names him 'Polly,' he do."

Still Jerry sat silent, and Joe could not read him; but the suggestion took hold of him with a sweeping grasp: why not take this power offered him—the power of the people—and match it against the power of money ? why not take hold of the opportunity now before him, and make the first bold stroke for his fortune: why not take the lead and be the 'people's man'?

So he sat and brooded, while Joe smoked diligently and spoke occasionally of the brilliant future that might be before Jerry.

" An' Durden's Mine is jest fuller gole "—he said at last as if to himself. There was something in the tone that made Jerry think Joe had unintentionally betrayed himself, and he looked up suddenly into Joe's eyes; but after one little flicker of the eyelids they did not flinch. Steadily the men looked at each other, and many things surged into Jerry's mind,—steadily he looked with knowledge growing in his eyes and shining on Joe,—steadily, until Joe rose restlessly and knocked the ashes out of his pipe.

" It's time to turn in," he said, and left Jerry sitting in front of the dying fire.

Long he sat there revolving many things: piecing together many tiny circumstances; mere straws of circumstances that now pointed straight through the mystery he had not allowed himself to try to solve—the mystery of Joe's money. He remembered quite distinctly the night Joe had first shown him a piece of gold, how he had heard other pieces jingle in his pocket: he recalled the strange stories that were kept afloat as to the horrors of Durden's Mine: and he remembered that Joe had offered to buy land for him; and yet Joe worked neither in Durden's nor in Eureka.

Joe had never trusted him—the doctor had turned from him,—yes, he was alone.

Slowly the cinders fell and were buried in the gray ashes; slowly the great logs burned through and broke, sending wild flurries of red sparkles up the broad chimney,—slowly the night waxed and waned. The long procession of his days passed before him and left him longing for a weary, ragged, silent woman with gentle eyes. He turned from this first real problem of his life that stood up and faced him so relentlessly, and almost he longed to return to the dense ignorance of his childhood, if so he might touch again the love that had died for him. He seemed to hear the thud of the blow that killed her, and his blood crept cold and tingling through his veins!

" Mammy—mammy ! " he whispered, while the dead

ashes piled in gray heaps, and the cold dawn crept under the door—"Mammy—mammy!" with a death-like longing to hold the poor work-hardened hand in his.

What were all the world without some love on which to base his life?

CHAPTER VI.

"Great Need, great Greed, and little Faculty."

THE next morning the crowd was about the schoolhouse door again, and the reporter standing in the shade scribbling. Jerry regarded him now as a personal enemy; for he must be the one who gave such false pictures of him and of Eureka to the world. And yet, should not he thank this creature who had swept away the film of imaginary friendship which had blinded him?—clearing his eyes that he might more fairly judge of this friend who, when he cried for bread, gave him a stone?

Jerry did not linger this morning, but kept up his long swinging stride until he reached the schoolhouse door; and when the people closed about him, he did not take his pistols out.

"Well," he said, looking about him; and the spokesman of the day before came to the front.

"These fellers," he answered, pointing to the house where the doctor's workmen lodged, "these fellers gits two dollars an' a half a day."

"Do you pay it?" Jerry asked.

The man shook his head.

"That aint the question," he answered; "the rale thing is jest this-away: day in an' day out we men have been a-payin' the doctor at the price of a dollar a day when we worked out a sickness"; then pausing a moment, "I do allow that there was never no charge for widders and orphins; but I aint no widder," with much animation, "an' I've worked for every blessed baby at a dollar a day!"

"An' me!"

"An' me!" came from many in the crowd.

"And what work did you do for the doctor?" Jerry asked, determined to be just, and feeling bitter enough to humanity at large to keep to his determination.

"We chopped wood."

"Any negro could have done that."

"An' raked the yard," was called out.

"Or that," Jerry added scornfully.

"An' worked on the road."

"And that did you as much gocd as it did the doctor," Jerry cried.

"An' hauled rock."

"But did not get the rock out."

"No," fiercely, "but I'm a man, I am; an' if my work aint wuth but a dollar a day, there aint nary a feller that is wuth more."

"Very well," and Jerry put his hands in his pockets; "it has taken me more than ten years to learn enough to teach this school, and do any of you pay me a dollar a day?" looking around scornfully—"one dollar a month is what the richest man in Eureka pays me for teaching his child; and when a man sends me two children, he pays me one dollar and a half a month to teach them both. Did it take you ten years of hard work to learn how to rake a yard, or to chop wood, or to haul stone? You know that it did not,—you know that there is no fool who can say it took him more than one day to learn these things; and yet you claim a dollar a day. You say your time is worth that much, and you know that is a lie; for if you had not been working for the doctor, and paying him for curing your wives who support you, you would have been lounging about in Dan Burk's or Dave Morris's shop, and drinking up at least fifty cents a day. You are not worth a dollar a day, any one of you, and you should pay the doctor for keeping you away from whisky. Now I do not want to hear any nonsense about this land question; I said it was a sin to speculate in land, and I say it still. But I say it is a blacker and more damnable sin to drink; to starve your children; to work your wives to skin and bone, and then to kill them in some drunken fury!"--his eyes flashed viciously on the crowd: it was only a few hours ago that in the early dawn he had recalled the thud of his mother's death-blow. "Have none of you ever beaten your wives until they could not move? Have none of you shed the blood of an unoffending fellow-man because you were crazy with bad whisky? I know you have: and there is not one man in this crowd whose wife is decently clothed this day, or his children decently fed.

"These men who have come to work for the doctor are men who have paid much money to learn to work as they are working now, and they deserve what pay they get. You," with infinite scorn, "could no more do this work than your miserable cur dogs could, and you know it. I am not afraid of you, and I will tell you the truth if I have to kill you afterwards: for my pistols are better than yours, and I shoot equally well," putting his hand on his belt. "But this I say: you would be greater fools even than I take you to be if you attack the doctor or his men. You have lost this chance for making money, but I will see that another opportunity comes to you. Only save your money and do not sell what land you own; promise me this and I will be your friend through all."

"It's all blamed true," the spokesman acknowledged, "an' if you'll watch for us we'll be satisfied; eh, fellers?"

"There's been some damned hard words said," one man demurred.

"But pisen true," another amended.

"If you say much more, Jim Davis," Jerry cried, "I'll flog you like a dog!"—he was bitterly angry; he hated his kind; he would have liked to beat and beat, like a brute and cruelly hurt something. The words he had said helped him because they were so venomously true. He scarcely knew himself, so vicious was the change that had come over him; and he stood glaring at Jim Davis and almost longing to see him step into the ring that at his challenge the crowd had instantly formed.

And the reporter across the road watched, and listened, and scribbled, and Jerry thought what a fine heading he was making. The least thing that could be said was that he was whipping the mob into his views.

And at last, when Jim Davis backed down, Jerry longed to thrash the reporter.

"Well," and he looked around the ring of disappointed faces, "you wont fight if I have said hard words; I think you are sensible, although I will be honest enough to say that I should like to beat somebody to-day."

"Good for you!" was called out.

"I would," Jerry went on; "I would like to whip that man over yonder who is writing lies about us to the Eastern papers."

The crowd turned instantly, and as the clear voice reached him the reporter looked about anxiously for a place of retreat.

"But none of you must touch him," Jerry went on,—"do not dare to touch him, for his lies are going to help us. I only want you men to keep sober; to save your money, and to save your land; and the day will come when we can show that Eureka and Durden's have men in them as good as can be brought here."

"You bet, Mr. Wilkerson!" and a cheer went up from the crowd.

"And if the strangers determine to build up one town, we will build up the other, and if you will help me, I know the race will be an even one."

Again the applause rose heartily, and the young man felt the thumping of his pulses and the surging of the blood in his veins.

"But you must trust me," he went on, "and if the

time of waiting seems long, you must not grow impatient. I will promise to watch and to work honestly, for I long to see things change in these towns. I came here half dead, and one of your number took me in; and the doctor saved my life as he has saved the lives of many of you. No man must touch him: no man must dare to lift a finger against him or his, for I promise to kill the man who does," pausing while the crowd swayed uneasily; then more slowly, "and you know I am not afraid?" looking about as if waiting for an answer,—an answer that did not come. "I have nobody in this world, and death means very little to me: but while I live I shall try to help those about me. I am one of you: I am poor as you are: I belong to the same class that you do, and ever since I have had sense enough to think, I determined to do all in my power to help my own class."

"An' we'll stand by yer, Mr. Wilkerson."

"I hope you will," more slowly, "for if you will not help yourselves, I can not help you. I do not wish you to come here to the schoolhouse again, but I want you to work. Take work from any one who will give it to you, and put up your money somewhere else than in the whisky barrels. Now I must go to my work; and remember, I do not get a dollar a day."

He turned and went into the schoolhouse with all the excitement gone from him, and a weariness creeping over him that made him long to lie down and die.

What a fool he had been! what a wild scheme this was that had laid its hold on him, and how could he dare to make any promises to these people?

He shook himself savagely: his scheme was as good as many schemes of which he had read—schemes that had succeeded. The doctor had taken Eureka as his hobby; all of his and Paul's investments had been made there; why should not Jerry take Durden's? It was only two miles away; it had plenty of land about it that was still untouched; it had gold!

Eureka would fill up rapidly and overflow; these

men who promised to stand by him must be made to buy the land about Durden's—must be made gradually to sell their lots in Eureka. And some day,—if he could possibly without ingratitude or treason,—he would open a grand new speculation that would make Durden's shoot far ahead of Eureka! He put his face down in his hands,—for the children had not come yet, and his scheme grew and grew before his covered eyes,--grew and glittered with applause and gold, and he saw himself a great financial and political success!

But behind the gilded picture a far-off memory came of a dull, gray evening, when the ghastly snow-clouds hung low, and the wind cried up the gorges like a human creature; of a wild leaping stream that wailed as it fell, and wrung white, helpless hands; of a child whose soul went out in dim, unrealizing sympathy for the water that came from the far sun-lightened heights to the gloom of the valley. Had it come to him then, some dim foreshadowing of his life; some prescient dream of the failing from the high endeavor to die on the sandy plain? The path roughened and the gorge darkened in the picture, and the blackness of desolation gathered about it, and the water that dropped forever! Never ceasing, never failing; dropping on and on, and never making a stream—dropping on the stillness like a sob or a sigh—heavy, regular, slow. He could hear it now with the broad morning light all about him: and he tried to shake himself free from the vision of the drawn dead face that had so terrified him years ago. He was nervous from loss of sleep: he was weakly superstitious: he was a fool!

And he was glad when the children, trooping in, brought him back to the tiresome reality of his life.

Maybe the gold and the success did lie down among the dead in the darkness; still it was more enticing, more worth than the narrow, high path of duty he had imagined himself traveling when he put his shoulder to this educational wheel. Who would ever realize the earnestness of his labor? who among these careless, ignorant little beasts would ever look back on him as anything more than the man who had taught them their letters? who would know the sublime truth of his endeavor, the great end he tried to put them in training for? Among the hundreds of thousands of schoolmasters, how many had been even thanked or reverenced—how many remembered?

So he reasoned from the gospel of Justice—scarcely knowing the *gospel of Love.*

CHAPTER VII.

> "Friends, this frail bark of ours, when sorely tried,
> May wreck itself without the pilot's guilt,
> Without the captain's knowledge."

IT was a bold, wild scheme that he had thought out in his long night's vigil ; and one too rash for any but a young and practically ignorant man to have imagined. He had no realization of the difficulties that stood in his way ; he had no conception of the mass of work to be done, nor of the great confidence he must not only inspire, but retain, before he could make even a beginning.

He had no thought but of the bitterness and anger that had sprung to life in his breast under the injustice of the doctor's treatment, and the insulting patronage of Paul's manner. He would succeed, he would obtain this power and hold it ; he would make these people, who scorned and distrusted him, at least remember him.

But how should he begin ?

The question was a momentous one ; one wrong move at the beginning and he could never recover himself. And yet he must begin at once ; he must take some steps to keep up the feeling he had inspired already. The people were in an excited state, and unless something were done to fix them, their energy, born of disappointed avarice, would disperse in a series of street rows.

He must formulate his scheme at once, and make his first move.

He taught absently, and dismissing his school earlier than usual, walked down to Dave Morris's shop. A little crowd of loungers were grouped about the door, and sitting on the counters; the long, narrow room was dark and dirty, and pervaded by the mingled smells of rancid bacon, bad whisky, and stale tobacco smoke; and the floor almost could have been plowed and planted, so dirty was it.

Dave Morris's shop was, in truth, the most miserable specimen of a poor country-store; and its frequenters seemed to be among the lowest of the low.

There were women there, too, lounging and drinking as the men were; and girls, and boys, and little children. Involuntarily Jerry paused on the threshold: it was the first time he had seen his class in one of its natural and favorite lairs, and the sight was a shock to him. Joe and the doctor had kept him from even the sight of these things while a boy, and since he had been his own master, he had never thought of investigating this place that had been but a name to him. He had read of such places, and had heard this special place discussed; but he had not realized the degradation of his fellows.

For a moment he felt ashamed of having come there at all, or of having in any way associated himself with these people. Then the thought came back to him, that when first he had looked forth to his life in search of a worthy work, he had intended to help these people. He had intended being a benefactor; now the scene had shifted—his motives had changed, and he intended to be a master. Still this memory of his high motive comforted him a little. He had not begun his mission in the way he had at first dreamed of doing, and it was well that he had not; for he found that to work for these people for love or for charity was simply to insure a loss of all their faith. They were incapable of understanding any such high motives, and what they did not understand they would not trust.

In all the years that the doctor had worked for them, they had come to look on him only as a person whose learning had had some strange effect on his brain. It had taken many years for them to learn to trust him; and at the last, it was only because some leaders like 'Lije Milton and Dan Burk had stood up for him.

It was hard to convince them that a man in his right mind would have done all he did for them for thanks only. They had never been brought firmly to believe it, and the last few months had made them know, to their own satisfaction, that their distrust was not misplaced. Now they hated him; while Jerry unconsciously had made himself a hero by taking his honest and uncompromising stand on the land question. They saw, too, that Jerry was not afraid of them: he had not spared words, and if the occasion came, he would not spare bullets.

He was the town's talk, and the people's hero!

Jerry was not aware of this when he stood in the doorway of Dave Morris's shop; but through all his reasoning and excuses he was aware that he had let go the only thing that could excuse his being in that low place—he was lowered in his own sight, and felt penetratingly the disgrace of using such tools as these. And yet, though the moving motive of his schemes was no longer their elevation, yet the success of his scheme must elevate them.

He paused a moment in the doorway, thinking angrily how ugly these men and women were. Seeing them one at a time in the sweet sunshine of the plains, or in the shadows of the mountains, they were not so revolting; their surroundings were not fitted to them, and so in a manner mitigated their wretchedness. But here, where everything had been selected with a view to suiting their tastes—where everything was an outgrowth of their own natures, the picture was horrid in its degradation and filthiness.

"Mr. Wilkerson, you do me proud," and Dave Morris, the proprietor, stepped forward—"what will you have, sir?"

"I want the latest paper you have," and Jerry laid a small coin on the counter.

But Morris was not as yet, nor in small coin to be paid by this rising man; and he spun the little piece of money back to Jerry, and slapped the greasy paper down in front of him.

"Notter cent, Mr. Wilkerson; notter cent, sir," he said grandly, "I'll be damned if Dave Morris is the feller to take 'spons' from the friend of the people, sir; no, sir!"

The little coin still rolled as he spoke, and Jerry with his hands in his pockets watched it as it neared the edge of the counter and at last dropped on the floor at his feet; then he looked up.

"I came to buy a paper," he said, with a slow disgust that even these people could see, "and not to beg one, nor to hear you swear at yourself," and he turned away, taking the paper up carefully because it was greasy, and leaving the money on the floor.

In an instant Dave Morris was over the counter, and standing in front of his customer; Jerry stopped and looked full in the bloated, brutal face, and the thought flashed through his mind that this was not the wise "first move" he had intended to make. But it was unavoidable, and if it ruined his influence in the towns?—The thought was like a reprieve—if it ruined his influence he could get out of this wretched position. "Well," he said; and the crowd made a ring as if they had been drilled to it.

"Do you think because you've got a little damned learnin' that I'm agoin' to take your impidence,—durn you!—you—"

There was one swift blow that scattered the words which would have been spoken, and a heavy thud as Dave Morris measured his length on the floor, and Jerry dropping the paper stood with a pistol in either hand.

"I want fair play," he said, looking round him in the dead, startled silence that followed his quick blow;

for the crowd was as much stunned almost as Morris; "You can help Mr. Morris up, if you like," Jerry went on, stepping back a little, "but I want all to understand that I will take neither words nor favors."

His words rang clear and angry, and the reporter in the doorway and the outsiders in the street paused to take in the meaning. "Take no favors!" this man was crazy. But Jerry did not think of them as he stood over his fallen foe, who would not get up. Several moments he stood there; then with a scornful smile he put away his pistols, and picking up the paper turned to the door. "I shall be in town all day to-morrow," he said significantly; and the crowd made way for him to pass. He felt more disgusted and angry with himself than ever; he felt dirty and low, but he knew that the people were looking at him from every hovel,—for the noise of the fray already had sped from lip to lip,—and that even in the midst of his self-contempt he must appear as if nothing had happened; so he opened his paper.

Involuntarily his step slackened as again he saw his words and his name heading a column. Fiery words that he had not written, vile actions that he had never contemplated committing.

He read on and on, walking slowly, while his temper got up and his self-disgust died a natural death, and as in the morning he longed to beat somebody: almost he could have turned back and again attacked Dave Morris. His first feeling of relief in thinking that perhaps by striking Dave Morris he had destroyed his own growing influence, and so had freed him from the difficulties which were gathering about him, had vanished; and the consciousness that possibly he had done the most unwise thing that could have been done for his cause, in thus hopelessly offending one of Eureka's potentates, now added to his irritation.

Dave Morris was a leader; a man who held in his hands the fates of most of the people; for as they were all in debt to him, they were all afraid of him.

Through him Jerry could have swayed the town; could have ruled even the whisky trade, which was his greatest enemy.

Surely he had made a dangerous first move.

Once out of the town and away from the oversight of his kind, his pace slackened, and he trailed his paper at his side. A dangerous first move: and if it ruined him, would it not be better to live in peace and quiet up among the rocks, pursuing the literary life the doctor had trained him for? live there quietly with his own thoughts and books for company?

Then the sudden recollection came to him that now that he could no longer go to the doctor's library, he had no books. The blood stole slowly up into his dark face; how much he owed that man! how boundless was the debt of obligation!

He folded up the paper and his step became firmer; his scheme must not fall through. Already he had changed too much, changed through learning and unlearning, ever to settle again into the still trustfulness of his past life; and he began to review his latest action more quietly. He had knocked Dave Morris down, thus making an enemy of the chief man of the town; but also he remembered that Dave Morris had refused to get up; and that the crowd had seen this: would not this tell in his favor?—their chief lying prone before them, entirely conquered?

His eyes flashed a little; perhaps, afte̊r all, it had been the best and wisest thing that could have happened; and his step became more brisk. At all events he would tell Joe, and hear his judgment of the matter. He made the fire and cooked the supper as usual, and when Joe came in there was no extra excitement either in Jerry's voice or manner.

"I had to knock Dave Morris down to-day," he began.

Joe looked up slowly.

"Dave Morris?" he repeated.

"Yes, Dave Morris," and Jerry poured out the

coffee; "he cursed me," he went on, "and I knocked him down. He was afraid to get up," he added, with a little satisfaction creeping into his tone, "and I told his friends that I would be in town all day to-morrow."

Joe took his cup of coffee.

"I'll be thar too," he said quietly, "Dave knows me, an' he knows thet nobody pesters me ner mine, 'thout thar's a buryin'."

"You must not take it up, Joe," and Jerry's voice had grown softer; it had been so unexpected, this sympathy—"me or mine"—this man loved him. There was no duty nor expediency here. "I can manage him, Joe," he went on; "you must not get into any difficulty for me, I am not worth the trouble."

Joe cleared his throat.

"Thet's orl right," he said, "an' you makes me feel bad, Jerry; makes me feel bad like I did when I picked youuns up out yander," pointing over his shoulder; "you kep' on a-cryin' 'Mammy, I aint got nobody!' an' it jest knocked me orl to pieces, it did," pausing thoughtfully in his eating, but never raising his eyes to Jerry's face, "you talked like me in them days, you did."

"And I wish that I had never changed," and Jerry's slim, nervous hand clasped Joe's rough, work-hardened palm. He was tired and excited, and this unexpected championship, coming so quickly on the heels of the doctor's desertion, shook his self-control more than he would have thought possible. "I remember when I began to try to be like the doctor," he went on more rapidly, "and I made a mistake, Joe. I would rather be like you."

"Youuns do me proud, Jerry," was all Joe said, nor did he turn his hand to take Jerry's: his class did not understand this kind of sensitive demonstration; they said few words and made few motions, and both words and motions were clumsy. But this man was true; and Jerry felt it with a force and keenness that became pain. This man had sheltered, and fed, and clothed him for all these years, and now was ready to fight his battles.

A love that had done all, and had asked no return: for the first time this fact flashed across Jerry's mind, and with it the pain that came with the knowledge that he could make no return.

He did not love Joe, and never had; from the first he had felt himself Joe's equal, and later on his superior; but now the relation between them came home to him in a new light, and he realized what it was that had made his life so smooth. And now—love from him to Joe was not natural, and never had been cultivated. All these years he had loved the doctor, day and night his effort had been to please him; but it had gone for nothing: this love had been shivered and broken into invisible poisoning fragments, and would wound him evermore.

Love Joe? The question was a new one, and he withdrew the hand Joe had not taken. He had been a fool to try to climb to any height—did not height mean loneliness? Why had he striven for any more than his class usually needed: was it only because the doctor had led him on? Must there not have been something in him that answered to the impulse: who knew what there was in his blood.

He finished his supper in silence, and when all was put away he spoke again.

"There is no need that you should go to Eureka, Joe," he said.

"Mebbe I knows morer about Dave Morris 'an you do, Jerry."

"Well, he can but kill me," Jerry answered.

"That's orl," Joe granted, "an' killin' wouldn't mean nuthin' to you, ner nuthin' to me, rightly; but," taking his pipe out of his mouth, "it'd mean a heap if you wuz a-lyin' har, an' couldn't lif' a eye ner a han' when I come home," drawing a long breath, "it'd make a heaper diffrunce," then a silence fell between them until Joe spoke again: "Ever sense you usen to squat over thar nigh the fire, an' ax me, 'An' what's a buryin', Joe?'—when you never knowed nuthin' ceppen what I telled you; ever sence then I aint been satisfy to steddy 'bout doin' 'thout you, Jerry, an' I aint agoin' to be satisfy."

Jerry rose, and stood looking down into the fire; was it an abounding love that remembered the pitiful sayings of his childhood; or was it that in a life as empty as Joe's, small things would be remembered as long as life lasted. There was no rush of thought nor of feeling to raise the annihilating storms that sweep through lives that are educated and sensitive; there never had been anything for Joe but the monotonous living from day to day. Jerry's train of reasoning failed him abruptly, and all the unexplained things in Joe's life rose up before him.

In this common life there was a mystery he had guessed at only, how could he say what there had been? What did he know of Joe's life?

He turned slowly.

"Tell me all about your life, Joe," he said.

For one instant Joe looked up, and there was a thrill in the voice that spoke to him, and a light in the eyes that looked down on him, that he did not understand, and that made him look away.

He could not grasp the longing for companionship that was moving Jerry—he thought only, "Jerry is cur'us, sure!"

His life?

Joe had never summed it up—had scarcely realized that he had had the spending of a life.

"I 'llows as I don't jest onderstand youuns, Jerry," he said slowly.

Jerry walked across the floor, then back.

"You have lived a long time," he said.

"Moren sixty yeer," Joe answered, "Moren sixty

yeer ; but I dunno rightly the day, not the rale day," and he wondered how this concerned Jerry.

"And how have you managed to live all these years ?" Jerry went on, with a hopeless tone creeping into his voice.

"I most allers had ernough to eat," was answered calmly.

Enough to eat.

Jerry walked to the door, and out along the little path that led to the trail. The stars glittered ; the wind that came so far seemed to speak to him ; and he thought "Is the soul of Nature the only soul that mine can touch ?"

Did he stand alone, in that he reached above the formula—"enough to eat" ?

Up he climbed, unheeding the roughnesses, unheeding the fatigue ; up until he was above the billowy mist that hid the plain—the flat, helpless plain that could not reach to any height.

And for him, was it any use that he should reach up for ever ? The people he thought to raise, did they have any other wish in life than Joe had ; did they know or want any other answer to his question than "I have enough to eat" ?

Long ago he had toiled, and journeyed, and hoped, and at the end had found a barren height and the far plain glorified !

All about him as he stood the moonlight fell broad and shining ; the ragged shadows lay clear-cut and black as ink ; the wind rose and fell ; the stars looked down like patient eyes, and at his feet the silent mist waves gathered and broke—noiseless spirit-waves tearing themselves against the cliffs.

Was it any use to leave the plain ? Did not the light reach it as surely ; did not the streams reach it ; and from the heights what else did one see save only the plain glorified ?

Money was all that was needed to glorify anything : Money !

And up there in the darkness he seemed to see the bewildering glitter of gold; he seemed to remember all the things done and sacrificed for gold since man was made; since the world smiled in its beautiful youth. What caused this enchantment? What had given gold this weird power that so enchained all the world; that brought from men their bodies and hearts—their lives, and honor, and souls?

Had God made all this fair world, and then in all the cracks and crannies put this snare,—this bewildering, shining ruin, that the poor souls he had created might destroy themselves for it; delve and toil through all their lives for this one thing that in itself was nothing?

Why should not anything else have the same value; or why should not the world find enough to surfeit poor humanity, and make gold a drug in the market. Think of all the vast sums that had been gathered and lost; think of all that was in use; think of all that still lay hidden in the earth! Why not gather it all together; work it all out; scatter it broadcast through the nations, and so destroy this devilish snare? Scatter it until the world could spend and hoard no more, and it would be like the autumnal leaves, or "like as when one heweth wood"; like the poor chips that are not worth the gathering.

How they would glitter and gleam in the sunlight, these piles that would be gathered for the nations! how coldly they would shine when the moonlight fell upon them!

He shook himself.

He was losing his mind. He must go home; Joe would want to shut up the house; and he turned and with deliberate slowness retraced his steps. He had climbed a long, rough way without knowing it, and the return was very slow.

He would carry out his scheme: but first he must win the people entirely; and then when all was ready he would tell Joe, and search into the worth of Durden's Mine. Money was needed for the scheme ; and it must be saved, or begged, or borrowed ; and to what extent would Joe help him ?

It was wild and rash, maybe, this fight he was beginning against money and station ; but it would be a fair test of the stability and worth of the masses. Money would be entirely absent from their ranks, and the fight would have to be fought before any capital could be won. It was an interesting problem, and one he was beginning to long to work out.

And after ?

He drew a long breath : and after would be the gold, and the luxury, and the power which would place him on a level with his rivals,—which would let him look the doctor in the face and say—" I am successful, and in my success I thank you and say, ' I have been true to you always.' "

Success could humble itself and be called nobility—failure could be servile only.

CHAPTER VIII.

"We are men of ruined blood;
Therefore comes it we are wise.
Fish we are that love the mud,
Rising to no fancy flies."

IT was a still, gray day, with an unhealthy coolness and dampness in the air for August. The clouds hung low and heavy; not a leaf stirred in the gloomy gorges, and on the spreading plains there was not a movement. An unnatural, blank stillness, as if the world were dead.

Jerry walked the long way with even, quiet steps; Joe had gone away long ago, but whether to his usual work or to the town, Jerry had not asked. No words had passed between them as to the possibilities of the day, and Jerry thought it not unlikely that Joe had repented him of the rash and generous ardor of the night before.

Slowly he pursued his way, his hat drawn down over his eyes, his pistols well at hand, and his eyes, and ears, and mind all alert for any sign of an enemy; for if Dave Morris struck it would be in secret: a shot from behind some tree or rock.

And what difference would it make? If his life were taken, all this difficulty would pass away with one or two triumphant shouts from the opposite camp, then he would be forgotten save by Joe, perhaps. Would be buried out in the rain-gullied graveyard, near 'Lije Milton, maybe, whose dead face had come to him in Durden's Mine. He remembered so well as he tramped along in the gray stillness, the terror and wonder of that time, and the signs that Joe had read in the circumstances. And the doctor's explanations, that he well remembered explained nothing. The doctor had turned his mind away only; had thrown on him the burden of an explanation.

"Do you expect to buy Durden's Mine?" he had asked, "else, why should 'Lije Milton come to you?" Buy Durden's Mine? how strange it all seemed that now he should want to buy Durden's Mine—and the question came up to him, how could he find out about it, and who owned it now?

The doctor would know, and perhaps Engineer Mills, but they were enemies: could he ask Joe?

He paused a moment: he had had so many suspicions, would it be quite honest to ask Joe? Of course it would; it showed a darker suspicion still for him to hesitate. If he knew where to find Joe he would go back at once and ask him.

He walked on slowly: his school would be waiting, and if he were not there Dave Morris would declare him a coward; and all the unwise impatience which he had shown yesterday, and which he might at this juncture turn to good, would be used against him. Twenty-four hours would make no difference in his knowledge of Durden's Mine.

At last the town was reached, and all was as quiet as if no creature had ever heard of a railway. The doctor's corps of workmen stood about the door of their house waiting to start to their work; and up and down the street Jerry could see the children loitering, waiting for the school-bell to ring.

There was no sign of any excitement, and Jerry unlocked the door with a little feeling of surprise that his orders should be obeyed so literally.

Slowly the hours of the morning came and went, and at last the miners' bell for dinner rang, and, the children dispersing to their homes, Jerry opened his dinner-bucket.

He was provoked almost that he had heard nothing of his yesterday's broil: he had expected certainly, before this hour, some threat or overture from Morris, and was a little disappointed at the quiet of the day. Later he would walk up the street and get another paper; the mail came in again this day, and he wanted to see the latest accounts of himself, and of the town.

Would Morris sell a paper to him, he wondered? A knock came at the outer door, a quiet, respectful knock as of one who hesitated to disturb him.

"Come in!" he called.

And, hat in hand, Dave Morris stood before him.

"Good-mornin', Mr. Wilkerson."

"Good-morning," and Jerry rose with his hand well round on his hip.

"Hope you don't bear no malice, Mr. Wilkerson?" Morris asked, leaning on the back of the chair Jerry had offered him.

"I have no need to bear malice," Jerry answered, looking him over from head to foot.

"Thet's true," slowly, not looking up, "the knock come from you;" then sitting down, "but I've come for peace to-day, durned if I aint."

"No cursing, please," and Jerry before he sat down laid a pistol on the table.

Morris paused a moment, while a dull red heat crept up his face; why did not he kill this young man? but this question found no utterance, and he began slowly:

"I've come to say, Mr. Wilkerson, thet if there's anything I kin do to help you on a bit, I'm ready: I'm your friend, I am."

Jerry gathered up the remains of his lunch and put them back into the bucket.

"An' if you want me to stop the fellers from buyin' whisky," Morris went on, "I kin do it," looking up slowly; "I heard you the mornin' that you said for the fellers not to put up their money in my whisky barr'ls; an' I'm agreed to it provided," pausing and fixing his eyes on Jerry's eyes that looked at him so steadily—"provided I know your idea," cautiously.

"I have none," and Jerry cocked and uncocked his pistol carelessly.

By some means—whether fear, or hope of gain, Jerry could not decide—this man had been made anxious to join him, and Jerry saw his advantage. Again the trigger of the pistol clicked sharply in the silence.

Morris moved his chair uneasily; a loaded pistol turned about recklessly in another man's hands is not a pleasant or reassuring sight,

"You had ideas the mornin' you talked to the fellers," Morris said at last.

"And you heard them," Jerry answered.

"I did, but I think I'd like to hear 'em again."

There was a moment's pause, then Jerry answered: "I told them that I wanted them to take all the work they could get, never mind who gave it to them; I told them I wanted them to keep whatever land they owned either in Eureka or in Durden's; I told them that I would watch for them, and that whichever town the strangers built up, we would build up the other; I told them that when the time came we should need money, and that they must save all they could." He ceased, and Dave Morris's small, bleared eyes watched him keenly.

"An' you'll build up a town without no money?" he asked.

"I have said we would need money," Jerry answered curtly, "and that the people must save it."

"Live at a dollar a day and save money?"

"It can be done easily."

"An' then what?" skeptically.

Jerry looked up coldly.

"I do not know why I should tell you my plans," he said.

"You don't, don't you?" and Morris put a piece of tobacco in his mouth with a swaggering air, "I tell you I kin save more money for you in Eureky, than all the men there."

"Do it, then."

Morris looked at him with distrust in his eyes; no man who was not entirely independent would speak so shortly; and he answered slowly:

"Thet's right easy said, Mr. Wilkerson; but I don't know that I'm goin' to stop a good whisky trade without knowin' what's to do after*werds*."

Jerry was silent for a moment: what Morris said was true; it would be useless to try to save the people's money as long as Morris sold them whisky; nor could he expect him to stop his chief trade without some prospect of compensation; yet to reveal his plans would be ruin; and Jerry was puzzled.

Dan Burk! the name flashed into his mind like a beam of light. Burk was a higher type, and could manage Morris and Eureka too.

"Very well," Jerry answered carelessly, while his plans formed themselves rapidly in his mind, "if you can not trust me, you need not help me. Besides, I think my work will lie in Durden's, and there are those there who will do as I wish and ask no questions"; then laying down his pistol, and crossing his arms on the table, he looked straight into Morris's face. "I will give you a friendly warning," he said; "your trade is going to fail you: the men who live here, soon will have no money to spend at your shop, for the new people who come will rather employ the new men who come with them, and there will not be work enough for all. More than this, new people who know what decent things are will not trade with you, and you will be simply crowded out."

Morris's face flamed with color; he shuffled his feet restlessly, while his hand sought the leather belt about his waist. Jerry did not seem to heed him, and only changed his position sufficiently to begin again his idle play with his pistol.

"This place will be taken in hand by great capitalists," he went on quietly, "and the people here can expect to hold their own only a little while longer; then they must move further west, or retreat to Durden's. They have made enemies of two of the leading men, and must expect no favors."

"An' you done it for 'em!" Morris broke in angrily.

"And am glad that I did," was answered coolly, "for now I can put them in a better condition than ever before; and make money faster for them: only they must trust me."

Morris's whole expression changed, and he leaned forward eagerly.

"Is Dan Burk the feller?" he asked, "is he the feller you think of to help you?"

Jerry laughed a little.

"So long as you are not the man," he answered, "I do not know that any part of this scheme is your business."

Morris rose hastily.

"Damn—" then his voice died away in his throat, for Jerry's pistol covered him, and its little mouth looked huge, and the shining hammer was drawn far back! One moment he glared on the quiet, dark face opposite, then sat down slowly; and Jerry, who had not moved, laid his pistol down and waited for Morris to speak. He had not long to wait, then Morris asked sullenly:

"What'll you pay me to stop the whisky trade?"

"Nothing."

"An' how's it goin' to help me?" anger creeping into his voice again.

"You will be a more honest man," Jerry answered, smiling, "and will allow other men to be more honest and decent, and you will be better in health."

"An' my fambly'll starve."

"Not more than other families you have ruined."

"Mr. Wilkerson—" menacingly; but the children began to come in, and Jerry rose.

"I will be here this afternoon at five," he said, "and to-morrow at twelve if you wish to see me again."

Baffled and angry, Morris rose: there was something in this young man that he could not grapple with: he hated him bitterly for his insults and slights that would have cost any other man his life, but he was afraid of him. Morris had killed men for far less. But now he stood twisting his hat about in his hands, while Jerry watched him, and waited for his going—watched and waited silently, with his eyes fixed on the ugly, sullen, face. It was only a moment or two he had to wait, then the greasy old hat was donned, and Morris turned to the door. "I'll come to-morrer," he said, and made his way out through a group of children.

Jerry drew a long breath, partly of satisfaction, partly of doubt. Had he been wise to refuse so entirely this man's support and assistance, basing his plans on Dan Burk, to whom he had not as yet spoken on the subject? And would Morris come again to-morrow, or would he form a rival party?

The long, gray afternoon dragged its weary length; the children droned through their lessons; and in the pauses the crickets cried their ceaseless monotone. Nothing stirred in the clouded stillness; and when the tasks were done and the children dismissed; when the gray day showed its death by growing yet more gray and still, Jerry heard the bugle-call rise soft and clear—echoed back by the great mountains until it died slowly from the world.

There was an inexplicable pain to him in the sound of that horn, almost as if he had been called and could not answer—could not go. As if he had left all he cared for; as if in some unwilling way he had descended from his sphere and station.

Then with a bitter scorn of self he would remember that he had been born to no station, as the meaning of the word was taken; and the sphere he had moved in until it seemed his by right, had been opened to him through charity. He was only one of the "common herd"—a favorite phrase of Paul's—one who would have to make a name and place; and who would have only such foothold in life as he cut for himself.

He laughed a little bitterly.

"A key of gold fits most locks," he said to himself as he went his way up the rough mountain path.

CHAPTER IX.

> "We pant, we strain like birds against the wires;
> Are sick to reach the vast and the beyond;—
> And what avails, if still to our desires
> Those far-off gulfs respond?"
>
> "Contentment comes therefore; still, there lies
> An outer distance when the first is hailed,
> And still forever yawns before our eyes
> An *utmost*—that is veiled."

JERRY was glad that he had the fire to make and the supper to cook, for this every-day work brought him back to a realization of his position and of all he owed Joe, for whom he now had a much higher respect than for either himself or the doctor.

The corn-bread was assuming a most approved brown tint; the bacon was crisping and curling; the coffee was bubbling and muttering in the pot, sending out a grateful fragrance. Homely, coarse fare, and Jerry knew it. He had read of the banquets and feasts of ages gone, and had read modern novels about the many alluring ways of feeding people which fashion invents and money pays for. He had read it all with a sort of scorn at first, but later with a changed feeling that grew to be a longing to see the sights and hear the beautiful sounds of music and laughter that must fill in these pictures. And lovely women: he had read of them too, and paused a moment as he turned the bread that was browned on one side; how would they look? He had never seen one save once when he was alone in the doctor's study, and before him on the table lay a case, a red morocco case. It was different in shape from any he had ever seen before, and what could it contain? It did not occur to him that there was any wrong in opening it, and he unhooked the clasp without one tremor of his honest boyish heart.

A sweet fair face, that was more delicate than any he had ever seen: he did not know if it were beautiful, for he had no standard; he had never seen any faces since he could remember, save those of the work-hardened, slovenly drudges about the towns where he lived; but there was something in the picture that held him. It looked so small and fine, like some of the flowers he had seen among the rocks, but had never picked because somehow he knew that one touch would kill them.

The eyes met his with an expression as if they once had pleaded for protection, but afterwards had learned a look of bravery; and the mouth was pained.

"Poor little thing," he had said, and had sighed as if he knew the sorrow that looked from her eyes. He felt that he would have spent his life in saving her from ill!

Of course he was a fool, and that face was only a picture, maybe of the doctor's mother or grandmother who had died long ago.

Poor woman!

Then he shut the case; a new thought had flashed on him; maybe this face had been the one face that the world had held for the doctor? And had she died? and so he had come out to waste his life on the people. Was this the secret of that life?

But the memory of that face never left Jerry entirely, and it became the nucleus about which all his youthful dreams grouped themselves. If he could only know a face like that: could only move in a world where such refinement was common. Paul could, but he could not: could not until he made a golden key.

He turned the bread carefully while he pondered on the discontent that had culminated so suddenly in his heart. If the doctor had not turned from him he would have been satisfied always with the old life ; but now all was changed and he was filled with a restless ambition and jealousy : feelings which he fully recognized, and a year ago would have despised. Now he must rise—if it took a lifetime to mount one step !

Perhaps when he was an old man he would see such faces about him. When his eyes were too dim to see almost, and his ears too dull to hear, and his heart too weary to love, then all these things would come to him !

"Well," and Joe stood in the doorway.

"How are you ?" Jerry answered, and turned to the table.

"Thar's a paper," and Joe laid the printed sheet down, "it cusses youuns wuss an' wusser ; durned if I'd stan' it."

Jerry put the paper on the shelf.

"I will have my say some time," he answered.

"An' Dave Morris says as youuns is welcome to the paper when you wants it."

"Dave Morris ?"

"Thet's what I said," sitting down near the table.

"You have been there to-day ?"

"I hev."

Jerry poured out the coffee in silence : questioning was not customary between them, and what else there was to be told must await Joe's pleasure. The supper was over and the few things washed and put away ; then Jerry lighted the lamp and took up the newspaper, and Joe filled his pipe.

Truly, as Joe said, the abuse and misrepresentations seemed to culminate in this paper. There was nothing too false to be said—nothing too wild to be predicted ; and at the end a comment by the far-off city editor, that many of the idle and worthless in the city were coming out to throw in their lots with the "redoubtable Jeremiah P. Wilkerson." Jerry read it over again—"the idle and worthless," the paper said : what should he do with them ? His heart sank within him. The little ball he had set rolling was taking such appalling proportions.

"Dave Morris says as youuns is the peskyist varmint as ever he's knowed," Joe broke in, taking his pipe from his mouth, "an' I says, says I, 'Dave, Jerry'll kill you 'thout thinkin',' says I," and Joe chuckled contentedly to himself.

This described his ideal hero, a man who "killed without thinking," and that Jerry should hold this proud position, and hold it in the estimation of the man who harried all Eureka, was to him an infinite satisfaction.

Jerry put down the paper; he was anxious to know of Joe's interview with Dave Morris.

"Morris came to see me to-day," he said.

"An' come back mashed jest as flat!" Joe answered with a readiness that showed his pleasure. "An' I axes him, 'Dave, did you skeer Jerry?' Lord!" slapping his leg, "you jest oughter seen him, Jerry; I 'llow he'd a-liked to eat me jest whole, he would; says he, 'Joe Gilliam, youuns aint got but one hide,' says he, cussin' awful, 'an' if you keeps on a-pesterin' me I'll jest use it up,' says he."

"And you?" Jerry asked.

"I jest knocked him down," pleasantly, "I gin him a eye thet'll not look purty fur a while," and Joe chuckled a little—"but I tole him as a rotten apple were mighty good fur it." Then Joe returned to his pipe.

He had gone to Dave Morris's shop to intimidate him, and had succeeded in doing not only this, but in addition had knocked the man down. This had been his day's work, and he had been happy in it; Jerry had knocked Dave Morris down one day, and he, the next; what more could Eureka need to prove to her that these men from the Durden's side were superior?

Knowing the people, Joe knew that his and Jerry's reputations were made now; and that no man in either town would touch them without much thought and calculation as to the consequences.

It was a happy feeling that came over Joe ; a calm assurance that he had done his duty by Jerry, and at the same time had won renown in Eureka. Surely a good day's work.

Then Jerry looked up suddenly.

" Who owns Durden's Mine ? he asked.

The fire still threw its quaint shadows ; the lamp still burned with unwavering brightness ; it must have have been Joe's eyes that flickered and winced until the room seemed dark—flickered for a moment so that he could not see the face of the younger man—and when he spoke his voice had changed.

" Durden's Mine ? " he repeated—" Durden's Mine ? I dunno fur rayly."

So Jerry *had* heard what he had said by mistake the other night.

And Jerry took the shade from off the lamp, and looked at the wick as if something ailed the light. " I thought you would know," Jerry said slowly, while many surmises as to Joe's words flashed through his mind unbidden—" and that you would tell me about it ; for if I know who owns it, and can find out from the owner its value, I can the more easily persuade the people to buy land in Durden's."

" An' open the mine agin ? " was questioned in a lowered voice as of one in fear of some catastrophe.

" Of course that would be the plan," raising the paper again between him and Joe, " that, or find gold somewhere else near at hand ; I suppose it lies all about here."

He had not looked at Joe since he asked the question about the ownership of the mine, and now went back to a pretense of reading in order to be able to collect his thoughts and reason them free from his suspicions.

And Joe sat still with his pipe going out, and his eyes fixed blankly on the fire.

It had been many a long year,—many a long year since he had been warned that some bad end would come; many a long year since he had been pleaded with to come away and let the place alone; many a year.

He glanced furtively at the corner where the dog Buck lay sleeping; then vaguely up along the rafters; then back again into the leaping fire that, even though it was August, did not seem able to warm him now.

The Devil had made gold, she had said; God had never made that thing that ran men crazy; the awful gold that shone in their eyes until they could see nothing else. And she had made him bury her in a place where there was no mark of gold; no trace of the kind of rock that held it, else somebody would come some day and dig her up to hunt for gold, and she and the baby wanted to rest. And gold would break his heart some day, she said: would it?

It was very long ago since his "little Nan" had warned him—very long ago, but dead people surely came back—surely! And he knew the path so well and every rock by the way; and everything was so convenient there; his eyes knew the darkness, and his back knew the angles and curves in the rocks; and his lantern, would it burn anywhere else—or his pick break any other stone? And the nuggets;—the little shining nuggets,—he had found so many of them washed down by the water that dropped and dropped forever, and that far back in an unknown corner helped to make a stream that flowed away—lost itself. And all that he gathered was for Jerry, all of it; and if others came in all else that would be found should have to be divided.

No, of course there was no gold in Durden's Mine! and he drew his chair nearer the fire.

"Thar's gole in the water thet runs down the mountain," he said at last; and Jerry looked up.

"I suppose there is gold all through that gorge," he answered, "even if the old mine is worn out";

then more slowly, "It is not the mine that I want so much as it is all the land about it."

Joe knocked the ashes out of his pipe and filled it freshly; "I 'llows as it aint lucky, the gittin' of gole," he said; "my Nancy Ann says, say she, 'Joe, don't you tech no sich work,' says she, ''cause I 'llows the devil made gole; God never done no sicher thing as thet,' says she, 'to shine an' shine in a man's eyes tell he can't see nothin' else,' says she—" puffing slowly at his pipe, "an' youuns done hed a warnin', Jerry, a rale warnin'," almost angrily, "an' you 'llows thet it's a sin to speckylate in lan', an' is jest a-bein' cussed out 'bout it, an' now you is jest a-hankerin' atter it."

"Not as a speculation," Jerry answered; "I want it to help those who have been hurt by speculators. I want to givē our people who have lived here always, as good a town as these new people expect to have; I want to give them mines to work in that will cause the railway to build a station at Durden's also; I want to give them a good school; I want to make the men more sober and decent, and the women more clean and respectable; I want—"

"To maker fool of yourself, Jerry Wilkerson," Joe struck in unexpectedly, while the angry color flashed into Jerry's face. "Youuns hes been a-livin' in the doctor's steddy—a-drinkin' books an' papers; an' Durden's an' Eureky's been a-livin' in dirt, an' a-drinkin' whisky; an' they loves it, yes, jest like youuns loves the books an' the papers, they do; an' lemme tell you jest one perticler—if you wants to start this po' trash off, you'll hev to promise 'em money, an' piles of it; an' if you don't give it to 'em, they'll kill you in a minute; jest you 'member thet!" shaking his head, "orl they wants, or knows 'bout, is whisky, an' terbackey, an' dirt; they's usen to it—an' born to it—an' likes it. Lord!" taking a puff at his pipe, "an' the wimmins is satisfy 'cause they 'specks to be beat, an' needs it too."

Jerry had turned away, and again had raised the paper before his face.

"I do not agree with you," was all he said when Joe's voice ceased.

"Orl right," and Joe chuckled to himself, "but thar's one thing I'm gettin' to be powerful sure 'bout, an' it's thet the doctor onderstan's these mean critters better'n I 'llowed jest at fust; he do thet."

Jerry moved his feet impatiently.

"It's the Lord's truth," Joe went on; "an' when they've jest plum killed you out, they'll stan' squar' up to the doctor an' to Paul, jest you watch an' see" —looking anxiously at the paper behind which Jerry hid himself—"'cause the doctor an' Paul jest stomps on 'em 'thout axin' no questions, they do,—jest stomps 'em clean out;" then more slowly, "I aint got much larnin', but I knows a pig loves its mudhole, an' a dorg is better fur beatin', an' it aint agoin' to do no good to tuck them things away. They's mad alonger the doctor now, 'cause youuns is done showed 'em thet they's been 'posed on; but they aint agoin' to 'member thet long; an' when they gits to doin' nothin' ceppen steddy 'bout youuns—Lord! you'll hanker atter gittin' shed of livin',—you bet!"

"And you do not know who own Durden's Mine?" Jerry repeated coldly.

"No, I dunno," he answered slowly, then moved his chair outside where no more such questions could reach him.

CHAPTER X.

" and also this
Fell into dust, and I was left alone."

DAN BURK would know.

This thought had come to Jerry in the night, and he determined to follow it up. As far back as he could remember, he had heard Joe speak of Dan Burk more than of any one else save the doctor; and Jerry felt quite sure that Dan could tell him all he wanted to know, and more, for Dan was an older inhabitant than Joe, and would know more of the local history.

Another fact of which Jerry was now convinced was that Joe got his money from Durden's Mine, which made his lack of knowledge as to the ownership seem more strange. But Burk would know, and Jerry was determined to make Burk tell him all that was known of the mine. Durden's had been always a strange story to him; as long as he had believed what the doctor had told him, that the better find was at Eureka—and had remembered what Joe had told him in his childhood about Durden's as a fairy story,—he could understand the desertion of Durden's; but if, as Joe had lately revealed, Durden's mine was full of gold, why had it been deserted—surely not for a ghost story! It was true that the people were not aggressively energetic; and as the Doctor and 'Lije Milton had invested in Eureka it was natural, perhaps, that the people should follow; but still, Joe's assertion of the richness of the mine made the facts hard to be understood. And now that he had committed himself so far that he could not go back, he must get at the truth of the story.

His scheme was far within the bounds of possibility; and success would bring him money, the one thing he needed to put him on a level with Paul, and to compel the doctor to respect his shrewdness at least.

He would go to Dan Burk in the morning before school, and if he gained any information it would help him in his interview with Morris.

He left home as early as Joe that day, only waiting until he was out of sight. He thought he had never known Joe to take so long to go; he was excited and restless, and the waiting was trying.

The paper he had read the night before had put new thoughts into his mind; he was known out there in the East much more than where he lived, and was looked on as a crafty mob-leader—as a violent communist—as a dangerous demagogue; and men were coming out to cast in their fortunes with his—to follow him wherever he should lead.

This sudden thought had demoralized him for a little while, but now he had recovered himself, and was determined to be ready for all who should come. A new excitement was creeping into his veins; his army that was to do battle against influence and capital; that was to win for all who came after a foothold and a hope; that was to make him triumphant—this army was fast doubling itself. The "halt, and the maimed, and the blind" were coming, "with neither scrip nor purse"—coming to test a great question, and to prove once more, in the long, dark history of the world, the power of the people!

He walked more rapidly to keep pace with his thoughts. Of course Joe would not have worked in Durden's Mine all these years, his thoughts ran on, unless there was gold to be found there. It would hurt him to stop, but the avarice of one man could not stand against the gain of the many; Joe had had long years in which to lay up store, now he must stop; indeed, he was too old to do such hard work, and once well started, Jerry knew that he could support them both easily.

Early as it was, Dan Burk's door was open, and he and his shop were both dirty. There were no loungers about as yet, however, and Jerry felt he had done well to come at this hour; for besides the quiet, Dan had had nothing to drink.

"I wanted to see you, Mr. Burk," Jerry began, "and had no other time; can you spare me a half-hour?"

"I reckon," and Dan placed a chair for his visitor.

"Who owns Durden's Mine?" the question was so sudden that Dan started, with a betraying look of wonder in his eyes.

"Durden's Mine?" doubtfully.

"Yes," and Jerry did not move his eyes.

"What do you want to know for?" cautiously.

"Tell me; you will not lose anything by it," and the two men looked fully and searchingly into each other's eyes. The suspicious, treacherous eye of the shopkeeper—the tired, keen eyes of the clever schoolmaster who had just now begun to measure his strength against the world.

"All right," and Dan laid his hand on Jerry's knee, "it's Mis. Milton's."

For a moment Jerry looked at him in silence; was he telling the truth? Could this be the truth and Joe not know it?

"I'll go with you and ask her," the man went on, his face reddening angrily under his companion's eyes; "has Joe lied?"

"That will do!" and a look flashed on him that made the words die on his lips; he had heard of the difficulty with Morris.

"And she owns all the land near it?" rising.

"She does."

"Will she sell?"

"She will, an' be glad."

Then Jerry turned away, looking out the door and down the road to the doctor's house; he could see the chairs on the piazza, and some one tramping up and down; how strange it was that he could not go there now, and ask advice—when, and where, and how had the breach between them begun?

"You will not mention this," he said at last, turning his eyes again on Burk, "if you do—"

"It's all right—all right, Mr. Wilkerson, all right," the man interrupted eagerly, "it's for you to remember, please, that I aint said nuthin'."

"Very well," and Jerry walked away.

Joe *had* lied! and he drew a long breath. Joe, whom he had trusted more than he would have trusted himself; Joe, whom he had looked on as the one honest man he knew; Joe, whom in the last few weeks he had put far above the doctor for the exquisite quality of sincerity!

He walked rapidly, and his heels struck sharply on the hardened soil.

Who could be trusted?

Slowly the long story unwound itself, this one clew showed him all. 'Lije Milton had owned the mine; had been unable to put workmen into it because of the mysterious sights and sounds that haunted it; had gone in himself—

Jerry's thoughts stopped, and a cold sweat came out on him, and his mind went groping back to that day when he had gone to see 'Lije Milton buried; what were all the circumstances—what had Joe told him?

He could not remember, save that 'Lije had met with some injury in the mine from which he had never recovered.

He drew his hand across his brow, and sat down on a stone. If only he could recall and be able to put together all that had been told him. How long had old Durden been dead; how long had Joe been gathering gold on his own account; how long had

'Lije Milton owned the mine? He remembered that 'Lije had been the discoverer of the new mine in Eureka, and reaping gold from there, had been content, probably, to let his old property go.

Jerry rose slowly: he would not think these thoughts any longer; he dared not formulate any theory on the slight basis he had, and the suspicions that had come to him were too dreadful to be retained for a moment. Besides, if 'Lije had met with any tangible foul play while in the mine, he would certainly have had his revenge. He felt relieved when he reached this conclusion, and put all thoughts away from him save that Durden's Mine had a bad name, and so would be sold at a great discount. He must by some means get money to buy the property, so securing it to his scheme; and he must find some person who would be figure-head to hold this land and sell it out in lots to the people from Eureka.

The scheme grew as he walked, and took clearer and clearer shape in his mind.

Faster and faster he tramped; his eyes shining, and a slow color creeping up his dark face; and he saw himself a rich, successful man.

And Joe?

The memory came over him like a cold wave, and he tried to put it aside. Joe was a liar, but not a murderer of his friend; facts disproved that.

And most men seemed to be liars?

He took his hat off; his head was hot and throbbing, and he hated himself that he had found cause against this man who had clothed him and fed him. It was treacherous to judge him. Joe had gathered gold secretly, and had hoarded it all these years; why not, if he found pleasure in it? He had gathered it from another man's possessions!

The thought came unexpectedly, and put yet another face on the question: Joe had stolen his money. And yet, could it be called stealing if he had made a find in a place that others had deserted? had deserted from stupid superstition, while Joe had been brave enough to go in and work there? Could it be stealing?

Perhaps not; yet, who was it that he had heard talk of the horrors of the old mine; who had said it was death to go there; who had been so mortally terrified at the nervous vision of his childhood?

Had it been a nervous vision?

Even after all these years he did not like the memory of it.

He put on his hat; it was ridiculous to deal in such fancies, and be swayed by them. If Joe had stolen the chance and the gold, it was not his care—he was not the keeper of Joe's conscience.

He walked steadily on, and into the town. He would have to turn Morris away again to-day; he had not learned enough to answer him yet. He would have made overtures to Burk that morning, but what the man had told him had shocked him from his purpose: he would go again to-morrow and make his inquiries the more sure from having had time to think them over.

The day seemed endless: the children stumbled and struggled with their lessons in a way that was exasperating; they seemed bent on making mistakes, on disobeying orders, on being kept in and whipped. The atmosphere was heavy and clinging; the smell of onions and dirt was intensified, and Jerry's nerves seemed to strain, and tingle, and long for freedom. He must have something better than this.

The day waned, and the tasks and punishments were settled; the future statesmen, and presidents, and "reigning belles" had gone home to their hovels; and Jerry, locking up his desk, heard the horn ring out so fine and clear. He listened; when he became rich and could claim success, he would have a band of instruments such as he had read of, and would ask the doctor to come and hear them play. He would have this horn multiplied a hundred-fold, and every note his own, and calling to him.

Always he had read of music with a longing: it would mean something to him: once in the night a traveler had passed down the trail thrumming a guitar, and Jerry had heard the sound; heard it coming like the throbbing of a heart—coming with a cry so vague, so unfinished—only a cry with so much left unsaid. Coming nearer and nearer until it seemed to throb all about him as he sat up in the darkness listening. Beating, crying, pleading with him to fill out the unworded measure.

Fading down the black gorge, the sobbing, broken cry passed away.

Would music be like all the other things he had found in life—a fragment? Would he be striving always after some unfinished measure?

Again the sound of the horn swept by him, and he listened with an impatience that was unbearable. Why had he been for all these years an idle dreamer, wasting so much time preparing himself for the cramped, chance life of a writer: feeding himself ill on dreams and vagaries that seemed now to possess him and to weaken him?

He closed and locked the door with an angry vehemence that had no foundation save dissatisfaction with himself. He had been *such* a fool! Would he be able now to gather himself together, and to stand entirely alone; could he put aside all associations, all qualms of conscience, all feeling, and conquer success? And he wondered vaguely if many of those whom the world called successful had consciences.

CHAPTER XI.

> "Then every evil word I had spoken once,
> And every evil thought I had thought of old,
> And every evil deed I ever did,
> Awoke and cried."

IT was very dark, and the entrance was dwindling to a point of light. Still Joe seemed to know the way with wonderful accuracy, and walked the rough path with the stealth and swiftness of a cat.

A little further and he paused, felt along the wall, fitted his hands slowly and carefully into a crevice, then swung himself over some danger so well known to him, that dropping safely on his feet he drew a short, sharp breath. He stopped a moment just where he had dropped, until he lighted a small lantern which he took from a ledge in the rock, then moved on. Carefully and slowly he went now, crawling like a great spider, scraping himself against the wall. Only a little space was lighted by the lantern, but the ledge of rocks on which he walked stopped far within that radius. Steadily on, looking neither to the right nor to the left, but only on the next step he must take; carefully, cautiously, slowly, with his eyes shining and his breath coming heavily. One misstep and he would never be heard of again: one man had made this misstep; he was sure of it, although no one else was; he knew because he had heard the legend of this narrow way from Dan Burk, who had been the near friend of old Durden.

And beyond this narrow way he had found the cave the story had told about; and where, unknown to Burk even, the old man had hoarded great treasure.

There was something strange about this mine; some devil of greed and deception seemed to inhabit it.

He was safe over the narrow way now, and putting his lantern down, he began to change his clothes with rapid, stealthy movements. The whole man seemed transformed and alive; seemed to have shaken off the stolid heaviness he wore in the outside world, and instead moved about with nervous quickness. Having arrayed himself in a rough, worn suit of clothes, he put his usual apparel in a corner, then paused and made a little wailing cry,—a peculiar sound that in an instant seemed to be repeated by a hundred voices; taken up again and again; coming back sometimes loud, sometimes low; seeming to die away, then waking suddenly to one more repetition; weird, startling, awful!

He listened, and seemed to know when it was finished, then made the little sound again,—this time not waiting, but going deeper into the gloom, leaving the little cries to wander up and down the hopeless darkness until they died,—up and down until the merciful silence hushed them.

Joe lighted two more lanterns standing in niches in the wall, then looked anxiously around the low arched recess that almost was a room.

The walls look dull and dead, and here and there were worked into deep holes; especially on the side overhanging a stream which ran the entire length of the room: a stream that appeared without visible reason in one corner of the room—foaming white and strong against the fretting barriers, and disappeared suddenly through a low arch in the corner furthest from Joe's place of entrance. Across its place of exit was stretched a net of finest wire; and deeper in the narrow crack, a web of cloth.

Low Joe stooped and peered with his glittering eyes that seemed to enlarge and gleam as he caught sight of the shining particles washed by the water against his catches.

"A good haul," he muttered, "a rale good haul," then he rose, and took down from the jagged ribs of the cave fresh nets of wire and cloth. Carefully he fixed them in place before he removed the standing catches, waiting patiently for a few moments that the disturbed water might resume its usual flow;—no smallest grain must be lost. Carefully he removed the nets that held the gold, emptying their hoard into a flat pan of water; dipping them again and again; examining them with 'bated breath.

"Orl fur Jerry," he whispered, stirring the glittering particles with his hungry-looking hands, "an' a good lot; an' he dunno, damn it!" tying a fine cloth tightly over the whole pan, "dunno nothin' jest ceppen hisn's books: talkin' so fine 'bout t'other folks, an' what he 'llows they orter hev: he aint got good sense 'bout thet, God bless 'im! an sich shinin' eyes."

Carefully the string was untied when the last drop of water had been drained from the pan, and the cloth, with the valuable sediment inside, was gathered together and tied like a bag, then hung near a small iron stove filled with charcoal.

Slowly the fire lighted and grew red and glowing—glancing through the one opening in the cylinder like a great red eye, dull, burning, watchful of the poor warped soul that only lived while in this den! who seemed endued with new life; who vibrated and glowed as he watched the steam that floated about the wet bag. It would not take very long to get dry, then he would get all the particles out, even to the least dust; shake it clear and clean into the little leather bag that soon would be full enough to take to Eureka.

If only Jerry would have a little sense; just a little, he thought, as he squatted before the charcoal stove, looking steadily into the red eye.

If only Jerry knew anything besides books: he had learned too much; he had learned more than Paul,—his thoughts ran on,—for Paul only knew how to get and spend money; he did not know that a man ought to think about other men having money: Jerry had learned too much.

He rubbed his hand back on his stubbly gray hair: if Jerry only knew gold; if Jerry could only see what gold could get—could only spend gold; Jerry would be like Paul, he would take all he could get and never ask where it came from.

Maybe if Jerry could be sent to where Paul came from, he would learn to be like Paul.

The idea crept into the anxious mind, and the deep-set eyes seemed to catch fire from the red eye of the stove, and to light up as the new possibility loomed before them.

Jerry must go East.

At last the problem was solved: Jerry must learn to spend money; he must learn to love it, then Joe would be left in peaceful possession of his den.

The red eye of the stove seemed to flash—the stream seemed to lift up its voice almost into a laugh; and from the black abyss the cries seemed to wake and come back to the lonely worker. He listened.

"I hears it sometimes," he whispered, "when I aint never made no soun'!" and he looked over his shoulder as if he expected to see a vision. "It'd orl a-been fur youuns, Nan, if youuns hed a-lived; I swar afore God!" putting his hands over his face—"I swar!"

The stream laughed on and on, washing high up against the nets; the eye of the stove glared at the dull wall; the lanterns flickered and flared as mysterious draughts of wind reached up and touched them with invisible, ghostly fingers: and the cries—were they echoing still through the blackness of that awful passage? Were the souls wrecked by this fatal den waking and sobbing in the distance?

"I swar, Nan!" and the lean, work-hardened body swayed back and forth where it crouched—"I sw'ar!"

Surely the dead came back—surely.

The man rose to his feet hurriedly; he must make

some movement. Close over the stream was his work, and standing in the cold water he swung his pick with even, regular strokes; breaking the rocks into very small pieces that dropped into the stream. The water and his hammer would do the rest of the work for him.

On and on he worked, his strokes falling fast and hard,—his breath coming sharp and thick. On and on only stopping now and then to step from the cold water that he might warm his feet near the stove. It would be his death some day, this standing in the water: he had seen many a miner ruined in this way; either drawn up with rheumatism and left a helpless cripple, or dying suddenly from some congestion caused by cold. He knew that in this place and in this work he would meet his death; he knew that sooner or later the end would meet him here. Maybe walking that narrow ledge he would slip over with a last long cry that would live to haunt some future worker.

Steadily the strokes fell: it was all for Jerry. And he must persuade Jerry to go East; to see the things that made money valuable. There was nothing but here in the wilderness to make men love money. But he had seen such things long ago when in the East he and Nancy were nearly starved; it was then that a man had persuaded them and a lot of other people to move West where a friend of his, Mr. Durden, had found a mine. They had had hard times that made him long for money, and made him come to this wild country. But when they reached the place they found that old Durden had disappeared in the mine some time before, and the place was closed because the people were afraid. They were simple, superstitious country people—content if they had room to plant a little patch, and live from hand to mouth. There had been no regular miners nor adventurers among them.

His Nan would have been content with a little patch; but Joe had dreamed golden dreams; and besides it was too late that year to plant a garden. Then it was that in despair he had explored the mine, had found the black hole, and on its brink a little nugget that some creature must have dropped there.

He remembered now the intense, wondering joy of that find ; and how he had taken it to Dan Burk, the one shop-keeper of the whole region, who was at that time reduced to as great straits almost as Joe. It was then that with much cautious questioning they measured each other, and determined to trust each other. Joe was not so much afraid of the mine as he was of hunger and death for himself and his Nancy ; and Burk, who was afraid of the mine, knew all its secrets or thought that he did.

He knew that the shaft beginning in a cave opening into which the stream, turned out of its course by Durden, had once flowed,—that this shaft had run into an awful abyss which the people said had no bottom, and into which the stream must have fallen originally : that on the other side of this abyss there was a large cave about which the Indians had left a story.

When by accident the workmen had broken into this hole, the last Indian left in the settlement came to see it and told his story. He said that on the other side of this hole there was a cave in which there was a stream that washed out quantities of gold ; that his tribe hearing of this treasure-house had conquered the tribe owning it. The battle had been fought out on the plain, and the conquered tribe, when desperately pushed by their enemies, had driven their wives and children through the cave and into this hole, themselves jumping in after, doing this rather than become prisoners, and lose their places as braves. He went on to say that, after this, no good luck had come to his tribe any more, that the Great Spirit fought against them in every battle, until in the days of his father they had closed and concealed the entrance to the cave. That he had never known where it was.

Long consultations had been held between old Durden and his few helpers; but the men refused to brave the dangers of such a crossing for any amount of money. The huge bonfire built on the edge of the hole showed a narrow tunnel that seemed to have neither bottom, nor top, nor end; the only vestige of any foothold being a narrow ledge of rock that could be reached only by swinging across a section of the hole. There was talk of a bridge, but there was no skill there to throw one across the hole,—and even while they talked strange sounds had come from the hole; they were made to listen by the Indian: it was the crying, he said, of the murdered women and children.

So the last man of the victorious tribe had spoken; with his hand resting on the shoulder of old Durden, and something shining in his eyes that made old Durden advise against the bridge.

Later, old Durden had heard further from the Indian: a whispered story of hidden treasure, that made him risk the dreadful passage; and Dan Burk said he had found much.

The shaft that in the first instance had diverged from the bed of the stream, but that in breaking into the abyss had come into it again, was once more turned aside; and the men, who would not attempt to cross the hole, agreed willingly to work there.

So all day long the men worked busily, and in the night the old man went and came on his dangerous journeys; for day and night were the same in that black place. For fear of having to share his gains, Durden revealed his find to one man only, and to him only because he needed a place of exchange for his nuggets and dust.

Dan Burk had agreed to keep his secret for a certain share of the spoil, and had made money on the bargain, until once the old man went, but came no more.

Search was made until they came to the hole that so held all in awe, and no man would go further. They heard dreadful sounds and cries, they said, and saw strange shadows looming up in the darkness, so that they turned back in terror, and the mine was deserted.

The people had hard times then until the doctor came and took command, and 'Lije Milton, who had bought Durden's on a speculation, found the new mine at Eureka; then peace came again, and old Durden was forgotten save as a ghost.

But during those dark days one man dared all, and crossing the dreadful abyss crept along the narrow ledge. He found the hidden treasure, and found also that his predecessor had not shared fairly; but carefully in strong boxes were little bags, clumsily but safely made, and full of dust: and in another box a shining pile of golden coin.

The old man had not carried out for exchange all that he found hidden, but he had brought back and stored afresh all the money he had gained. And all his tools were there, and the charcoal stove, but no other sign of him; and Dan Burk's theory was that he had lost himself in trying to find the old entrance to the cave. Joe, who knew so well the perils of the passage, said he had fallen into the hole.

And Joe, was he to reveal all that he had found? It was surely his, he had risked an awful death to win it; a death Dan Burk would never have risked. No, it was not stealing; and when his friend 'Lije Milton wondered about the old story, he did not tell his secret: 'Lije had plenty, and where he worked was not Lije's mine, but an old Indian cave that belonged to no one.

Of course it was not stealing; and if Jerry would only let him be,—or if he could only find the old entrance to the cave!

He stopped in his work and laid his pick down: there was one place he suspected as the end of the old entrance passage, and once he had explored it for a little distance; not very far, but far enough to realize that the dangers of it were too manifold for him to dare a hurried investigation : and he could not be absent for any length of time without an explanation.

He took up a great stone pestle to crush the pieces of rock that had fallen into the water.

Jerry must go East to learn to love money, then Joe could have his days free from observation.

Surely Jerry *must* go East: the thought took stronger and stronger hold on him : Jerry must learn the worth of this money he had won from the hands of Death.

He had worked hard to get it ; had spent sparingly to hide it, for he had learned to love the shining stuff for itself. It seemed to get into his eyes as his Nancy had said, and to shine and shine until he could see nothing else. How heavily freighted he had been sometimes, when crossing that narrow ledge ; how carefully while Nancy slept had he dug a hole in the corner of the house ; how secretly night after night had he put away his treasure. And was it all to be cast to the crowd to be scrambled for when Jerry came into possession ?

He had not divided the found gold-dust with Dan Burk, nor the box of money ; but only divided a part of what he got each day. He had found in the engineer of the Eureka Mines a man who paid more fairly for the gold, and who asked no questions, as he was in constant receipt of private stores of this sort. Every man who had a little "find" of his own tried to hide it from his fellow-man ; and all these little hoards went to enhance the value of the Eureka Mine. Of course it all came from this mine ; and the shares ran up ; and the engineer's salary was increased ; and his speculations grew ; and Joe's secret was safe. As to Dan Burk, his share diminished steadily, and Joe grew more importunate in his demands ; for he could get a better price, he said.

Of what use was it that Dan threatened to tell of the cave ; Joe's retort came readily—"Tell 'em, an' show 'em the way."

It was hopeless ; no one would attempt that passage

when gold was so easily found elsewhere: and Dan was quite sure that even Joe would not attempt it for the small amount brought to him as his share. He knew quite well that Joe was cheating him, but what redress was there? So Dan determined to make what he could by holding the secret; but was very willing to sell any information to Jerry when he came to him with his eyes gleaming so dangerously, and his words coming so sharp and quick. He had not thought it safe to thwart Jerry; and by helping him he might gain something.

Poor Joe!

Long ago he had removed all the treasure from the cave and stored it where a written paper would reveal it. And the paper was sealed and in the doctor's keeping: he knew the doctor would see his wishes strictly carried out if he did not know where the money came from; but once acknowledge the source of his gains, and he knew that strict justice would be done: justice such as Jerry believed in; and the money would be divided out to every soul who had the remotest claim on the mine. So the paper revealed nothing save where the money was, how hidden, and declaring it all to be for Jerry. Nor was the doctor to read this paper unless Jerry willed it so; and since the recent misunderstanding Joe felt an extra degree of security in the thought that Jerry would not show the paper to the doctor.

It was all well stored now, and if any misstep left Joe's place vacant, the money he loved so well, and the young fellow his love bade fair to ruin, would both be safe.

But the old lost entrance: if only he could find that, no law nor justice could disturb him, for none could prove that he was working in Durden's Mine.

The cave was his own find; Dan Burk had heard of it only as a tradition, a wild story that meant little: Joe, however, had worked his way to it, and surely had a right to what he found there.

Only he must find that old entrance.

CHAPTER XII.

"Hadst thou understood
The things belonging to thy peace and ours!
Is there no prophet but the voice that calls
Doom upon Kings, or in the waste, 'Repent'?

O rather pray for those and pity them,
Who through their own desire accomplished bring
Their own gray hairs with sorrow to the grave—"

THE papers came daily now; filled with warnings, and vituperations, and news of the horde that was preparing to come to Durden's.

Only too swiftly were the shortening days flying by; and the railway seemed to loom terribly near to Jerry, while day by day his fame grew until he found himself a hero.

Dave Morris and Dan Burk had voluntarily come into his plans, and had agreed to advance money for the scheme on any terms he chose to name.

Burk accepted the position as "Land Agent," and bought all the land about Durden's Mine. Dave Morris put so high a price on his whisky that none but the best-paid miners, and the new civil-engineers belonging to the despised "doctor," could avail themselves of the luxury. And of the first new people who came, Morris made good use: he persuaded them to give great prices for the land about Eureka, so relieving the Eureka people of their properties, and allowing them to move to Durden's with money to invest.

Jerry watched with intense interest the extraordinary sales that Morris made for his Eureka friends: listened as the strangers were made to read the pamphlet put out by the engineer of the Eureka

Mine, in which all the lands in and about Eureka were represented as gold lands: listened afterwards as the Eureka people were persuaded to buy lands in the Durden's settlement: and listening wondered that Morris did not stand higher in the world.

Morris's own Eureka lot went for the highest possible price, part of which was invested in Durden's land, the rest being generously lent to forward the new scheme.

Eureka was in a state of the wildest excitement: lands changed hands from hour to hour; were sold by telegraph even, the operator making a small percentage in the general upheaval; and all the money, following Dave Morris's, fell into the hands of the new land agents, Daniel Burk & Co.

Even to Jerry who stood behind the scenes—who pulled the wires—even to him it seemed like magic. And when with Dan Burk he went to see Mrs. Milton about buying the mine, he felt as if some strange power, other than he knew, was working for him.

Instantly she acceded to their request.

"Durden's hes allers been onlucky," she said, and willingly gave up the mine and all the adjacent lands for relatively a small amount.

And Joe, left outside of all plans and arrangements, watched, and listened, and wondered in his own anxious mind how Jerry had accomplished it. Things were taking such a strangely sudden turn that he could not satisfy himself with any solution save that Jerry, and not Dan Burk, was the moving power; even though Jerry kept himself well in the background. No one but Jerry would have had the sense to direct such a move as this, and carry it out so successfully.

Land in Durden's could have demanded almost any price; yet stranger than anything that had ever happened in his experience, Joe saw that the price was never increased; and this convinced him that Jerry was manager.

Rapidly the people from Eureka began to erect

their small houses in all directions : their small houses that they were allowed to move from Eureka to Durden's. The lots were not laid out with the beautiful regularity of the great tract of land about Eureka, but they were sold or rented much more rapidly. Durden's was surely favored in its situation ; high up from the plain, and with plenty of water, it was cooler and more healthy than Eureka; and Jerry wondered that the doctor had not chosen it instead of Eureka as his center of operations. And every day as Jerry went to his school, he was stopped and consulted as to the future of Durden's, and the advisability of buying land there. Was gold to be found there—was there money to be made by holding the land—was it better and safer than holding land in Eureka?

And to all these questions he answered yes; and revealed his position further by saying that this was the chance he had promised to find and secure for the people ; and he wanted them to understand that it had his fullest sanction. To prove this, they could see that no matter what the demand for land might be, the price of the land was never raised. He came forward now when this last fact had been sufficiently observed and proved, so that he could act without being suspected as a speculator, and took hold of the scheme with a strong guiding hand ; and the people flocked to him.

Three new "finds" had been made in Durden's gorge, and the regular miners, thrown out of work in Eureka, were leading the way in opening them up most successfully.

Jerry's heart burned within him : money and people came in rapidly : Burk and Morris carried out his every wish, and rendered a strict account of every transaction. A committee had been appointed and called the "Town Committee," and of this Jerry had been elected chairman. The first resolution passed was one prohibiting the sale of liquor in the settlement : a strange law, the old inhabitants thought; and looked on Jerry as a sort of supernatural creature. After this a corps of workmen had been detailed to cut wood for the Community, and to bring it down from the mountain-side: this the "Town Committee" shared out according to the number in each family. The "Town Committee" had in their hands also the opening of the mine, in which every Commune man was to buy shares, and be paid regular dividends as soon as they could be declared. Any gold found on private lands was the property of the land-holder; every man who held shares in .the public mine had to do a certain amount of work there, or put a man in his place; for private finds must not be worked to the detriment of the public good.

Eureka stood still and breathless: would this marvelous enterprise prove entirely disastrous to them? It was a question that grew more grave as day by day there were fresh defections from the Eureka colony: day after day men came and cast in their lots with the Durden's Commune; for so Jerry had named it; and the Eastern papers, taking it up, rang with it, and Jerry became more and more notorious.

But, amid all the toil and tumult, one came and went silent and unnoticed. Going out from his house before day; before the brisk new town that fast was climbing up to the mine's mouth was astir; and coming down in the darkness when all were at their evening meal.

Like a bent shadow he came and went; every day stooping a little more; every day the frost gathering a little more thickly on his stiff hair. He was unheeded in the general rush: left outside of all plans: left outside of all that filled Jerry's life. He knew that Jerry was the leader; he knew that Jerry had stopped teaching the school that now had been moved from Eureka to Durden's; he knew that Durden's Mine had changed hands; he knew that Jerry had lost all confidence in him; he knew that the man,

Dan Burk, whom he had saved from starvation, he knew he had betrayed him : and deeper down in his old heart he knew that not for much longer could he walk in his old paths, and reap his golden harvest.

The old mine was like a home to him—like mother—wife—children : all the ties of life were for him concentrated in that black hole, and in the glittering particles he found there. How could he live his life day after day, and all the object gone out of it : hour after hour sit and smoke idly by the fire ; hearing in imagination only the laugh of the stream, that in these years had come to seem the voice of a friend ; and seeing in memory only the great red eye of the stove ?

For many years he had lived there, working alone in the darkness ; with at first the need of the money for spur—afterward for love of the money,—later for the love of the wistful eyes of the boy who looked to him for everything.

The little, thin voice and patient, humble face, so sorrowful, so lonely.

Somehow the boy had taken a deep hold on him, and all the gold he gathered was to provide for this little creature. It had made him work all the harder : he had been happy in paying for his education and clothes : in each winter providing for all his wants ; in making the house and the living gradually better for him, and in each day adding to the store of gold. He had been proud of Jerry's absorption in books and dreams ; proud of the gradual change that left such a distance between him and Jerry, and lifted the boy to the level of Paul and the doctor. It had never occurred to him but that Jerry loved him, although toward the last Jerry's devotion to the doctor had hurt him a little. But now ?

Now his boy had turned from him entirely—had joined with a stranger in betraying him—was living his life apart, without any reference to him.

It had been for Jerry's good that he had deceived him about the mine ; yet from that night Jerry had never uttered one word in his hearing of the hopes and wishes he entertained for his scheme.

The more Joe thought and suffered, the more surely he came to one conclusion. Only one thing was left to be done; only one plan that could save him and teach Jerry wisdom: it was to send Jerry East that he might learn to love money, and while he was absent, find the old entrance to the cave. This done, he would be safe in his possession—safe to gather and hoard the gold that Jerry would one day appreciate, and appreciating would come back to his old relations with his truest friend.

But how could he accomplish this end? He had not been near Dan Burk for a moment's speech even, since the mine changed hands; a tacit understanding made them avoid each other; and now all Joe's gold-dust went to Engineer Mills of the Eureka Mine.

He must approach Burk once more, however, to get his assistance in sending Jerry away; and he felt quite sure he could find means to make Burk persuade Jerry to go.

He had stopped work while he brought to a conclusion these thoughts of many weeks; and now storing in his pocket the last little bag of gold that he had gathered, he set his nets to last for two days, for to-morrow he must go into Eureka to sell the dust. He did not know what might happen any day, so he busied himself making all safe behind him; there was nothing there to tell any tales except the nets and the little black stove, things of little value; friends who could not betray him.

It was late now, very late; Jerry would be at home by this, and the supper ready, but for all that he must see Dan Burk.

Carefully he chose his way through the new settlement that had climbed the mountain-side, down into the old village which was nearer the level of the plain: carefully, for people might ask questions if they saw him in the town at night.

Dan Burk was at home, sitting in his shop, that looked much improved: it was clean, and without the smell of bacon and whisky that had never been absent before. The Community had provision depots now, and Dan's place served only as a shop for clothes and tools. Besides, his business as land agent kept him busy, and in the future would pay him better than selling whisky.

More than this, Dan's shirt was clean, and his black hair brushed to a painful state of sleekness. He turned when the door opened, and recognizing his visitor, he rose.

For a moment he paused, then pushed his chair back and came forward with a suspicious profusion of welcome.

"H' are you, ole pard, h'are you?" he said, "durned if I aint real glad to see you," holding out his hand.

"I'm well as common," Joe answered, and stood still with his hands in his pockets.

There was a pause while Dan rubbed his overlooked hand down his sleek hair, with a doubtful look creeping into his light eyes.

"Take a cheer," he said at last.

"No, I'm 'bleeged," and Joe took one hand from his pockets to push his hat back, "I aint got much to blate 'bout."

"All right," and Dan cleared his throat that had become strangely dry.

"You knows orl of Jerry's doin's," Joe began, with both hands again in his pockets, and his keen, deep-set eyes fixed steadily on Dan's half-averted face, "an' I don't; an' you knows somer my doin's, an' agin you don't," pausing solemnly after this last thrust that made Dan look round, "no," more slowly, "you dunno orl, damned if yer do!" with an angry light gleaming in his eyes that made Dan wince a little.

"But I aint come jest to jaw, ner to tell you

nothin' 'bout me," more mildly, "but sumpen 'bout Jerry."

"About Mr. Wilkerson?" and Dan was all attention.

"Thet's what I said," Joe answered, "'bout youuns' Mr. Wilkerson an' 'bout my Jerry: an' it's jest thet he aint got no sense ceppen 'bout books. Great-day-in-the-mornin'! why, man, Jerry dunno nothin' mo' 'bout money an' a baby, he don't," and Joe shook his head solemnly.

"He knows how to git it, all the same," and Dan laughed in a relieved way.

"Orl the same he aint agoin' to keep it," Joe said, "ner he aint agoin' to let you keep it, an' don't yer furgit it! An' he's jest agoin' to shar an' shar alike orl roun' this town; jest you watch," waxing more earnest; "I knows thar aint nobody agoin' to make no forchins 'roun' this town tell Jerry larns to love money: durned if they will!"

"Learns to love money?" Dan repeated slowly, "Lor, Joe, you're plum crazy!"

"Orl right," and Joe shook his head slowly, "orl right, an' when you keeps on a-seein' Jerry jest a-spreadin' orl the money roun' even; an' keeps on axin you fur 'counts; an' a-buildin' a meetin'-house, an' a schoolhouse, and a-stoppin' folks from cussin' an' whisky,—you'll 'member me, an' mebbe you'll say, 'Ole Joe warnt crazy nuther.' Mebbe you'll 'member, an' mebbe you'll cuss 'cause you 'members."

"'Members what, Joe Gilliam?" and Burk uttered some oaths even now before the prophesied time.

"'Members as Joe Gilliam said to sen' Jerry to the East whar he'd larn to love money; 'cause when a man don't love money hissef, he's jest sartain to 'spise them as do," pausing as if to give his words more weight, "an' thet's the reasin as Jerry 'spises the doctor 'cause he spekylates in lan' to make money; an' thet's the reasin as Jerry 'spises me, 'cause I tole him

I bet on money, I did. An' if a man 'spises money he aint agoin' to save none, ner to let nobody save none; an' don't you furgit it."

Burk stood without motion, and looked at his companion, while a great wonder grew slowly in his eyes: was the old man losing his mind?

Joe went on slowly.

"Jerry aint never seen nothin' as money kin buy," he said, "an' he don't keer nothin' 'bout it; he kin git vittles, an' cloze, an' books, an' thet's orl he wants, an' he dunno nothin' mo'."

"Darnation!" and a new light seemed to be coming to Dan.

"I knows it's true," Joe went on, "an' Jerry aint agoin' to let nobody hev no moren thet, he aint; an' he's agoin' to make orl go to school, an' go to meetin', 'cause Jerry don't know nothin' ceppen books."

Burk stood silent: this model community, with no possibility of private gains, was not his ideal town; so far he had rendered a strict account of all money in his hands; but he had not made his calculations on this senseless honesty lasting forever, but only until the enterprise was fairly started. He had voted for schoolhouse and church, thinking they would look well in the circular which the Town Committee had put out, and would make the place more attractive to outsiders.

"An' he'll tuck in orl the trash as'll come alonger the railroad," Joe went on, "'cause when orl the lan' 'roun' Eureky were sold, Jerry were jest a-rippin' 'bout folks not a-gittin' a shar' of lan'. Youuns hearn him a-talkin' 'bout God a-makin' the lan' fur orl, jest like the sun and the wind wuz"; then reflectively, "Mebbe it's so, then agin' mebbe it aint, 'cause if God 'llowed fur orl to hev the lan' I reckon it 'ud a-been fixed up thet away like the sun an' the wind wuz; thet's what I 'llows."

"An' it's true as mornin'," Dan granted.

"An' I dunno as orl God made were made fur ever'

pusson," Joe went on instructively, "'cause I knows as God made me, an' I'm durned if I'm fur ever' pusson; durned if I are!"

"That's so," and Dan looked still more grave.

This "all things in common" arrangement was a mystery to him; his ideas of justice and equality were circumscribed; it was not just that any one should have more of this world's goods than Dan Burk, he thought, but if Dan Burk gained more than his brethren, it was because Dan Burk was a sharp fellow. As he had realized Jerry's enterprise, it looked like a fair opening for a few to make fortunes; but now Joe had put a new face on it; and Dan paused and thought very deeply. He realized the truth of all that the old man had said; and looking back he could see plainly very convincing proofs that Joe's warning would benefit all who heeded it.

For how could they know of the wild desire for wealth and success that now possessed Jerry; how could they know of the deep plans he was laying for the future—thinking night and day of ways and means to persuade some capitalist to interest himself in the mine,—growing thin and careworn with the strain and longing that was on him. How could they know of the consuming bitterness that held him—that almost would have caused him to sell himself if that would secure the success of his plans.

To Dan Burk, he was the cool, calm, far-seeing man, directing with consummate skill the workings of the little community; a controlled, fearless man who commanded the confidence of the people.

To Joe, he was still the wild dreamer who could realize nothing but the injustice of existing laws, and the needs of his fellows; who had no want nor care for money; who despised all practical things.

"I'll gie him the money to go, an' to spen'," Joe went on, breaking the silence that had fallen, "you'll wanter feller what onderstan's; a rale engynar to open Durden's agin," slowly.

"That's so, and Dan looked interested.

"Sen' Jerry to git him," Joe pursued, "jest you come to my house to-morrer night, an' tell Jerry 'bout goin', an' I'll fix the ress; jest you come," then Joe turned away, but paused as he turned, "an' if you tells Jerry thet I've a-been har," he said slowly over his shoulder, "you'll never git in Durden's Mine, 'cause I knows the way of keepin' folks out," mysteriously, "but if you'll do my say, I'll pint the way myseff: farwell," and he walked slowly out, shutting the door after him, and leaving Dan Burk pondering deeply.

This was the best opportunity in the world; and the pay Joe required for leading the way into this mysterious mine was that Jerry should be persuaded to go at his expense to get an engineer—the engineer who was now the greatest need of the community.

It was strange pay, that this young man must be made to love money. What motive lay hidden under all this? In Burk's estimation old Joe did not have much sense; and think, as he would, Dan could not solve the problem.

But of course he would accept the offer; that part was plain enough. He would go the following night to Joe's, and make the proposition; then Joe must manage the rest.

And old Joe, toiling up the steep path, felt his point was gained; rejoiced that he had been able to spread the toils for the feet of him he loved the best; had been able to set forth the temptation so that the young heart might most surely be led astray and be absorbed by the meanest of passions!

Poor old man; doing in his loving ignorance the greatest ill to the one creature he loved—the creature for whom he would have given his life!

CHAPTER XIII.

> "O we live, O we live—
> And this life we would survive,
> Is a gloomy thing and brief,
> Which, consummated in grief,
> Leaveth ashes for all gain.
> Is it not *all* in vain?

HOW strangely the way had been opened! Jerry could not account for it; could not understand Joe's action in the matter. Since the beginning of his enterprise he had been wearying himself over the problem of how to get an engineer and assayer, and have the mine opened before the railway and the general rush of immigrants should come.

The new "finds" which had been made had been sufficient to give work to those who had come already; who had toiled down the long stretch of plain that lay betwen the rival towns, and the place where the railway was crossing the mountains; they had drifted slowly down with the circulars of the Durden's Commune in their hands, and had passed Eureka by!

Durden's had smiled over this; and Jerry had gotten a post-office list and mailed his circulars to every postmaster in the East; and looking back he had laughed at the demoralization caused by the first notice he had had of emigrants coming to him. Now he saw the advantage to be reaped from his notoriety, and put aside his fears. Only he must be prepared: the mine must be opened; the railway must be extended to Durden's, and timber and tools must be ready for the building of houses. And how was all this to be accomplished?

He had grown thin and worn thinking it over by

day and by night, and seeing no solution. Suddenly, the way had opened before him plain and straight, with not one difficulty to perplex him.

It was yet three months to the day on which the railway had promised to reach Eureka ; and though railway promises were seldom kept, yet even four months, if they took so long, was a short time. Still, going immediately, he might accomplish all his work and get back in time to meet the incoming tide of people. Another thing that he had worked for and had gained was the defection of one of the doctor's imported land-surveyors ; a young fellow named Greg, whom Jerry had discovered to be the son of one of the Eureka syndicate. After identifying Greg, Jerry, worked hard for him, and at last won him from Eureka to Durden's by the fair method of showing him the new "finds," and by allowing him to look over the Durden's land that lay up the long, dark gorge.

So Greg had come over ; had bought a lot, and had built a little house for himself ; telling the doctor that as he had come to seek his fortune, he must go where he saw the best opportunity of making it.

This was a serious blow to Eureka, and more of the inhabitants sold their little lots, and brought their houses over to Durden's.

And now Greg was the very man Jerry needed ; he could vouch for the promise of Durden's, and for Jerry's honesty of purpose and success. Greg was the very man !

Already he had written a letter to a leading paper in the East, telling them the truth about Jerry and Durden's. Telling how that Jerry had been driven into the position he had taken ; telling of his honest aversion to the land speculation ; telling of the wonderful success of the little colony he had undertaken to care for and protect,—the little colony that had left Eureka because it had felt itself wronged.

Greg was young himself, scarcely so old as Jerry ; and all his youthful enthusiasm had gone out to Jerry when he heard from Jerry's lips the story of Jerry's venture. It was after he had agreed to buy land in Durden's that this history was told him, for Jerry would not, however much he needed Greg, win him on any but practical grounds.

But now Greg was heart and soul a "Durdenite," and wrote his letter with all the fervor of a new adherent.

Jerry was a hero; Jerry was a genius; Jerry was quixotically honest and strong. And the greedy-pocketed old men of the Eureka syndicate looked in each other's eyes with solemn doubt as they read the ardent letter. Could it be that they had made a mistake—and been deceived?

And a communication of serious import began its journey out to the doctor.

And now when the way seemed so clear for Jerry to go East, Greg rose to still greater importance. He could give Jerry letters to his father, who was president of the railway, and so could secure him a hearing in the Board; also he could introduce him and his enterprise to numbers of fabulously rich men.

Durden's was enthusiastic, and Greg was elected to the town committee immediately, and was appointed also one of three commissioners who were to regulate things during Jerry's absence. Dan Burk, Dave Morris, and Greg were the three; and Jerry felt sincerely thankful that Greg was there, for could he have trusted either of the others? But to Jerry, Joe's action was a mystery still, for immediately on Burk's making the suggestion that Jerry should go East, Joe had volunteered the money.

"What little I'se got is agoin' to be yourn, Jerry," he said, "an' youuns mise well tuck it now if you wants it."

The old man was smoking in his regular place near the fire, and did not turn his face toward the two who were talking near the table.

Dan came to the fire quickly.

"What's that, pard?" he asked.

"I says as I'se got the money fur Jerry to go," Joe answered slowly, taking his pipe out of his mouth and looking up into Dan's face, "I aint got much," he went on, looking into Dan's eyes steadily as if defying some accusation he saw there, "but it's all to be Jerry's when I'se gone, an' he kin hev it now if he hes a mind to it; thet's what I says?"

Jerry sat quite still, suffering more acutely than ever before in his life. His conduct seemed to blacken to the darkness of sin as he listened to Joe's words. He had thought himself so true, and Joe so false; himself so magnanimous, and Joe so avaricious as to hold back a whole community for his own gain when he refused to give the name of the owner of the mine.

And now; now after he had cut the old man off from all interest or knowledge of his plans and hopes; —after this he had come forward and had given all his hardly won savings that the venture might not fail and that Jerry's fortunes might be secured.

What could Jerry say?

He sat still with one hand shading his eyes from the light: and Dan Burk, standing silent by the fire, looked anxiously from one to the other. There was a long silence while Jerry repented and Joe smoked; then Jerry rose and stood behind Joe's chair.

"I thank you very much, Joe," he said, and the two practical minds, listening, wondered why his voice trembled so, "and if ever the Community succeeds," he went on, "they will have you to thank."

"Orl right," and Joe moved his pipe to the other side of his mouth.

Even Dan was embarrassed in the silence that followed Joe's words, and shuffled his feet uneasily for a moment, until Jerry suggested that he should call a meeting of the town committee for the next morning in order that these plans should be laid before them.

"An' say thet he pays hisn's own way," Joe put in, —"an' don't name Joe Gilliam's title; 'cause Durden's aint nothin' to me, an' I aint nothin' to Durden's."

"All right, pard," Dan answered, "an' the day after thet, Mr. Wilkerson, you kin start," then more slowly, "an' you kin have my nag to ride to the pass"; then Dan said good-night and went away, and Joe and Jerry were left alone together.

It was a painful moment to the young man; he could not change the fact that Joe had told a lie about the ownership of the mine; he could not blame himself for not ignoring or not condoning the falsehood, and without implying some such action what could he say?

"An' if you'll stay thar awhile, an' spen' orl the money I'll gie you," Joe said, breaking the silence so suddenly and unexpectedly that Jerry started, "an' spen' it on seein' orl thar is to be sawn; an' on gittin' orl the books an' good cloze like Paul; if you'll do as I say 'bout this, I'll show youuns' engynar orl thar is in Durden's Mine; an' I'll do it sure."

Jerry listened with a growing wonder in his mind; what could be Joe's motive? But he promised, and at the meeting next day made a speech in which he announced his plans with such clearness and precision, and showed such a firm conviction of their success, that Mr. Titcomb, the editor of the Eureka *Star*, who had been invited to attend the meeting, rose and declared his intention of moving his whole business to Durden's if the committee would permit; and of changing the name of his paper from the *Eureka Star* to the *Durden's Banner!* And the permission being given instantly, the meeting broke up with cheers and a general congratulating of all parties.

The news was all through both towns before the sun set; the news that Mr. Wilkerson was going east with letters to Mr. Greg's father; that he was to ask for an extension of the railway to Durden's, and to bring back an engineer to reopen Durden's Mine. Further, that the *Star*, the pride and glory of Eureka, was going to desert them for Durden's, and be called the *Durden's Banner !*

Even the doctor looked grave when this news reached him, but he said no word. Large sums had been spent in buying the land about Eureka, and in laying it out ; large sums had been spent in extending the Eureka mine,—in improving the machinery, and in raising the wages of miners ; and larger sums still, in bringing lumber from long distances that the emigrants might have it for building.

And now must all this fail—could it fail ? Was it possible that he was to be thwarted by Jerry's venture, that at first had seemed so small and so wild as to be ridiculous ?

At first he had watched with some amusement what he thought to be the vagaries of a very young man's course ; withdrawing all counsel and sympathy that the course might be untrammeled. Later, he watched with interest, and a growing appreciation of Jerry's power over men ; but now there was some wonder, and a little anxiety mixed with his opinion of his protégé. Would the little waif he had trained and educated succeed at his expense, and at Paul's ?

He rose from his chair and marched up and down the room as in the old days when Jerry came to learn his letters.

Strange results had come from that long day's watch up on the mountain-side, when he had waited to save the boy's life ; strange results, with stranger things yet to come ; and the doctor felt a growing irritation within him, and a determination not to be conquered. He must go East and fight the battle there.

But Eureka was almost discouraged.

The land-agents had bought in at very high prices all the lots the departing inhabitants would sell ; had built houses, and fences, and laid out garden plots and small fields; had improved the one street, and reestablished a shop on a more decent footing than Dave Morris's shop had ever occupied ; finally, had whitewashed the whole town until it shone and gleamed far across the wide plain. All this was very well: and all about Eureka's outskirts was the doctor's vast tract staked off in streets and lots that were all neatly numbered with white numbers on little black boards, giving it the appearance of a Government graveyard. But in spite of all these advantages, Eureka was standing still. The land-agents, shaken in their belief of her future success, watched with great anxiety the few scattered emigrants coming up the plain from where, to the south of them, the railway was crossing the mountains; watched them solicitously; even went out to meet them, but only to find the Durden's circular in their hands, and a Durden's man guiding them on to the daring little town.

When Greg left Eureka there was a general failing in spirits; but when the news came of the defection of the *Star*, their hopes followed their spirits, and the people began one by one to go to the doctor where he lived in the midst of Durden's prosperity, to ask his opinion.

"Things look dark," he answered them gravely, "but I think I can right them by going East; and I shall go as soon as I can put things in a condition to be left."

And Paul, fuming and fretting, cursing his fate and Jerry's impudence, grew thin, and white, and worn with hatred. It was the first time in his life that he had ever been thwarted except in the doctor's training; the first time that he had been unable to dictate terms save in that one never-to-be-forgotten battle when he and Jerry met, and Jerry conquered. Was this greater battle of later life to have this same termination?

It should not, if he died in the struggle! And one of them would have to die, for it was a struggle that could end only with life.

Meanwhile, he declared that he could not live in Durden's without the doctor, and during his absence would go over to Eureka and stay with Engineer Mills.

So the old place was shut up for the first time in more than twenty years; for it was as long ago as that, that an unknown man had ridden into the town, and bought old Durden's house, paying cash for it; a fact that had raised him to a great height in the estimation of the people, and also had put hope in their desponding hearts: for the mine was closed, and they were out of work, and without a leading spirit among them.

For more than twenty years the doctor had lived there, lost to his former life and friends; lost to all the world save the little circle about him. And now he was going back to his old haunts, to look in eyes that would scarcely know him; to clasp hands whose touch he had almost forgotten; to hear voices whose tones would bring back to him times and things he had striven through all these years to bury!

After he had given his word that he would go, he walked the long, dark library back and forth the live night long—back and forth—back and forth: and open on the table the picture of the fair face Jerry had seen. The face he loved to look on—the face that had wrecked his life—but not the face that haunted him. The face that haunted him was the face of one whom he had deserted—whose sad eyes had looked at him last from behind Convent bars.

And now he was going back, he would see her again, the woman he had loved to his ruin—he would hear her voice—would touch her hands—once more would have to say farewell, and come away—once more would have to fight to the death the remorse and the longing that had darkened all his days!

Would the battle be as hard—would it hurt him now as it had done once?

Still, he must go.

CHAPTER XIV.

> "Gold? yellow, glittering, precious gold? . . . .
> Thus much of this, will make black, white; foul, fair;
> Wrong, right; base, noble; old, young; coward, valiant.
> Ha, you gods! why this? What this, you god? why this
> Will lug your priests and servants from your sides;
> Pluck stout men's pillows from below their heads:
> This yellow slave . . .
> Will knit and break religions; bless the accursed;
> Make the hoar leprosy ador'd; place thieves,
> And give them title, knee, and approbation,
> With senators on the bench."

IT was a bewildering scene that lay spread before Jerry's eyes; and nothing that he had ever read or imagined had prepared him for it.

He had seen many strange things since he had left Durden's in the early dawn of a cloudy day; with a valise borrowed from Greg, strapped on behind his saddle; and all the gold Joe had given him converted into a check on Greg's father. It was safer than to travel with so much loose gold, Greg said.

"An' jest you tell youuns' par, Mr. Greg, to gie Jerry jest as much money as he hes a min' to spen'," Joe had said, when at last he had been brought to trust the check, "an' what he gies Jerry over thar I'll gie you over har; 'cause Jerry's my boy jest like you is hisn."

And Greg had promised, while Jerry protested, until Joe came near enough to whisper:

"If you don't spen' the money, I aint agoin' to show no way to the mine; and don't you furgit it."

So Jerry said no more, and Greg added a postscript to his letter of introduction saying that Jerry was to have unlimited credit, himself standing security for the money.

More than this, Greg had written to his father to take Jerry to his own house during his stay in the city. The letters had gone the day before, immediately after the meeting of the committee; and also a telegram to Greg's brother to meet Jerry on his arrival.

So Jerry had started on his journey with a feeling that he would meet friends at the other end; but even with this assurance he had many more doubts and difficulties in his mind than he had had long ago, when he set forth, a poor, friendless, half-starved little creature, on the one journey of his life.

The first car he traveled in from the Pass to the first station on the other side, where the regular trains came in, was a battered box-car that seemed strangely like an old friend; and if only it had been full of loose hay, he would have imagined himself back in his old trousers and ragged shirt, with his little bundle under his arm. Poor little wretch!

At the end of the journey, when he was transferred to a ferry-boat, and felt the shiver and the thud of the engine—heard the clang of the bell, and watched the water slipping by—he remembered, with a pity that was pain, the deadly terror of the friendless child. And how wonderful his escapes had been!—surely he had been spared for something.

Then in the rush on the docks he had seen a face so like Greg's, that he felt as if a piece of Durden's had reached this great center of life before him.

He was sure it was Greg's brother, and introducing himself was warmly welcomed, and then stowed away in a carriage that seemed to run on velvet wheels.

"Of course you know you are to stay with us," the young man said, "my father and mother are very anxious to meet you, and to hear about Charlie; indeed, my mother wanted to come down after you herself."

"Your mother!" Jerry repeated, "how very kind!"

then he fell to wondering how a civilized mother and children behaved to each other.

It all had been very strange to him; the grand house that seemed so deadly still after the din of the street; the stately woman with kind brown eyes like her boys, and soft gray hair, who came forward to meet him with both hands held out in welcome; and soft lace and ribbons and silk floating about her almost like a cloud.

Then afterward the tailor had been a strange experience; and his new clothes a still stranger one; and he laughed as he looked at himself, and wondered if Joe would know him.

It had been stranger than any fiction he had ever read; but this sight that sketched before his eyes now, was the strangest of all!

The glittering horseshoe of lights and brilliant colors; the soft rustle of silken garments; the shimmer of jewels; the delicate faces that seemed to beam and smile from every side, and that all seemed beautiful; the graceful courtesy of the men who bowed or rose, or sat as some fair woman willed; it was marvelous to him!

And this was what education and civilization did for the human race; this was what gold wrought?

He sat silent and observant; watching from his place in a silken-lined box, with a jeweled fan in his hand, that he had been taught laughingly by the fair girl at his side to wave gracefully; watching while his heart sank within him, as he wondered how his daily life would seem when this dream was ended. Ended, and he had gone back to live with those creatures among whom he had grown up: those creatures who yet were men and women with the same hearts, and souls, and humanity as these people; those dirty drunkards and bedraggled drudges out in Durden's and Eureka were free, and equal; had rights and votes; had everything except money!

No wonder the world worshiped money; no wonder

there was magic in the gleam of gold ; no wonder men toiled and slaved for it. What were life worth lived as those poor creatures lived it out where he had come from? Who would not rather die striving for the glittering power, than sink to such degradation? He had read and thought about life as he was living it now; he had watched the doctor and Paul, and the differences between them and the people about them ; and now he was among people who were as they were—people with soft voices and gentle ways: and he longed with a bitter longing to have been born one of them.

"Honest toil," and "self-made men," and all the other cries built up to comfort those who could not do better, rang very false in his ears.. Good things and to be commended, of course ; and he hated himself and cursed his low blood that must be the cause of these weak longings.

Yet, he knew that many of these about him were newly risen to this grade of life ; that to them he looked as they did ; and, successful, he would command to all appearances a station equal to theirs : this was all true—and yet ?

He watched Mrs. Greg as she sat, an exquisitely finished picture of what a woman should be ; if he had had such a mother !

The thought died in its birth—his mother? His face burned ; no love could have been truer than hers—none could do more than she had done for the one she loved—she had died for him.

Suddenly the lights about him were darkened ; the hum of voices was hushed, and from some unseen place he heard the sweetest sound that ever had come to his ears. The cries of the wild creatures that he used to hear in the white winter nights when the snow lay over all the dead land ; the wail of the wind as it swept up and down the gorges, whispering humanly among the black pines ; the blackness of the mine and the water that dropped forever ; and the stream that fell from the far sun-lightened heights into the blackness of the gorge, its voice was there too, and its white hands thrown up in despair ! He heard it all in the music that stole about him ; rising, sweeping over the silent host of people ; falling, sighing down to a far-off whisper.

And all his longings were there ; and all his fears and hopes ; and all the tumult of his soul seemed to thicken and darken, until he longed to hold up his hands like the falling stream, and cry aloud ! What was it that made him find in that music a tone that told all the loneliness of his life ; all the pathetic pain, and hunger, and fear of his childhood ; the love of his mother, and her wild cry as she caught him from his death ; the wistful look he remembered in her eyes ; it was all there in that music played for the rich, and the happy, and the beautiful ; and what right had he to find his poor ragged life there ?

Slowly the beautiful picture that hung before him rolled silently away ; the music faded from about him ; and the people on the stage began a mimic representation of life. It was well put on the stage, the critics said, and all the parts were well sustained. Jerry could not tell ; but he heard every word, and to him it was all real ; real joy, real sorrow, and at the end real failure and despair. He lived through it all, and when the curtain rolled down again, he was sorry that the people about him spoke to him.

"We will wait for the farce," they said, "the play was too sad to finish the evening with" ; so they waited, and the music floated about them once more.

Something drew his eyes—caused him to look up—he never knew what the power was ; but opposite him, looking down on him, was a face that surely he knew ; a face that was neither old nor young ; but it held his eyes.

How was it he knew it so well ? how was it that, like the music, it mingled with all his memories, so that it seemed a part of them ?

"Who is she?" he asked of Miss Greg.

"I do not know," she answered, "we have lived here only a little while, and we do not know many people."

Through all the silly farce, that only provoked him, he watched the face that haunted him so strangely, and mixed itself in with his past. He had no eyes for the girl who sat with this almost phantom woman; he had no eyes for anything but the exquisitely sad eyes that now and then looked at him so earnestly.

Who was she?—how and where had he ever seen her? And while he puzzled the evening wore away, and they drove home through the glittering streets to an entertainment given in his honor.

"You are a lion, Mr. Wilkerson," Mrs. Greg said kindly, "so many have read of you in connection with the gold-fever in Eureka, and with the new railway; and since you have founded a rival town and mine, the interest in you has doubled."

"And Paul Henley, do you know him?" Jerry asked, while his heart beat a little faster for her words. She shook her head.

"Only through my son's letters," she answered, "and Charles does not seem very favorably impressed," she went on in a lower tone; "he says that Mr. Henley's temper was never very pleasant, but since your success he has been unbearable; because, I suppose, you have outwitted him and his guardian so entirely."

Then the people began to arrive, and Jerry was introduced to numbers of portly gentlemen and slim dandies,—to anxious mammas and pretty daughters, and discovered that all he said was listened to with the most marked attention,—so marked that almost it embarrassed him.

The older men plied him with questions as to what he had done, and what were his intentions for the future; but here his natural reticence helped him. What he had done he told frankly enough; what the plans for the future were, he told them was not his secret.

But, as the evening wore on, Jerry found himself more and more the attraction. Bewilderingly the truth began to dawn on him that he was a success; that in the eyes of these people he was a rising man; that these men who had millions at their command looked on him with confidence, because in their estimation he had proved himself clever enough to outwit their trusted agent, and so undermine a plan that was supported by all these millions. Could this be true?—had he done it, and how?

"And the railway, will I be granted an extension of that?" he asked.

Then they shook their heads and rubbed their fat chins, and said that this question was now before the Board; and they would give Mr. Wilkerson a hearing just as soon as their man should be on the ground to state the case for Eureka. And it would not be long now, as he had telegraphed that he would be with them shortly.

The doctor was coming!

Jerry passed his hand over his eyes as if to clear them.

At last they were to meet face to face, and tell their stories openly; at last he would hear an explanation from this man he loved so well; this man for whom he would so readily give his life!

Then the evening was over, and the people went away, and Mrs. Greg said an especially gentle, kind good-night to him,

"How proud your mother would have been!" she said, with her jeweled hand on his arm, and in her soft eyes bright tears of sympathy.

His mother.

And he looked into her face with a strange pain tugging at his heart; he had forgotten his mother, and this stranger remembered her.

"She is dead," he said slowly, "dead long ago."

Dead long ago—poor, weary mother; poor, wornout drudge that this fine, lady would not have looked at; —dead in his place!

And turning away he went to his room, while all the pride and triumph faded from him.

CHAPTER XV.

"Who calleth on thee, Heart? World's Strife,
With a golden heft to his knife:
World's Mirth, with a finger fine
That draws on a board in wine
Her blood-red plans of life:
World's Gain, with a brow knit down.
World's Fame, with a laurel crown,
Which rustles most as the leaves turn brown—
Heart, wilt thou go?"

DAY after day passed for Jerry in sight-seeing; in dinners and lunches; suppers and operas; plays and drives. Each director of the railway entertained him, and many people besides who had children to place well in life. And Mr. Greg gave him careful instructions and advice as to the tone to take with each important person he met; and Jerry heeded with rare wisdom, and being possessed of much natural tact, was winning day by day more and more favor and influence.

In company he found himself remembering and copying the doctor in his ways and words, and Paul too: almost it seemed to him that he was a different person; he could not be the same Jerry who fed the pigs, and chopped the wood, and cooked Joe's supper. With money slipping like water through his fingers; going for all sorts of things of which he had not known until now, but that now seemed necessities; with each day brimful of change and pleasure, and luxury,—he wondered how he had lived the narrow life of the past; and he wondered how much money Joe had.

For now at any cost he must have money. The thought had grown into a desire; the desire had spread into a longing—a longing that pervaded every moment of his life. A thirst, he had called it once when speaking to the half-starved creatures in Eureka. Hard words for those poor wretches who had no greater longing for gold than these grand people. And now, as if in judgment, the thirst for gold was on him; the fatal plague-spot had appeared, and had spread until to him success meant life—failure meant death!

And so many chances against him still.

At last one day they said that the doctor had come. Two weeks, that had seemed like two years, had passed by him in this new life; and now came the climax—and Jerry wondered as to the results.

He had never lived before: he knew this now when he felt the fever in his blood that made him long to face and conquer the world! He longed for the hearing that would be given him before the Board; he longed to tell his story, and watch that grave, severe face, whose calm he had never seen broken.

Long ago he had been chilled by this calm, and had learned to keep his dreams in the quiet of his own heart.

"You are a dreamer, Jerry," the doctor had once said, "and dreamers are never practical."

Now he would have a chance to prove himself; now the doctor would find that he had made standing room for himself among these worldly men, who were nothing if not practical money-gatherers.

More practical in their winning and hoarding than poor old Joe was, who toiled day by day in the bowels of the earth; closer in their transactions than stingy Burk; more anxious about their gains than besotted Morris! Yes, even among these he had made himself a success; and the doctor would see it, and feel it, and hear it on all hands. It was worth ten years of life, this success that was as much social as it was financial.

The music was more beautiful, if that were possible, than it had been since the first evening he heard it: and the scene, though more familiar, was equally bright. Jerry leaned against the side of the box, with a gay party all around him, who were impatient that the play should be over and leave them free for the ball that was to follow.

But to Jerry the music came as of old it came to Saul; and he listened thankfully, while the burning spirit within him was laid to rest. Yet the music seemed in some sort to take its keynote from the thoughts that held him; seemed to vibrate and quiver with the struggle that would fill the next day. For on the following day he was to plead his cause—to stand or fall before the man for whose commendation he would have done anything. Would he be able to rouse him; once to shake him from that calm; once to make him break his self-control?

He looked up to the box opposite, where he had always looked for the face he had not seen since the first night, but that nevertheless had haunted him; he looked up now—

Now, and almost a story was told him—almost a mystery was revealed. She was there, looking up into the doctor's eyes.

Jerry drew a long breath; he knew now where he had seen her face; he remembered even the shape of the case, and the red of the morocco; he remembered the trick of the little catch, and the face that had met his eyes.

"There is your friend up there with Henley's mother," Mr. Greg said, bending over Jerry; "it was strange her husband should give away his boy Paul, give him away so that his own mother should never see him again"; then Mr. Greg turned away to auswer some remark.

Paul's mother?

Jerry could not account for the involuntary shudder that had thrilled him at Mr. Greg's words. Why should he object to this woman being Paul's mother; why should he feel as if for her sake he must hate Paul? The fact of her being Paul's mother would account for the doctor's interest in Paul; for one glance as they stood together told Jerry that the doctor loved her. If so, why should not they finish their story now that she was free? And could it be this that had silenced the life of this man—that had driven him out from his place in the world? Just for the love of this woman who had meanwhile loved and married another? Jerry shook his head.

This could not be all; there was something deeper than this, something no mortal eye could see,—some overwhelming sorrow to warp so strong a life.

And Jerry seemed to see the long, low house without fence or garden, with the black mountains for a background, and the wide plains stretching shadowless in front. He could see the dim library; he could see the flickering of the firelight, and hear the clanking of the doctor's spurs as he strode up and down. Which was real, that lonely home on the plain, or this life that seemed to have caught the glamour from the "Golden Age"?

And this man, so perfectly dressed, standing with such easy grace, so at home amid all this richness, was this the real man, or was the reality the one he had known out yonder in his rough hunting suit?

Which was the real man—which was the real life? And Jerry's mind wandered during the play; and the music mingled and wove its way through all his thoughts and questions.

But the next day would tell all; the next day, that would stand a mark forever in his life!

And a cold, dreary day it was, with the rain falling down persistently on the drenched world. Trickling in little streams from the omnibus drivers' hats, and from their thin horses; falling mercilessly on the poor scraps of humanity hunting greedily in the garbage barrels; making hasty little runlets around the corners of the pavements; and seeming as if striving with its thousand little tones to drown the noises of humanity.

Jerry stood watching the passers-by,—watching the omnibus men and horses—watching the drenched barrel-pickers. They were very pitiful, the blurred pictures he saw between the raindrops that trickled slowly down the shining plate-glass windows. This was the wrong side of the gilded picture of city life, the wrong side of which he had read, but as yet had not seen. These figures were some of the poor creatures who were crowded out of life; who were pushed to the wall to die; who were looked on as surplus population that had no right in the world; who should never have been born, and for whom disease and starvation were the only remedies.

These were the people he had planned to help; these were the people for whom he wanted the land saved, the people no one cared for, who had no chance in life. Had he stood to his purpose?

He moved his hand across his eyes slowly.

In all these weeks he had had but one thought—the success of his venture as a speculation; and now he was pledged, almost, to have no other thought.

Having accepted favors from these rich people, he was under bond, almost, to succeed; had promised almost that money should be made for them from Durden's. If the railway went there his plan would succeed; if the railway went there it would be to make money for these rich people.

As a looker-on, how he would have despised such a state of things, how he would have launched all his power against such seeming injustice! Yet, as an actor he was bound and held down, a slave to the money of these people, to the money that had become a necessity to him.

More and more gloomy his thoughts became as he stood in the rich, warm room, looking out on the falling rain that seemed to sing a requiem for the darker side of life.

How would the day end—how would he stand to-morrow at this hour? It was in vain that he made an effort to arrange the words he would say—they slipped away from him hopelessly; he could trust only that when the time came his excitement would help him. But through all one thought haunted him—one thought that he was afraid would take all his strength away, and leave him without a case,—the thought that he had not been true to his earlier purpose. He had begun to work for the good of his own class; now he was working only for the success of his venture. Its success *might* mean the good of the people, but he knew that if it did not mean this, he would pursue the success just as eagerly. He had not been true.

So he brooded gloomily, looking out on the falling rain, and behind him the women near the fire conversed in their soft tones, and worked their useless embroideries.

He had no right as yet to such a place as this in the world; he had not been born to it, nor as yet had reached it through any work of his own. Joe and the doctor had brought him up and educated him through a pure sense of "mercy and loving-kindness"; he was now spending Joe's money, and by its power holding an undeserved position in society. He felt that he was an impostor, and the feeling had driven him into telling his story to these kind women. He had tried to tell it truly; he had tried not to soften any of the roughnesses, nor to lessen any of his obligations; and yet, when he finished, they gave him the gentlest sympathy; and Mrs. Greg's eyes had filled with tears over the poor little ragged waif!

"Think if my boys had suffered so," she said.

Was this a woman's natural way, Jerry wondered, to take the pathetic part of a life and spread it over all the sins and wickednesses; were women always so merciful? He did not know enough of women to draw any conclusion ; but he felt sorry that he had said anything, it made him feel weak and pitiful, as if he had been complaining, or asking for sympathy. Among men it would have been different : how he had arrived at his present position, to whom he was indebted, would make no difference to men ; all they would want to hear would be how he intended to make a success of his town. It would be no concern of theirs whose lives or teachings served as his steps to success ; their only question would be, is he successful, and how much advancement can we count on from this man's success ? If he ruined the doctor in this struggle, if he took from old Joe the one occupation and joy of his life—it would be nothing to these men—nothing to the greedy crowd watching out in Durden's, following close on his heels with hungry eyes fixed on his every movement, ready with grasping hands to tear him down if he but seemed to fail them for a moment !

He looked out at an old, bent, ragged creature stirring in a refuse barrel ; hooking out scraps of meat, moldy bones, decayed vegetables ; fishing in the dust-barrel of the Gregs ; and Mrs. Greg's eyes were still wet with tears over the story of his life.

Suppose Joe had wept only ?

He turned from the window and walked hurriedly down the room ; he was becoming more and more vile every moment. How could he think of anything except the kindness of these people ; and that if he failed he would have no better place in the world than the beggar he had been watching. Never ! never while he had life and strength ; never while he had a mind to conceive and guide, would he yield one inch of this position he had stormed. He must lead—he would lead ; he would have this money that made the world so beautiful to those who gained it : that left all bleak and cold to those who were worsted in the fray. And some must fall in this wild, grinding conflict ; a man could take care only of himself ; and with all their efforts some could not accomplish even this. This was the new lesson he had learned from the civilized and educated.

Then Fred came to tell him that the carriage was ready, and it was time to go: and Mrs. Greg insisted on his buttoning his overcoat more securely—and Isabel pinned a pansy to his buttonhole. "You must succeed," she said, while Fred laughed at them for having any doubt.

"The old gentleman has had a fresh letter from Charlie," he said by way of comfort, "and he intends reading it to the Board before Wilkerson begins his speech."

"Then I will not fail," Jerry answered, while a new light came into his eyes; his eyes that had never lost the wistful look that had won him so much in his life; "it will seem like a piece of the old life come to urge me on to better it and to help it up"; then he and Fred went away, and Isabel waved a farewell from the window.

CHAPTER XVI.

"'Be strong,
Take courage; now you're on our level—now!
The next step saves you!' I was flushed with praise,
But, pausing just a moment to draw breath,
I could not choose but murmur to myself
'Is this all? all that's done? and all that's gained?
If this then be success, 'tis dismaller
Than any failure.'"

IT was a handsome room in which the Board met; richly furnished and warm, and with plenty of light and space. But this day it was a little crowded, for many of the stockholders were there to hear and vote on the road being extended to Durden's.

They were a little late, Fred and Jerry, and Mr. Greg, who was chairman, was impatient over the delay.

"Do not look anxious," Fred said as they mounted the stairs, "else they will think it a personal matter."

Jerry started a little, the advice was so good,—and mentally he thanked Fred for it; aloud he said, "Our being late does not look like too great anxiety."

And truly as he entered the great room, with a smile on his lips, and a pansy in his buttonhole, he did not looked troubled. The doctor watched him curiously as he came in: tall, well-made, easy in his movements, meeting all with an air of quiet equality; being cordially welcomed by the great bankers and stock-brokers, and railway men; and seeming to think nothing of it.

Could this be Jerry? His clothes fitting him perfectly; with even an air of distinction about him; and, stranger than all, come to meet him on equal ground—come to cross swords with him!

Things had changed marvelously.

Then their eyes met, and Jerry felt the hot color creep slowly up into his face as he remembered the day that now seemed so far away—the day when this man had shaken him off so coldly. But he had a clew to the secret now; he had found it the night before in that woman's face. She had absorbed the doctor's heart and life; and he, Jerry, was only a part of the missionary work he had done either to fill up his life, or as atonement for something in his past.

This last was a new thought, and flashed like a stream of light on Jerry's mind; and he turned to look again on this man who puzzled him so. What was hidden in that life; hidden behind the inscrutable sadness of that grave, cold face?

A bow was all their greeting, and they took their seats the width of the room apart. Only a moment; then the meeting was called to order, and Mr. Greg rose to say that, before introducing his young friend Mr. Wilkerson, he wished to read a letter he had received that morning from his son, who being in Durden's could give the latest news.

Then he read a letter telling of the success of everything that had been touched; that the new lodes increased in riches as they went deeper; that even if the old mine were not reopened, and even if the road was refused them, it would pay to transport by wagon all that the town needed, and all that she would have to export. That it was an ascertained fact that much of the gold-dust purporting to come from the Eureka Mine had been gathered in Durden's gorge and sold to Engineer Mills. Then the young man added: "Never shall I cease to thank Mr. Wilkerson for the opening he has given me, and for the way in which he showed me my best advantage. He used no persuasions, he asked me only to look for myself and decide on the truth of his representations. Now, I consider myself a rich man in owning the land I at present hold in Durden's gorge."

There was a little murmur when Mr. Greg finished;

and it was moved that Mr. Wilkerson should now state his case and his wants.

It was a tremulous, exciting moment for Jerry; he had never made a speech in his life save to the people in Eureka, and how would he do it? One moment he paused, and in that moment heard an inimical stockholder say in an aside:

"I suppose his talent lies in addressing mobs."

The blood sprang into Jerry's face as he laid aside his overcoat and mounted the platform where Mr. Greg sat. The aside had made him angry; they should not scoff at him; he would make his speech and carry his point.

He shook himself a little, as if his clothes were not quite in their usual place; then drawing himself up, he put his hands in his pockets and looked out quietly over his audience.

He knew nothing of the usual etiquette of bowing first to the chairman, and then to his hearers; he knew nothing of beginning, "Mr. President, and gentlemen of the Board"; he knew nothing of gestures; he knew only that he had something to say, and must say it convincingly or fail; and that these people were willing that he should fail.

"I heard a gentleman say a moment ago," he began, and his voice rang clear and fresh, and a little angry, "that he supposed my talent lay in addressing mobs; it may, or it may not; but I can say truly that in all my life I never have made a speech save to what this quiet company would call a mob. I saw them called a mob in your newspapers, where I had the honor of being called their leader; and both about me and about them a great mistake was made. They were poor, and they were ignorant, if that constitutes a mob; and they were human creatures who had been wronged; and, rightly, this should have converted them into a mob"; the color in his face deepening, and his eyes flashing as he looked over the upturned faces. "Those poor people had lived in that far-off, lonely region for more than twenty-five years; a region that had ceased to have even the excitement of being on the frontier, or near an agency; had lived there on scanty wages, contented with the thought that if any good days ever came, they would have their share in them. The good days came, and they were pushed aside! They had been improvident, had been wasteful, had been ungrateful to one who had spent much money and time in helping them; and they deserved to be pushed aside?

"Perhaps, but remember that they were as ignorant as beasts—mentally and morally they were blind!

"Long before this issue, I had determined to help them; determined, if such a thing were possible, to raise the whole class, because it is the class I spring from," and he looked straight across at the doctor, who was watching him intently. "So these people believed me that I was their friend; believed I meant to work for them, and yet I had to abuse them roundly—had to knock one man down before I could make them see things as they should see them for their own good"—and a hearty "Good enough!" that sounded strangely like a Eureka comment, came from some one in the audience. "Maybe all this made them a mob," he went on, "but they are quiet enough now. They followed the advice given them, and held their lands in Eureka until the price offered was as high as it could be forced; they then sold, and bought the land held for them in Durden's gorge: and they got it, good gold-land, for half the price which had been paid them for their lots in Eureka.

"We then elected a town committee, printed circulars which we sent to every post-office in the East, opened three new finds within a quarter of a mile of each other; and we stopped the sale of liquor.

"This is what we have done without capital; the money to buy the land and the old mine was advanced by a man who made it selling gold-dust to the Eureka Mine; he has been selling them gold-dust ever since the Eureka Mine was first opened," he paused a moment, arrested by the intent look on the doctor's face; "this man's name is Daniel Burk," he added, while the interest faded from the doctor's eyes. "For the future we need an engineer to open the old mine, which has been closed for all these years only because the people were superstitious. The original owner disappeared in the mine, and the people deserted it.

"If we can secure an engineer, I and others have pledged ourselves to go with him to the end of the tunnel in order to reassure the Durden's people; the new miners who come in will not heed the old story. But we need machinery, and a competent man to direct us. You have spent millions in sending your railway out to this gold region, and already you have made millions from the speculation: this is well, but it is better still to know that a little further on there are as many more millions waiting for you: extend your railway to Durden's, and take stock in Durden's Mine.

"If you will not help us," and he paused a moment, "we can wait, and grow slowly: we can save money until we have enough to open the mine without outside help: then the tide of immigration will flow in on us, and we will succeed in spite of all odds, and dictate terms to Eureka and to you."

Now they applauded him, and he felt his heart rise up within him.

"For or against Eureka," he went on, "I have nothing to say; and most unintentionally was I led into making the towns rivals. I heard of the railway and I warned the people against the land-sharpers; I warned them, and explained to them that simply holding the land they had would bring them money in the end. I persuaded them that to buy land as speculation only, so depriving the poor, who were coming out to find room enough to live, of all hope of new homes, was a sin. Suddenly, enough land was secured to make a new town, and their little lots seemed valueless! It was hard, and I did not blame them that they turned on me. Then I had to seek something for them, and like a revelation it came to me to build up Durden's again--and I will do it," proudly, "for when failure means death,—success will be fought for hardly! These people have put all they own in Durden's, and can not hope to make another venture if this fails them.

"If you will help us, it will be the best investment you ever made: if you turn from us, we will be patient."

Then he sat down amid a clapping of hands and words of commendation, and waited with a sick heart to hear what the doctor would say.

Would he undo him? Were there any points kept in abeyance that would pull down his whole venture? His speech had not been as good as the words he had said to the poor people out in Eureka: he was not as angry—he was not as earnest—he felt trammeled and bound; the people and the occasion seemed unreal, and the life about him was a sham! They had enough, these people; and should be compelled, not begged, to help those who needed. Something, surely, was very wrong with humanity!

"Mr. President, and gentlemen of the Board," the doctor began, standing in his place, "all that Mr. Wilkerson has said is true, perfectly true. But all that I have written you of the Eureka Mine is true also. That Engineer Mills has bought gold from outsiders, is no wrong; and it was not to be expected that he should label each little lot. The land that was bought around Eureka is my private affair; and if it fails I shall be the only loser. As to extending the road to Durden's, I can see no objections to it; and as I have at heart also the greatest good of the greatest number, I hope it will be done. The work of Mr. Wilkerson needs no word from me; his plans have been well conceived, well executed, and surprisingly successful. You can not lose anything by investing in Durden's Mine; nor will you lose anything that you have invested in Eureka.

"I have come here at the request of the land-agents who have invested in Eureka. They have been very much disheartened by Mr. Wilkerson's success.

"They have not capital enough to enable them to hold the land they have bought: if they sell at a loss it will injure the reputation of the town, and for a time the mining interests. I came to advise for their good, and for your good, that the company buy the lots the agents now hold, and hold them as private property. The two towns will be one eventually and their interests be merged into each other: one can not grow without helping the other; and for the sake of the money which already you have invested in Eureka, I strongly advise that the land values be not allowed to decline.

"I have with me a map of the town, and of the number of lots that will have to be bought in—also their values. I can vouch that no higher price has been put on the lots than the agents paid for them."

Then he sat down amid a surprised silence.

Where was the expected struggle between these rival towns and leaders: where was the great excitement that had possessed the company when they met: where was Jerry's enthusiasm!

He sat quite still through it all: listened while the short, quiet sentences fell so coolly and calmly: felt that he had made a fool of himself; and discovered a slow, dull anger creeping through him.

The two towns to be made one: their interests to be identified; only that Durden's was allowed to grow first!

Where was the opposition; what could he do? whom could he antagonize? And he had not injured Paul; but only a private venture of the doctor's, about which he knew as little now as at the very first.

No explanation had been made; no light had been

thrown on anything, save on the one fact that his attack on the doctor had served only to strengthen Paul's fortunes: for, of course, it was more safe that the company should own the town of Eureka, than that chance adventurers should hold the land. Of course the company would see that the town succeeded; and if they extended the railway to Durden's, and put their money in the Durden's Mine, there could be but the one issue for the whole matter: the towns would be made one, and their fortunes rise and fall together. And from the first, the doctor had intended this—had foreseen it.

He longed to be alone; he longed to walk for miles and miles; maybe he so could still this throbbing anger that was increasing every moment; he wished that the people in front of him had been the poor Eureka mob that he might abuse them!

How had this thing happened; how had he been such a blind fool?

All about him there was a hubbub of voices; a group gathered about the doctor; a group about Mr. Greg, and close packed about himself Jerry found the mass of the company.

Congratulating him—shaking hands with him—telling him that his success had brought Eureka and the Directors to terms; and that now his fortune was secure.

So it was: and he talked and laughed, and shook hands, and understood that his point was gained, although no official action had been taken as yet.

Then he and Fred found themselves outside in the pitiless rain that still fell; but a liveried servant held an umbrella over them, and the carriage waited with open door.

The ladies were enchanted, and at lunch Mr. Greg rubbed his fat white hands over the morning's work.

"And you can go to the ball to-night, my boy," he said, patting Jerry gently on the shoulder, "feeling yourself rich because of the land you own in Durden's."

Rich because of the land he owned!

A new and dreadful realization came to Jerry—he owned no land. Durden's might make millions, and not one cent would come to him!

The room and all its beautiful furniture seemed to waver for a moment.

Dan Burk—Dave Morris—Charles Greg,—indeed, every man in Durden's was secure in his possesions,—secure in the protection of the Commune.

He only had been left out.

Blind to everything except the success of his venture, and the triumph over Paul Henley and the doctor, he had forgotten himself until now—now when all the best land had been sold, and not one foot of it his.

And even if it were still there, he had no money to buy it with. He was spending money fast enough now, but it was Joe's money, which he had bargained to spend that the old man might be persuaded to show the safe way into the mine. Once back in Durden's he would not have a cent.

He dressed for the ball with a heavy heart: how could he rectify this mistake?

He was still more of a lion in the glittering assembly where he was taken at the end of the exhausting day; for besides the wit and wisdom he had made evident, it was said that he possessed acres of undug gold!

So of course he was courted and smiled on, and Isabel Greg was looked on as the young woman most likely to capture the prize. Even beautiful Edith Henley looked with interested eyes on this "ruffian" and "wretched ragamuffin" of her brother's letters. He was a success, and surely looked like a gentleman; and the next day she wrote Paul a letter that roused every evil passion of his nature,—an innocent letter, save that it was full of Jerry's success, and the doctor's compromise!

And under all these admiring eyes poor Jerry stood, longing for one moment's quiet where he could collect his thoughts, and look his situation in the face. To betray his position or his anxiety by word or look would be ruin; for after such an acknowledgment who would believe anything but that the whole scheme was a fraud. It was not usual for men so to leave themselves out of reckoning; and these people would not believe him.

Poor Jerry! he longed to be back in the wilds where a man could look as he felt, and where every man carried law and redress in his belt. There one was free, here one was bound by a thousand little fetters that galled at every turn.

At last his chance came; for a moment he stood alone, and in that moment he stepped through a long window near which he stood, into a conservatory.

All about him beautiful flowers, and at great distances the dim lights: inside the throb and swell of the music,—outside, the stony street—the cold wind, and the rain falling ceaselessly.

He sat alone in a dark corner with his face down in his hands, trying to still the tumult within him,—saying over and over to himself that he must be calm and strong, for now a great question lay before him.

"The land you own makes you a rich man"—these words had never left him, nor the knowledge that had come with them—the knowledge that he was as destitute now as when Joe had picked him up.

His head sank lower.

More destitute: then he had been conscious of cold and hunger only; now he was filled with knowledge, and knowledge revealed a thousand wants that served to make his poverty infinite. A thousand wants that all centered in money.

His thoughts paused for a moment, and a calm,

clear light seemed to shine within him. Let all succeed; let the prosperity and the good he had instituted live and bloom about him—live and multiply a hundred-fold, yet not touch him save through the peace within his soul! Go back to his old ideal—realize his first high calling—show the world a man higher than these paltry ends of fortune!

Sink out of men's minds—go back to nothingness? And what would the world say—"A wild dreamer—a fool!" Suddenly he lifted his head, for voices approached him, and one voice was so familiar.

"Things have not changed, Judith," the voice said, "and you are as far from me now as then; for the wrong I did lives still; even if within convent walls, she lives and I am not free,"—and a little way in front of him Jerry saw the doctor standing, holding in his hands the hands of the woman whose face had so haunted him.

"I am not free," the deep voice went on, "and my life is now too near its close for me to hope for freedom, even if that hope were righteous."

"And must your whole life be one great sacrifice, Paul?" and the voice was so low and sweet that Jerry listened to it as he had done to the first music he had heard, "one long self-annihilation?"

"One great expiation, rather, even as hers has been," and the doctor put the two hands he held together, folding his own about them, "and I must say good-by, dear, and this good-by will mean forever!"

Then they passed on; and the dim lights made broken shadows; and the flowers cast out their sweetness recklessly; and the distant music rose and fell for the glittering throng to dance to!

Good-by forever!

The young heart listened with a dim sense of the infinite sadness that lived in the words; and in the music that was meant to be gay—in that pulsing, throbbing waltz with a minor cry through all its chords!

This practical, money-getting, soul-crushing age;

is this the music it dances to? This proud, hard Nineteenth Century that vaunts itself that it neither fears nor loves—that glories in tearing the veil from the "Holy of Holies" that the mob might be as free to touch and see as the "Anointed of the Lord"! that analyzes every throb of brain and heart; that laughs faith and hope to scorn, holding only certainty: that shuts charity into hospital wards: that teaches the "survival of the fittest"; that tests prayer and crowds down the weak and the poor to death and annihilation. Hailing "labor-saving" inventions with a shout of triumph, and trusting to disease and death to clear the overcrowded garrets and cellars!

Clamoring and battling for gold; and legislating on the crowded prisons and lunatic asylums! This great "Iron Age" that has no heart save the thud of machinery—is this the music it dances to?

Do the eliminated, foolish heart and soul find their refuge here? Sobbing through all the songs and dances—crying out to the throb of beating feet!

Do we hear the heart of the Nineteenth Century pulsing in its music—the saddest music the world has ever heard?

CHAPTER XVII.

"Oh, Soul!
To stand there all alone
And without hope!
To watch the years come one by one,
Sad faces from the old days gone—
Eyes full of memories pale and wan—
And hands that grope
About thy weary heartstrings, without hope!
Waking old chords, and long-hushed cries,
And loving tones—
And warning words, and patient sighs—
And pleading prayers from long dead eyes
And trampled hopes, and broken ties—
And sins and joys that restless rise
With smothered groan—
And tears that weigh like lead! Aye, writhe,
Thou Soul!"

THE excitement was all over now, and the reaction was a most painful thing to Jerry.

The day before had been one bewildering whirl of astonishing events: the success of his appeal; the revelation of the condition of Eureka; the realization of his own position; and at the ball the little scene that had passed before him like a dream.

There was a weariness over his body and a dull pain in his head when the daylight stole through the window, finding him still awake; turning over and over in his mind the chances for his future.

All was accomplished now that he had come to arrange: a company had been formed called "The Durden's Mining Company,"—the railway was to be extended, and a mining engineer and assayer to be sent out.

All this had been decided the day before, and there

was nothing left to do now, but for Jerry to go home and put things in motion there.

For Durden's he had been entirely successful; but for himself what had he done?

He dressed very slowly, for he dreaded the time when he must appear as the successful man; and longed to go away and hide from all whom he knew. The rain was still falling, but the scene within was bright enough when Jerry entered the breakfast-room, humming softly one of the waltzes that had been woven into his thoughts the night before.

The table with its shining silver and glass, and delicate china, and flowers that made all sweet; the fair women; the successful old man reading his paper by the fire. Jerry paused a moment to take it all in: if he had had such a home. And yet, young Greg left it all to gather gold? He must gather too; for years he must gather, then he could have all these fair possessions about him as this old man had.

A pleasant "good-morning" greeted him as he sat down; and a "By the way, Wilkerson," from Mr. Greg as he laid his paper across his knees.

Jerry looked up quickly.

"You had better let me take stock for you to-day in your mine," laughing; "you are bound to take it, you know, in order to give us confidence."

"Of course," Jerry answered, while there flashed through his mind the memory that he had nothing.

"Your credit with me is unlimited," Mr. Greg went on, "those were Mr. Gilliam's instructions."

"I know," and the cup that Jerry took from Isabel's hands trembled as he put it down.

"How much shall I put you down for?"

The point-blank question was startling, and Jerry paused a moment: it seemed hard that Joe's savings should have to go to buy shares in a mine that for more than twenty years he had worked alone!

"Of course the stock is bound to rise," Mr. Greg went on, "for we can make it rise: in two weeks it shall have doubled its value ; after that, much will depend on how you manage things in Durden's ; but now—"

"I will take as much as I can get," Jerry said quietly.

"As much as you can carry ?" Mr. Greg suggested doubtfully.

Jerry shook his head.

"As much as I can get," he repeated with a smile ; "I know Durden's, and I should like to own the whole thing."

Mr. Greg rose and stood before the fire, brushing his hair back with a quick, nervous motion, while a new expression seemed to change and sharpen the whole shape of his face.

"Are you in earnest ?" he asked slowly.

Jerry stirred his coffee quietly.

"I am," he answered, "I know Durden's."

Mr. Greg walked the length of the room and back again ; was this young man trying to play the game on the company that the company intended playing on Wall Street ?

"Do you know how these things are worked up in the market ?" he asked, pausing near Jerry's chair.

"No," Jerry answered, while he wondered if they could hear the thumping of his heart, "no, I know nothing of such things ; but I know Durden's, and I know that gorge can not be exhausted ; you can gather gold for ever, and never find the last," with a laugh ; "almost one drinks it in the water," and the eyes that looked up into Mr. Greg's glittered with a new light—and the old man turned away.

"I shall come out there myself," Fred put in ; "you and Charlie shall not have it all your own way."

Mrs. Greg shook her head.

"One is enough out there, Fred," she said ; "put your venture somewhere else."

"I shall make a fortune, and then draw out," Fred answered.

"And I shall stand to it and make millions!" and there was an exultant ring in Jerry's voice that gave Mr. Greg more confidence in the venture than the visible gold would have done,—"I will gather in piles and piles of gold," the young man went on, while the color crept up his dark face, and the light in his eyes gleamed brighter, "I will pile it up as I used to pile the chips when I cut wood," the old simile coming back to him that had been in his mind when he stood alone in the midnight high up among the rocks—the old simile that had been with him when the thirst for gold first seized him,—"and if I get so much it will not be worth any more to me than the chips," he added, with a sadder tone creeping into his voice.

"Hurrah for you!" and Fred put back his head with a hearty laugh, "Mr. Western Millionaire growing melancholy because he is apt to have money scattered about him like chips—very good!" and he laughed again.

Jerry looked up slowly.

"What will be left for me to do when I have enough?" he asked.

Mr. Greg shook his head slowly, folding up the paper. "We never get enough," he said, "it is a want that is never satisfied"; then to Jerry, "Will you come down to the office later?"

"Yes, Mr. Greg, by twelve," and the door closed on the old man, grown more thoughtful over the Durden's venture; and the young people and Mrs. Greg were left alone.

"Remember the matinée at two," Isabel suggested.

"I will," Jerry answered slowly, "as it is my last."

"Your last!" came in three different voices.

Jerry nodded.

"I must get back now as quickly as possible," he said, "to gather in all those millions Fred laughs at";—they had grown very friendly in the time they had been together, and had fallen into the way of saying "Fred" and "Jerry," for Jerry, somehow, seemed to be one of them,—"and you must have all your packages for Charlie ready to-day, for I shall leave in the morning," and he walked to the fire.

"We shall miss you so much," Mrs. Greg said kindly, while Isabel looked into her cup pensively. "You have come to seem like one of my own boys," she added.

"And you have been so kind to me," Jerry answered, coming and standing close at her side, "you have shown me what a home and a mother can be."

And strangely across his memory there drifted the vision of a humble grave built round with rails, and covered in with brush!

Then he went down among the crowded offices; up and down the narrow streets; in and out the great Exchange where lives and souls are brought and sold; in and out, learning the way in which great ventures are put on the market: signing away hundreds, and running up the value of Durden's even in the mind of Mr. Greg.

Then to the luxurious lunch, and glittering theater, where the music throbbed, and humanity imitated its own sorrows and joys; pictured misery for happy people; and made false mirth for the weary and heavy-laden. And Jerry listened as to a dear voice that he would never hear again,—it was the last time!

* * * * * *

And out in the far-off blackness of Durden's Mine an old man struggled vainly almost. It was very dark,—"a darkness that could be felt"—he had heard that read from the Bible once; and he put out his long arms vaguely.

He was very weary and weak, for his food had given out long ago; he did not know how long; and his light had gone too! He put his hand over his face as if he needed more darkness, and a little groan broke from his lips.

Had old Durden died in this way? Some one had said that he had set out to hunt for the Indian way into the cave, and never had come back. Maybe he had died just here, and had not fallen into the hole; and maybe his bones, grown white and dry, were close beside him!

A great shudder went over the crouching form, and the long arms felt about on the ground hurriedly; but all was smooth and cold.

If he sat here he would starve; he must go on or die!

Die! die, shut up in this black darkness without a voice to comfort him, or a hand to give him strength; without a soul to breathe a prayer, or tell him God was good!

He flung his arms up, and clasped his toil-worn hands together.

"My God—my God!" he cried, and the hoarse, deep voice rolled back and forth through the black rents and chasms. "Good God, cuss the damned gole—cuss it,—cuss it!" and the wild prayer faded away in a faint whisper.

Once more he sat quiet, with his head down in his hands. If he sat still he would starve; he would die here in this darkness; anything would be better than that! And he crawled on slowly on his hands and knees. He was afraid to walk,—afraid he would step off some awful chasm, and for days lie maimed and dying. So he moved cautiously, and the movement gave him hope. Why should not this long passage, that seemed so endless, be that lost entrance to the cave?

It always tended upward; this was what made him so weary; it was always going up and up; it had not dipped for a long time now, he could not say for how long.

But he had prayed too earnestly; God could not let him die here.

"An' Nan, her prayed fur me too," he whispered, then crawled more slowly as the thought came to him that it made no difference that he had hidden safely such store of gold : and again his whisper fell on the silence, "Orl fur gole, an' it can't he'p me now, not now—an' it can't he'p me when I'se dead an' gone—notter cent !"

On and on through the darkness, slowly, painfully.

"An' I'se done sent Jerry to larn to love gole ! oh, God, I never knowed—I never knowed !" sobbing as he crawled, with the penitent tears dropping on the hard, smooth floor. Tears that were too hopeless for such old eyes to shed !

On and on, muttering to himself ; praying aloud ; stopping to feel about nervously for the bones of the dead man that he might find anywhere—the poor old man who had died for gold, as he might die if his strength gave out before he reached the end.

Was there any end ?

He had heard the doctor say that all through these mountains there were long caves and cracks that often had no openings. It was strange how everything he had ever known or heard came back to him now ; he remembered even things his mother had told him when he was a little boy. He remembered the first furrow he ever plowed, and how across it the sunshine slanted up the hillside to the door where his sisters fed the chickens ; and the spring where all the washing was done. He could remember the wooden trough his father had placed there and the gourd that was always near. And the tubs were blue, he remembered that distinctly ; and the soft lye-soap was kept always in an open gourd. And Jim Mabry had given 'Liza Jane a ring, and she took it off always before she washed the clothes because it turned her finger black. Yes, he could remember it all as if it were yesterday ; remembered it as he crawled, and prayed for his life in the awful darkness.

A poor old man who had nothing to show for his days save a hoard of gold !

Poor little Nan, she used to come there too, to wash clothes at the spring ; and had "given her word" there, and Preacher Rowls had married them—poor little Nan!

And again in the bitterness of his memories he cast himself down on the rocks.

"My God—my God, I never knowed!"

Would God help him now? It had been so long since he had prayed. Yes, and he gathered himself together once more, and urged his much-tried strength to its utmost limits.

He was old, and he was weary and weak from hunger; and an awful thirst burned in his throat. That was what made him think of the old spring and the dry, brown gourd. Ah, that was the sweetest, freshest water he had ever tasted.

Oh, for only a mouthful! Then the awful memory came to him of the rich man down in hell crying for a drop of water. He had heard a preacher read that once: all his money could not help him then—burning up with thirst and fire, and praying for one drop of water.

Had many people died for gold? Judas; yes, that was the name; Judas sold his God for money; Judas, he remembered that now. He had heard the doctor read that once to poor 'Lije Milton when he was sick; and 'Lije had died for gold! 'Lije? A deeper groan broke from him, and he cast himself down on the floor.

"An' I he'pped to skeer 'Lije!" he cried, beating on the rocks with his clenched hands. "Oh, God, it were the gole done it—the gole done it!" writhing in his remorse. "I never knowed as it would a-killed him—I never knowed!"

Then he lay quite still; he had thought of 'Lije before, and the thought had driven him on and on until he had come too far to turn back; and now, if he thought of him again, he would be too weak to go on; he would lie where he was and die. And if he died in here the doctor would give Jerry the paper that told where to find all his money; and Jerry would take it and love it, and he would not be there to tell him of the awful curse that came with the love of gold. He must get out if he could, to warn Jerry ; and he raised himself and crawled on.

Little Nan had said that God did not make gold ; that the devil made it and put it in all the cracks of the earth to buy men's souls with : and it was true. How many dug through days and nights down under the earth, bringing up gold, and yet men never had enough.

Little Nan was right ; God did not make gold.

Poor little Nan : but God would help him, because she had prayed for him so often : yes, God would set him free from this black hole—this cursed mine, that had murdered all who entered it : God would surely set him free.

His breath seemed to leave him,—his lifted hands touched a wall in front of him !

Was it so ? Had he not turned in some way and touched the side wall ?

He was afraid to feel, and make sure ; for suppose the passage stopped here ! He could not go back, he had not the strength ; besides, after he had left the cave a long distance he had come to a place where the way was very narrow, and hung over a stream that roared until it confused him, and now he was so weak he would fall in.

Must he feel all about him, and find that cold stone wall ? He drew himself together and put his face down between his knees.

"Oh, God ! she were good—she were good," he pleaded, "an' she prayed fur me ; oh, God ! she prayed fur me." What else could he pray ? what else did he know ? One had prayed for him long ago, when life was fresh and strong, and he knew she was good, and God must have heard her prayers—surely.

He put his hands out cautiously—the poor, work-hardened hands that had done many kindly deeds, which the terrified heart did not seem to remember now, when in his dire distress all his mistakes and sins loomed up before him.

Poor old weary, tremulous hands; surely God would set them free!

Carefully he felt over the wall on one side, across the low roof, down the other side, then again up to the roof. He knew which side he had come from; he knew that behind him stretched that endless black passage; but in front?

He paused with his hands above him, touching the roof—

"She were good, God, and she prayed fur me," he said.

Then slowly down in front of him he moved his hands—slowly—slowly—and the wall was there! A moment he paused—one moment when all his life seemed to rise and sweep before him; all his life, and all the faith he had had that for her sake, the one creature who had loved and prayed for him—for her sake God would save him—her sake who had been good!

All came over him now, and he was shut in here to die by inches—to die!

"Oh, God!" a long, wild cry—a last supreme appeal in his agony, and he fell forward against the wall—the wall that shut him in from life and hope!

The sinking sun shone clear and red, wrapping the plain in a rose-stained cloud of light, and sending long rays of gold up to the highest peaks, tinting and glorifying all the scarred, storm-beaten mountain-side. It beautified Eureka, lying still and white on the plain, and Durden's, climbing bravely up the gorge; and far up among the cliffs it touched a thin slab of rock that had been pushed from its place, and in its fall tearing from their hardly-won homes all the lichens and little vines that had grown about its edges. The sun touched all this very gently, making silver lights in the gray hair of the old man lying face down across the fallen slab, with his long arms stretched out above his head.

Was he dead, lying there half in and half out the black hole ; had he died in his search for the way that was lost so long ago? But at last he had found it: high up among the cliffs overlooking the wide plains and busy towns, overlooking his own little home, and in touching distance, almost, of the place where he had buried his little Nan!

In a dip in the rocks where the earth had so gathered and deepened that even some trees could grow there,—there she had chosen to be buried ; and now very near the old man was the rough headstone he had put up, with her name clumsily chipped on the surface.

The sun touched that, too, and the little shadowy pines.

Had Joe made his last find right there by her grave?

CHAPTER XVIII.

"The past rolls forward on the sun
And makes all night."

"HAS the doctor come?" and young Greg looked anxiously in Paul's face as he opened the door of the doctor's house in answer to Greg's knock.

"Yes," and the door was opened wide enough for Greg to enter.

Down the long hall he went, and into the library where the glowing fire was grateful after the keen November winds that swept across the plain.

The doctor rose, holding out his hand to Greg.

"How are you!" he said; then, "I left your family quite well."

"Thank you," Greg answered; "I heard from home to-day; but it is a greater satisfaction to hear of them from one who has seen them face to face."

"Won't you stay and dine with us?" the doctor went on, when they were seated.

Greg shook his head.

"I can not this evening, thank you," he said; "I have come to you on very anxious business—old Gilliam"—the doctor looked up quickly—"is in a very precarious state, I think."

"Fever?"

"No, nor can I satisfy myself at all as to what ails him," Greg answered, "he was missing for two or three days; I know this, because Wilkerson begged me to go up and see him every evening, and I did until a little while ago he was missing for four consecutive evenings. I felt uneasy, but I did not like to make inquiries, for he is such a peculiar old man ; so I waited until four days ago, when I went up and found him in this strange condition. He eats very little, and refuses to leave his house, or to give any account of his health. His only admission is that he wants to see you, and he wants Wilkerson. Can you come ?"

"Of course," and the doctor gave orders for his horse. "Wilkerson ought to be here this evening," he went on, "for he was to leave New York twelve hours after I did."

"That is fortunate," Greg said in a relieved voice, "for the old man will not last much longer."

"Is it so bad as that ?" and the doctor paused in his preparations ; "you really think the old man is going ?"

Greg nodded, and the doctor made more haste.

"Perhaps you had better go back to him," he said to Greg, "and I will follow ; have you brandy ?"

"Plenty," rising ; "I have kept him alive on it." Then he went away, and Paul, leaning gloomily against the mantel-piece, asked if the doctor would be gone all night.

"Probably," was answered shortly ; then he gave orders to a servant to take a horse to Eureka for Jerry ; to make a point of meeting the wagon that came in, and to tell Mr. Wilkerson to make great haste. Then he was gone in the falling evening, gone as swiftly as might be up the lone trail.

Was the old man going out on the "lonely road," to-night, he wondered ; the old man who was only a gray-headed child ; the old man who had come to seem a part of the place, almost like one of the storm-battered rocks, so gray and quiet was he. He had known him so many years, he would miss him.

It was strange how things fell out in this life ; the old man going just when Jerry, the pride of his heart, was beginning his career.

"And Jerry will be successful," he said to himself,

buttoning his coat more closely against the cold wind; "he knows how to manage men; but he stands in a dangerous place."

The lamp was burning brightly, and the fire was flashing brilliantly into every corner of Joe's house when the doctor entered. The clock ticked busily: the dog breathed heavily in his corner; Greg sat still near the fire; and on his bed, fully dressed, old Joe lay with his eyes closed, and his hands crossed on his breast.

"Well, Joe," and the doctor laid aside his coat and hat as he stood by the bed, then put his slim white hand on the old man's hand, grown so thin and tremulous; "how is it you are sick?" he asked.

"I aint sick, doctor," and the dim eyes opened slowly, "I'm jest called, I am."

"When, Joe?" looking down sadly.

"It aint a-been long sence; but I've done sawn orl my sins, I hev, an' God's done sawn 'em too," panting wearily, "an' I'm jest a-waitin' to see Jerry; jest a-waitin' fur thet, 'cause I've got a word fur Jerry, I hev."

"Will you drink this?" and the doctor held some brandy to the white lips.

"I'll drink it fur youuns, doctor; but I aint a-goin' to say nothin' tell Jerry gits har," drinking slowly; "he's a-comin', I kin feel it, he aint fur," then he lay down again with a long, tremulous sigh.

"Kin youuns read to me, doctor?" he asked after a little; "Jerry's gotter leetle Bible sommers—sommers roun' on the shelf."

And the doctor found it, the little black Bible he had given Jerry to teach him the way to the "Golding Gates"—poor little child.

The deep voice read on and on; the firelight flickered over the rough walls; the young man sat still and listening, and the old man on the bed breathed heavily. At last, far off, the clang of a horse's hoofs on the rocky path, and a silence fell in the house—all were listening. Again the sound came sharply on the wind, and the old man rose on his elbow.

"It's Jerry," he said, "I knowed I were a-feelin' of him; I knowed he warn't much fur; I knowed as I were called fur to-night, an' he'd come," and the deep-set eyes lighted up strangely; "gie me a leetle dram, doctor, 'cause I hes sumpen to say," then he lay quiet again until the doctor poured out the brandy and raised him to drink it.

"An' I reckon Jerry's powerful honggry," the hoarse voice went on, "powerful honggry, and thar's bread thar, but thar aint nary time to eat now, I mus' talk fust; I've got sumpen to say."

Nearer came the ringing of the horse's hoofs, nearer and nearer; as fast as any horse could come on such a night, up such a path: at last it stopped at the door that Greg held open, and Jerry stood among them.

"Lord!" and Joe passed his hand slowly over Jerry's face, then down over his shoulder and arm—"Jerry," he muttered, "leetle Jerry a gentleman,—a rale gentleman," then he closed his eyes, and Jerry looked anxiously from one to the other of the watchers.

The doctor shook his head; and Jerry bent low over his old friend, with a dull pain growing up in his heart—how had this happened—had he had anything to do with it?"

"How did you get sick, Joe?" he asked softly.

Joe shook his head slowly.

"I aint agoin' to tell you thet, Jerry, ner nobody; nobody aint agoin' thar no mo'—no mo'—" then he opened his eyes slowly—"you is got the paper, doctor?" he asked.

"Yes, Joe."

"Gie it to Jerry when I'm done buried; an' bury me up yander by my Nancy Ann—leetle Nan, I calls her; thar aint no gole thar whar she's a-layin'; an' hev it writ on the stone as this is Joe Gilliam's las' find—hev it writ jest thet away;" then rousing up suddenly he grasped Jerry's hands, his eyes burning brightly, and his breath coming thick and fast—"Thar's damnation in the gole, Jerry, an' death in the mine! Don't go thar—don't go thar. An', Jerry, I done sent you over yander to larn to love money, an' to see what it could buy, an' to larn to love it; but don't you do it, Jerry, don't," with pitiful entreaty in his eyes and voice, "my soul'll never res' if you gits honggry fur gole; an' I aint agoin' to tell you whar I got mine; I aint agoin' to tell!" taking his hands from Jerry's and wringing them together as he sat propped up against the doctor's shoulder, "an' I'm rale glad you is done gotter lot of folks in the mine to shar' an' shar' alike—I'm glad," his voice falling lower, "an' the way is mighty easy to find if you never tu'ns to the lef'—never to the lef'; thet's death—death!" closing his eyes.

The doctor put some brandy to his lips and he swallowed it with difficulty.

"I were honggry fur gole," he muttered, "honggry; an' leetle Nan 'ud cry when I were gone orl day—pore leetle Nan! I sees her aheaper times a-layin' thar buried in the gole-dust—an' it's a-chokin' her an' the leetle 'un!" starting wildly, "a-chokin' her an' her can't git it out—it's in her eyes, an' in her mouth—her mouth!" struggling, and wringing his hands, "Leetle Nan, I'll bresh it out—bresh it out," slowly the voice faded.

Greg covered his face with his hands; the doctor prayed with his lips close to the old man's ear; and Jerry stood white and still as a stone.

Slowly the death-dimmed eyes opened; the words of the prayer had reached the darkened mind—"Fur Jesus' sake?" slowly; "leetle Nan usen to say thet; I hearn her in the night time—"fur Jesus' sake"—then he lay quite still listening to the low voice. The breath came slower and slower—the chest heaved laboriously—the hard, brown hands twitched nervously. One more breath—was it the last?

The old face looked gaunt and gray—the sunken eyelids quivered ;—again a long, tremulous breath ; the eyelids lifted slowly, and a whisper swept past them—

"Thar's death in the mine, Jerry ;" then all was still.

PART THIRD.

" Be not deceived ; God is not mocked : for whatsoever a man soweth, that shall he also reap. For he that soweth to his own flesh shall of the flesh reap corruption."

CHAPTER I.

> " Dark, dark was all ! A mist,
> A blinding, whirling mist of chilly snow,
> The falling and the driven ; for the wind
> Swept round and round in clouds upon the earth,
> And birm'd the deathly drift aloft with moans,
> 'Till all was swooning darkness. Far above
> A voice was shrieking with a human cry ! "

THE wind was howling wildly, and the snow falling in swirling sheets, was scurrying across the wide plain ; driving the snow against the great cliffs, and banking, dangerously almost, on the frail new houses. It had not been falling for an hour, and yet all the land was covered. The fire burned hotly, sending a vivid glow over Joe's chair that stood in its accustomed place, and seeming as if it strove to touch with one little shaft of light Joe's pipe that lay in the crack between the logs where for years he had kept it. Buck slept in his box ; the lamp shone brightly, and Jerry, with his arms crossed on the table, and his head bowed down on them, sat alone.

There was nothing to indicate that Joe might not come in at any moment ; except that his clothes hung long and limp against the wall—that his hat was on the peg behind the door, and that his boots stood in the corner with some mud still on them, and their tops drooping over one another.

The bread browned in the spider ; the coffee-pot steamed on the hearth—why should not the old man come in ? Because the door was barred—or because the window was shut fast, blind and all—was that a reason ?

Lonely ? Jerry had never realized that such loneliness could be felt.

Fresh from the whirl of gayety and excitement; fresh from the midst of luxury and praise, to this. He raised his head and looked about him; this was all he owned; all he owned, for the old man had died with the secret of his "find" kept close. Jerry was in despair: he had spent hundreds, and had pledged himself for far more; and now Joe was dead, and the secret of where he found his gold was dead with him.

It was not in Durden's Mine; that appalling truth had come home to Jerry in the midst of that awful death-scene like a merciless blow. For he had been so sure that Joe got his gold in Durden's Mine, and Dan Burk, who professed to know, had confirmed his surmises,—and now?

A groan broke from his lips.

"Great God!" he cried, "what *shall* I do!"

What, indeed! The next week the engineer would come, and the examination of the mine begin. Never go to the left, the old man had said, but had added "There's death in the mine?" Death. Death was nothing compared with failure. He would suffer a thousand deaths rather than fail.

What should he do.

He turned his head from side to side to deaden the dull pain that had never left it since that bewildering day in the Board room; a heavy, heavy pain that would not go.

He looked back all along his course; how he had been pushed and driven; how his present position seemed to spring on him full-armed, and he so unprepared; how blindly he had gone into this wild scheme that no man with any experience would have dreamed of attempting. It had wound like a coil about his feet,—a net spread so plainly that any eye could see. Nothing but invincible ignorance would have dared so much so regardless of all consequences. And now the consequences were on him, and he was lost in a mist of despair.

Would it not be better to put the engineer at work

on the new finds; while he searched for Joe's place of work?

Again he shook his weary head; this would lose to him the people's confidence: and a slow feeling of resentment began to burn in him against the poor dead man. He had not money to live on even, now that Joe was gone: he was afraid to ask Greg if Joe had repaid all of Mr. Greg's advances: he was afraid to ask any question; to meet Dan Burk; to look any one in the face; for what better was he than a pauper and a fraud? At last he rose and shook himself; whatever else he might be, he was surely a fool and a coward. He must not dream of flinching now, but must fight this thing through whatever the end might be. He must put the engineer to work in Durden's Mine; must go in himself regardless of the death that was prophesied for him there.

He laughed.

It showed what an idiot he was to remember even an old man's superstitions: and he tramped up and down the little house until the floor shook. To-morrow he would put on his old clothes and move into Durden's; he was going to live with Greg now, and the change and new life would help to rouse him from this wretched weakness and despondency: he would move everything and shut up the old house for a while.

Up and down he tramped until he felt better; well enough to put his supper on the table.

One week ago he was at that ball. He put his cup down; he seemed to hear again the minor chords of the waltz that passed by him when he sat alone among the flowers, and heard that last farewell! He took up his cup again, and emptied it; he would lose his mind if he allowed himself to brood in this way. He must eat his supper, and then must read the sealed paper the doctor had given him that morning after the funeral. He had put off the reading hour after hour: he had said that when he finished cooking his dinner he would read it; then, when he had finished eating his dinner—then, when he had finished cutting his wood because the storm was coming; and then, when he had finished cooking his supper. Now all was done save the eating of his supper, and he could have no further excuse. The paper was in the inside pocket of his coat, he could hear it crackling a little every time he moved: he was silly to put it off any longer; he would finish his supper and then open it.

Resolutely he set to work and made himself eat as usual; then he washed the few things and put them away as he had done for so many years, then sat down by the light.

It was a large, yellow envelope, with inky finger-marks on it, and a long smirch where it had been glued down. Jerry turned it over slowly; no living creature knew its contents: this thought gave him a tremulous feeling as if a ghostly company were waiting to see him read it, and to watch his action!

He looked over his shoulder hastily, and the clothes of the dead man hanging limp and straight against the wall, fluttered slightly as a more violent gust than usual, struck the house. A cold perspiration broke out on Jerry's forehead! For one moment he sat quite still, then rose and took the clothes down, putting them on Joe's bed. Of course the wind had stirred them; the wind was unusually high.

Then once more seated near the lamp, he took the ugly envelope from the table, turned it over once, then tore it open.

Was there anything in it?"

Nervously enough he held it before he looked, then one little scrap of dirty white paper was all he found, and on it in cramped, laborious, printed letters, these words—

"Een the dorg korner—een the rafters—een the j'ists—een the korners"— that was all!

Jerry put the paper down and looked about him bewildered—what did it mean?

The dog's corner; that was mentioned first; should he go there; and if he went what would he find? In the dog's corner—he must look!

He called old Buck from out his box, putting all the remaining supper on the floor for him,—then pulled the box away. Carefully he rapped the floor,—it was hollow; but all the floor was hollow. He took the lamp from the table and looked more closely; all the boards were short, and were more compactly fitted together: more carefully still he looked, and in the darkest part of the corner he saw a place worn almost smooth, and on the edges of it many finger-marks.

He thought for a moment, then put his fingers in this place, and the floor came up!

Jerry drew a long breath, and dropped it. He walked up and down the floor once or twice: was he dreaming, or was he a coward?

Once more he approached the corner, once more fitted his fingers—it came up readily, and looking he saw that a square of the short boards turned on well-greased wooden hinges.

He had often seen such hinges, why should they so astonish him? Then he saw something else; was it another floor, or a box? He ran his fingers over the whole smooth surface, then carefully examining, he found more finger-marks; he fitted his fingers to them—one second—then a lid was lifted!

Had his mind deserted him suddenly?

He passed his hand slowly over his eyes and brow, then knelt by the open hole as if turned to stone!

Was any one knocking, or crying, or was it the wind?

Hastily he sprang up, shutting down both floors, and putting the lamp on the table.

Buck was eating his supper quietly; the wind howled despairingly, and he could feel the snow banking against the window. He could feel it falling flake by flake, he knew he could,—and some one was walking and wailing outside!

He covered his face with his hands—was it Joe? A shudder ran over him—Joe longing once more to count his hoard!

With a wild shriek the wind came down the gorge, striking like a human hand against the door and window—Jerry stood still, and cold, and white—it came across those lonely graves: those lives had been sacrificed for this gold!

Greg had left a flask of brandy on the shelf: he needed strength now, and he would find it in that flask.

He took a tin cup and poured some in it; how Fred Greg would scorn to drink from such a vessel; and yet, this was the same brandy Fred drank in the East. It looked like melted gold as the light shone through it: then he tossed it off. He stood still for a moment: he was on fire—there were broken stars before his eyes, and red-hot blood in his veins! He walked to the book-shelf—those were his books, he knew every one of them—and there was Joe's ax in the corner, and Buck lying full length before the fire.

Nothing ailed him, he had taken only a little brandy to steady him after a day of unusual excitement; he had often seen men take more than he had taken.

Now he had strength to open those floors; and after that—"een the rafters—een the korners—een the j'ists,"—he laughed aloud.

Poor Joe, he said always "een" for "in." He felt better now, quite strong and well, and had been a fool to think he had heard voices, or footsteps, or snowflakes falling—a perfect fool!

He walked to the corner, he knew what was there now; he knew that his reputation was saved—his name made good.

Eagerly, greedily he lifted the two floors—ah, those little bags; they could hold only one thing—gold! Gold dust—gold nuggets?

Anxiously he opened one,—one, two, three of

them—five, ten of them—and a cry burst from his lips!

Gold money, firm and solid from the mint! He heaped more wood on the fire—he spread a blanket on the floor—a blood-red blanket—how the gold would sparkle against it!

And then bag after bag he emptied it—how it clinked—how it rang—piles and piles of it! He was drunk with the sight, and sat on the floor and smiled at it, and talked to it like an idiot; then suddenly rising up with arms outspread he cast himself upon the glittering heap!

"Mine, all mine!" he cried aloud; a wild, sharp cry that seemed to still the wail of the wind as it passed, and an awful silence fell! Had he made that sound?

He got up slowly: what ailed him, was he mad? of course not; but foolishly he had emptied many of his bags of gold: he must fill them all again and put them back; that corner was the safest place in which to keep them.

Then the words came back to him—"een the rafters—een the korners—een the j'ists—" he looked up; could gold be hidden up there in the rafters? he put his hand up in the lowest corner of the roof; and something was there—something soft and round. He paused a moment: should he take it down and examine it now, or wait until he had put away all his gold, and replaced Buck's box. Poor dog, he waited so patiently, so still and watchful near the fire. Perhaps he was accustomed to see those little bags taken out and emptied,—emptied and counted over and over again. Old Pete had had those patient ways too.

Slowly Jerry filled the little bags, packing them tightly;—had he done it too securely? He looked about him bewildered; he must have, for there was no gold to fill the last bag which he held in his hands. He passed his hand slowly over his forehead and eyes—had an unseen hand filched any from him?

Out again, hurriedly, eagerly, came all the little bags; how many pieces had there been in each? Many of them he had not touched as yet; he would count the pieces in these, and fill the others with the same number of coins.

Bag after bag was carefully set apart on the floor; the unopened ones opened and counted, and the rest filled accordingly, and enough was left for the last bag—none had been taken.

Then he put them back; shut down the floors; drew the box into its place, and watched as without any command the great dog stepped into his resting-place.

While he had been dreaming of the equal distribution of land and money, and making maudlin speeches about the inalienable rights of humanity, old Joe was gathering, and old Buck was guarding!

Humanity had no inalienable rights—had no right to anything save what he could get and hold by his own strength. Buck and Joe had been wise—had gathered and saved the one thing that would make these ignorant hordes respect him, and stand back from crowding him down; the one thing that would give him power in the world.

He laughed a little, then stood still in front of the fire trying to calm his excitement, and decide what he would do. Should he hunt for and examine his treasure now, or wait until daylight?

For a moment he wavered; he might lose some in the night; but in the daylight Greg might come upon him at any hour—he was more secure now.

He again took up the blurred, rudely written paper; "een the rafters—een the korners—een the j'ists"—he would have to tear the house down! Had the old man designed this so that no one should have the house he built so long ago for his little Nan? But now he must look.

The rafters were rough logs with the bark still on them, and ran the length of the house; nor were they very far apart, for the clapboards that stood for shingles were nailed to them without any intervening sheeting. Jerry was tall, and the house was low; he could reach up and touch every rafter except the three in the peak of the house, and these he could reach by standing on a chair.

He took it all in; almost he could see Joe's long arms reaching up, and his bony hands fumbling about the rough bark; and now he could understand why he was not allowed to whitewash the inside of the house, nor to move Buck's box. What a blind fool he had been! If he had had any sense he could have read the secret of Joe's life long ago, and the mystery that kept him aloof from his fellows; it was all clear to him now—so clear that the only wonder was that he had not seen it sooner.

Now he went back to the place where he had put up his hand, and had felt the soft little bundle he had been afraid to take down. He went back now and lifted his slim, nervous hand that trembled foolishly; it was there, he had not been mistaken, and he brought it to the light eagerly. A little roll about the size and shape of his finger, and wrapped in a piece of leather that looked as if it had been cut from the top of an old boot, and tied round with a leather string.

He sat down by the table, he was so nervous, and untied it—slowly it unrolled before him, an orderly pile of bank-bills!

One hour ago he had looked on himself as a ruined man—a pauper—a fraud! Now, who could say how much he owned?

He got up and poured more brandy into the cup, but before he drank it he wound up the clock; this task would take hours, and he must know when to look for interruptions. An intense, excited quiet seemed to have fallen on him now: he must work steadily and systematically; he must know exactly when he began his search, and carry it on quietly from that point. He marked the place, then went regularly on, putting all he found on the table. Strange little rolls wrapped in scraps of leather, or in pieces of the skin of animals, or in squares of felt that looked like the remains of old hats, and all of them carefully tied. Some were hard, as if they were rolls of gold or silver, and some were soft as the first bundle had been. Carefully, slowly up and down the long rafters he felt his way; up and down all the higher ones, filling his pockets that he might not have to move too often.

How careful and ingenious the old man had been in hiding his treasure! no one could possibly have found it without some clue. Then he emptied his pockets on the table; what a pile it made! and how should he store it away? One or two of the little packages he had found stuffed in between the clapboards,—how many more might be there he did not know; but he would find out,—find out if he had to pull the house down piece by piece!

Carefully he went over it all again, very carefully; he must not miss one inch of that roof. He was not trembling now, but he was cold, cold as death! He piled more wood on the fire; the blaze mounted up higher and higher—the room was in a glow. Then he looked about him; there was his trunk he had bought while he was gone, and his valise. Not in the valise, but in the trunk that had a false bottom that opened with a secret spring. A new invention the man had told him; he would put all his money there; the bills would not rattle, and would lie flat; and he could put the extra covering on the rolls of coin to stop any possible sound.

In a moment the trunk was open, and all his clothes out on the floor, all his fine new things that had cost so much money, and been put on with so much pride and pleasure; what did they matter now—what did anything matter! Down, down to the bottom, down into the false tray that was so deftly concealed; one touch and it flew open. Only one thing was there—one small bundle tied up in old newspaper. Jerry stopped; his hands fell at his side, and the light died out of his eyes. "Mammy—mammy!" he whispered.

What came to him that he looked all about him; stood up, and turned, and looked about as if listening; what did he see or hear?

He turned the soiled, crumpled bundle over and over in his hands. The same old paper he had put about it as a child—the same old paper he had left there because he had not known that it was wretched and dirty—and that later he had left because of a nameless pathos that appealed to him from every smirch, and every wrinkle! Now it came to him like a voice or a touch from another world; his life was cut in two, and that other life he had lived had died and been buried long ago.

He was another person: he could not be that wild dreamer who had thought to equalize all the possessions of the earth; who would now have had him give a roll or a bag to every person in the town; How strange he had been! no wonder Joe had laughed at him.

And this little bundle that, for all his life until now, had been his only possession: poor little bundle, the only inheritance of his life.

He turned to look at the table where his treasure lay in piles and heaps—now! He thrust the bundle far back in the bottom of his trunk—far back in a hidden corner: the night was going and he must work. Hurriedly he began to drag the trunk across the floor; midway he stopped and lifted it; it might jar some of the little bundles from their resting-places in the joists; and he put it down very carefully near the table, and began to pack. All the bundles of bills he smoothed out evenly, laying them in exact piles in the false tray; then the rolls he covered more securely, putting them in even rows, and there was a great space left.

"Een the korners," the paper had said. He took

the lamp, and moving his cot looked carefully on the floor in the corner, while visions of another double floor, as in the dog's corner, flashed across his mind.

But carefully as he looked, there were no marks; he tapped the floor, he tried the boards, but with no success, and a feverish impatience began to pervade him: what had Joe meant "Een the korners"?

He lifted the lamp and looked up and down where the logs crossed each other—ah—! In each joint there was a crack, an innocent natural crevice, but they meant much to Jerry. There they were, little rolls and bundles hidden away, pushed in carefully and systematically, hidden entirely. Slowly but surely he pulled them all out; one after another with an absorbed, intense expression on his face, and a burning light in his eyes. One after another they came out; how many more were there, and how many more in the other corners? How much would he have when he gathered it all together, how much; and would he ever find time and place to count it?

Each corner yielded up its treasure, and he put it away as he had done the rest, then paused and looked about him.

He was very weary, and the night was nearly done; should he put away everything and rest until the day came, or should he search further. He was very weary, and his head felt strangely heavy; was it the brandy, or the pain that had worried him for so long, turned to heaviness? It was something he had never felt before, and he must rest.

It would not do for him to be ill and all this money about; no, he must put the house in order, and rest; perhaps a little sleep would send the feeling away.

Slowly and heavily he moved about, shutting down the secret tray, putting his clothes back as they had been, and carefully rolling the trunk against the wall. The fire; yes, he must make that safe, it would never do to let there be any danger of that kind, with all this money about. How reckless he had been all these years, not knowing the wealth hidden all about him!

But now he was very weary; he must rest; but he would not put the light out,—a light would be a safety to the house; seeing it thieves would think him awake, and be afraid to break in. But yet the light might guide some wanderer there, some traveler lost on the trail; so he must turn it very low, for it would not be safe to take strangers in with so much money about.

He must be careful now, very careful, for no one must know of his wealth; no one must know. Nor must he undress, that would not be safe; and the old rifle must be loaded and cocked by his bedside; that was what Joe always did; Joe, who was so clever to gather and to hide!

He felt better lying down: but had he left any of the little rolls in his pockets that he could not lie easy? And he felt about him on the bed and in his pockets; no, they were all safe in the trunk; unless he had dropped some on the floor. He did not remember hearing any of them fall, and yet they might have; would it not be better to get up and look?

Only he was so weary; let him rest a little while longer, then he would look; yes, he would look, for perhaps he had left some on the table, and that would betray him to Greg.

Was Greg there in the room—had he come softly over the snow from Durden's?

He must get up; he must! If Greg found it out everybody would know, and they would force him to share it out—never—never!

He must hide it: he must send it to old Mr. Greg to buy shares, and make into millions and millions; until it would be scattered about him like chips around the woodpile—yes, like chips!

And so he tossed and dreamed, half asleep—half awake—while the night waned, and the wild wind blew the snow-clouds away and let the morning stars shine and glitter, and the moon turn all the snow-covered world to silver.

Clear and crisp, and cruelly cold when the red sun rose and shone on the work of the busy snow clouds, and stole under Jerry's doorway, following a little drift of snow that had driven in, and lay across the floor a beautiful, unheeded stream of gold; stole in to show that a new day had broken over the land, and a new time and chance wherein man might begin his life afresh.

A beautiful new day; a resurrection from the death of sleep; a clearing of the soul from troubled visions that once more it might look up to God's glad light and turn away from sin and darkness; one more gift of time and opportunity sweeping in a golden flood before each life!

CHAPTER II.

> "Howbeit all is not lost:
> The warm noon ends in frost;
> The worldly tongues of promise,
> Like sheep-bells, die off from us
> On the desert hills cloud-crossed!"

IT was late when Jerry roused from his restless dreams, and he wondered vaguely what had come to him, and if he had slept at all. The fire had smoldered into a gray heap; the sun shone under the door, and old Buck lay with his nose up on the edge of the box blinking at the unaccustomed darkness at this hour.

Jerry sat up and looked about him: it surely had been a black, wild, snowy night when he lay down, and now the sun was shining.

He got up slowly, staggering a little just at first, and his head was very heavy; that was the brandy,—yes, he had taken some brandy. Then slowly across his memory came all the scene of the night before; and he covered his face with his hands—could it be true possibly?

He walked to the window and pushed open both sash and blind, and the sight of the whitened world reassured him that he had not lost his mind. But it was cold, bitterly cold.

Quickly he made the fire and put on the kettle; now he would go out to the bathing pool and put his head under the spout of the spring,— that would clear his brain so that he could think.

The fire burned brightly, and Buck came out of his box to sit near it; things were beginning to look more natural.

Jerry took out a suit of the rough clothes he had worn always, and that Joe had put away for him in the old wooden chest: he would put them on when he came back from the spring, and things would seem more real.

Once out in the crisp cold air he started at a full run up the little snow-covered path: he used always to run on cold days, and somehow he had a wish now to do as he had done always; he wanted to take a fresh hold on the old life that had been so real and so happy! Yes, it had been happy, but he had not realized it at the time; this new life, into which he had stepped so suddenly, seemed like some strange dream from which he must soon be roused; he seemed to be able to stand off and look at himself as if he were some other person. He could see himself smiling, and talking, and bowing in the beautiful rooms that were full of light and music and lovely women: he could see himself down among the busy offices with his face grown keen and sharp after gain: he could see himself mad with joy over his heap of gold! And the person who looked was a grave young man, with rather a sad face, who trudged back and forth to the humble schoolhouse in Eureka; a sad young man with a heart all wounded and embittered by the love cast back on it.

Ah, that had been the turning-point! If only the doctor had not cast him off.

The thought was bitter to him still, and hastily he pushed his head under the rough spout. The little icicles hanging on the side broke and fell clinking down with a sharp rattle; he laughed a happy little laugh, the sound took him back so entirely into the old days. And the water was so cold, his head felt clear and sound in a moment.

Now he could go back and cook his breakfast and make his plans in a cool, sensible way.

He rubbed his hair round and round with a rough towel; Joe had made him do it in this way always, and he was finding Joe to be a very wise old man in many ways.

And they had been happy together in all those long, quiet years that were gone—they had been very happy. And the study under the doctor had been so pleasant and good, and he had found when he went out into the world that he knew more than most of the young men; nor had their ways and manners been strange to him. Yes, his life had been happy; picking his way slowly back to the house; but there was no reason why this new life should not be happy also—why not? He took off his "city clothes" and put on the rough suit that seemed so much more real and substantial; and made up the bread for his breakfast, and the coffee, and sliced the bacon that he would fry when the bread was nearly done. It was all so much as usual that he felt quite sure Joe was at the spring and would come in soon.

Busily he swept the floor, stepping softly lest he should jar some of the little bundles out of the joists; but when he remembered all the years that he had been coming in and out, and Joe, stamping heavily, he thought there could be no such danger.

Then looking up, his eyes fell on the little flask; that was what had made him so wild the night before; so miserable this morning, and it should not stand there to tempt him, he would pour it out—Greg had plenty more. It made a little hole in the snow as he poured it—a little round hole like a bullet, and the smell sickened him—bringing back the horror of the night. He put the empty flask back on the shelf, and arranged the table for his breakfast: it was better to do things with the usual regularity, it would help to calm him from the excitement of the past week, and allow him to think quietly of his future.

He would send his trunk down to Greg's, and whatever else they would need out of the house; and Joe's clothes and tools he would give to some poor emigrant—there were plenty of them who would be glad to get these things.

His books he would pack in the old chest, and take them with him too: he paused, and a sudden thought came to him that made him turn and look at the chest. Surely it would hold all his books even with a false bottom put in, and his gold bags packed between. And books were heavy, so that the weight of the chest would not be noticed, and he would pack the gold so as not to rattle; this was a good plan, and he felt relieved.

As to the house; and he paused again in his slow eating to look up at the roof—it would have to come down, and what excuse could he give for taking it down himself? This thought worried him; he could not say it was from love to Joe, affectionate recollection of the old man who had been all to him. A real pain—an acute, accusing pain for the poor old man, crept into his heart. Until now, no thought of love or of mourning had come to him; it had been painful, and he had missed Joe, but that had been all.

And he hated himself for the coldness of his heart.

No, he could not claim love as a motive for pulling down the house himself; he could not use the kind old man's memory in this way. He would pull down the house and say nothing about it, and when it was all down he would move it into the town, it would make a good house for somebody. This was the best plan, and surely it was nobody's business.

The dog was fed, the things put away, then he went to the bottom of his trunk once more; all was safe, and he put his clothes back more carefully, and on top he put the rest of his coarse clothes: it would be best to dress as he had always dressed, and to live as he had always lived, for too much public money passed through his hands for it to be safe for him to change in any way.

And not even Greg must know of the extent of his fortune, for no one would be loath to suspect him of knowing Joe's "find," and of concealing the knowledge in order to reap all the advantage.

Now he must prepare the chest; and the lid from the second floor in the corner would make an excellent false bottom, for it was thin and light.

The tools were all there, and he knew pretty well how to use them; it would not take him long; then he must go down and see Greg.

Quickly the hours slipped by, so busy was he, but all the little bags were safely stowed away, with space left for what he might find in the joists.

And gradually, as he worked, the absorbing thought of his future took hold of him again; in the morning the reaction from the troubles of the night had made him long to go back to the wholesome old times; but as the hours went on, and he realized for what he was preparing, the same excitement crept again into his veins.

So soon as these minor matters were made safe, he would map out his future course, and pursue it steadily to the end.

Durden's should succeed—Durden's should swallow up Eureka—Durden's should be the creature of his hand, and call him master as long as life pulsed in his veins. Only wait a little while—only be patient,—and soon all the world should see what he could do and be.

He cooked his dinner and ate it, then locked the chest, and the trunk, and the house, and set off down the trail toward Durden's. He must see Greg, for it had occurred to him that it would be better to put up another room in addition to the two which Greg had already; it would be much more convenient for them to have such a place, and there was lumber to be bought in Eureka and plenty of men anxious for the work.

Certainly it would be best, for things had changed, and they could not now have all affairs in common.

To-morrow the Town Committee would meet, and

the sub-committee make a report; after that he would have to report, and he must make out his papers to-night, and the feeling of a pressure of work seemed to lighten his heart and his step.

He had risked a great deal in giving his notes to Mr. Greg for such large amounts—had done wrong, perhaps, but it had been Joe's fault—Joe had given him unlimited credit. Then again there came into his mind the question of the motive that had instigated Joe's course. On his death-bed he had said that he sent him to learn to love money—to learn to love money. A light seemed to break in on him: Joe had been afraid that Jerry, not valuing money, would share it all out! Was this his only motive?

He remembered Joe's distress when mention was made of buying Durden's Mine; the distress that more than anything else had convinced Jerry that Joe worked in Durden's Mine.

Now that theory was done away with, what caused that distress? And his death, what caused that? something mysterious which he would not tell; and Greg's story of his absence surely looked as if he had some resort and place of work other than the mine.

All this came back to Jerry now that his mind was free from the awful anxiety that for two days had possessed him—the anxiety about his notes falling due, and there being no money to take them up—what would have happened? The whole scheme would have failed, and he have been branded forever as an impostor.

Now all was secure, perfectly secure; he could take up his notes, and invest more—could himself run up the Durden's stock a point or two, so that even those keen, cautious men in the Board would feel secure. In a day or two he would take Greg and go in the mine, but he would not suggest any of the men going with them; for until they were accustomed to the idea of people going in and out of this haunted place, it was best not to ask them, so risking a refusal, for a refusal would set the whole town talking, and he must be very cautious about this.

And besides his report, he had a proposition to make to the committee; it was to buy all the lumber now lying in Eureka. It would be sold at cost, now that Eureka was depressed, and it all would be needed in Durden's as soon as the rush began. It would be a good investment for the committee to build the houses, so that the community would own them, and when rented or sold, the money would come back to the treasury. It was a good plan, and he would suggest it.

And now he began to whistle merrily as he walked, for his heart grew light as he planned his future, and felt that in the present he was safe. Yesterday the world had seemed blacker than the grave—to-day there were no tints needed to brighten it. But it would not do to be too gay suddenly,—Greg nor the doctor would understand it, and he sobered down before he entered Greg's house, where he found him writing letters.

"Letters for you too, Wilkerson," he said; "the old gentleman has followed you up quickly."

"A note of mine falls due next week," Jerry answered, opening Mr. Greg's letter first. "And good news, too," he went on, "Durden's stock on a steady rise, and Fred anxious to join us."

Greg shook his head.

"I shall say no to that," he said. "Too many of a family or a class coming in will look like a ring, and we can not afford to lose the least bit of ground in the confidence of these people."

Jerry looked up from his letters.

"Is it well for us to live together, then?" he asked.

"I have been thinking about it," Greg answered rather hastily, "and scarcely think it wise; and for Henshaw, the engineer, I have taken a room at Dave Morris's. I tell you, Wilkerson," he went on more gravely, "that since I have worked on that committee I have not the least faith in these people; they would turn against either or both of us in a minute. They can not understand anybody's working for the common good, and immediately grow suspicious of any one who says that he does. Constantly I hear them going back to the doctor's case, and saying how he deceived them. They have to be held with a strong hand, or they will turn on you."

Jerry sat quite still; these were Joe's own words,—"They will kill you in a minute,"—and they would, if he did not kill them first!

Still, he did not blame them altogether now, for his own views had changed as to the rights of the masses, and as to the masses themselves; and perhaps it was well that they had changed, for now, instead of trying to work out some romantic dream—some philanthropical impossibility, he would take hold of these people and rule them as the ignorant needed to be ruled.

"I will manage them," he answered, "and perhaps we had better not live together, although it would have been very pleasant."

"Very," Greg assented, drawing idly on a piece of paper that lay near him on the table; but the voice was not hearty, and Jerry wondered why the wisdom of not living together had come to Greg so suddenly: yesterday he had insisted on it.

Did he know of anything these people were plotting, and so had grown afraid of being connected with him? Jerry would not look up while he thought, for he was afraid the suspicion would show in his eyes; and it was a mean doubt to have, but since the doctor had failed him he had come to doubt everybody. "I shall try to get a room at Mrs. Milton's," he said, "until I can move my own house nearer the mine; it is too far from my work now"; then he went on opening and reading his letters.

Three or four applications for places under him from young men of good standing: two or three inquiries as to the real worth of land in Durden's, and of the true future of the place; and numbers of answers to his circulars sent out two months ago. He read them all through gladly enough, for they all promised well; and in a general way he told Greg their contents; but thought that as things between them were turning out so differently from what he had expected, it would be wiser to keep his own counsel. Nor did he mention his plan of buying lumber and building; he would keep this to himself also. And he was glad that Greg had declared himself so early in the campaign, thereby giving him time to strengthen himself so as to stand alone. It had all turned out very well, and it would be a good thing to read out these answers to his circulars,—then propose the building plan to the full meeting of the Town Committee, and let them see that Greg was no more in his confidence than they were.

And he would not, as he had thought of doing, send more money to Mr. Greg to invest for him: but after taking up all his notes he would employ a regular broker to transact his business for him; for of course all that he told the father would be used to help the son, and maybe the son would join with any party that might form against him—might even form one.

And in the half-hour that he sat so sociably by his friend's fire, the whole plan and temper of his life had changed; and the thought came to him, as he left the house, that it seemed to be ordained that he should stand alone.

He had grown up with two men whose lives hid mysteries, and so touched his only on the outermost surface, leaving him to live within himself; and now when he thought that he had made a friend; had found one of his own age with the same views and ambitions, this friend suddenly withdrew from him; because their ambitions *were* the same, perhaps. It was disappointing, but maybe it was best; his life would be much more to the purpose, and much more intense, if he lived entirely within himself, and frittered away none of his strength or energy on love and sympathy!

A little laugh broke from him as he walked, that was not pleasant to listen to, and he said aloud—"Love and sympathy!" and said it with great contempt. It seemed to him that he had given so much, and to what purpose—to have it all thrown back on him, not because of lack in him, but because of a love given long ago to a woman.

And as he stood knocking at Mrs. Milton's door, that weary delicate face rose up before him. A strange story—a sad fate that often he dreamed over: and who was the one shut away in the convent—and why was Paul with the doctor?

"Bless my heart, Jerry Wilkerson!" and Mrs. Milton stood in the doorway looking him over from head to heels. "Come in—come in," she went on, after Jerry had shaken hands with her and had knocked the snow off his boots—"it's rale wittles an' drink to see you a-bowin' aroun' an' a-talkin' fur orl the worl' like the doctor; tucker cheer," and she dropped into one of the rocking-chairs that had figured so many years ago at 'Lije's funeral; only now it had grown rusty and bare of varnish, and the arms were tied in place by pieces of string.

"An' how did you favor down East?" she asked.

"Very much," Jerry answered, "but I could not live away from Durden's."

"Gosh, no!" scornfully; "I aint got no stomick fur the pulin' way folks lives down East, thar aint no grit 'bout nothin'—notter specker grit!"

Jerry laughed.

"But it is very comfortable over there, Mrs. Milton," he said.

"Durden's 'll do me," she answered, taking down a black clay pipe, "an' it did fur Joe Gilliam, an' it did fur 'Lije Milton, an' them were good men as ever wuz daubed outer clay; an' you orter 'gree to thet, Jerry Wilkerson."

"I do," and Jerry looked into the fire sadly: certainly Joe had been faithful to him.

"I 'llows thar's sumpen on youun's mine, Jerry Wilkerson," the old woman went on, reseating herself and looking at him keenly from out a cloud of smoke; "when a man's wittles don't sot easy, or ther's the least little thing a-pesterin' him, he allers looks like he's a-hankerin' atter a-buryin'—what's up?"

Jerry ran his hand over his face, trying to change his expression; this old woman was so keen.

"I came to see if I could board with you, Mrs. Milton," he said quietly, "my house is too far from my work."

"I knowed it," nodding slowly, and looking into the fire, "Joe's gone, an' you is a-goin' to spen' what he saved, a-boardin'—mussy me, boy, you kin live a heap cheaper to you seff."

The color rose in Jerry's face.

"I want to board only until I can move my house," he said, "and I am going to work, Mrs. Milton, not waste."

"Jest so, thet's better: but movin' thet house aint a-gointer pay, them logs is plum rotten by now; git youuns a little new lumber, an' put up a shanty,—it'll pay a heap better."

"Maybe so," Jerry answered: this was a good idea to have in people's minds; they would think the old house had rotted away; and as no one used the trail now, no one would know it had been aided in its fall.

"I shall send my trunk and my bed down on Monday?" he suggested.

"Well, an' the price?"

"You must settle that," rising, "you know best what it will be worth."

"You makes a fine trade, Jerry Wilkerson," standing between him and the door, with arms akimbo,

"Joe'd be rayly proud to hear how peartly smart hisn boy were."

"I don't think you will cheat me, Mrs. Milton; at least I did not think so," laughing.

"Thet mout be so, an' agin it moutent; an' I'd sot a heap mo' sto' by you if you'd try to maker trade, I would. You tried it on me when you come alonger Dan Burk to buy the mine, an' you made a rale good trade, you did," putting her head on one side and taking her pipe from her mouth; "I reckon you is got mo' truck sence Joe's gone, an' don't feel so pertickler bad off; ain't thet so?"

It was in Jerry's mind, indeed on his lips, to say that then he had been buying for the people, and now he was making only a little arrangement for himself; but he remembered Greg's words that these people did not believe in such motives—words he knew to be true, so he said only:

"Yes, Mrs. Milton, I have more money now than then."

"I knowed it," nodding her head, "an' nobody need not to prophesy to know it; kase orl the town knowed thet Joe Gilliam were a savin' creetur, an' lived lonesome," she went on more thoughtfully—"an' did orl fur hisseff an' fur you; I'll be bound, Joe washed youuns' cloze, now aint thet so?"

"Yes," Jerry answered, "and mended them too."

"Great-day-in-the-mornin'! an' a heaper gals jest ready to tuck up alonger him—Gosh!"

Jerry laughed, he could not help it,—the idea of Joe's marrying seemed so queer, it had never occurred to him before; and the other idea of the young woman being willing to take him—that was still more strange; marry old Joe! and he laughed. The old woman joined in with a grim sort of chuckle over her own wit, walking with him to the door.

"Go 'long, boy," she said, "an' don't fotch no beds—I'se got beds, I reckon, an' Milley kin rub out youuns' shirts onest inner while: an' you is jest right thet Mandy Milton aint agoin' to cheat you, I were jest a-foolin' : come along when you hes a mine to, an' you'll fine the inside of Mandy Milton's han' jest sure, you will," and she slapped him on the back too heartily for comfort almost ; "I aint furgot thet Joe Gilliam, an' me, an' 'Lije come from the same ole State, an' thet fur awhile Joe Gilliam an' 'Lije were kinder pards—I aint furgot—farwell," and she stood in the doorway to watch him.

"Poor creetur," she muttered, "to think as he's pards alonger Dan Burk, the p'isen-meanest parry-toed creetur as ever were growed, drat 'im ! " then she shut the door.

And Jerry went his way up the lonely trail, thinking deeply, and readjusting his mind to the new order ot things that had come to him since he had left his home light-hearted and sure of his future.

CHAPTER III.

"Friend, who knows if death have life or life have death for goal?
Day nor night can tell us, nor many seas declare nor skies unroll
What has been from everlasting, or if aught shall always be.
Silence answering only strikes response reverberate on the soul
From the shore that hath no shore beyond it set in all the sea."

SETTLED at Mrs. Milton's, Jerry felt more himself than he had done since the time that seemed so long ago, when he had waited to warn the doctor. It was better for him to be always among his fellows; the lonely life up on the trail allowed him too much time to brood and see visions; this busy life was more wholesome.

His report had been received with great applause by the committee, and his proposition to buy the lumber from Eureka, and to build houses, had been accepted, and a committee on building appointed, of which he was chairman.

Engineer Henshaw had come, and had been settled in his rooms, and now the investigation of the mine was to come the next day.

It was very late; Mrs. Milton and the town of Durden's had been long sleeping the sleep of the weary, but Jerry's light burned still, and he wrote busily. All day he had worked for the Commune—to-night he worked for himself. His private affairs were in the most prosperous condition; he had taken up all his notes as they fell due; and had spent three days in riding to and from the nearest station—to send his money to be deposited safely in bank. His broker had telegraphed its safe arrival, and his certificate of deposit and bank account had come to him that afternoon. He knew now how much he owned; at last he had counted all the savings of old Joe's long life, and of old Durden, whose money Joe had found—had counted every cent won by those lives of unceasing toil and saving, and knew himself to be a rich man.

It had taken time for him to get the money together: log by log, and board by board, he had taken down the whole of Joe's house; he had gotten all that was hidden under the floor, and had searched the roof most thoroughly. If ever it came to his memory that he was destroying the place that had sheltered all his happiest years, the thought did not stay his destroying hand; rather, there was a haunting fear always that some of the treasure might be lost; and his most constant dream was that the little bundles were rolling away from him in the snow and the rain.

Relentlessly he pulled down all the little shelves and conveniences that one after another Joe had arranged for him. The first shelf put up for his school-books; the larger one put up later for books that Joe had given the doctor money to buy for him; the little cupboard nailed against the wall, that served to store his papers in—all these came down one by one! Whatever was of any use, he gave away: Joe's clothes, and tools, and bed; the rest of the things he kept to put in his own house that was now building.

All his money was safe now,—what did these old things matter? But he kept the little bags that had held the gold; somehow he could not destroy them; and in one of them he had found a strip of paper, and the words on it puzzled him; but he could not destroy the little bags.

His face had grown very sharp in the last few weeks, and his eyes burned more brightly than ever before, as he sat writing under the full glare of the lamp.

He was a rich man now—a rich man! Sometimes he said the words over to himself until they rang in his ears and his heart,—a rich man! And the respectful letters from his broker, and the paternal notes from

Mr. Greg, were but the forerunning voices of what the world would soon sing around him.

His broker had advised him not to take any more stock in Durden's just now; he carried enough to assure people of his confidence in the venture, and to take any more would look as if he wished to prop it up. So some of his money was invested in other ways, and people in business circles looked on him as a "solid man." But in Durden's he was still only "Mr. Wilkerson," the chief man of the Commune; the man who had the responsibility of the whole town and its affairs on his shoulders, but who expected to make his money as the Durdenites made theirs. No one knew of Joe's treasure, and his strange sickness and death were soon forgotten.

Mrs. Milton had said, and every one believed it, and thought it most natural, that Joe Gilliam had saved a little money, and young Wilkerson was living on it; but no one knew of the bank account, nor of the investments made in his name in various prosperous railways: only Dan Burk wondered in his heart where Joe's money was. He knew how much he had saved, and he knew that Joe must have saved twice as much; yet no word had come to him—no whisper of Jerry having found but the little he was now spending on his living; and he wondered if the old man had hidden it too securely, or purposely had put it out of Jerry's reach.

Burk had been to see Joe once during his illness, but Joe had not vouchsafed to notice him except to say that there was "a curse on the gold, and death in the mine"—and this looked as if he might have buried it out of sight forever. Then Dan remembered Jerry's visit to the East and hearing that he had spent a great deal there; maybe it had gone in this way, maybe; but then this would not account for Joe's great desire that Jerry should learn to love money. He could come to no satisfactory conclusion, and fell to watching Jerry closely for any betraying word or action; he went to see him at all hours, hoping to surprise him in some way, but gained nothing for his trouble. Jerry lived quietly at Mrs. Miller's—he was building for himself a small house in no way better than the houses built for the emigrants; only two small rooms close under the cliff near the mine's mouth; he gave no sign in his dress, nor in any of his habits, that he was in possession of any great amount of money: and Dan Burk was puzzled.

The others who watched Jerry were Greg, with always an anxious look in his eyes; and Paul Henley.

The doctor came and went silently; he attended carefully to his work in Eureka, and kindly to all the sick and dying; his life seemed to have lost all interest, and he went about as one to whom duty has become habit. His great tract of land lay under the sun and rain untouched and unsought: his great stacks of lumber had been sold to Durden's; his imported workmen had followed their leader Greg, each buying his little lot, and building his little shanty; and the land-agents whom he, more than Jerry, had foiled, had been bought out by the railway company, and in a body had gone away in search of further prey.

All things rested in Jerry's hands now, and he had begun to think he could not fail—that all he touched must succeed. Nothing surprised him unless it went wrong; then he was provoked. He ruled the town committee, never hesitating to tell them the most biting truths: he dictated to the building committee: he asked no advice, and told none of his plans. When a plan was fully matured in his own mind, he systematically worked things in that direction, then laid the plan before the committee, quite sure of its adoption.

He was fully armed always, and people said he was not afraid of the devil. More than once Dave Morris had bragged of his defeat, elevating himself along with the reigning hero—a friend intimate enough to knock him down ; and Dan Burk often had repeated old Joe's words—"he would kill without thinking"—and, if true or not, this was believed.

And Jerry's laws were stringent.

No whisky was allowed in the town save as rations to men who were working; and it was said that Mr. Wilkerson would shoot any man he caught selling anything stronger than beer. Long ago he had established a school and church, where services of some kind were held every Sunday; but he had no reading-rooms; no lending-libraries; nor any news-stalls: those who wished newspapers might take them privately, but the fewer the better; he did not think them good for the masses, they only fomented discord and discontent; he had seen this, and as the people were satisfied with the *Durden's Banner* he made no move to introduce papers from the outside world.

As it was, his power was scarcely realized; and Durden's, surprised by the order and method with which she was governed, followed Jerry quietly and blindly.

His letters were finished now, and he pushed aside the coarse curtain that shaded the window and looked out. The autumn was very late, fortunately for his plans, with only the slightest snowfalls at long intervals; allowing him to build and prepare for the new-comers, and to push the work in the new "finds"; a little more good weather, and the old mine would be reopened, and the railway in; and of course the weather would hold.

There was a slight covering of snow on the ground now, as Jerry looked out, but the stars were shining overhead, and the moon so brightly, that he could see the stone meant for Joe's grave, leaning against the fence.

"*Joe Gilliam's last Find*" was the inscription cut on it, with the date of his death.

Jerry turned away; his last find,—where had his first find been—where had he worked all these years—wnere had he found all his gold?

Up and down Jerry walked: to-morrow for the second time in his life he would enter Durden's Mine. Would he find anything there to tell of that long toil and saving? might he not have mistaken Joe's last words?

He had found no mining tools among Joe's things; no lanterns, nor miner's lamps, nothing but common saws, and hammers, and hatchets: no clothes that looked as if he had worked underground. Would he find them all in some black passage in the mine; all piled carefully in some far recess, put there by the old hands that could handle them no more: or had Joe said true, that he had not worked in the mine,—that it was all safe unless you turned to the left.

He paused in his walking: some day he would examine that turn to the left. Die—he could not die yet—he *would* not die! If the devil had filled all the cracks of the earth with gold, he would dig it all out and give it to men so that there would be no more power in it to tempt them: and he laughed a little, remembering his foolish visions.

He went to the window again; his head was hot and heavy, and lifting the sash he leaned out into the biting wind.

"*Joe Gilliam's last Find.*"

The stone leaning against the fence seemed to speak to him. Something connected with his work had killed the old man; and his last find, did that mean his grave, or the thing that had caused his death?

He could never find out; and to-morrow he would go into the mine that the old inhabitants looked on as fatal to all who entered it.

Mrs. Milton had uttered sad forebodings.

"My 'Lije were a good, strong man, an' he were gone two days," counting slowly on her fingers, "two days, a Thursday an' a Friday, thet were orl—orl the time he were in thar; thet were orl, but when he come home a Saturday, he were done—plum done!"

and she wiped her nose with the corner of her apron; "thar warn't no mo' sperrit in him, no mo' sperrit in 'Lije Milton," shaking her head; "he never said anether cuss, ner tuck anether dram, ceppen what the doctor give him; an' he never tole what he sawn in thar—he never tole it."

Then Jerry had left her: he had heard that story long ago from Joe, and later had had suspicions of Joe's connection with this same story—dark suspicions that he had stilled: now they all came back to him as he thought of the next day, and looked at the stone leaning against the fence.

"*Joe Gilliam's last Find*"—that narrow grave up among the rocks—the common pine coffin—the quick forgetfulness!

He came in hastily from the cold night, and shut the window; he must get some rest, or he would not be fit for the next day's work.

Carefully he put the fire together, and drew the curtain, then looked at the clock; it was time almost for Mrs. Milton to get up.

CHAPTER IV.

"When wealth shall rest no more in mounded heaps,
But smit with freer light shall slowly melt
In many streams to fatten lower lands,
And light shall spread, and man be liker man
Thro' all the seasons of the golden year."

"AND this was the original bed of the stream?" Mr. Henshaw asked, standing in front of Jerry's unfinished shanty, and looking up the gorge, that was untouched by the sun as yet, "and formerly it flowed into this opening and disappeared?"

"Yes," Jerry answered, "and Mr. Durden, seeing indications of gold in these rocks, turned the stream aside by building a dam up yonder," pointing to where a dam, running up and down the ridge, turned the stream into a shallow ravine on the other side, "and worked in this cave opening. It is said," looking at the engineer keenly, "that the Eureka Mine, which has also a cave opening, was the outlet of the stream."

"Indeed?" seriously; "I doubt it; there is no sign of a cave opening there."

Jerry laughed.

"The only way to settle it," he said, "would be to turn the stream in again."

The engineer shook his head solemnly. He was too poor a man to joke about trying experiments on gold mines. "That would be ruination, you know," he said.

"Of course," and Jerry brought himself back to the strict business of the hour: this man was literal and earnest, the very man to have on an exciting search, as this might prove: and the traditions were nothing; indeed, it would be for the benefit of all if they could be forgotten. And the scrap of paper, that now he understood, had better be burned. For with the opening of the mine all the most far-fetched and most weird of the legends had come to the surface.

Mrs. Milton had poured into his ears all that 'Lije had revealed to her, of the sounds like women and children crying and calling for help—of a great red eye that glared at him—of twinkling lights that shone in impossible places; and Dan Burk had told him the old Indian's story of how the tribe had driven in all its women and children to death in a bottomless hole, rather than they should fall into the hands of the enemy. But the Indians had not gone in through the mine's mouth, of course, but through another opening into a cave that lay on the other side of this hole—a cave that was "lined and floored with pure gold!"

Before day that morning Dan had come to tell Jerry this story, and to warn him not to turn to the left. "Joe were the only feller as knew the way," he whispered, "and 'Lije Milton's death come from there, and Joe Gilliam's death come from there!"

So Jerry went to meet the engineer in the early morning with his nerves all strained and tense, and his mind all alive to every least sign or mark. He had not told Dan Burk that Joe already had warned him about the turn to the left, nor had he mentioned to any one Burk's story of the abyss that Joe had crossed daily; but the whole thing was clear to his own mind now. He could understand now Joe's anxiety as to the mine being occupied,—it was his only entrance to this cave beyond where he had found his gold; and amid the chaos of new surmises that were coming to him, the dreadful suspicion that Joe had aided in terrifying 'Lije Milton away from his work of exploration grew stronger and stronger. He had given up the thought that 'Lije had been hurt in any way, for from Mrs. Milton he had heard that the illness had lasted for months, and had been what she called "a dwinin'."

"'Lige stayed in thar as long as he said he were a-goin' to stay," she said, "'cause he never let go onest he tuck er grip, but what he sawn an' hearn in thar never leff him, an' he worn't never wuth nothin' no mo'."

"It promises well," and Mr. Henshaw's voice roused Jerry from his dreams; "the stream fell in here," he went on, "and the opening was enlarged from the top; see?"

"Yes," looking up where the marks made by the picks so many years ago were still visible; "but here come the men," and he leaned over the opening, that seemed to descend much more rapidly than he remembered.

The men came up; all of them were new men, anxious for the work, and anxious for the success of the mine in which they had shares: what were legends to them?

One after another they descended, Jerry leading the way. He was a man now, and educated sufficiently to be above all superstitious and ghostly fears, yet he looked back longingly to the light as they went down into the darkness, and for an instant held his breath to hear the water that dropped for ever—and what would he see?

"This is still the bed of the stream," Mr. Henshaw said, as they paused for the men to light the lamps, "and it turns to the left."

Jerry looked; surely it did, and he looked about him carefully for some mark or track—some little, beaten way that would tell that the place had been frequented—but there was not a sign: the worn bed of the stream held no marks.

"And they tunneled here straight in front of them, and up," Mr. Henshaw went on solemnly, holding up his lantern to prove his words. "They should have followed the bed of the stream."

"Shall we?" Jerry asked doubtfully.

"It will be best," was answered; "but follow very carefully, for being the natural opening they would have followed it as least expensive unless stopped by something impassable."

Jerry listened quietly; he could never have reasoned in this way; surely this was the man for such an expedition.

"I will go first," Jerry said, and no one demurred. The bed of the stream tended steadily to the left, dipping slightly, but lay several feet above the floor of the tunnel where they stood, so that a little climbing was necessary to put them back on this level they had left.

"They did not tunnel here," and Jerry lifted his light to show the scarred roof, when once more they were in the bed of the stream.

"Yes," Mr. Henshaw answered, "strange they should have left it."

On they scrambled, Jerry leading the way, and going most carefully; what might he not find?

Presently the light from his lantern struck against a wall,—the next moment it traveled indefinitely into the gloom!

He paused, and the men behind him stopped as if moved by machinery—they were not timid men, and were seeking their fortunes, but they stopped as one man and listened.

Was it water or wind that they heard—a sigh?—a cry?

"It is the echo of our own voices," Jerry said sharply—"listen!" and he raised his voice in a high, long cry: the men started—even Henshaw felt his nerves jerk a little as the cry went on, and on, and on—coming back again and again—fading, and rising, and dying like a sob! Then a dead silence fell, and Jerry leaned against the wall he had reached, unnerved and weak.

Was it a sob or a sigh that swept past him, or the last wave of sound from his own cry! It came again, and he started, lifting up his lantern—higher—higher! and he stepped back slowly, carefully.

"Stand still!" he commanded quickly, for the men were moving forward; then picked up a stone and cast it down in front of him.

The men all saw the movement by the flickering lights, and waited in silence. Would it never reach the bottom? then far off there came a sound, then another, and another fading down in the depths.

"Great God! if we had gone on!" and the men moved back hastily; but Jerry did not move, and Mr. Henshaw came to his side.

"Drop another stone," he said; "we can time it and judge the depth."

Jerry picked up a stone, and the man of business took out his watch.

"Now—" and the stone flashed across the belt of light and disappeared: down—down—down. What would it fall on—bones? poor whitened bones that would be crushed and powdered by this touch from the upper world—by this stone their feet had trod on years ago—ah, it struck them then!

"Very deep," and Mr. Henshaw looked up in the darkness to make his calculations.

"One hundred feet at least," he said; "a very good reason for not following the bed of the stream,—it fell here"; then he went back to where the men were grouped. "That echo was a fortunate warning," he said, "and we must put a railing there, it is too dangerous."

But Jerry had not left his position: the corner where he leaned was polished as by constant rubbing—the spot where he stood had regular marks worn into it; he waved his lantern out into the darkness, and there not four feet away was the corner of a ledge; he paused: was this Joe's path—did he daily cross this awful gap a hundred feet deep—jump across that space trusting to that ledge? He drew a sharp breath; he would not find anything of Joe's, they were in the cave at the end of the black tunnel down which he looked;—and the ledge he had seen must run along the wall, and be the path to the cave.

And this awful risk for gold!

Mr. Henshaw called him, and he went back to where the men were turning over sand and rubbish that had been brought in by rain and wind; and Mr. Henshaw peering at everything closely.

"Very rich," he said at last, "but worked most carelessly—most carelessly."

In a moment Jerry was at his side.

"They made a great mistake," Mr. Henshaw went on,—"they worked overhead and in front of them,—a great mistake,—all lies under-foot—all of it; rich, most rich!"

"Good enough!" and the men went to work more busily than ever to clear the rubbish away.

"It will be well to work this tunnel that is cut already, until we get the proper materials to sink a shaft," Mr. Henshaw went on, "but we must go down; for this vein, the richest I have ever seen," his eyes gleaming as he spoke, "widens as it descends."

Eagerly the men listened, and Jerry, with shining eyes, seemed to drink in the words.

"There are millions in this mine—millions!"

Jerry stood quite still, and his old dreams, that only last night he had laughed at, seemed to sweep over him,—and fill his brain as a mist: all his visions of piles and piles of gold—piles that would satisfy the nations, and stop all greed and longing! Gold should be a drug in the market: and what would the world do for a medium of exchange? In the latter days there was to be "perplexity of nations"—nations that could not buy nor sell to each other—nations reduced to barter! All the great exchanges in ruins; grass growing in the streets of great cities, and the nations spreading out over plains and hills, seeking for places to plant and reap!

Back, further still, they were searching into the tunnel, and Jerry followed mechanically, walking as one in a dream.

No wonder the devil had worked to drive men out from this great treasure-house; his power was to be taken away; his charm wherewith he charmed all men to sin and death—the root of all the evil and suffering under the sun; this gold for which men sold their souls—this thing was to be cast among them until it was like the dust in the road, and the chips!—yes, as when one "breaketh and heweth wood"—then the devil's power would be done!

And Mr. Henshaw turning over a rock in his hands muttered, "Millions—millions"—he must borrow money and invest in the venture; and he would write to Sue that soon he would be a rich man—a rich man! Then to Jerry—

"Your fortune is made, Mr. Wilkerson, already made," he said, and Jerry started from his visions as if some hand had struck him. "You have made a most wonderful discovery," Mr. Henshaw went on,—"and your townspeople, and all who come here, should be most grateful to you, for I understand that you entered into this scheme with great odds against you."

"I did," Jerry answered slowly, "but all is in my favor now"; then looking up, "Have you shares in this venture?"

Mr. Henshaw shook his head.

"I had nothing to invest," he said sadly.

"Let me lend it to you?" Jerry rejoined quickly, "and you can repay me at your leisure."

"Sir!" stepping back in his astonishment, "Sir, are you in earnest?" and the workmen looked from one to the other questioningly—then into each other's eyes longingly; they had shares, but if only they could double them!

"It is nothing," and Jerry turned away; "I have money my adopted father left me, and I shall be glad to lend it to you," and the men looked at him kindly: he was a "fair, square man," they said afterward; he could have taken double shares himself, but instead lent the money to a poorer man; he was a fair-dealing man, a man they could depend on.

And Mr. Henshaw felt his proper, middle-aged heart beating hard and fast under the shining seams of his coat: he could build a little house, and Sue and the children could come out! His mild blue eyes were strangely dim behind his spectacles as he looked after Jerry walking back and up to the black hole. A strange "mob-leader," he thought, a strange disturber of the peace,—and an honest Communist! Surely he was sharing his goods.

And in his report warmer words were said of the venture than ever he had said of anything in his whole visionless, unenthusiastic life; and the Board felt new confidence in Durden's, for every man sent out, from the keenest to the dullest—from the most enthusiastic to the most prosaic—all seemed to become imbued with perfect faith in the project, and in the young leader Wilkerson.

And now the stock ran up higher, and Jerry's man of business had orders to sell out all his other investments, and to put all the proceeds in "Durden's"; and Greg told his father that he could not invest too largely: and Mr. Henshaw bought and felt his life begin afresh; and Durden's rose to such a pitch of enthusiasm and delight that people almost cheered Jerry as he passed.

Eureka came over in a body, settling themselves anywhere that a house could be built; selling all to buy shares in the mine, and privileges in the Commune; and the doctor rode about among the sick, lending money to those who did not have it to invest—and watching Jerry's course with tired, kind eyes: and Paul, refusing to come back from Engineer Mills' house in Eureka, worked, and thought, and spent money and strength to build up Eureka—to outdo Jerry! Once more the "dirty little beggar" had the best of it, and had overcome him; but life was all before them yet,—and where would death find them?

CHAPTER V.

> "But O blithe breeze! and O great seas,
> Though ne'er—that earliest parting past—
> On your wide plain they join again,
> Together lead them home at last.
>
> One port, methought, alike they sought,
> One purpose hold where'er they fare,—
> O bounding breeze, O rushing seas!
> At last, at last, unite them there."

THE weather had held good as Jerry had expected, until the work in the mine was well under way; the railway also was near, for building on the plain was easy work; the town of Durden's was spreading up the mountain-side, and down, and out on the plain; and Eureka seemed dead, save for one grog-shop. Mr. Henshaw was spending most of his time now working on the dam that kept the stream from the mine; and was impressing on the Committee and the Company the grave importance of keeping the dam in perfect order. Once let that stream break through into its old channel, and the mine would be flooded to a ruinous extent: for now all the work in the mine was on a level far below the old bed of the stream, and all the new shafts and tunnels would have to be filled before the stream could find its old outlet down the chasm. And Jerry had made a speech to the people on this subject that had caused their pockets to feel empty, and their hearts to ache. For himself, he dreamed night after night of an awful battling with overwhelming floods of water; waking with cries and struggles that made Mrs. Milton announce to her gossips that "Jerry Wilkerson air the mos' onres'lessis creetur as ever wuz, an' if he eats nothin' or no, he's allers a-walkin' aroun' an' a-hollerin' in the night."

So things had gone until now the open weather seemed over; all the new houses, clean and tight, and ready for occupation, were covered with a light fall of snow: only a light fall, but to all weather-wise eyes the low clouds promised much more in a little while. The Committee added steadily to the stacks of wood gathered for the common good, and all the people did what they could in preparation, for it was prophesied on all hands that the winter, though late in coming, would be a hard winter—a very hard winter. A bright December made always a black January, the old people said.

It was Sunday, but Jerry had not gone to the church, as usually he made a point of doing, even if no better man than Dan Burk or Dave Morris was there to preach to him; but, instead, he was going to ask the doctor to come to Mrs. Milton; she was not well, and Jerry had volunteered to bring the doctor.

He had not been down that road for months, not since he had gone to offer his services, in case the doctor needed help. That had been in the spring; and since then a life seemed to have passed!

Now he walked slowly; it was cold and still, and all the town seemed dead: everybody was in the church, or shut safe in their houses; his own little house that he used as an office, but into which Mrs. Milton had begged him not to move until the spring, was shut tight, and looked desolate; indeed, lent desolation to the scene as he caught a far glimpse of it before descending the hill toward the doctor's. Down the long, ugly road he went, then turned sharply across the gullies and rents made by the snows and rains, up to the steps. Nothing had changed since his first visit there, as a child: all was the same—no fence had been built, no whitewash nor paint had been put on the house: as dark, as ugly now as then, only now seeming more still.

Slowly Jerry mounted the steps—slowly took his way across the piazza, and knocked at the door. A step came down the hall—a step that made the color mount to his face, and Paul opened the door. One moment they eyed each other, then Jerry asked—

"Is the doctor at home?"

"No."

"When will he come?"

"I do not know"; then more curtly, if that were possible—"I do not live here, perhaps the servants can tell you," and shutting the door he went back, and Jerry heard him call the doctor's man, then turn aside into the library. Presently the servant came, and Jerry saw on his face an anxious look.

"Doctor's been gone since yisterday—since yisterday evenin' late," he said.

"On horseback?" Jerry asked.

"No, sir, he walked off," and Jim scratched his head anxiously, "he hed his dinner, an' read a letter, an' walked off without sayin' a word—notter word; an' Mr. Paul's been here since mornin' nigh crazy to see him."

Jerry's face was as anxious now as the servant's; this was not like the doctor to go long distances on foot, and he asked slowly:

"Where did this letter come from?"

"I don't know; I couldn't read the mark of it, but it was black all roun' it: I had it a-waitin' fur him a long time, an' plum disremembered it tell he was done his dinner, then I give it to him, an' he took it like it were a snake, an' he went to the liberry, an' after that I heard him go out, an' he aint never come back."

Jerry leaned against the door-post.

"Have you told Mr. Henley this?" he asked.

"No, I aint, because when he come he cussed me black an' blue, but he never axed me nothin', but he's been a-stompin' roun' in the liberry consid'-abul."

Jerry stood still a moment, then drawing a long breath straightened himself up.

"Tell all this to Mr. Henley at once," he said, "and say that I have gone to hunt for the doctor—that I have gone to the rock over the mine,—the doctor often went there."

The man looked aghast.

"But all night, Mr. Wilkerson, all night!" he said.

Jerry turned away quickly, a nameless terror coming over him.

"You tell Mr. Henley," he repeated, "and tell him to come to the mine"; then he went down the steps and turned toward the old trail that led past Joe's house. This was the easiest way to the shelf of rock he wished to find.

What news had come in that letter with the black edges. What news had come to make Paul stamp and curse? only one person could touch them both. He paused a moment in his rapid walk: had anything come to that woman? Faster and faster he made his way up the slippery path, scarcely thinking what it was that made him come to this place. Higher and higher, while the low-drooping clouds seemed to touch him with their shadowy, cold hands, and in their folds he seemed to see that woman's patient eyes looking out on him—eyes that looked as if they had shed so many tears. So often had he gone over the few links of that story, that at last it seemed as if it were his own romance: had the one in the convent died? and what was the mystery that lay behind?

Up, past the ruins of Joe's house, past the broken tree where the doctor always tied his horse during his few visits—then beyond, and down the narrow path that led to Jim Martin's house. He remembered so well the first time he had come here to get hogs, and they had stopped to look at the stream that fell so far,—and on the shelf of rock they had seen the doctor. Often in the years that had passed since, Jerry had found him there, and many times since the opening of the mine, looking up from below he had seen the flutter as of a white handkerchief, and knew that the doctor was there. And now his instinct had brought him here first, sure that in any trouble it was to this quiet place the doctor would come. And the last time he saw him—the last time! He shook himself—what nonsense to think of a "last time"! he would see him many more times—could go to him in his success and say, "I love you, Doctor, and have loved you always, and you misunderstood the stand I took"; then the doctor would clasp his hand so kindly, and his voice would soften as sometimes in the old days it had done, and all would be well between them.

It was fortunate that he had put his hand on that boulder—else he would have fallen down to the mine's mouth!

He stood pale and trembling—what was missing? surely he had always stepped down just there—surely? Something was gone, and some low bushes and vines seemed to have been pulled up by the roots, and some of them were still hanging—still hanging!

He passed his hands over his eyes—his hands that trembled so and were so cold. But the weather was cold, very cold, and this freeze had caused the thin slab to fall; or perhaps the jarring of the work in the mine; something had caused this rock to fall—this rock that had been there yesterday: yes, up to the time when the workmen left the mine, for he remembered looking up and seeing it. It had fallen in the night, for the night had been such a cold one.

His thoughts stopped, his heart seemed to stop, and he leaned against the rock: something fluttered from one of the uprooted bushes—something that until this moment he had not seen against the whiteness of the snow. He pressed back against the rock—he looked up at the low gray clouds—looked all about him over the ghastly world—looked at everything save the white token which the sudden flaw of wind had lifted, and he could not look at that! He knew what it was—he knew whose it was.

Then he straightened himself up and walked steadily toward the loosely hanging bush, and untangled the handkerchief from the briers that held it: it had been a perilous act, for the bush hung so far over, but he had the handkerchief safe, and put it in the breast of his shirt slowly. He sat down for a moment, for his head seemed going round and round, and he wondered if it would be safe for him to go on. The path by Jim Martin's house was very steep, and with snow on the ground would be dangerous. He staggered to his feet—of course he would go on—how could he stop to question it! and he began carefully to find his way over the snow-covered rocks down the steep path. There was smoke coming from Jim Martin's house, and a face watched him from the window, but not for long, it was too cold to stay near an unglazed window. Down, still down; he had not travelled this path since he and Joe had come together, and had imagined the vision of 'Lije Milton. This day was just as that one had been, gray and cold, with the ghastly snow-clouds hanging low. But it was harder now than then to reach the mine's mouth, for now there were huge piles of débris all about, and huge timbers waiting to be put in place: and all was quiet with a death-like stillness, save for the wind that came in gusts up the gorge, and the stream that cried as it fell!

But the town, scattered up and down the sides of the gorge, seemed supernaturally quiet. He stopped to rest for a moment, for he was very tired, and the dizziness was returning; it was hard work climbing up and down with that slippery snow under foot, and he had come a long way round, and had come rapidly.

The last hillock of rubbish was reached, and he stopped to look: the black entrance yawned before him; the timbers lay about just as he had seen them the night before, and the snow had blown a little way into the mine: that was all he saw.

Nearer he crept, with ever an unanswered wonder in his heart as to why he crept—why was he afraid—why did he tremble.

One second's pause—no cry—no exclamation, only a deadening of every faculty—a stiffening of every fiber!

So still he lay.

Slowly, as one walking in his sleep, Jerry climbed down the rocks that slipped from under his feet with a noise that struck sharply on the silence; bounding down, and down as if they were alive; and one—he held his breath—how far it was rolling, how far—on and on until, oh, God! it struck him lying there so still, with a white face turned to the sky—struck him dully on the breast!

How Jerry crossed the intervening space he did not know—what need to know?—he was there kneeling, crouching, lifting the poor cold body, drawing it up into his arms—brushing the snow from out the silvered hair!

And the rock he took from off the pulseless breast—he would break it, he would grind it to dust, for it had struck his friend lying dead and helpless!

Dead? dead, and cold as the snow that lay in little lines in the creases of his coat, and in his hands some dry grasses, and a leafless twig—he had tried to save himself?

He drew the dead man closer with a passionate, remorseful strength; how had such an awful thought as suicide crept into his mind. The rock had fallen with him; he had been too strong for such a thought as self-destruction. It had been dark, and he could not see to save himself, and had caught only the little grasses and the tiny twig. Oh, the awful horror of that fall—falling in the black, lonely night! Had any cry gone up for help?—gone out on the wild winds, and none had heard it!

Jerry's face drooped until almost it touched the dead face resting on his shoulder: why had he not made his peace with this man?

"Oh, God—oh, God!" he whispered, "have mercy!"

He did not remember then that this man had let him go; he remembered only his love, that had turned to bitterness in his heart, and now had become bitterness that would never die!

He started a little, for something dropped on his leg: he raised his friend and stretched out his arm, leaning over to see: a dark stain, almost black, was on the sleeve of his flannel shirt, and on his trousers a smaller spot that shone red on the gray of the rough jeans. Blood—he shivered a little; then he saw the great gash on the back of the head and the neck. He laid the head again on his shoulder: why should he shiver at blood that had pulsed with this good man's life; the blood of the only creature that he loved on earth!

Again the blood dropped, and Jerry's weary, racked mind slipped away to the memory of the water that dropped in the mine,—the water they never had found,—that dropped with a catch in its fall like a sob.

Did Nature weep far away under the rocks; weep her tears in silence where no eye could discover them? weep out all her sorrow for the beautiful dead years that could not crown her with their glory any more?—the beautiful dead years that had spent all their life and strength for her. Did she weep for them in the darkness tears like the tears that kill humanity—tears that never leave the heart?

He did not remember shedding many tears; his mother had trained him not to cry for fear of his father, and he could not remember many tears. All his sorrows had seemed to lie still in his heart until they died.

He looked down on the dead face: this sorrow

would never die. His head seemed to swim a little ; the cold wind seemed to strike through him like a knife, and it was with an effort that he kept his mind from wandering. All sorts of vague dreams and half-memories seemed to float about him, and the visions he had lived among and loved through all the lonely years up on the trail.

Some one ought to come ; if the servant had given his message, Paul ought to come. Or would they leave him here to watch with the dead until his own blood was frozen ? Then his mind slipped off again to vague wonderings as to the news that had come in the letter with the black edges ; was it any trouble that had come to the woman this man had loved so truly—any trouble for her that had hurt him, and made him come out to the darkness and stillness for comfort ?

His head drooped lower : he was so cold and weary, and the women were all in the church, and the men in Eureka, and there were good fires in most of the houses, good fires.

What made him think of this ? he was losing his mind, and freezing to death, sitting still with the dead in his arms—freezing to death !

If only his tears could drop as the blood was dropping, maybe his head would not feel so heavy, nor his thoughts wander so wildly.

Ah, there was a step ! Surely no rock would roll else : certainly it was a step, and a hurried one : would the person come near enough to see him, or must he call. Call with the dead in his arms ? he could not do it.

He watched anxiously as a hat, and then a face, appeared above the nearest hillock, and Paul stood looking down on him.

For an instant that seemed hours they stared in each other's eyes—then Jerry's voice, all changed and hoarse, broke the stillness.

"I found him here," he said, "dead," and he

pressed the white face against his breast as a mother might press her sleeping child ; saying the words made it seem so much more real—made his mind come back from its desolate wanderings.

Then Paul climbed down slowly, and stood beside him. "My aunt who was in a convent died," he said in a slow, dazed way, "and the shock killed my mother, and I came this morning to tell him."

The words crept slowly into Jerry's mind ; the one who bound them had died—and her death had killed the one who longed to be free.

"They say my mother had heart disease ; and I came to tell him," Paul went on in a low, unnatural voice.

Jerry pushed the hair back from the dead man's forehead—of course, her heart was broken—broken long ago, her eyes told that.

"He got a letter with black edges," Jerry said, "your servant told me so."

A letter with black edges : the servant had told him also, but he had forgotten it ; a letter with black edges ; so his guardian had known the news first.

A strange change came over Paul's face, a strange change that grew in his eyes as he faced Jerry.

Always there had been a mystery about Paul's life that he could not solve, that had kept him watchful and suspicious always, and that now came up before him : why had he been given to this man—why had he never been allowed to go back to his mother for one day even ? And now she was dead, and this man, hearing it, was dead also ; a strange, unaccountable death—was there any connection ? What right had this man to die because his mother had died ?

Suddenly he became conscious that Jerry had laid his burden down, and stood before him with eyes that burned and glared on him, and Jerry's hands clutched his shoulders almost to pain!

"The rock fell with him, do you not see it ?" his voice rising to a sharp cry ; "look there in his hands where he tried to save himself—look!" and he pushed Paul back and stooped by the dead man—"look here in his hands, the grass, and the bush he caught hold of; it was dark, and he could not see," a pleading, soothing tone coming into his voice as he looked down on the dead face, "he could not see to catch a rock—he could not see," laying the cold hand down softly.

But Paul did not answer; he stood there where Jerry had pushed him, still and white, with a hard look settling on his face, a hard, evil look. This man he had looked on more as a jailer than a friend, had no right to die now—no right!

"You seem to have had that same thought yourself," he said harshly, but stepped back as he spoke, for Jerry sprang up tall and straight before him, with that strange light in his eyes that had gained for him the reputation of a man who would kill without thinking!

He could have killed Paul with one blow—he could have shot him, for instinctively his hand clasped the butt of his pistol, and he longed to kill him—longed to give vent to the wild rage that surged within him; but the old loyalty to the doctor held him still.

The gathered jealousy and hatred of all his life seemed tearing at his heart—he could have struck and beaten Paul like a beast—he seemed to hear the blows falling dull and heavy on this enemy—he seemed to see the beauty bruised and driven from his face! The love that he had so longed for all his life, had had been given to this false creature—this vile creature who now cast it all back in the face of the dead: who would now cast black suspicions upon a defenseless grave! Death was too good for this creature who trampled on a never-failing love—a love that protected him now, as it ever had done, from Jerry's anger.

Further back still Paul retreated, never moving his eyes from Jerry's face; his own face was white, and his heart beat tumultuously—had he roused a madman?

But Jerry did not touch him; not any more now than he would have done when the doctor was with them; it would be treachery. But he could tell him all the scorn he felt for him; he could accuse him of the lies he had loved and made to separate him from his only friend; could curse him!

And the awful words fell deliberately from his dry lips—the awful words that seemed to throb through Paul's brain, and to ring and echo through the cold, dead silence—would he never stop?

To Jerry his words seemed like blows he was hurling at this man—oh, if only they would follow him forever! "And I shall listen," stepping close to Paul who now was braced against the cliff, "I shall listen with every faculty I have, and if ever I hear a whisper that he died in any way save by an accident, I will kill you like a dog—I will beat and stamp the life out of you—now remember that."

And Paul answered slowly:

"There is Greg behind you, and he has heard you."

There was a sharp, short, gasping sigh, and Jerry turned on his heel to see Greg and the doctor's servant standing behind him. How the scene and his words might strike them never entered Jerry's mind; his only thought was to prevent any surmise on their part like that he had seen in Paul's eyes; and he approached them quickly.

"The rock fell with him," he said hastily, pointing up to where the fresh break showed clear on the cliff,—"see all the pieces about him, and the grass and twigs in his hands?"

Greg looked anxiously from one to the other as the eager explanation went on, then down at the dead man, and at the blood on Jerry's clothes.

"And he struck his head," Jerry went on, gently raising the dead man in his arms. And Greg could see, as Jerry held the body, how the blood had gotten on him; and the snow had gathered in the dead man's clothes—yes, the rock must have fallen with him. And now he could remember that one day he had seen the doctor standing up there and looking out; and he drew a long breath of relief as a dreadful suspicion lifted from his mind; a dreadful suspicion that Paul had seen, but that Jerry had not dreamed of. No thought of suicide had dawned on Greg's mind; what he had first seen, and the words he had heard from Jerry, had filled his thoughts with but one idea—murder.

And Paul had seen the thought; and Paul knew he was the only living creature who could refute it! But now Paul saw that Greg's mind was clear of the doubt, and on his face was only the deepest sorrow.

And Jerry, kneeling by the doctor's body, looked up into Greg's eyes questioningly. Then the servant told his story, making it still clearer to Greg that Jerry had nothing to do with the tragedy: and Paul found the black-edged letter in the doctor's pocket, a short note from Paul's sister telling the sad news, and asking that Paul and the doctor would come to her immediately.

"He and my father were friends," Paul said slowly, and Jerry stooped low over the mute, dead lips.

Then the servant was sent to bring help; and the three men sat watching with the dead.

CHAPTER VI.

> "Life crowded on him, and the days that swept
> Relentlessly all trust and love from out his heart.
> Where could he put his faith, where clasp a hand,
> That would not turn against him if occasion called."

"YOU will have to be very cautious and very watchful," and Greg paused in his idle whittling of the table; "Henley is bitterly opposed to you, and only has been held from molesting you and your plans by the positive orders of the doctor; I found this out when I was surveying in Eureka."

"Do you think Henley will use unfair means to hurt me?" and Jerry rose and leaned against the chimney.

Greg stuck his knife up in the table once or twice thoughtfully, not looking up.

"I do not like Henley," he answered cautiously.

Then Jerry put on his hat, and Greg went to the door with him.

"I will watch and listen for you," he said rather hurriedly, "and will warn you; but do not trust any one."

"Thanks," and Jerry stepped out into the black night and biting wind: he took off his hat to the cold air and drew a long breath—he felt as one standing in front of a desperate battle!

For, though estranged, he found that through all the doctor had protected him against Paul,who now stood revealed as an enemy whose strength and bitterness could not be measured. And the last time they had spoken together, that dreadful day down at the mine, he had cursed Paul with unexampled fury, and had done it for the sake of a man who in his death had struck him the cruelest blow that the most careful malice could have designed.

It had not been designed, he could reason that out; still his heart grew hard as he remembered, and said to himself, "It was only a piece of the doctor's cold, careful wisdom."

It had been a great pain to him that the doctor had died estranged from him, and that the people should know this, and so think it all right that Paul should arrange everything for the honoring of the dead; that even strangers should be called in and he shut out. It had hurt him deeply, and when after the funeral Engineer Mills had asked all the company to return with him to the doctor's house, as the will was to be read, Jerry had turned away, until stopped by a special message that he should be wanted. Then he had followed the crowd, angry when he saw them hustling and jostling into the empty house that to him was sacred; then crowding out again as the will was to be read on the piazza where all could hear it, he among the rest. It had been hard, and had grown doubly so toward the end,—almost too hard.

Twenty-four hours ago it had happened, yet Jerry could see still the gaping crowd looking black against the snowy background; still could hear them stamping with dull thuds to keep their feet warm—stamping that ceased as Engineer Mills read aloud a little note from the doctor, appointing that the chief man of the towns should read the will aloud to the people, and see that it was carried into effect honestly. And then the murmur that had swept up from the crowd—

"Mr. Wilkerson—Mr. Wilkerson!" Yes, he was the chief man of the towns—it was his glory brought him pain! It had seemed a most cruel sarcasm, but the bitterness of the moment brought him strength, and when Mr. Mills called to him, and the crowd parted to let him mount the steps, he went forward without a second's pause and joined the group on the piazza.

And the men on the piazza knew what was in the will, and watched him as he read—he could feel them watching.

It was short enough,—a clear, concise statement that the doctor had cast his fortune in with the people of Eureka and Durden's, and sincerely wished for their success and prosperity, in proof of which he now left all his property to endow a free school for the children of the miners of both towns, and a home for the widows and orphans of the same; that the tract of land he had bought, had been bought with this end in view: it was surveyed in suitable lots, that were to be rented, and all rents used for the purposes above mentioned. That trustees and guardians had been appointed for the property, the mayor, or chief man of the towns, being always chairman of the same.

That was all: not a word of the distrust the people had shown him; no mention of his difficulties and disappointments; a fair, free gift to the towns, and Jerry to see it given!

He had read it all through clearly, slowly, distinctly; and in the silence that followed, a silence so intense that he seemed to hear it, he said no word. He stood there white and still, and folded the paper carefully, and the crowd watching him seemed scarcely to breathe.

He would not speak of the misunderstandings and mistakes of the last few months, any more than the dead man had spoken; and the silence hung about them like death. Then there was a little movement, and he heard Greg speaking to the crowd and explaining what had been done for them—that widows and orphans would never suffer want again, and that education would be free to all. Then the crowd separated and went away quietly to their homes; and Mr. Mills told Jerry that he would send him all papers relating to the property and put him in communication with the trustees. Only twenty-four hours ago all this had happened. He walked wearily up to his room: his burden seemed too great. For some noble end men might strive like this; but he had let go his aspirations, and his highest motive had come to be the excelling of an enemy: could he sink any lower? There was one lower depth—he could sell secretly and leave in the lurch all who had trusted him.

He threw himself face down across his bed; he despised himself, and realized a dreadful self-abasement that galled him every moment he lived.

And yet, the highest he had known had let him go astray. His heart hardened within him: what use to love or trust? Old Joe, whom he had not loved, loved him; had been faithful to him. And this love he had won he had not cared for—and the love he had longed for, he had not won.

The only eyes he need please now were the eyes of the world; and in the eyes of the world money was the highest good: the world grown greedy and sordid in its old age. Money bought love, and honor, and power, and friendship, and souls, and bodies; and the free and enlightened Nineteenth Century saw more slavery and subjection than any other age of the world. And he, he could not serve, he must rule—he must have money!

And to-day a new fear had come to him, and he realized that the money he had so longed for,—the money that when he found it had seemed salvation to him,—this money had become a terror!

Paul Henley had that day gone East, and intended spending the rest of the winter there. Nobody could know what possibilities to Jerry lay hidden in this simple announcement that Greg had made to him. A few weeks or a month would not have been such a risk, for Paul would have been too busy settling his own affairs to trouble himself with the transactions of other people; but the whole winter would leave him much unoccupied time.

And yet what had Jerry done that he need fear being found out? He had only invested money that had been left to him,—this was all he had done. But he had no proof of this; he had not told any one at the time; he had not shown any one all the curious places in which this treasure had been hidden; for then a vague fear had possessed him that once let Joe's fortune be known, and claims would be put in against it as having been taken from another man's property; and this fear had proved true.

He had known that Dan Burk had at all times been aware of Joe's place of work; and after Joe's death he felt that Dan Burk watched him; what he did not know was that at one time Dan Burk had shared Joe's spoils, so giving him a hold over Burk. At the opening of the mine Burk had revealed to him Joe's secret, which revelation had confirmed his worst fears. And now once let Burk know that Joe had left a fortune, and he would either claim hush-money, so holding Jerry always in subjection; or he would tell the secret and ruin him. Jerry had not known all this at first, but he had known enough to make him very cautious, and he had had what was a still stronger motive for secrecy—a great longing for the money! And this longing was what had made a coward of him, and was the net that had closed about him.

A year ago he would have told the doctor what he had found, and have dealt justly by all; if Joe had done wrong, he would have righted it;—a year ago when no evil passions had been roused in him; when he was strong in his carelessness of men's opinions, and the world's honors.

Now—and his heart seemed to grow cold within him as he realized his own position; now, Paul Henley, his declared enemy, had gone to the East; what would prevent his hearing of Jerry's riches; what would prevent his searching and finding out all that Jerry owned, and raising ugly stories as to the sources of his wealth? A man who handled public money lay open always to suspicion and attack, and for a man in such a position to be discovered suddenly to have a large fortune, was a black enough story.

And Paul would sow distrust in the East by declaring Jerry a poor man; and distrust in Durden's by telling of Jerry's possessions. Paul would not now hesitate.

Jerry got up hurriedly and went to the window; he must have fresh air; he must shake off these dreadful forebodings, or lose his mind!

All his accounts with the town had been read to the committee, and put on record; would not that prove his innocence?

Dan Burk knew that Joe had been saving all his life; would not that be proof as to the source of his wealth? Aye, too sure a proof; a proof that would let in claims for all his fortune! The Durden's heirs who he knew were still living somewhere, and who had sold the mine to 'Lije Milton, they could present claims—and Mrs. Milton would own all that was left.

But now, when he needed all his strength and determination; now, when the struggle was growing harder, and the plot more intricate, he must not flinch. He could not go back; there was no retreat that would not end in ruin of character or fortune: there was no explanation that would not weaken his position most terribly. He must be careful hereafter to have a witness for every transaction to which he was party; to this extent he could and would guard himself; and, for the rest, must wait until the attack came.

This was all he could do; there was no avoiding the daily anxiety; there was no way of pushing aside this new fear; no way of lessening the strain on mind or body; and there was only one comfort he had,—it was the knowledge that failure would kill him!

The terrible tension of always watching—always fearing—always suspecting; the hard work by day and by night; the absence of any creature in whom he could confide, this would wear him out even if at the end he were successful: if he failed, then he knew the string must snap.

He shut the window slowly, as one who had faced and weighed all the dangers about him, and had made his own course clear to himself; had realized all to the end. There was no need of hurry even in the shutting of a window: his work and his path were plain before him, and behind him an immutable Fate born of his own deeds!

He stirred the fire to a brighter blaze, turned the lamp up, and sat down to his table, where lay a pile of papers relating to the doctor's property, which Mr. Mills had sent that afternoon. His heart throbbed a little faster when he first looked at the familiar writing. But he put aside the memories; they were not his any more, and it was with anger that he remembered the remorse he had felt when he found his friend dead, and peace not made between them. He had been only a duty to the doctor, not a love; the end proved this.

His mind was clear and quiet now, and he went over document after document, making notes and memoranda, then gathering his materials together composed a letter to his co-workers in this bequest.

He told them that having been educated by the doctor, he thought he could give them a clear idea of the system on which he would like the school carried out; that having taught in Eureka himself, he knew that this system would answer. He then went on to state his views as to the present and future values of the doctor's property in Eureka, including the shares held in the Eureka Mine; giving them the present condition of the towns, and their prospects; and the present and probable future cost of building.

A clear, succinct letter that caused a meeting of the three trustees, and many inquiries as to this Jeremiah P. Wilkerson. Inquiries that widened out until they penetrated the inner circle of moneyed men, and Jerry was reported as a man of solid means.

After this, Paul was asked to meet these gentlemen: after failing them many times he came at last, but with his temper unimproved by the examination of his mother's affairs and property. His sister Edith,—whom he found not to be his sister, but his first cousin, the daughter of the aunt who had died in the convent, and who had been adopted by his father and given the name of Henley; she had a large property—but he had little or nothing: further he found, to his exceeding disappointment and surprise, that he had inherited nothing from his guardian. He had not realized this before he left Durden's, for the only will found there was the one giving the Durden's and Eureka property to the towns; and a memorandum referring them to his lawyer in the East for further information as to his affairs. So Paul came East with high hopes. Of course there was city property, and high rents all to be his, and visions of himself as a rich man floated fair before his eyes.

But the visions had come to nothing.

He felt an unreasoning anger against the poor of Durden's and Eureka, who seemed to have defrauded him; for he found that the doctor had sold everything to buy the great tract of land which had caused such a stir, and had changed so many lives.

A wild, mad scheme, Paul called it, that had left him scarcely enough to live on: he thought that at least the doctor might have left him the management of the property, and the small salary which would accrue therefrom; but even this went to Jerry,—Jerry whom he hated, Jerry who had been so successful.

And meeting the trustees in this frame of mind, he had to listen to Jerry's letter, so clear and strong, and to praises of the writer expressed in slow, precise language by these mighty men, who seemed willing to leave the whole property in the hands of their "competent fellow-trustee."

"Whose wealth and business qualities," they said, "as well as the high esteem in which he is held in business circles, make us feel sure that he will manage this great property with honesty and skill."

Paul sat still; did he hear aright? Were these men talking of the Wilkerson whom he knew?

And he asked what seemed to them a silly question: "Do you mean the Wilkerson from Durden's?"

The three old men looked at him from over their glasses, and the eldest answered:

"Of course, Mr. Henley; the same Mr. Wilkerson whom your guardian educated; you must have known him all your life: the same Mr. Wilkerson of whom Mr. Charles T. Greg, one of the most solid men in the city, speaks in the highest terms; of course you know him, this man who has risen from the people to the highest respect and esteem, and whose success,--material, moneyed success,—is well known on Wall Street."

Jerry Wilkerson in Wall Street—Jerry Wilkerson a moneyed success—Jerry Wilkerson indorsed by a man like Charles Greg! His guardian had told him nothing of this—Jerry had not whispered it. And Paul felt himself in the heart of a mystery, and walked home slowly, and questioned Edith Henley closely as to all she knew or heard of Jerry. Then to Mr. Greg—then to Wall Street—day after day following closely in the track of his successful rival. And as he went the mystery deepened: it took him a long time, for he had to seem to know it all, and so had to grasp a few facts before he could pretend with any success. He was several minutes in placing the "Mr. Gilliam" spoken of with such respect; the "Mr. Gilliam" who had requested Mr. Greg to give his adopted son Wilkerson unlimited credit, and who had paid all notes and bills with remarkable promptness; and Mr. Greg had been very sorry to hear of his sudden death.

Old Joe Gilliam! the surprise was too great, and Paul had to remember suddenly an engagement, and was obliged to leave Mr. Greg.

"Yes, Gilliam's death had been sudden; but he would call again if Mr. Greg would allow him."

Old Joe Gilliam giving Jerry unlimited credit—and Paul walked three blocks in a driving snow-storm before he took in fully this piece of information, or remembered that there were such things as cabs.

And from all he could hear, Jerry had not spared money. Edith spoke of him always as a rich man, and represented the doctor as looking on Jerry in the same light.

"The doctor said Mr. Wilkerson was already rich, and would be in time among the richest men in the country," Edith said one day, but she did not look up from her embroidery, so did not see Paul's face; but a valuably-hideous cup fell from a stand with a little crash as she finished, and she wondered that Paul seemed so angry about it, and swore so openly as he picked up the pieces. Paul had lost some of his polish in the West, and it grieved her.

Paul's life, meanwhile, was becoming almost unbearable; he realized his inability to cope with Jerry, and had not only to listen to commendations of him whenever his name was mentioned, but was allowed to see that some of the attention he received was due to his supposed brotherly connection with Jerry, whom people imagined he must love, as they had been educated by the same man. And he had to bear in silence, day after day, all the slow suffering born of his hatred for this man; suffering that can not be measured,—can not be equaled: the suffering born of hatred is the only suffering for which there is no balm!

It was working through all his nature, this hatred; a dreadful corroding rust that was destroying his heart and soul; that turned his blood to gall. And his anger grew deeper when he heard Isabel Greg's name coupled with Jerry's, and the invariable comment—"Of course the Gregs will forward the match, as Mr. Wilkerson is so rich."

So rich! and nobody in Eureka or in Durden's had heard a rumor of it!

And he would sit for long hours pondering on this strange revelation. If it had been a moderate sum that was named, Paul could have understood how old Gilliam might have saved it; but when he heard of "unlimited credit," and heard Fred Greg tell with much admiration of the "plucky way in which Wilkerson had run up the Durden's stock," and of the "large amount he carried," the question became one that Paul could not solve.

Where had this money come from? Jerry had been decently dressed always, and never had seemed to have anything to do but to study and read in the doctor's library; and Paul had come to know, somehow, that old Gilliam supported a poor woman in the village, instead of paying the doctor for Jerry's education. And until now these things had never seemed strange to him, now when from a distance he looked back and saw the great difference there had been in Joe's action toward this boy he had picked up, and the actions of his class toward even their own children: of course Joe must have had money to be able to do all this, yet this had never occurred to Paul before.

But this fact, having been established in Paul's mind, did not advance him in the least in the solving of the problem as to where Joe got his money.

He could not remember that he had ever heard Joe spoken of either as a miner, or a special worker of any kind; indeed, as he looked back he found that he had never heard anything of Joe Gilliam except that he had found Jerry lying on the trail half dead, and had adopted him. He had accepted old Gilliam as one of the facts of the place; something that had been there always—had been there even before the doctor moved there, which seemed to Paul like some event back in the middle ages.

Then his thoughts would slip away to the strange features in his own life. He had found no papers to tell him anything, and if any ever had existed they had been destroyed most carefully. In the doctor's possession he had found two pictures, one that he recognized as his mother, only younger and fairer than ever he had known her; and the other not so regularly beautiful, but a brighter and more girlish face, and on the back the name "Edith Henley"—this was his aunt then, Edith's mother who had died in a convent.

He had put the pictures aside, unable to understand how they had come into the possession of his guardian; photographs might have been explained, but carefully executed miniatures told a different story; his own banishment to the care of this same man had puzzled him always, especially when he remembered his mother's tears, and his father's stern, harsh orders; stern and harsh even though he was dying.

He hated mysteries, and would sigh most impatiently; then return on the old track—"Where had Jerry gotten his money?"

He became quite friendly with the Gregs, almost intimate; he won the entire confidence of the three trustees of his guardian's property; then by a free use of the doctor's and Jerry's names, and by means of Mr. Greg's patronage, he won his way gradually among the directors of the "Eureka, Durden's, and the Great Western Railway," and at last fixed his certain hold on the "banker and broker" who had Jerry's interests in hand. It was a great discovery, and Paul drew a long breath when accidentally he made it; and instantly determined to lengthen his stay in order to follow it up.

A keen, cautious business man, no cleverer man in the city; and Paul put his own affairs into his hands immediately. Daily meetings and conversations ensued over proper investments. Jerry was not mentioned, but Durden's stock was, and after many discussions, during which Paul let fall many dubious hints and candid fears, he allowed his new friend to invest for him in Durden's.

"But hold it lightly," was Paul's parting injunction, "I must watch and be more certain before I carry Durden's as steady weight." Then he went away, and the disinterested broker turned over all his own Durden's stock to Jerry, writing to say that he had obeyed his orders to take any Durden's that might be on the market, especially as it had still an upward tendency.

And Jerry, under the steady pressure of his daily work, that seemed to gather force and velocity as the days went on, listened and watched with strained attention for every sign that might tell of Paul: listening with painful eagerness to any word that concerned him or his work; and felt that a fortunate chance had put him at Mrs. Milton's, where he could hear every rumor or surmise about every creature or affair in both towns; could, as it were, feel the pulse of the community without ever seeming to do so, or to wish to do so. And when the letter came from New York telling of the increased amount of stock that had been taken for him, with the further information that Durden's was on the rise, he drew a long breath of relief, for it seemed that he had not been injured as yet: and he went about his increasing work with a better hope.

CHAPTER VII.

> "But at the last
> A great contempt and hatred of them took me,
> The base, vile churls! Why should I stain my soul
> For such as those—dogs that would fawn and lick
> The hand that fed them, but, if food should fail,
> Would turn and rend me?"

AND this hope was a godsend to Jerry.

The autumn had been late, allowing everything to work prosperously, and encouraging Jerry to believe that he was destined to succeed; but following the favorable December had come weather that was unprecedented in its severity. The snow-falls had been so heavy and so continuous, that all available labor had to be put to the work of keeping the gorge clear; else, who could estimate the danger to the lives and property of the whole town. Only once since Durden's had been settled had there been such a winter, and then many lives had been lost of people who lived in the bottom of the gulch; so that after that the people had built in sheltered places only, where great bodies of snow could not slide down on them from higher points. But during all the safe years that had followed, this precaution had been forgotten, and now the houses were everywhere, and the danger was great.

"It were the awfulest time I ever seen," and Mrs. Milton finished her relation of woes with an ominous shake of the head, "an' many a pore creetur worn't never dug out tell way in the spring; an' the Lord hev mussy fur the water thet come down when the snow melted!"

And Jerry listened with a heavy heart, and urged

Mr. Henshaw and the men on to every exertion possible, to make the place safe.

And still the snow fell.

The work on the railway had been stopped, and the workmen had gone back over the mountains ; the men had been taken from the mine, so that the work there was at a standstill, and no dividend could be declared ; money was scarce in the treasury ; wood was getting low : there was no doctor in either town to attend the sick, and no priest or minister of any kind to bury the dead. Colder and darker the winter settled down ; each hour drawing things nearer to desperation—each day coming as a freshly armed enemy !

So quietly the danger had crept upon him that Jerry did not realize it was a danger. So many things culminated so silently ; the continued snow that stopped all communication with the outside world ; the stopping of work in the mine that caused the dividend to be postponed ; the emptiness of the treasury that the dividend would have filled ; the stacks of wood that were not sufficient to meet the extraordinary run on them ; the public store of meat and meal that could not be replenished because the roads were blocked. Who could have foreseen all this—who would have realized it until it was too late.

Jerry was appalled, but he gave no sign ; instead, he made as if he did not hear the murmurs that at first were disjointed, but that now were growing more and more continuous : he made superhuman efforts to rectify things and to satisfy all wants ; but he would hear no murmurs.

He grew thin and white with the dreadful strain, and his eyes shone with an unnatural luster.

Suppose the people should revolt—should throw all their shares on the market !

He ground his teeth : a sudden fierce anger, that was like madness when it seized him, swept over him when he remembered that these ignorant creatures had it in their power to ruin him ! And as he heard the sullen grumbling grow louder, and knew that insolent words were said for him to hear, he longed to beat and stamp upon them, and to drive them from the town : and his anger grew almost more than he could bear !

At last there came a break in the clouds, and for one week no snow fell ; this gave some hope, and the discontented murmurs were lessened somewhat.

A party went out to hunt, that the people might have fresh meat ; another party went after wood, and those who stayed at home spoke cheerfully of spring.

Two weeks without snow : and Jerry asked Mrs. Milton, in a half-frightened way, if she thought the winter had broken ; and hardly dared ask the question, lest the snow should begin again.

At the end of the two weeks Mr. Henshaw advised that the men be put to work on the dam before any snow melted, as when this happened it would be too late to help matters. Jerry agreed with him, and put the matter before the Committee, and for the first time since he had been their leader, he met a repulse. He had expected it, for he knew that the men thought the work in the mine would now be resumed, and a dividend declared : nevertheless, just at first it gave him a shock, then his accumulated anger flared up!

How dared they oppose him—these ignorant fools ! and he rose to his feet with a light in his eyes that made the bravest man there wish himself out of the difficulty.

With his hands in his pockets, he stood for a moment looking coolly and scornfully over the crowd. Men grown gaunt and white during the long, hard winter for lack of proper food and warmth : men of desperate characters and fortunes who had come to Durden's expecting immediate wealth : disappointed men who had grown sullen and hungry and were not to be tampered with lightly.

But Jerry was more desperate than they ; he had more at stake : to them it was a chance speculation only, that had not answered their expectations: to him it was success or disgrace—it was fame, fortune, life,—or death!

Slowly, and in a voice that showed the restraint under which he was holding himself, he began his speech. He reminded them of how this venture had come to life and been carried on; how he had built up the town of Durden's and had had the railway extended: how they had been cared for and helped through the hardest winter ever known in that country: how the Eastern shareholders of the mine had consented that the work might be stopped if the miners were needed to work for the protection of the town.

"And now, when the winter is breaking," he went on, raising his voice, "when the time has come to make the thing pay,—to save the thing from destruction, you stand back like fools and refuse to work!

"Protect the mine by a week's work, then work it so that a dividend can be declared. You know, as well as I do, that to-day this town is in better order, and the people more free, and more justly dealt by, than in any other mining town in America. You know that as long as the present government of this town continues, things will go on as prosperously as now; but change it, and what will be the result? With the entrance of the railway the place will be flooded by a mob of 'placer miners'; the Eastern shareholders will look only to their own interests, and you will lose all the work, and much of the money you have invested in Durden's. I say that if you change the present organization you are fools; I say that if you do not make the mine safe, you are fools. You can shoot for these words, but so can I: it will not pay, however, and you will not do it.

"Now, I want you to think of two things: first, without a strong government the railway will ruin us; second, that unless twenty-five men are at work on that dam to-morrow morning, I wash my hands of this whole business,—I will resign every position and leave Durden's to-morrow!" and he took up his hat and walked down through the crowded room, where a way was made for him, and out of the house.

He had made a desperate move, and how would it be taken? Every nerve was quivering, and he strode through the snow to Mrs. Milton's house, scarcely heeding that he did not follow the beaten track, made safe but hideous by ashes being sprinkled on it. Even down to so small a matter as this, he carried his rule: one woman had slipped on the ice and broken her arm, which Jerry could set but very indifferently; and after that each householder had to save ashes, and sprinkle the pathway for a certain distance.

Young Greg had watched with wonder the way in which Jerry controlled these people, who were many of them no better, nor more educated, than beasts. What was the source of his power, and how had he won their confidence so entirely? At the time of the doctor's death Greg had watched for some outbreak; would they distinguish between Jerry's words against abstract land-sharpers, and the doctor? Would they remember that the doctor had indorsed Jerry and his plans, or would they remember only that he had left his money to benefit them, not once mentioning past ingratitude?

He had expected some revulsion of feeling in the people that would carry them violently in an opposite direction, and dethrone Jerry; but he watched in vain. The money had been left to them; a good man had vindicated his name and proved his interest in their welfare: this had been done, but the money had not come to them in a way that would arouse any enthusiasm. The good they were to reap from it was not personal enough for the men to feel any special gratitude for it; and the women had no word in the matter. They looked on the will only as another "curus doin'" of the doctor's, who had been a mystery to them always. Indeed, on speaking to one or two of the men about it, Greg found that they thought that Mr. Wilkerson had done much more for them, and in the future would make the fortune of the town and all the people in it.

As the winter went on, however, and the cold grew more and more intense, and the prospect of work and money more and more precarious, Greg once more began to watch and listen anxiously.

It had become a great wish with him that Jerry should succeed, a great wish outside of his own interests in the town. Jerry had worked so bravely, and his success had been so unprecedented, that it had come to be like the watching of some exciting game of chance. He knew for what high stakes Jerry was playing: he saw that it would be life or death to him, and that the instinct of self-preservation inspired some of the moves Jerry made.

But beyond this, he had played so boldly and so skillfully, that sometimes when a difficulty was overcome Greg would draw a long breath, and wonder how long this man's highly strung temperament would stand the strain!

And as he sat in the council-room lately put up over Burk's shop, where the public meeting was held to call for men to work on the dam—as he, going early, sat and watched the gathering of the crowd, he realized that a dangerous crisis had come, and wondered what the upshot would be.

Greg watched anxiously as Dan Burk explained that the meeting had been called to hear a plan of Mr. Wilkerson's; that now the working season had come again, Mr. Wilkerson had something to say to them.

This was received in silence; then Jerry told them that he wanted them to work on the dam and so make it safe before beginning work in the mine: and when he ceased there was the same ominous silence—a silence that made Greg lean forward and listen and watch intently.

There was a little shuffling of feet—then a man rose

and said that work in the mine they were willing to do, for that meant a dividend to them and to the town, and money was needed badly enough; but that "work on the dam," pausing in his slow drawling speech to give full effect, "wuzn't wuther damn, an' all were free men"; then he sat down amid great applause!

It was then that Jerry rose and attacked them so unhesitatingly, and threatened to throw over the whole scheme. And when he was gone Greg looked about in grave anxiety: how would they stand this? But nothing was said, and after a little while he saw the new men, who had come after the town was well under way, rise one after another and leave the room; and from the window he could see that they had congregated outside, and inside the old inhabitants sat in sullen silence, looking at him rather suspiciously. But he did not move, and these also left the room one by one, making another group in the road, and Dan Burk, left alone with him, stroked his sleek, straight hair slowly.

"It'll bust all to pieces if Mr. Wilkerson gives it up," he said.

And Greg asked impatiently:

"Why do not you tell the men so?"

But Burk shook his head.

"They knows it just as well as me," he said, "an' they aint agoin' to let nobody talk no sass to them except Mr. Wilkerson: an' you kin rest damn sure, Mr. Greg, that if they want to go to the devil, talkin' won't stop 'em; just be sure of that," then he rose, and Greg followed him down the ladder to the shop below.

Evidently there was no way for him to find out the probable course of events, and having a letter he wanted to show Jerry, Greg turned his face in the direction of Mrs. Milton's.

It was a letter from his sister that surprised him a little. She said that they had seen a great deal of Mr.

Henley, and liked him better than at first; that he told them a great deal of the life at Durden's, and "spoke most pleasantly and affectionately of Mr. Wilkerson, whom," he said, "he had known most intimately; but laughed when we called him wealthy." And Greg was much puzzled.

Of the extent of Jerry's fortune Greg knew only what his father and brother knew, and this knowledge did not include Jerry's transactions with his broker; and to Greg, as to Paul, it had seemed a strange thing for a common man like Gilliam to have so much money, but it had never entered into his mind to ask the how of the fact. Indeed, life in Durden's was to Greg so new and unique, that he seldom wondered or was suryrised at anything: each individual enjoyed perfect freedom of action and thought, while comment and questions were careful and few.

Jerry was the only man that Greg could find, who was in the least hampered, and that only because he had made the people depend on him; and he, if he would sell the town to the railway and the mining company, could free himself and go East a rich man. But Greg could not imagine Jerry as doing this; his ambition was higher than the mere making of a fortune: he wanted to create a community—he wanted to control great interests—to be known as a "Money King"—he wanted to raise the people; and this last made Greg sigh. Still, he thought Jerry bid fair to win even with this weak philanthropical joint in his harness. Things looked dark just now, and Paul Henley was a dangerous enemy because an unscrupulous one, and Greg felt anxious; but he had great faith in Jerry's keenness, and power over the people. His speech that day had been dangerous, but it had dealt a telling blow in that it had divided the party that was against him. The old and the new had separated completely: the new were favorable to the present government, with much contempt for the old Durden's, of which they had heard much: the old settlers looked back angrily to the old times because they were learning to be ashamed of the old ways, while yet they had a weak longing for their license. But all parties were fully aware that there was no man in either town who could guide affairs as Jerry had done.

For himself, Greg felt that he had been cool to Jerry, and by his father's advice had abstained from being intimate with him for the present; but he could not help feeling a sort of pitying admiration for this man fighting so hard a battle, and standing so entirely alone! Yet sometimes, as he watched Jerry, his mind would fill with doubt, and his father's warning would seem wise.

Jerry's door stood a little open, and Greg walked in to find him seated at the table with his arms crossed on it and his head bent down on them. Greg stood quite still; the whole man and position looked so despairing, and he feared, as he had never done before, for the fate of the mining venture.

Jerry rose, not hurriedly as if he wished to hide his feelings and the anxiety that possessed him, but slowly as one who was thoroughly worn out. He had made a rash speech—had pronounced a rash ultimatum; what if he had been taken at his word? Where would he stand with all his fortune invested in the mine?

It would look like base desertion for him to sell out; indeed, he did not believe that he could sell the stock if the facts of the case should become known. His only alternative would be to sell secretly; in this way he could save his money.

And if the men did not come to their work in the morning, would he do this?

But now Greg interrupted him, and he rose wearily—

"I have brought you this letter," Greg began, ignoring all the morning's troubles, "because I can not make any thing of it, and I thought that you might read something between the lines; it is from my sister," and he handed Jerry the letter, opened at the page that mentioned Henley.

The paper was rich, and a little perfume seemed to float up from the folds of it; a faint, sweet smell that took Jerry back to the luxury, and beauty, and pleasure that he remembered as a dream!

He did not see the words just at first, but stood wondering at the past and at himself as he had been then. He passed his hand wearily over his brow, a gesture he often made now, and with an effort brought his mind back to Greg and the letter. He read it slowly once, then more carefully the second time, standing quite still in front of the fire, while Greg watched him anxiously.

"He is winning their confidence,—the women first, Fred and your father later,—in order to injure me," he said, then walked over to the window.

"How will they help him?" Greg asked a little hotly.

"He speaks of me in this way to them, so that when the time comes to attack me, they will be persuaded to his side, not looking for any personal motives behind his actions."

Greg sat down thoughtfully: this ridiculously simple solution was not all that Jerry read between the lines; of course Jerry saw more than this—he had not mentioned the allusion to his wealth.

Jerry handed the letter back slowly—he liked to hold it, it was so dainty and refined; and he watched it while Greg folded it and put it away, and caught himself wondering how it was he had such a longing for things so entirely out of his sphere.

"I am much obliged to you, Greg," he said, "for taking the trouble to bring the letter here, and for your kind interest in my small difficulties," then sitting down near the fire, "Has your father written you anything of Durden's stock lately?"

"Firm, with an upward tendency," Greg answered; "the report of Henshaw has made a great sensation; then the doctor's will has brought us into notice."

"I knew it would," and Jerry took a letter from the

table; "The trustees leave the whole matter in my hands," he went on, "asking for a yearly report of the property; they have empowered me to employ a secretary; do you know of any one who can fill the position?"

Greg shook his head.

"There is no one out here, but I dare say they can send you one."

"I prefer that they should," Jerry answered, "and send me a man clearly instructed to watch the destination of every cent," his voice growing harder as he went on, "I prefer to be watched in my transactions."

Greg moved a little; this did not have a pleasant sound; did Jerry think he could be attacked from that side by Paul?

"You have been watched in all your town transactions," he said, "you do not know how closely: Burk never allows anything to escape him; you need have no uneasiness about that."

"I do not know that I am uneasy," Jerry answered, "but I prefer to be watched, for then I can have witnesses always."

"Unless those who watch you are unscrupulous, and enemies," and Greg rose to go. He felt repulsed, and yet could not blame Jerry, for in the first instance he had turned from Jerry: but the man seemed so lonely that unconsciously Greg had cultivated a feeling that at any time that he held out a hand, Jerry would take it; but now he found that even though very lonely—even though entirely without friends, Jerry would not let him return to his old position.

It hurt him just a little at first, this stiffness, but when he thought over it quietly, he was not sorry. It was interesting to stand and watch this game as it was played; it was exciting even, but he did not want it to be any more so than at present; if he cast in his fate with Jerry it would grow too exciting, and he would have to stand or fall with this man. As it was, he was secure outside of Jerry's venture ; on his own land he had found gold, and besides his investments in the town and in the mine, he had this private vein that already paid him. He was doing well, and was glad that Jerry had withdrawn from him ; for now he was not only financially safe, but his conscience was clear, for he had made an advance to Jerry, and had been repulsed.

On the whole he was glad, and his father had been wise.

CHAPTER VIII.

> "Who bettering not with time,
> Corrupts the strength of heaven-descended will,
> And ever weaker grows through acted crime,
> Or seeming-genial venial fault
> Recurring and suggesting still!

THE daylight seemed to come reluctantly the next morning; at least so it seemed to Jerry, who was watching for it with a weary excitement. Sleep had been impossible to him: all night long he had lain with wide-open eyes trying to rest,—trying to push out of his mind all memory of the disasters that might meet him when the day dawned. And he watched the firelight that played on the wall, and the wan gray day that marked so gradually the square of the window.

The sky was leaden-hued, but no snow was falling: he sighed a little, for the snow would have solved this difficulty. But the snow was waiting for some time when he would not want it; and the issue stood before him unsettled.

He dressed slowly; he would give the men the benefit of every moment of time; and he ate his breakfast slowly—very slowly, by the light of a smoking lamp—for Mrs. Milton had it ready for him always before the work-horn blew; then slowly made his preparations for going out to the dam.

"Hev a leetle patience, Jerry Wilkerson," Mrs. Milton said, as she followed him to the door, "Orl the boys is been right smartly honggry sence the cole sot in, an' they aint got much onderstandin' no how; so hev a leetle patience."

Jerry felt that his pistols were safe; then lifted his

hat; but he said no word in answer to Mrs. Milton's exhortation, and left her watching him anxiously as he walked away.

"Techin' hisn hat fur orl the worl' like the doctor," she muttered, "an' a-killin' hisseff fur this pore trash jest like the doctor," and she turned away with a sigh.

Jerry found it a hard climb over the snow that was mashed into ice,—a slow climb that gave him full time to think, and now that the issue was on him, he could no longer drive away his anxiety: every step brought him nearer to this decision; every step brought him nearer to an awful temptation!

He looked down anxiously for the tracks that would show that the men had passed on their way to the dam, but the frozen snow held no marks. Beyond the end of the street he would be able to see tracks, but he would have to go to his office for something, and this would take him off the main road which the men would have followed; so that until he reached the top of the dam he could not know how the issue had been decided. He might have gone and looked for tracks, but this would have been too great an acknowledgment even to himself.

His office was dark, and cold, and dusty, and in one corner the things he had brought away from the old house. Dead memorials that had gained a human aspect from long association with living souls; things that looked as if they had regular habits, and were distressed by their homeless, useless condition; by being huddled into a corner with dust and spiders' webs about them. Did they suspect that they might pass into strange hands before this day faded?

He turned away hastily: if the men were going to obey his orders, they would be at work by this time; if not he would need all the day for the arrangement of his own affairs: and locking the door, he took his way up the gorge.

Up where the wind cut him more keenly, and the dry snow blown from off the higher peaks came about him in sudden swirls and eddies; up from the white valley that yet was checkered and smirched with the black marks of civilization;—up to where he could see so clearly the unsullied because unhumanized mountain tops shining white against the leaden sky.

Half-way up the gorge he paused, and listened intently; he heard no sound of pick or spade, he heard no sound of voices. More intently still, with his hand to his ear, and his head turned away from the wind: his heart sank within him—had they turned against him as Joe warned him that they would?

Up higher, and still no sounds nor voices greeted him; not even his own footsteps could be heard as he worked his way through the soft, dry snow: on the highest ridge that he would touch he paused again to listen; it was strange he could hear nothing,—the strokes of the pick would reach him at this distance surely!

The day grew brighter; the work-horn was sounding from the village, and he waited to hear it—it was his horn now! Clear and distinct, ringing up and down the white, dead stillness; and a little thrill of scorn for himself went through him as he listened. It was a small thing he had done in establishing that horn to mark the work-hours—a small thing that he had done to mark himself as victor and master: and he had worked,—secretly, of course,—to get the same horn, the very same horn he had heard that evening when he had been shown his place:—the evening when his old life died—died with such painful throes! Yes, it was small.

Then the last echo faded, and once more he plodded on; if the men were coming they would be at the dam by this time and he would not stop again. Steadily forward; and on the top of the dam he stopped: below him the small ravine into which the stream had been turned, a pile of wood lay ready for lighting, and kneeling in front of it there was a man striking a match, and all about it a mass of silent workmen showing black against the snow! He stopped still to recover himself, for they had not seen him as yet, and his heart was beating strangely, as with a halt in its throb; and his head seemed full of blood; he had had the feeling once before when he found Joe's money!

Then Mr. Henshaw caught sight of him, and hailed him, and Jerry climbed down among them. The fire was lighted now, and the men stood about it quietly. "We get to work none too soon," and Mr. Henshaw pointed to the sky, "this freeze will not last much longer; all indications point to a warmer change."

"And so we must work the harder," Jerry answered, selecting a pick from a pile near at hand, "what shall we do first?"

The revulsion of feeling had been great, and he felt weak from it, but he had nodded to the men as if nothing had happened, and now followed down to where the engineer thought the bed of the stream should be widened to lessen the weight against the dam. Besides, the stream would be so full from the unusual amount of snow, that it might flow over the artificial bank if room were not made for it. The dam could not be made higher in a freeze like this, and in any event this would not be so advisable as the other. So the work was laid out, and the men told off in gangs to work at different points: fifty men, Jerry counted, with a strong feeling of exultation; fifty men who yesterday had defied him almost!

He struck good blows with his pick; strong blows that rang clear and sharp: he led his gang in work, but said no word to them.

And when Greg came, he stood still and watched how Jerry took the lead even in this work; and when the short day was done, how easily he resumed his place as chief, giving his orders for the next day clearly and peremptorily, and directing the men who had worked to come and draw extra rations : then he gave his pick to be put in with the rest, and walked home with Mr. Henshaw and Greg.

Greg watched it all with the question ever in his mind "How does he do it ?" What was the source of this man's power over these men of his own class and standing ?

And with his head bent, and his hands in his pockets, he walked in silence, not even hearing the talk between Jerry and Mr. Henshaw, but wondering if his father's fears about Jerry would be realized ever.

This crisis was past, and Jerry lay on his bed exhausted. All day long he had worked as hard as a common laborer : after a long strain of responsibility suddenly increased into a dreadful anxiety and temptation, a tense state that had been relieved as the sudden snapping of a cord too tightly drawn ; he had worked as if his life, like the men about him, had in it only the questions of food and raiment ; and now the reaction was too great.

Through all the day's work the exultation had found vent in the quick regularity of his blows, and the short clipping of his words when he gave his orders : an exultation and relief that were over now, leaving him exhausted and bitterly humiliated by a realization that had been pursuing him all day, ever since he had mounted the dam and had seen the men gathered below him : a realization of himself that was new to him, and being new was still dreadful : a realization that had come close to him, and had wrapped him in its hateful folds. He abhorred himself, for he knew that if the men had refused to work, he would have sold out by telegraph, and at this moment would have stood free, and rich, and a legalized thief. He would have withdrawn from the venture secretly—would have escaped free with the spoils—would have failed to every trust in order to save his own money !

And as he dragged himself from the bed wearily,

the question came to him, would the greatest success, even, repay him for this? What would the greatest success mean—the success for which he found he would sell his soul—what would this greatest success mean?

He leaned against the chimney and looked down into the fire: the greatest possible success could mean only the gathering of a colossal fortune for himself—and then?

He turned quickly to the door; then he would have to hunt for somebody to love him—for somebody to put faith in—for a new level of self-respect—for a new ideal of a man!

And he went downstairs slowly.

Already in his pursuit of money he had lost his trust in every human creature with whom he had come in contact: and with a fortune in his hands how black human nature would seem! And yet, there was nothing left for him to believe now, but that money would compass most of the things he desired—would make him happy! And he would gather and gather gold until it would mean nothing to him,—and die. Aye, but he would leave his gold so that the country would ring with his name!

He ate his supper hurriedly, and walked rapidly to Dan Burk's shop where the public stores were kept; he had to issue rations, and to order out more men to work, for the wind had a new and sudden warmth in it that meant a thaw. Swiftly down the rough road, and in at Burk's shop, glad to reach the piles of meat and bins of meal—to reach and measure out the crude, ill-smelling liquor from the great barrels that stood in the inner room—glad to do anything, or go anywhere that would deliver him from this "self" he was learning to fear,—this "self" he was not brave enough to contemplate.

How he had fallen from his high ideals! how recklessly he had striven and fought for this money that had seemed to satisfy!—and he had gained it.

Gained it? he spilled the whisky a little as he measured it out by the light of a flickering torch the men held; and he knew that he had not gained the gold, but the gold him! It held him fast and strong, and drove him in ways he abhorred—held him down until his old self became a haunting spirit that made him loathe this new creature born of covetousness.

The men had gone now, and twenty new hands were coming to the work in the morning: his task was done, and he locked the doors and walked up the street with Greg, who had come to help him.

"The men have worked well to-day," Greg said, wondering if Jerry would allude to the crisis in any way.

"Yes," Jerry answered, "it is not often they are blind to their own interests," but that was all, and at Mrs. Milton's door he said good-night without the least suggestion that Greg should come in.

And Greg turned away provoked, yet he felt uneasy; he must make peace with this man to-morrow—did he care for him really?—strange what power he had.

CHAPTER IX.

"The weariness, the fever, and the fret
Here, where men sit and hear each other groan;
When palsy shakes a few, last, sad gray hairs,
When youth grows pale, and specter-thin, and dies;
When but to think is to be full of sorrow
And leaden-eyed despairs."

AND so the winter passed with its sufferings and crises; with its strained watching and excitement, and at last the weather had broken, and a chilling thaw set in. Worse than the dry, iron freeze of the mid-winter, this thaw seemed with its death-like dampness to search in among the bones, and to creep up and down the shrunken blood-vessels.

The roads were half-frozen slush, and the stream already boiled white and angry down the mountain-side, while as yet the upper snow had not begun to melt. There was a fascination in watching its eddies and foaming waves, and Jerry would stand on the dam and wonder how much higher it would rise when the real spring-weather came; and would the dam hold it?

Wretched weather that brought to the people all the ills with which cold and dampness could afflict. Many of the little children died, and the old people, and the murmur of regret for the doctor swelled and grew into rooted discontent. Mr. Wilkerson ought to send for a physician; and Jerry, who had appealed to his friends in the East already, made another statement of his needs, and asked that a clergyman should be sent also; for he felt a strange reluctance to read the services over the dead, which thing he had to do because the doctor had done it always,—a superstitious feeling about it that made him afraid almost, and a knowledge that he was not fit to do it. Yet, many, many times he had to stand in the rain-washed graveyard, and commit to their last resting-places the children, and the men, and the women he had known; had brought out there in some cases; had watched sicken and die with no creature near with knowledge enough to help them!

He could not do everything.

But the work on the railway was going on briskly now, and soon the advanced corps of workmen would be in the town, and the physician of the company be near enough to help them.

As yet, Jerry had heard nothing from the East that could in any way advise him of Paul's movements, save the letter from Isabel Greg which her brother had shown him. But he had not much time to brood over this now, for the mine occupied all his attention. Mr. Henshaw's work was thorough, but he worked with a deliberation that to Jerry was maddening almost. Mr. Henshaw could not realize the importance of making one quick dividend that would keep the people patient and fill the treasury; he had perfect confidence in the mine himself, and wrote it up most diligently; and the capitalists in the East were perfectly satisfied, but the people in Durden's, who were doing the work, began to murmur.

They were not in want, for the town supplied them with all the necessities of life, but they had no money: the chance laborers who were paid from the treasury had more money than the governing members of the Commune.

Jerry spent much weary thought on the subject, but could find no solution for the problem; if he advised these men to sell, it would affect seriously the mining stock; if he broke up the Commune system, and paid back to these men all they had invested, he would have to sell much of his own Durden's stock, which would look more like a loss of confidence than any other move he could make. Henshaw could relieve him from his difficulty entirely, if he would make a little haste, but this he did not seem to understand, and Jerry knew that if he tried to hurry him by telling him all the motives and necessities of the situation, he would not comprehend the position, and might kill the whole scheme with his slow, blundering, literal explanations to every soul whom, he thought, contributed one cent to the very handsome salary that made him and his "Sue" so comfortable. There would be no dishonesty in the quick dividend which Jerry wanted, but Henshaw's elaborate explanations would be sure to make it seem so.

Jerry thought of every possible, and impossible, plan to satisfy these ignorant people who were hampering him so cruelly. If his money had been an accepted fact among them, he would have bought out the half of every discontented man's share, and so have satisfied them; as it was he could not do this without explanations which would seem like fairy tales to these people, and more surely than anything else would ruin him. One last plan occurred to him: it was to double the working force in the mine, and compel Henshaw to be more active.

And he could get the men easily, for now that the terminus of the railway was so near, numbers of new men were coming in every day to ask for work; but how pay them? It came home to him with harsh force how foolish he had been to invest everything in Durden's; if any part of it were now free, or was invested in anything it was less ruinous to touch, he gladly would have withdrawn it all in order to pay these men and quicken the declaration of a dividend.

His only alternative was to borrow; again and again he had turned away from this thought, only to come back to it whenever a louder and more angry murmur came from the people. Borrow money to carry him over this crisis, and all would be well: borrow money in his own name, and buy out the shares of these discontented people in the name of his broker—why not? This would be easy, very easy; and he wrote to the broker the amount he wanted to borrow.

It took nights of thought, coming after long days of labor, to decide this, and he felt very weary when at last he wrote to his broker; and was in despair almost when he saw the rate of interest charged him. Still, to have the money was a relief, and the broker's name to shield him.

Louder the murmurs swelled; but Jerry waited; every day that passed without actual disaster in the shape of a strike was so much gained. Louder and louder, then quietly he stepped in and bought in the name of Mr. Glendale the half of every stockholder's interest in the mine: then made a biting speech about their cowardice and short-sighted policy; a speech that made every man regret his action, and on the first suggestion agree to advance all that had been paid them, that the body of workmen in the mine might be doubled.

And Mr. Henshaw was delighted, and promised to make his work still more sure and honest; with a doubled corps of workmen why need he hurry and so leave careless work to mar his reputation? This mine was bound to succeed, and with its success his name as an engineer would stand or fall.

So the spring days came and went, each one a little warmer and giving no sign of the late snows prophesied, but melting the frozen masses that had gathered during the winter: and the streams were many and unusually full.

The people in the two towns were quiet now save for the coming of the railway, and the rumor of a great excursion. For now the time was approaching when the Board of Directors of the "Eureka, Durden's and Great Western Railway" were to come out in special trains, and drive "last spikes," and make speeches, and spend money to make the venture better known. It was a grand affair, this railway, and must be advertised that in the future it might give grand results: and these great Directors must be entertained,—and the treasury was low.

If only Jerry had kept in hand old Joe's patiently gathered treasure—or if he could have been his own engineer and have declared a dividend.

But new hope came to Jerry in the news that more "Durden's" had been bought for him, as it was still rising, for this assured him at least that Paul had not injured his scheme as yet. So he borrowed more money and set about making the greatest arrangements possible to Durden's, for the reception of the coming magnates; and galvanized his dead enthusiasm to rouse the people to a more proper sense of the coming event, and to awaken in them the high hopes that he was now too weary to entertain. For now he felt that he was driven on and held up to his purpose more through fear of failure than through the realized value of what he was striving for. But also he knew that now for him there was no choice, for as he looked back, every barrier that had hindered his onward march seemed to have doubled in strength once he had passed it: what had been hard to pass, now became impossible to repass; and he saw with growing despair that there was no retracing his steps: his mistakes held him in worse than Egyptian bondage. There was no middle way for him now, the end must be either an absolute success, or an overwhelming failure; and even the *thought* of failure had become torture too exquisite to be borne; no toil that might avert this could be too hard,—no risk could be too dangerous that might gain success for him!

And two bands of silver came in the dark hair on his temples, and the light in his eyes had become an unhealthy glitter.

CHAPTER X.

" ' Waiting to strive a happy strife,
To war with falsehood to the knife,
And not to lose the good of life—

' As far as might be to carve out
Free space for every human doubt,
That the whole mind might orb abcut.'

' Yea,' saith the voice, ' thy dream was good
While thou abodest in the bud,
It was the stirring of the blood.' "

JERRY made a speech in which the people did not see the effort, and a small sum was gathered to provide for the reception of the excursion party. "What weuns eats ever day is good enough fur them, I reckon," and Mrs. Milton gave a dollar, "an' I'll tuck in three 'thout chargin' no bo'de," and Jerry telegraphed that the sleeping-cars must be brought the whole way.

He thought much on the subject, and knew that he would be doing well if he could rouse the people to the necessity of seeing that the strangers had enough to eat ; more than this was impossible, and he would not suggest even any further effort. So he made a list of the strangers coming, and put them about with the people according to the number they each agreed to provide food for ; then wrote a letter explaining as best he might the customs and resources of the place, and the type of accommodations that could be furnished.

And the Directors laughed, and prepared as for a great picnic. What did they care for the feelings of these wild borderers—feelings Jerry had used all his power to rouse successfully into a state of hospitality; what did they think of the eager expectation of making a show, that possessed the hearts of the Durden's people; what did they realize of the willingness to help Mr. Wilkerson, and the latent pride the people had in this man who was one of themselves, yet powerful enough to have influence with these "money-princes"; and further, how could they appreciate the precarious position of this young man, who not so long ago had moved among them as one of themselves, but who had to be now one of the mob?

They stocked their train with every delicacy; they carried a full corps of servants; they spent great sums in transporting, without jarring, much priceless wine; and put on an extra car for a few wives and daughters who were "ecstatic and wild to see the romantic western life; the dear miners, and the heroic women who were brave enough to share their frontier life,"—which was not frontier life, but hopelessly within the border for the excitement of Indians, or of anything more romantic than wild creatures and tramps. An old mining town that had been deserted and kept in the shade for twenty odd years—that had been given over as a failure until one year ago. Of course the frontier was across the plains by this time, and all the Indian agencies and reservations seemed as far from Durden's, almost, as the great eastern cities.

But these people from the centers of American civilization and luxury did not realize this: to them the South and West were unknown parts of the earth—the South meant oranges, and flowers, and "*Ku-Klux*"; and the West meant Indians and gold mines. And Indians were all the "*Last of the Mohicans*," and gold mines were beautiful grottos where stalwart men, clothed in red and blue shirts and spotless white trowsers, carelessly gathered shining lumps of gold.

And Jerry worked hard to make the town look clean after the hard winter, so that the excursionists would not be too much disappointed.

"My mother and sister will come," Greg said, "but against my advice."

"You may have my house prepared for them," Jerry answered quickly.

Greg shook his head.

"They must remain in the sleeper," he said; "it will be for two days only. I can not make them as comfortable anywhere as they will be there; but I thank you very much. By the way," pausing doubtfully, "Henley is come,—arrived this morning."

"Did he?" and Jerry's pen moved none the less steadily because the beating of his heart had doubled.

"I have not seen him," Greg went on, "but he sent me the news of my mother's coming; I believe he expects to entertain many people."

"Your people?" and for the first time Jerry looked up.

"Not with my consent," Greg answered, coming nearer this man who puzzled him so often, "you know that I do not trust Henley."

Jerry returned to his work.

"I think we had better make your house or my house ready for them," he said.

But Greg would not agree; he was sure that the car would be the best place for them. Then he left Jerry to his work, and going down the road met Paul Henley—Paul Henley who grasped both his hands; who was dressed as would be Greg's civilized friends, giving him a home look; who rattled off the eastern news; who was grateful to Greg's mother and sister for bringing his adopted sister out with them, and who was dreadfully anxious that everything in the doctor's house should be in proper order to receive them.

"I suppose you know that your mother and sister will stay with me?" he finished.

"No," Greg answered bluntly, "no, I did not know it."

"Well, they will," and Paul watched Greg keenly.

"You are very kind," Greg answered, his brown face showing more color than he would have liked if he had seen himself, "but I think they had better stay in the sleeper."

Paul laughed.

"Your mother's only objection to coming was her dislike to the sleeper," he said.

Greg walked on a little space in silence: he did not trust Paul Henley; he was angry with himself that he had not warned his family against this man; he was provoked that they should have agreed to stop at Paul's house, and he determined to make an effort to change all these plans. His house could be prepared for them, or Jerry's house—he would go and see Jerry about it.

"You have never met my adopted sister?" Paul went on.

"No," and Greg looked interested; he could not but look interested when a man talked to him of his sister.

"She has no notion of taking care of herself," Paul went on, "and could not have come unless with your mother, and she and your sister are friends."

"Are they?" and Greg felt that his plans were becoming impossible.

"And you had better come to my house also," Paul went on, "and stay while your mother and sister are with me, you can then see so much more of them."

"You are very kind," Greg answered, "but I have made other arrangements for them."

"The 'sleeper'?" laughing amiably; "that is impossible, for I promised your mother that so soon as they reached Eureka I should have them transported to the most civilized house in the place, and that you should come and stay with them; so do not trouble yourself needlessly, and deprive me of this pleasure."

"You are very kind," Greg said again, then turned off toward the mine.

What would Wilkerson say? was his first thought; then angrily he asked himself, what right had Jerry to say anything? No right in the world; and in his secret heart Greg knew that Jerry would not say one word; probably he would not look at him, but go on quietly with whatever he might be doing.

This was the sore spot, that Jerry could and probably would listen to his words of explanation silently, then quietly put him and his mother and sister aside with Paul Henley, and go on his own way.

And if Jerry did, what matter to him? he had not espoused Jerry's side to any extent; he had not become an intimate of Jerry's: his father had advised against this, and he had acquiesced. Still,—and Greg quickened his pace, and drove his hands deeper into his pockets: he despised Paul Henley, and he was learning to value strangely Jerry's approbation and good will; was growing anxious to break through the reserve and silence in which Jerry wrapped himself. And that this should be thus was the heart of the problem for Greg: why should this man be of any special importance to him? Jerry had no higher aims now than many men Greg knew, no higher motives,—why should Greg wish for his friendship? Jerry had grown selfish, intensely selfish. At first there had been at the root of his work the desire for the good of the many; this had been the enthusiasm that had set the work in motion, as well as the force that had been at first the motive power; but Greg knew that this enthusiasm was dead: how he knew this, or when this force had died, he could not tell, but the fact of its death dwelt with him, and strange to say, had raised Jerry in his estimation as a practical man! The loss of the higher motive that had seemed chimerical, gave the venture a solidity that enhanced Greg's faith in it, and increased his respect for Jerry.

It had seemed weak to him at first, this plan to improve a town for the good of the town's people, and not as a speculation ; to build up a community that possibly would help all, but positively would make the fortune of no one person : it had seemed wild and unstable, and a mere waste of energy : it was against the spirit of the age that was for monopoly, even though it might go hand in hand with the theory of the age which was for humanity. This theory was wrong ; it would weaken any man to help all about him, and to be helped in return. Every man must fight through his own life, and shape his own fortunes ; every man must run his own race and win his own prize ; this it was that made men of Americans ! The national creed that every man was free to run ; every man had equal chances ; every man could have all he could get and hold against the odds brought to force his gains from him : this made men strong and hard for the battle, and this was what had at last made him look up to, and respect Jerry ; this very power to take all he wanted,—to guide all to suit his will, and yet to build all on the fair foundation of the public good !

Greg was forced into admiration—Paul was forced into envy and malice.

And Greg went home angry with himself that he had not guided his steps better than to wander from under the shadow of this man's power. This man whose power was bound to increase because daily he was learning the motto of the Age—" Every man for himself." If every man stop to help his brother ; to 'pour in oil and wine' and bring him to a safe resting-place, who could first reach the goal ? who could do more than win food and raiment, if this were the code ? The creed of individualism can permit no such weakness as this ; the narrower the aim, and the harder the heart, the surer the success !

The creed of Individualism and the Creed of the Christ touch but at one point : " Thou canst not serve God and Mammon."

CHAPTER XI.

> "For every worm beneath the moon
> Draws different threads, and late and soon,
> Spins, toiling out his own cocoon."

DURDEN'S was in a stir, and pulsed and throbbed under its ugly covering of slush and grimy snow: Durden's had never seen such times and in its wildest dreams had never pictured such excitement.

A shanty had been put up in Eureka and called the "Depot," and one small locomotive had made the run over the road that was barely laid, and entirely unsafe. Still, the directors could not come at any other time, and they had made it quite plain that the salvation of the two towns, the mines and the railway, depended on their coming to see and to advertise things. So the track was laid, not built, to Eureka and on to Durden's, that the imaginary last spike might be driven by some portly director or his wife, or his daughter; that the reporters might be there to telegraph this wonderful town-growth to all the important daily papers; that the artists in the great cities might make the pictures of the event so that the people in the provinces might see it all in their illustrated journals before it had really occurred! All this was necessary to the success of the towns, and to the welfare of the railway: things must be advertised else they should die. Every one having been convinced of these facts, a great excursion at half rates was advertised, and a suitable number of the moneyed elect invited to go out and patronize this new town of Durden's, that was different from any other town in that it was founded and organized on the newest theories, and worked on the plan of pure equality, that had been the problem of philanthropists and philosophers through all the ages! So the newspapers said.

Alas! a town that had become a dreadful burden and puzzle to its author!

And Durden's, reading all this in Dan Burk's paper, felt very proud and important; and was fully prepared to patronize these "city folks" who were coming out to see this remarkable town. And Jerry was glad, for the people were much more willing to help in his preparations and plans.

The paths that answered for sidewalks were put in order, the houses were thoroughly cleaned, a new path was made to the mine, and on the few sunshiny days everything in Durden's seemed to be washed and hung out to dry.

All was moving smoothly, when suddenly the temper of the people seemed to change, and Jerry heard murmurs about spending so much money and about the dividend that had not been declared.

"Paul is at work," he said to himself; and the clew was put into his hands by Mrs. Milton.

"An' you hed better know, Jerry Wilkerson," she said, while putting his supper on the table with more than usual emphasis, "thet if these city folks *is* rich, an' is youuns' frien's, they aint agoin' to stomp on noner us, ner change nothin' in this town, they aint, if Mr. Henley as knows 'em do say it; an' you hed better tell 'em so, Jerry Wilkerson, or Durden's will."

It was after a hard day's work that this revelation, for it was a revelation, came to Jerry; and he did not answer the old woman—he did not wish to until he had collected his thoughts somewhat, so went on with his supper diligently, as if this were his reason for not talking.

"Paul Henley, thet were borned rich," Mrs. Milton began again, "he don't take on like he were too good, he dont; he jes goes roun' alonger orl the boys, jest fur orl the worl' like he were a pore boy too, he does."

And now Jerry did not answer, because he saw that it would do no good. Paul Henley had produced his impression, and these people were not capable of receiving more than one impression at a time; and this silence was so often his way with Mrs. Milton that she scarcely noticed it.

It was her method to give her opinions and advice while Jerry was busy with his dinner or his supper, because, as she would explain—

"It's a good time to say youuns' say, 'cause thar aint the man livin' as'll stop eatin' to jaw back; jest you bet on that," and Jerry often verified her theory, and was glad to do it on this occasion; and without reply went away to the issuing of rations, and the doing of numberless odd jobs that were crowding on him more and more as the time drew near for the great excursion.

He could not stop to think now, it was impossible to pause long enough to gather together his thoughts; his thoughts that, notwithstanding his preparation and expectation of Paul's attack, were scattered wildly by the strangeness of the quarter from whence it came. He held the clew, however, to Paul's course of action, and to that extent was more safe; and while he worked even though with both mind and body, directing, measuring, counting, weighing, his scattered forces gathered themselves about this new center, and worked out counter-plans.

Mrs. Milton's words had revealed much; had connected much for him; had given him the key to Paul's intentions. Paul was trying to undermine him in the eyes of the people by telling them that the laws of the town would bind them, but not Mr. Wilkerson's rich friends. Not a very clever plan, Jerry thought, and one easily foiled. Next day at the meeting of the town committee he would move that all the laws of the Commune should be strictly enforced during the stay of the strangers. This would open the people's eyes: and the ease of his counter-move made him suspect that this was a ruse to throw him off his guard; Paul's plans must be deeper than this.

On the morning of this same day Greg had told him that his mother and sister would stay with Henley, that the arrangement had been made before Henley left New York: and Jerry had answered that they would be more comfortable there; but that he would not be able to see anything of them; then had gone on with his work in so undisturbed a way that Greg—though to some extent he had expected just this action—felt a little angry.

His people had been very kind to Jerry, he remembered, and Jerry ought to be more troubled about not seeing them: still, if he were not, it was not Greg's place to remonstrate.

Then Jerry had heard of Paul and Engineer Mills putting in order many of the empty houses in Eureka, and arranging them as lodgings for the excursionists. Paul was unusually energetic and interested; and Jerry listened and watched closely.

His move in the committee, that the laws be strictly enforced during the stay of the strangers, was warmly seconded and carried; no drink was to be allowed except beer, and men who got drunk over in Eureka must stay there until they recovered. No drunkenness nor rioting was to be tolerated in Durden's.

And Jerry walked home wondering what he would hear next. And he had not long to wait: the next day the news came to him that Paul had repaired and improved Dave Morris's old shop in Eureka, and had stocked and opened it as a "Bar-room and Eating Saloon." Dan Burk told him of it, and had added that his wife was to attend the eating-room, and a new man from the East was to keep the bar.

"It's to be fine," Dan added, "and good vittles for mighty little."

"That is economical at least," Jerry had answered, while his mind began to follow Paul's plans.

A very sure game for a man whom Greg had described as unscrupulous. And to put Mrs. Burk in the front of his venture was a clever move: as the standard of Durden's went, Mrs. Burk was a society leader; she could read and write, and took much to herself from the fact of her superior education, and the people regarded her as a person of some importance.

In the course Paul was pursuing, a woman was the best tool. Mrs. Burk's tongue was endless, which was one good way of advertising the "saloon," besides being most admirable for the spreading of any reports Paul might wish to have scattered abroad: added to this, she would make the place attractive for women, and the men would soon follow.

Jerry pushed the fire a little uneasily as he sat thinking: he had been such a fool; such a fool to banish so great a power as drink; such a wonderful factor as it was in keeping the people satisfied and unquestioning: such a wretched fool! Joe had warned him of this—wise old Joe had said that these people wanted nothing so much as corn bread, and dirt, and whisky, and that they would have it. And in the silence words came back to him, words he had heard that day, but that he had not heeded properly until now. A man had said "Mr. Henley aint above ownin' a shop, nor sellin' whisky,"—and Jerry had passed on, not seeming to hear.

And he understood it all, and could see the poison working in the minds of the people.

If only this wretched excursion were over, and he left free to counter-mine, he could play the same game: he would work things round until the people would not be able to understand anything but that things had changed; he would do anything, he would put half he owned into the town in order to win the game against Paul.

He paused suddenly in his thinking, and pushed the fire until it blazed and roared up the chimney: there was one easy way out of it all; and he leaned back in his chair with his hands clasped behind his head.

Run the Durden's stock up as high as possible, then sell out quietly from the whole affair. He could retain power long enough to accomplish this; and do it while Paul was involving himself in new ventures and expenses in order to undermine him: sell out quickly and leave Paul neck-deep in a troublesome speculation.

He laughed a little, and turned the thought over in his mind: it did not seem so black now as it had done. The people no longer cared for him; already they were becoming adherents of Paul Henley's; and they were not worth that he should sacrifice anything for them. For years and years the doctor had been their friend, and in a week they had all turned away from him: why should he think of them? True, they had invested in the town and in the mine because he had told them to do it; but in return he had kept them sober for months, had given them more comfortable homes and more decent habits than they had ever known: and besides, there was no reason why either the town or the mine should fail because he withdrew.

Give up the mine and Durden's—give up his millions that lay hidden down there under the earth where Joe's patient feet had trod day after day to amass the gold that now, strangely enough, had gone back into the mine—had all gone back to try to bring out more!

Strange, very strange! if he had thought of this he would not have invested all in the mine—Joe had warned him.

He got up and walked up and down the room once or twice: his pulse was beating faster, and he felt the blood burning in his face.

Give up Durden's and not make his millions—give up Durden's and his power and position: go away from the only place and people he had ever known; give up his individual glory and his little kingdom; admit himself foiled, and his scheme a failure,—leave Paul victorious even though the victory should be death!

He shook his clenched fist.

Never!

He would rather be buried under the ruins of the fabric he had created, than lay down his arms!

How foolish this was! Who would care if he failed and died; who would count him a hero for standing by this venture; who would mourn his loss?

To die now would be like dropping a stone into the water—one little swirl of the tide, then gone! And why should he hate Paul—Paul who had been the spur and power of his life. If he had never known Paul as a rival, as an enemy; as a creature who took and held the love and place he had longed for, he would have been an idle dreamer still, planning impossible schemes for the regeneration of his class. He would never have gone East—never have compelled the doctor to go there: and so to wrench the hope out of two lives?

Never have left Joe to go on that wild adventure, whatever it might have been: that cost him his life?

Never have found the money: nor invested it so wildly?

Not have lost his only friend and protector: nor involved himself in this net that was closing about him—binding him until he writhed and bled. Never have lost the peace and quiet of his days: never have fallen so low as he was now—now when he was willing to stoop to anything—to sacrifice anything to make and save money!

But for Paul he would have still retained his self-respect.

He laughed.

Now he was a fool. He was not obliged to make a decision at this moment: he could run up Durden's stock, and the manipulation would help him in any case; and he would write to his broker immediately.

It was a relief to have something to do, and he sat down and wrote rapidly. A peremptory letter it was, directing that every known mode should be pursued that could force the stock up: that his name and his credit should be used in any way and to any extent to further this end,—and after this Mr. Glendale was to stand ready to sell at a moment's notice—he would telegraph his orders.

And the broker read the letter with a satisfied feeling when he remembered that he had sold his Durden's stock to his client; and being uninterested, calmly began to make preparations to execute these very doubtfully wise orders.

CHAPTER XII.

> "We talked on fast, while every common word
> Seemed tangled with the thunder at one end,
> And ready to pull down upon our heads
> A terror out of sight."

DURDEN'S stood on tiptoe!

Preparations had been made that seemed grand and luxurious in the eyes of the town: the Town Committee had met and elected a "Committee of Arrangements," while the whole population turned out as a committee of reception.

As there was not even a shanty in Durden's which could be used as a station, Durden's had built a shed; a shed that meant money, as labor and lumber were expensive: a shed that, Durden's magnanimously announced, would not cost the railway company anything! A shed that Durden's was proud of in a reckless, careless, bountiful sort of way: when they did things in Durden's, they did them "rale han'some!"

Many had gone to Eureka to see the entrance of the grand train—the grand train that was obliged to come in very slowly on account of the insecurity of the track: these people intended to board the train, if possible, and come back as an escort of honor, and receive the guests in grand style under the Durden's shed, where the great body of the town's-people waited in hungry excitement for this greatest event of their lives.

Two nights before, a light snow had fallen, which melting within twelve hours had reduced the partially dried roads to the consistency of soft-soap, and had caused every small stream and rivulet to double its size instantly. Jerry and Mr. Henshaw were anxious, miserably anxious, though Jerry gave no sign; but his heart was quaking and his pockets felt empty, for the main stream was as full as could be esteemed safe, and too full to let the shareholders think of the mine as an entirely trustworthy investment.

"They will not know that this has been an unusual winter," Mr. Henshaw said despondingly; "they will judge of things only as they see them," and he looked at Jerry mournfully over his spectacles.

"Very true," Jerry answered quietly, "and we can only hope that the stream will subside a little before to-morrow; they will not have time to go to the dam to-day."

"So!" and Mr. Henshaw looked admiringly at Jerry, who seemed always to find the right way out of a difficulty, "I had not thought of that; of course they can not go up to-day—of course not," and he took his way down to the reception shed in a calm and peaceful frame of mind.

All the town was there; everybody in their best; everybody eager to see and to hear; everybody full of importance as to the guests consigned to them.

Jerry had told them that, with the exception of a few ladies who would go to Mr. Henley's, the people would live in the train probably, and only would have to be provided with food: he had made a point of telling them this, fearing dissatisfaction or misunderstanding. Also, he had spent much thought on his dress; should he wear his usual Durden's suit, with his rough trowsers tucked inside his boots, and his pistols in his belt; or should he put on the clothes he had brought from the East?

He felt foolish because he could not decide instantly, and angry with humanity that such a trivial thing should be of importance; but it was of importance, and he knew it. Would the people prefer that their representative should dress as they dressed; or that he should look on an equality with the people who were coming?

He spent much thought on it, at last deciding in favor of his usual costume: there was a fitness in it to the environment that would be missing entirely in his tailor-made clothes. He dressed most carefully, with an unacknowledged feeling that he would like to look well in Isabel Greg's eyes, and wondered if she would recognize him in this Western guise. Pshaw! if she did or did not, what matter? she would stay at Paul Henley's house, so that he could see nothing of her—what matter how he looked? Besides, she would have eyes for her brother only, whom she had not seen in a great length of time. So he hurried down to the station, being a little late, to find the town waiting and fuming over the delay in Eureka. The train had been heard and seen to stop in Eureka, at least twenty minutes before Jerry joined the waiting town.

Dan Burk and Dave Morris had gone over there, the people said, to see that things were properly managed, and the train properly welcomed. Twenty minutes ago the train had stopped, and since then there had been no sign of its moving on; and yet there was nothing to keep them in Eureka.

Jerry listened, but made no comment, even though he was surprised: he had expected them to pause in Eureka simply because it was Eureka, but only for five or ten minutes!

Gradually the grumbling grew louder and more impatient, as through strained eyes the people watched the train, announcing at short intervals that the smoke from the engine was rapidly lessening. Had any accident happened?

Thirty minutes passed, and many more in their wake, when a voice in the rear of the crowd said in a smothered tone—

"Hullo!"

The murmurs had been loud and continuous, and this exclamation was scarcely above a whisper, yet every man, woman, and child turned, for there was something in the tone that defied indifference.

Jerry drew a sharp breath between his teeth : driving by as rapidly as the road would permit, was Paul Henley with a large wagon full of ladies going to the doctor's house, and behind him another wagon full of gentlemen, and driven by Greg !

Jerry's heart seemed to stop its beating : Paul had outwitted him !

It was a stupidly simple plot ; so stupidly simple that Jerry had not suspected it ; and now, though he understood it all in a moment, he dared not act on his intuitions. These people could not understand anything but a plainly demonstrated fact ; and if he showed that he understood with so little explanation as two wagons full of people, the town would accuse him of being in the plot to give Mr. Henley all the great guests. He must wait always as they did, and understand as they did when ill was about to befall them ; but good fortune he could predict as far ahead as he pleased, and be esteemed a prophet !

The people watched until the wagons stopped and the travelers were lost to sight in the house, then once more they turned their attention to the train, over which only the thinnest cloud of smoke was visible : what did it mean ?

Jerry knew, and as the murmurs grew loud about him, he cursed himself bitterly under his breath ; cursed himself as the blindest of fools, and Paul as the most wily of villains.

He could read it as plainly as a book spread open before him : two days ago Greg had gone to meet his mother and sister across the divide ; and Paul had gone with him to meet his guests ! And now the train had stopped in Eureka, and Paul had driven over a wagon full of ladies, and Greg a wagon full of gentlemen to Paul Henley's house : had the rest of the excursionists taken up their abode in Eureka ?

The surmise struck him like a blow, and with it

came the memory that the railway company had most of its interests centered in Eureka. They owned all the land and houses in Eureka, of course it was to their interest that Eureka should advance. Had all stopped there?

Louder and more discontented grew the words about him; the people were becoming more and more angry; it was cold and uncomfortable even under the wonderful shed, and the waiting crowd were hungry. But not even one of the advance guard who had gone to meet the train had come back; nothing had happened since the thrill that went through the populace when the whistle of the engine was first heard, and now they were weary.

Curses were growing plentiful, and sarcastic remarks as to great public festivities, when a cloud of smoke was seen to issue from the engine, and a sound like a faint shout was borne on the air!

"She's a-comin'!" went from lip to lip, and a breathless, strained silence ensued: surely the train was in motion, very slow on account of the insecure track, but still it *was* moving! Once more the excitement rose to fever heat, and the people ceased their cursing and grumbling, and every eye watched eagerly.

Every eye save Jerry's.

He knew that the day and its triumph had been stolen from him; he knew that the end he worked for would never be accomplished through any good he would reap from this excursion: Paul Henley had undermined him. He was certain of this fact, but to what extent Paul had cheated him he could not know until the train arrived.

How many had gone with Paul did not matter so much, as the standing of the men; the people in Durden's knew the names of all these magnates who were coming, and from the new settlers, many of them sent out by these great Directors, they had gathered some knowledge of the moneyed worth and standing of these men, and had contested as to the entertaining of them ; a man's millions making him great or small.

More than once Jerry had turned away from the boasting of the Durdenites over the man "who was agoin' to eat with them !" And now he knew that all these triumphs were gone hopelessly : he knew that all the great men had gone to Paul Henley's ; and what would be the upshot ?

Slowly the train came on, crawling like a great worm, the more slowly when it felt the upward grade as it neared Durden's, and the excitement had time to grow intense : Jerry caught it, and his fears added to it made him angry,—what would the result be ?

Nearer and nearer ; the buzz of excitement growing into a cheer as the engine gave a last scream and stopped.

Instinctively Jerry turned and looked toward the doctor's house—what made him he could not tell, but he turned back quickly with a smothered oath, for on the distant piazza he could distinguish Paul and his guests watching the arrival !

"I'm blessed if it aint plum empty !" and Jerry, hurried on by the crowd that hustled and pressed the more eagerly after this exclamation, found himself pushed into the first car, that but for one or two men, well-known inhabitants of Durden's, was empty !

For a moment the crowd paused, too surprised to ask any questions ; then pushed on toward the next car, only to find it locked and a guard at the door.

"The provision car, sir," he said, touching his hat respectfully to Mr. Henshaw, who, like Jerry, had been hurried along by the eagerness of the crowd, "to go back to the other town, sir," the guard went on, "Mr. Henley has a lunch-room there, sir, for the gentlemen."

Mr. Henshaw looked at Jerry in mute wonder, and the people crowded nearer to hear.

"It must be a mistake," Jerry said quickly ; "Mr.

Henley does not know that preparations have been made in this town to entertain all the guests."

"I have it in writing, sir," now addressing Jerry, and handing him a card, "as soon as the back cars are emptied the train is to push back to Eureka, and unload the provision car there, sir," again touching his hat; "this is Mr. Henley's card, sir, and Mr. Redwood wrote the orders on it."

Durden's stood open-mouthed, and Jerry felt as if he were in a dream!

"This provision car belongs to Mr. Henley's guests, then?" he asked as calmly as possible.

"No, sir, to the directors, all the directors, sir; they are to have rooms in Eureka, and their meals to be provided for them at an eating-room of Mr. Henley's, sir."

"And these other people whom you have brought here," Jerry went on, striving to steady his voice that was shaken sorely with anger, "who are they?"

The guard shrugged his shoulders.

"Paying passengers," he answered, almost contemptuously, "people who wanted a cheap trip."

Jerry turned away; he had been foolish to push this explanation that was now almost irretrievable, and he could only hope that the people had not understood it.

He could not afford to stop and think now, and he pushed his way hastily through the questioning crowd to the last cars, that were disgorging rapidly a motley, tawdry crowd of men, women, and children; flashy, loud-talking creatures that even to Jerry's untutored eyes seemed far below the inhabitants of Durden's. Involuntarily he recoiled for a moment, and asked sharply for Dan Burk and Dave Morris; they should be there to help him; but they could not be found, and one of the men who had gone to meet the train explained that Mr. Henley had asked them to stay and see after the strangers who had stopped in Eureka.

There was a vow of vengeance uttered under Jerry's breath, then he turned manfully to his task. He had expected people like these to stop in Eureka, and be fed from the lunch-room ; and only that morning had been anxious lest this class should prove more attractive to the Durden's people, and so entice them away to the aiding and abetting of this new scheme of Paul's. Now things were completely reversed, and all his plans with them.

Hurriedly these thoughts streamed through his heated brain, as calling up man after man of those who had promised to provide for the visitors, he parcelled off to each his guests. Rapidly the crowd dwindled, and the spirits of the Durdenites seemed to rise as they led away the strangers to be fed and warmed ; and Jerry, watching and listening, had a faint hope that Durden's would be satisfied, and not fully realize the slight put upon her.

Very weary he was when he reached Mrs. Milton's with the three men she had agreed to receive ; very weary, and possessed by an undying hatred and anger. An honorable death by shooting was far too good for Paul : he would ruin him first ; would cause him to waste his substance—then he would stand and watch his life fade into a colorless failure !

If only he could compass this.

It was one o'clock, late for dinner in Durden's, and Mrs. Milton was more brusque in her ways than usual, in order to show that she was perfectly at her ease with these "pulin' town folks."

"An' har's some writin' as come fur youuns, Jerry Wilkerson,"—she said, putting down by his plate a carelessly folded note, "Jim Short he brung it from Paul Henley's house"; then with a chuckle that was more angry than amused, "Jim he 'llows thet Paul Henley's done crawled youuns log to-day," she said.

Jerry's eyes flashed, and the color surged up into his face; but it would not do to contest Mrs. Milton's words, especially before these strangers; and an effort at explanation would be ruination. Paul had over-reached him, and the more clear he made it to the people, the higher would be their respect for Paul, and the more faith they would have in him. He knew full well that the first claim he had on their regard was the fact that he had outwitted both the doctor and Paul, and now his safety lay in not acknowledging himself as worsted; so he answered with a laugh:

"My log is a slippery log, Mrs. Milton."

"Thet's so!" came heartily from the old woman, "an' I tole Jim Short thet Paul Henley'd better scratch mighty easy roun' you, 'cause thar worn't no sicher thing as raisin' dust ernough to make you shoot crooked: but keep the wittles a-stirrin', boys," she went on, more hospitably than she had done before, "I guess you all is rale honggry."

Then Jerry opened his note: a little scrap of paper from Mr. Redwood, who stood in Mr. Greg's place as chief officer of the expedition, telling Jerry that there would be a supper that night at the lunch-room in Eureka, to which he was most cordially invited; and that the next day the "Directors" would take great pleasure in going over the mines and the towns.

They had reversed the order of things, and intended entertaining him!

And he realized to the fullest extent that he stood in a most difficult and dangerous position.

"Did Jim say there was any answer to this, Mrs. Milton?" he asked.

"Nary," emphatically. "Jim's a plum fool any how."

So Jerry returned to his dinner, and to the entertaining of these three nondescript guests who had fallen to Mrs. Milton's share, while his mind followed an undercurrent of reasoning.

If he went to this supper from which the people were shut out, what would the people say? if he refused to go, what could not Paul say? Either way he was sure to be misjudged, for Paul would be ready to give either side reasons and motives unfavorable to him. He thought diligently while he talked to the men and to Mrs. Milton, who in her various journeys from the fireplace to the table made many telling remarks on the place and people; but she was stanch to Durden's, and told the most entrancing stories of the fortunes that had been made, and that could be made still.

"Sakes-alive, when 'Lije Milton come har, I'll be drat if he hed a livin' thing ceppen the cloze on his hisn's back; an' when 'Lije Milton were buried he owned the whole thing, he did," putting down some biscuits that were golden-green with soda.

The men looked at each other, and then at Jerry incredulously, so that Jerry added:

"Yes, and the town bought the mine from Mrs. Milton," and the men rose from the table much impressed, and Mrs. Milton swore a secret oath that she would stand by Jerry as long as she could "worry out one breath."

One strong adherent, and Jerry would need many. Still undecided as to the supper, he took the men out after dinner to where he had agreed to meet several householders, who would assist him in showing the guests the wonders of the mine, and the advantages of the town. They met many groups on the road who joined them, until quite a crowd took their way to the meeting-place. But there he found neither Dan Burk nor Dave Morris, nor was Mr. Henshaw anywhere to be seen. Added to this it was cold, and had clouded up as if for another snow-fall; and Jerry's own spirit being at a low ebb, there was not much enthusiasm to spare.

But Jerry did not falter; he could not falter; he had been obliged to change the base of his operations entirely, and from intending to push and advance the interests of Durden's, he had to retreat to the position of saving himself and his venture.

So quietly, so cleverly the thing had been done, that he had scarcely had time to realize it; and the only hope left him was to impress everybody with his past successes, and the future of the place.

Instead of taking the grandees about, and strengthening his position in the eyes of the people by the way in which these great men listened to him; and instead of securing himself in the estimation of the stockholders by the sight of his power in the town, he was reduced to the necessity of keeping this motley mob in order, and also in a good humor, that the Durden's people might be deceived into esteeming these creatures as guests who were worth pleasing, and to think of themselves as gaining importance by entertaining them.

This was necessary for to-day, and to-morrow he would take the real guests about, and have all Durden's out to escort them; if only he could tide over this one bewildering day he hoped that the occasion might yet be retrieved.

And after?

He put his hand back on his pistol for comfort, as he led the way over the carefully prepared pathway that he had intended should be trod first by the great directors! Alas! the rabble tramped over it carelessly and unappreciatingly, and Jerry thought with much impatience how impossible it would be for him to repair it before the next day! The whole thing seemed like a nightmare that he could not shake off; why could not he rise and denounce the whole transaction; why could not he explain the whole affair, and demonstrate the great mistake that had been made; explain to whom? Only to himself could the explanation be made, and the mistake be demonstrated. Mr. Henshaw had acquiesced in the whole arrangement, though somewhat surprised, and had been seen to go from the car-shed to Paul Henley's, where doubtlessly he took his lunch. Dan Burk and Dave Morris had never returned from Eureka; Greg's mother and sister were Paul Henley's guests: so who was there to listen to his explanation, or to agree that he had been badly treated, when he was the only dissatisfied person? All he could do was to cover as well as possible his defeat, and bide his time.

At last his task was finished: the mine had been explained and explored, the town talked about glowingly; then, a light snow beginning to fall, the people hurried off in groups, and Mrs. Milton's three guests having gone to Eureka to look at that mine, Jerry felt at last that he was free to examine his position and arrange his plans.

Stock-still in front of his fire, with his hands in his pockets, and his eyes fixed on the dancing flames: feeling too much to rest or to think connectedly; only realizing a hatred for Paul, and a desire for revenge that seemed almost to consume him: while a cold resentment against all humanity took possession of him.

Over this foundation of feeling a confused cloud of ideas floated: how had Greg explained his absence to Mrs. Greg and Isabel? in what light had Paul represented him to these people? how would he be received that night, and should he go?

Over and over again these thoughts drifted through his mind; over and over again he decided in one way, only to change to the opposite extreme.

Try as he would, he could not realize his position; he could not control the feeling that the whole fabric was melting before his eyes as suddenly as it had sprung up: there was magic in the whole thing,—magic that would destroy him! He was doomed—he had taken the wrong turn that lies in every path—the one wrong turn which there is no recovering, and now he seemed to be traveling fast away from all success.

Whichever course he took now could be misconstrued, and would be misconstrued: but he must decide on something, and take a firm hold somewhere;

to drift would be inevitable ruin. He might make a mistake in his action,—still it would be action; and he must act if action meant financial suicide. He must play Paul's game, and stop at nothing; let no tool nor thing be too low for use; and if he found that he could not hurt Paul in any more lasting way, he would kill him. And he laughed bitterly at the thought that death would not last as a punishment for Paul Henley! If there were any judgment or punishment hereafter, death should take Paul Henley to both: the doctor's love should shield him no longer.

Then the door opened and Greg came in.

"Not ready yet?" he began with a gayety that had something of nervousness in it; "the supper will be early so that we can sit long," he went on, rubbing his hands and holding them to the fire, "and of course you are coming."

"Yes," Jerry answered quietly, rising and standing in front of the fire, with his hands behind him, "but I will not change my clothes. How is your mother?"

"Quite well, thank you, and wishes to see you very much; so does Isabel, and Miss Henley asked after you most especially."

"They are very kind; I hope I shall see them to-morrow. Are you ready to go to Eureka now?"

The color flashed hotly into Greg's face.

"Not immediately," he answered hesitatingly: "I told my mother I should stop there a moment on my way over."

"And will go over in Henley's wagon," Jerry added in a matter-of-course way; then looking at his pistols carefully before putting them in his belt, he asked, "How are your visitors impressed with Durden's?"

"They seem to be immensely surprised," Greg answered, "especially at the government of the town; it seems that they did not believe what the papers said about us."

"I suppose it seems rather foolish to them," Jerry said; "rather whimsical."

"Well, yes," doubtfully, "rather impracticable for a speculation, they say; but I think they scarcely understand it yet."

"And would not, probably, after a week's talk," laughing. "To a capitalist and a speculator the scheme does not look so captivating as it does to the class I have been entertaining to-day: people looking down, and people looking up can not of course get the same view of a thing; and when I began, I was one of those who looked up."

"But now you look down, so can agree with the capitalists," Greg suggested.

"Do they propose to try any changes?" and involuntarily Jerry's voice sharpened.

"No, no; they can not, you know; but I believe they have some suggestions to offer."

"To-night?" tersely.

"No, to-morrow; they intend to enjoy themselves to-night, and talk and explore to-morrow; there is to be a public meeting in Eureka, and speeches."

"In Eureka?" Jerry asked quietly, although for a moment the ground seemed to slip from under his feet.

"Yes, the railway men, you know; they bought all the land at the doctor's suggestion, you remember; and now they are very anxious that the land values should rise, and think this is a good opportunity to capture settlers."

"And it is," Jerry answered, looking down into the fire, while there seemed a singing in his ears.

"And to-morrow Henshaw goes with Mills to inspect the Eureka Mine: of course the growth of one town will react on the other," he went on as if to comfort Jerry, "a sort of double-barreled affair that will help all."

"And I suppose I shall have to speak," Jerry said.

"Of course," quickly, "I shall call on you myself."

Jerry laughed.

"Scarcely," he said; "I do not think that would

quite do," then drawing a heavy pea-jacket over his flannel shirt, and taking up his hat, he turned to the door; "of course I shall be called on to render an account, and I shall do it: but now we must go," and he led the way from the room.

At the foot of the steep, blind descent of the stairway, Mrs. Milton opened a door and let a stream of light out on them.

"I wants to set eyes on you, Jerry Wilkerson," she said, "'cause you looks rale jimpsey in sto' cloze, you do; come in, come in."

Jerry laughed.

"I did not put on my store clothes, Mrs. Milton," he said; "I prefer to look like a Durden's man," stepping into the light.

"Great-day-in-the-mornin'!" Then Mrs. Milton stood in silent disappointment.

"You are the best friend I have in the world, Mrs. Milton," and Jerry's eyes seemed to glow as he laid his hand on the old woman's shoulder, "and what is good enough for you, is good enough for any one."

"An' nothin' but youuns' ole blue shirt an' jeans breeches—Golly!"

"A brand-new shirt," Jerry answered, "and of the very best flannel, and my pistols are cleaned and my boots freshly greased to keep the wet out; what more should a man want?"

Mrs. Milton turned away.

"You is a good figger of a man, Jerry Wilkerson, whatever youuns' cloze is," she said slowly, "an' allers looks rale nice; but them thar sto' cloze does look pisen fine, you bet: an' Mr. Greg," scanning him over the top of her glasses, "looks a rale buster, he do," and without more words she ushered them out of the door, closing it after them.

"She is an extraordinary character," Greg said laughing.

"The most extraordinary I ever met," Jerry assented, "she is perfectly true and honest."

"Whew-w-w!" Greg whistled. "You are hard on humanity."

"Only another case of people looking from different standpoints," Jerry answered.

Then they plodded on in silence for a time.

"It will be deucedly cold by morning," Greg said, at length, almost repenting the friendliness that had caused him to come and warn Jerry of the plans on foot, so that he would be somewhat prepared. Jerry had not seemed surprised, nor in the least thankful to him for the trouble he had taken, nor did he seem much upset by the day's doings; indeed, Greg felt defrauded of the sympathy that he had been spending on Jerry all day.

"And the snow is increasing every moment," Jerry answered; "if the worst comes, we shall have to illuminate one of the mines and have the meeting there; it will be warm, and have plenty of echo, so that their words can come back again and again, and so impress themselves on our minds"; then suddenly, "Why did not your father come?"

"My father?" Greg repeated in some surprise; "he could not leave his business."

"And Mr. Glendale?" mentioning the name of his own broker, who was also a director of the railway, "he could not leave his business either?"

"I suppose not, though I have not asked;" then Greg turned down the road to Paul Henley's, and Jerry went on to Eureka.

It had not occurred to Jerry before that the absence of these two men might mean something more than accident; but now, although he did not know that Glendale was Henley's adviser also, the fact of both staying away seemed ominous. They were the only directors who were in any way bound to him, and knowing that there were possible disagreements ahead, they felt that in Durden's they would have to take sides, while in New York they could remain neutral. It was a hard conclusion to come to, and it was harder still to bear, but fortunately for Jerry it brought its own strength in the shape of anger; a strength that upheld him as no rest nor sympathy could have done.

So they were to have a public meeting in Eureka; and the thing he had looked on as his greatest triumph, the compelling the company to buy the lots in Eureka in order to save what they had invested there already, this act that had been more than anything else the badge of his success, this had turned out to be the salvation of the rival town.

At the time of the transaction he had realized that this would be the case, but not so soon as this. It was a cruel misfortune that it should come now, and through the machinations of Paul Henley. And yet, was it any more than he had done to Eureka? He walked a little faster.

He had been working for the public good when he did that; his motive had been the raising and bettering of a whole class!

He laughed a little as he thought this, a scornful, ill-sounding laugh: what a complete fool he had been! The only difference between him and Paul Henley was that Paul had had sense enough to have but one end in view—the destruction of an enemy; while he, though thirsting for this same thing, had covered it over with a philanthropic cloak. He had not realized his hypocrisy at the time, perhaps, but this proved him only the greater fool. And now Paul was reaping the benefit of his unscrupulous honesty in working openly and unblushingly for a low end. The people could understand him and his scheme, and were forced into belief in him by the unveiled selfishness of his motives. All along he had known that Paul laughed at his venture, and the laws of the town that held these men to a decent way of living, and took care of them and their money by force.

And well might Paul laugh: laugh at a man who, with the experience of generations before him to show and prove the folly of forcing people into a right and just way of doing things, still made the experiment. Old Joe, even, had seen his folly. The Almighty Himself had left humanity free for good or ill!

The world would grumble at its condition always—always it would cry frantically for honesty and reform; but it had only laughter for the honest man—and woe for the reformer. All that the world wanted was money, and only the poor found the times evil: it was only the poor who could not hold their place in the battle of life; and no man could help them; weakness must fall.

And yet Almighty Strength gave itself to death for the weak. He looked up to the sullen sky—if only he had been strong enough for that kind of success.

And the doctor? Jerry paused a moment in his going; had the doctor believed in that grand atonement of love,—the doctor whose whole life had been spent in trying to strike a balance of good works against his sins?

If only this man had given him a little love, how his life had been glorified!

Even now it was not too late for him to make a grand sacrifice?

He walked on slowly: suddenly he turned into the one muddy street of Eureka, and stopped to take in the novelty of its appearance.

In front of every house up and down the road were hung lanterns, making quite an illumination, and in front of Dave Morris's old shop there was a long row of them; and boards laid down before the door; and an awning stretched overhead!

Jerry walked down to the shop, and found that inside things were as different as possible from the time when, in his youthful scorn and folly, he had knocked down Dave Morris. It had not been a year yet, since he struck that first blow of his career.

Dan Burk and Dave Morris were both in the shop, and Mrs. Burk, in all the finery she could buy or borrow in both towns, was sailing importantly, but condescendingly, about a table spread at the far end of the room. There were one or two women, faint copies of Mrs. Burk, who followed her obediently: and, in *blasé* and amused silence, the cook brought from New York was carving at a side-table; while a group of well-dressed imported waiters stood laughing near the stove.

And Jerry, in his rough dress, walked in unheeded by them. Dave Morris and Dan Burk were charged with the admitting of people, and now they hurried forward.

"Good-evenin', Mr. Wilkerson," looking anxiously in his cold face, for as yet they had not won their way with the new party sufficiently to be regardless of the censure of the old; "a paper, Mr. Wilkerson, and a chair?" and Jerry, accepting both things, sat down near a lamp.

The imported servants looked at him curiously; but he had given Dan Burk his coat and his hat with the air of a master, and wisely surmising that he was not made by his clothes, their mirth subsided into respectful silence.

Jerry opened the paper that already was rather soiled, and behind its protecting pages watched, and listened, and drew his conclusions.

Paul had worked well; for as the conversation of the waiters and the women drifted to him, and as he listened to the talk of a group of natives eating at the lunch counter near the door, and caught the remarks from Burk and Morris, he could hear "Mr. Henley" referred to as an authority for everything: a stranger would have thought Paul the great man of the towns; and the anger and revenge that out in the darkness he had subdued a little, seemed to take fresh hold on him, and to grow more quiet and more determined within him: it seemed now to reveal itself as the substratum of his whole being, over which all lighter emotions passed like the shadows of the clouds over the plain!

It would never leave him, this hatred,—it should lie still for a while yet, but it should grow and strengthen by day and by night until the right time should come. His thoughts and emotions as he walked over had been only another phase of his lunacy.

There was a sound of wheels and of laughter outside, then an influx of men in every shape and size of overcoat and wrap that could be thought of, and out of the crowd Greg approached Jerry.

"Here you are," he said heartily, "safe out of this beastly weather;" then to the party, who were most of them out of their wrappings by this time—"Here is Mr. Wilkerson, Mr. Redwood; of course you know him, Granger, and you, Van Dusen," and Jerry's hand was shaken by one man after another, and he was looked at from head to foot in a well-bred way. This the Wilkerson, the exceedingly gentlemanly young man they remembered in New York? What possessed him to clothe himself in this way?

Then Paul came forward, and a bow and a few words of greeting passed between them: Jerry's hatred must keep: and Paul's rôle was to make these people believe Jerry to be a rash, hot-headed philanthropist; and he the much-enduring friend whose advice and warnings had been scoffed at and disregarded: so their greeting was strictly unremarkable.

It seemed like a dream, to Jerry; a bad dream from which he could not waken: all the talk seemed to be against him, yet in a covert fashion that he could not take hold of: he talked busily enough himself, and was the recipient of many toasts and many fine speeches, so that the people and the waiters standing about looked on him with very different eyes from what they had done when the semi-royal feast eaten in public began. Yet under all he detected with unerring instinct an effort to keep him in a good humor: he was an amiable visionary who had no harm in him, and who had succeeded after a manner, but whose success could not last.

But Jerry made no sign: he would "bide his time"—wait until the moment came when his blow would crush some thing or person—then he would strike—strike if the same blow destroyed himself.

He had ruined Eureka once,—why not again? He had brought these men to terms once, why not again? No reason that he could see, save one, that sickened him with dread of failure; in his first struggle he had had a noble foe to deal with; now,—and his blood tingled as he remembered who opposed him now!

And while he talked and listened he found himself revolving in an idle fashion the question whether it would be wiser to fight Paul with Paul's own weapons—"fight the devil with fire"; but surely this would give the devil the advantage to fight him with his own weapons; and yet to fight a lie with truth seemed a losing thing. If he had but stood to the first principles he had laid down for his life, how idle this present strife would have seemed to him! How pityingly he would have looked down on the fray, and the poor squabblers wasting lives and souls on the idle dross of gain! What difference if one or the other won?—a little while and their graves would lie rain-washed and forgotten out there on the hill-side.

"Eureka is bound to succeed!" and Paul put his glass down with a clash.

"Of course," Mr. Redwood answered, tucking his napkin more carefully under his chin, "too many capitalists own land here for it to fail; we have only been waiting on the railway, knowing there was no need for any haste."

Jerry rallied his thoughts as Greg answered quickly—

"And Durden's *is* a success."

"Except that damned stream," Van Dusen answered, "it makes everything so confoundedly unsafe."

"What do you say, Mr. Henshaw?" and Paul held his glass up to the light.

Mr. Henshaw cleared his throat, and glanced at Jerry. "The dam is safe now," he said.

"And has been for more than twenty-five years," Jerry added.

"But the twenty-sixth might smash it," and Granger shook his head gravely.

"I am willing to risk it," Greg struck in sharply, seeing some of the natives drawing near and listening intently.

Paul laughed lightly.

"So you may be, Greg," he said, "for you have no one dependent on you; neither has Wilkerson; besides," looking Jerry straight in the face, then beyond him to the natives who were listening, "besides Wilkerson has enough to carry him over any failure."

"Of course," Van Dusen answered, innocent of the part he was playing, "every man on Wall Street knows that Wilkerson can afford to play with dangerous investments, but I have no fortune, and I have a wife and four children."

"I am sorry for you," Jerry said drily, filling his glass, while a laugh ran round the table; "I have only been imprudent enough to invest all that Mr. Gilliam left me in the interest of his town, Durden's," returning Paul's look, "and with Durden's I stand or fall."

There was a little sound from the shop as of applause, while Greg clapped his hands openly, and the color rushed into Paul's face.

"By the way," and Paul put down his knife and fork, "we are old friends enough for a home question,—how much did old Gilliam leave you anyhow?"

"Enough," Jerry answered, while he skillfully jointed the shapelessly fat ducks put down before him, "to run Durden's stock up above par in the market, and to keep it there," and his eyes flashed dangerously.

"And where did he get it?" Paul went on, feeling safe in the crowd, and too angry to restrain his venom.

Jerry's face grew very white in the moment's silence

that followed Paul's words, but his voice was steady enough as he answered slowly:

"He did not tell me, nor any living man: the secret of Joe Gilliam's find died with him," and Jerry paused in his carving to lay his pistols on the table.

"He refused to tell it even on his death-bed," Greg said, looking angrily in Paul's face, "for I was there and heard him."

Then a silence fell on the company that was not comfortable, until Van Dusen said with an uneasiness born as much of the look of Jerry's pistols as of Jerry as he silently and ruthlessly dissected the tender round ducks, as of the subject he was reintroducing:

"But that dam?"

"Perfectly safe," Greg answered firmly; then went on to tell the story of old Durden who had first turned the stream from its course; a story well known to all present, as it had been most carefully published in the pamphlet advertising the place, but which now was listened to with undivided interest, while the company, each in the silence of his own heart, tried to decide whether Jerry had pulled out his pistols as a warning to Paul, or because they made his belt too tight as the feast progressed. They had heard many well-authenticated stories of the Western mode of dealing with the slightest impertinence, and they were uneasy lest they should be treated to a specimen. Henley had been confoundedly prying, and Wilkerson was not a person who looked entirely safe; and he was not drinking much.

Meanwhile they listened to Greg's old story, making vague comments, and looking steadfastly away from the daintily mounted pistols that seemed to grow larger as they lay on the table-cloth. And when Greg finished, Mr. Henshaw, who was accustomed to seeing every man in the town armed always, and who did not take in the situation, went into a long disquisition on the present safety of the dam, and the work that had been put on it to make it perfectly secure. Then some one followed with a story of some recent flood, and the talk floated away from all dangerous topics: and the wine flowed freely, and the stories grew more witty and less decent, and songs from the younger men waked up the nearest inhabitants; and in the midst of it Jerry left, taking his ghastly pistols, judging rightly that no one could harm him now.

And through the crowd gathered about the door he found a respectful path opened, and the next day everybody knew that "Mr. Wilkerson had struck up to Durden's, and hadn't drunk but mighty little."

Steadily on through the dreary night; tramping heedlessly through mud and slush, breaking with sharp cracking the ice formed since nightfall on the roadway pools; unconscious of the driving snow, and the wind that cut like a knife; regardless of everything save the one great hatred; grasping with his fevered hands the pistols in his jacket pockets until the cold metal grew warm, and seemed almost to answer to his grasp. The one mad longing to crush and strangle the life and beauty out of the false face that had mocked him that night: he had read a book once, where a man after long waiting strangles his enemy. A slow, great agony of death, that he could watch growing in his victim's eyes; no sudden, merciful blow nor shot, but an awful creeping horror that would grant time for the realization of illimitable suffering—for the anguish of regret and failure to work its most dreadful pain. This man might undermine him; might in his crafty, snake-like fashion, compass his ruin; might stand and smile triumphantly over his fall; he would bear it, he would wait and watch, and when the hour of greatest success stood ready to this man's hand he would murder him.

He drew a long, sharp breath; he longed to cry aloud, that the awful excitement might find vent.

The wind came tearing down the mountains and out across the plain, driving the snow in great clouds before it, crying and shrieking as it went, and far off he heard the roar of falling water!

He stood still in the darkness—and in the lull of the storm he listened: often in the night he heard this roar. How easily an enemy might ruin him: one loosened stone—one little blast of powder unheard in the stormy night, and the wild water would rush like a mad creature back to its old haunts; dash in wild ecstasy down the black abyss where old Durden's bones lay crumbling; lash with its fierce caresses the stones that in the long ago it had worn down to patient smoothness! would it know that it had got home again, this water that fell so far, and cried so piteously as it fled away to the thirsty plain; would it know that it had conquered one man who stood without one friend to love in all his life?

He started on hurriedly.

No friend, no friend; but, ah, one enemy! one merciless enemy whose dead body should be cast down the abyss with the wild white water as its only winding-sheet, and find no rest down among the black, bruising rocks! That would be better than fortune or fame—better than any success!

A sudden memory came to him like a voice speaking in his ear: he must burn that little scrap of paper; no man must know that the same water would ruin both! It would be a sweet revenge to let Paul ruin himself. For the paper said—"What goes in at Durden's, comes out at Eureka."

And he laughed aloud in the darkness.

Paul would laugh as the water roared in at Durden's Mine—*he* would laugh as the stream flashed into the sunlight again from the mouth of the Eureka mine!

Joe had been wise, and faithful, and silent.

CHAPTER XIII.

"Let go thy hold when a great wheel runs down a hill, lest it break thy neck with following it; but the great one that goes up the hill, let him draw thee after."

WHEN Durden's opened its doors and windows the next morning, the world was white, and the snow was falling with dangerous swiftness. The excursionists were dismayed, and fears were soon floating about that they would be snowed up in these wilds; if they could get so far as the first station from which the road was properly built, they would feel safe; but with much more snow the loosely built track would be impassable.

The belated directors were roused by the conductor of their train at an unbearably early hour, considering it was the morning after a supper, and were advised to make an immediate start.

Soon the towns were in confusion, and the ladies, all of them at Paul Henley's, were in a great flutter of excitement. The people who had not been to the supper realized the position immediately, but it was a hard matter to move the exhausted revelers.

"A wagon!" Mrs. Greg cried plaintively, "and Charles, where is he!"

The servants were at a loss; where was Mr. Greg? where in the two towns was he to be found when his own house was empty?

"Ask Mr. Wilkerson," some one suggested, and Jim Short ran as fast as he could to Mrs. Milton's.

"Mr. Wilkerson?" he asked breathlessly of the old woman, who was smoking busily, with her knees in the fire almost.

"Jerry Wilkerson is done eat an' gone, Jim Short, an' you mighter knowed it if yer hedn't stuffed yerseff plum foolish las' night," and Mrs. Milton replaced her pipe in her mouth, and turned a stolid gaze on the fire.

Jim paused a moment in the open door; he must venture another question, and he asked desperately—

"Whar?"

"Whar?" scornfully, "go an' fin' out; an' if you don't shet that dore mighty quick, I'll jest git up an' knock thet same stuffin' outer you," turning to look over her shoulder: but Jerry stood there between her and the despised Jim, asking what was wanted.

"Drat if I knows," the old woman answered sullenly, and Jim taking courage gave his message that the ladies wanted Mr. Greg and a wagon, and he had come to Mr. Wilkerson to find both.

"And where is Mr. Henley?"

"Mr. Paul's deep in the bed, sir."

"Very well," and Jerry stepping outside closed the door after him, while Mrs. Milton walked to the window to watch him down the street.

"If he'd a-tole me hisn-seff," she muttered, "I'd a-made the folks stan' roun'; but to hev thet Henley an' Dan Burk a-talkin' 'bout it, an' a-tellin' it like it were stole—it jest hurted me to death, it did," drawing a deep sigh, and returning to her place by the fire, "an' I sets aheaper sto' by Jerry Wilkerson; an' I 'llowed I'd gie him 'all I hed when I gits ready to be planted: an' I *will*," wiping her nose with her apron, "Jerry Wilkerson is my man!" and she smoked vehemently.

The celebration had been a failure; a failure that was unexpected, but thoroughly realized by all parties.

"An' Paul Henley spiled it," Mrs. Milton said openly, "all alonger hisn sneakin', onderhanded ways!"

But good, or bad, it was over now, and the people

were going away helter-skelter, in dreadful fear of being snowed up, and expressing very unflattering opinions of the climate.

It was a melancholy end to all the high hopes of both the inhabitants and the guests, and no one felt the failure so keenly as Jerry. He worked with all his mind and strength to get the train off, for under the present circumstances the longer the people stayed the more harm it would work for him.

The owner of the horses and wagon was sleeping off the drink of the night before, and though the harness was primitive enough, Jerry had to hunt for some one to show him how the thing was managed. At last, however, it was ready, and he drove down to Paul Henley's, where the ladies, many of them in tears, were waiting for him anxiously.

Out they trooped, bag and baggage, with Paul bringing up the rear, and looking decidedly the worse for wear.

"Dear Mr. Wilkerson!" and Mrs. Greg clasped both his hands effusively, "you come like a guardian angel; do you think we can get away?—and where is Charles?"

"You can get away if you go immediately," Jerry answered literally, "but if you delay you may have to stay with us for a month."

There was a general outcry at this, and the whole party began to scramble into the wagon, with or without help.

"There can be no such need for haste," Paul remonstrated impatiently, "and Greg has not come yet."

"He must meet them at the other station," Jerry answered decisively, gathering up the reins, and taking his place next to Edith Henley, who was seated in front. "Will you come?" he added, without looking at Paul.

"Of course!" Isabel Greg cried, and Paul climbed in beside her.

The drive to the station was short, but it was heavy,

and the wind that had them at its mercy was cruelly cutting.

"I shall never again yearn for the West," Edith Henley said plaintively, "and I do not see how you and Paul have managed to live here so long, Mr. Wilkerson."

"I have never had any other home," Jerry answered, "and I like it."

"Paul does not," she went on, creeping a little nearer to Jerry so as to be more sheltered from the wind, "and says he will leave very soon."

"Finally?" came involuntarily from Jerry.

"Yes, just as soon as he has made arrangements out here that will give him plenty of money"; then there was silence between them until the shed was reached where the half-frozen, thoroughly demoralized excursionists were huddled together. The train was only waiting for these ladies, as the directors were to be picked up at Eureka, so the farewells were short.

"Good-by, Mr. Wilkerson, you have been *so* kind," and Mrs. Greg held both his hands, while her soft, brown eyes filled with tears; "you must come to us this summer at Newport; be sure you come!" Then Isabel and Edith shook hands with him; and the other ladies said things he could not hear, and Paul, and Jim Short, and the maids, all loaded down with innumerable packages, went in, and the door was shut.

Then the train backed slowly down the grade. It was a precarious experiment with snow on the track, and Jerry watched anxiously, afraid of some accident, and warned the Durden's people not to be surprised if the whole party were back on their hands before night.

But his watching could not help matters, and he took his way up to the dam: he wanted to be alone, and there was a fascination for him in the swirling water drawing down into black eddies, and dashing into angry foam over the rocks. Up and up he climbed until he reached the dam where the water spread into a lake almost. But above and below this lake, how the water tore along, flinging the spray far to right and left ; a mighty power,—and in the summer it was only a silver thread that wasted to spray as it fell !

Jerry stood and watched it, heedless of the bitter wind—heedless of the snow that was banking silently on the path—thinking idly and aimlessly.

How much had Paul injured him ? and what a lovely thing Edith Henley was ; if he made a fortune he could win such a creature as that, and if he failed ?—

His thoughts seemed to pass out of his keeping, and the bitterness of the night swept over him. If he failed he would commit an awful crime, and all the world would turn from him. An awful crime to kill the man who had ruined him ? It might be a crime over in the civilized states, but out in the wilds men were killed for much less—sometimes for nothing. Kill him ? Ay, if he were hanged for it !

The snow deepened marvelously while he stood on the dam, and his way to Mrs. Milton's was one long fight, so that the evening was falling fast when he reached the door. He was cold and tired, and stopped to rest by the fire in Mrs. Milton's room.

The fire was low, and the room in shadow, and the door into the kitchen was shut ; but he could see a light in there, and hear voices quite distinctly through the thin walls.

He did not heed them just at first, any more than he heeded the rattle of pans that told him supper was being prepared ; but presently Mrs. Milton raised her voice angrily, and her words caught his attention.

"I tell you, Dan Burk, thet Jerry Wilkerson come by thet money hones' ; I knowed all along as Joe Gilliam were a-savin' money, an' you knowed it too ; an' if Joe Gilliam's money wuzn't hones', an' b'longed to 'Lije Milton,—it's pisen sure thet youuns' money aint hones' an' b'longed to 'Lije Milton too !" and she slapped her hands together vigorously.

"Lord, Mis' Milton, don't git so mad," and Burk laughed uneasily, "I aint said nothin' against Mr. Wilkerson; but it do look reelly curious for him to have sicher lot; durned if these men didn't say thet he owns the most of Durden's Mine!—buyin' it for the people!" scornfully.

"An' Jerry Wilkerson did buy it for the people, Dan Burk," and Mrs. Milton's voice rang higher than before, "an' youuns is jest a-strainin' yerself to lie; 'cause Joe Gilliam warn't no deader ner you when Jerry buyed it, an' Jerry never hed no money then—consarn yer bleary old eyes!"

Then there came a movement, a scraping of chairs as if Burk meditated a retreat.

"Goin', is yer?" Mrs. Milton went on; "well, I'm glad, an' jest you 'members thet I'm agoin' to tell Jerry Wilkerson if I hearn 'bout this agin; an' you kin jest be skeary, sure, 'cause he'll shoot the gizzards plum outer the las' one thet lies 'bout him; an' don't you furgit it," and she slammed the door violently behind her vanquished visitor.

Jerry sat still for a moment while there came a clang of pans as if Mrs. Milton were venting her wrath on them; then he put off his hat and coat, so as to look at ease and unhurried, and walked slowly into the kitchen.

"Whom must I shoot, Mrs. Milton?" he asked, standing before her with his hands in his pockets.

Mrs. Milton started guiltily, dropping a pan.

"Lord! Jerry Wilkerson, you took me orl to pieces," she exclaimed, while Jerry picked up the pan and put it on the table; "did you hearn Dan Burk a-lyin' hisseff inside out?" she went on.

"He does not know how to do anything else, Mrs. Milton," Jerry answered quietly.

"An' you choosed him fur youuns' pard?" she asked, losing her usual stolidity in blank surprise.

"I chose him only because he seemed to be the friend of everybody, while I knew no one."

"Jest so," angrily, "friens alonger orl the folks," shaking her head slowly; "I've knowed him nigh onter thirty yeer, I hev, an' Dan Burk allers sweeps his leaves the way the wind's a blowin', he do; drat 'im!"

"And the wind is blowing away from me?" Jerry asked, with a smile on his lips—a smile that did not reach his tired eyes.

"You kin jest bet on thet, Jerry Wilkerson," she answered vehemently, stopping her work and gesticulating with a fork, "an' if you hed jester come to me, Jerry Wilkerson, an' a-said, 'Mis' Milton, Joe's done left me a heap of money, an' I'm a-goin' to sen' it down east,' I'd a-said, 'Orl right, Jerry Wilkerson, Mandy Milton aint agointer blab,' an' it would a-been as soff as mud when the folks commenst a-sayin' thet youuns hed a lotter money hidin' down east,—Lord!" going back to the bacon she was frying, "I could a-curled 'em up liker pig's tail; drat 'em!"

Jerry sat down, clasping his hands over his head, and tilting his chair back.

"It would have been better," he said slowly, "but I did not know you then, Mrs. Milton."

"Thet's true," she acknowledged; "Joe never let you go anighst nobody ceppen the doctor, an' thet blasted Henley; an' now it's him thet is a-doin' orl the mischief an' the meanness."

"I know it," Jerry answered, "he talked last night until I put my pistols down on the table."

"I'll bet on you," and the old woman chuckled grimly, "an' I'll bet thet them city men looked sorter onressless; like thar were a brier sommers on the bench."

Jerry laughed a little.

"They did," he said, "but Greg spoke well."

"Greg's a right tastey little chap," Mrs. Milton allowed, "but I reckon hisn's mammy made him go roun' in frocks too long; Greg allers wants sumpen to lean aginst; an' as fur thet Henley," stabbing the bacon fiercely as she took it from the pan, " he's done busted his'n gall-bag young ; drat 'im ! "

" How will they hurt me, Mrs. Milton ? " and Jerry watched to find out what she knew.

" They aint said yit," shaking her head, " but you'll know jest as soon as I knows."

" Thank you, Mrs. Milton," and Jerry drew his chair to the table where the supper had been put.

" It aint no thanks I wants from youuns, Jerry Wilkerson," and she poured out a great bowl of coffee and put it by his plate, " I jest wants you to stay har, jest so old Mandy Milton kin grip a han' as b'longs to her, an' hev a hones' creetur to tuck what she hes to leave. I've been a savin' woman, Jerry Wilkerson," pausing with her arms akimbo, and looking down into Jerry's astonished eyes, " an' I've done saved a right smart of money ; an' jest you live har so thet I kin know thar's sumpen as is Mandy Milton's, an' when I'm gone, you kin hev it orl ; sure enough," wiping her eyes with the corner of her apron as Jerry stood beside her with his hand on her shoulder.

Here was a true friendship given to him without any seeking on his part ; without any motive behind it save that the old heart that offered it was lonely. After all, he would not have to buy trust and truth ; it was here, offered to him freely, simply, by this ugly old woman, whose little eyes deep-bedded in wrinkles were shining with something like tears : and they were truer than Mrs. Greg's soft brown eyes, he could see that now ; and the hand held out to him was hard, and distorted by work, but it was held out to him when he stood on the verge of failure !

There was a strange feeling in his throat, and he could scarcely say the simple " I will, Mrs. Milton," that sealed their compact : then he sat down again, and Mrs. Milton put all the dishes about his plate, talking rapidly the while.

" My boys would a-been jest like youuns, if the

measles hedn't tuck 'em off; and when you goes a-trompin' roun', I jest 'llows thet it's my Sammy done growed up, I do," again resorting to the corner of her apron, "an' jest you let these pore creeturs roun' this yer town come a-howlin' about you," fiercely, "an' Mandy Milton'll make 'em pisen sure thet they's a-stannin' on the wrong end; jest you bet on thet!" sitting down vigorously and filling her plate with supper.

"I would not worry about it," Jerry said quietly; "people always think you are afraid when you explain things, and make excuses; I do not intend to say a word."

Mrs. Milton put down her knife and fork, and pushed up her glasses.

"Jest so!" she began sarcastically, nodding her head slowly, "thet's the way the doctor done; jest the way, an' the folks don't know this minute if he wuz a raskil, er a angil, they don't," again attacking her supper. "Jest you keep yer mouth shet, an' when the folks is done a-cussin' an' a-lyin' 'bout you, then jest fall off a rock an' gie 'em orl youuns' money; an' they wont keer a durn: thet's the way, jest you grip onter thet, an' they'll tuck orl youuns is got, an' furgit you ter-morrer. Golly!" taking a long draught of coffee, "I know what you don't, Jerry Wilkerson, thet cussin' is the best thing fur mos' folks; cuss 'em tell they're skeered thet you'll shoot 'em, an' they'll clean yer boots alonger their tongues, you bet!"

"Well," and Jerry rose wearily from his place, "they have not ruined me yet, and maybe they will not."

"Mebbe," slowly, "an' mebbe the snow'll not melt, mebbe; but it won't be fur lacker tryin'. Just you shoot a few, an' knock down the res', an' they'll think thet Jerry Wilkerson's the biggest man in 'Meriky—thar aint nothin' you've done thet's made you look so big as knockin' down Dave Morris."

Jerry laughed again ; the weary laugh that comes of despair,—that laughs because that is as good as tears or expostulations.

"Good-night," he said, pausing with his hand on the door, "and believe that I am truly thankful to you, Mrs. Milton, for your trust and friendship given me now when the world is turning away from me."

Mrs. Milton scraped the plates violently before casting them into the pan of hot water that stood near.

"Youuns is welcome, Jerry Wilkerson," she answered tersely, "but don't say nothin' mo' 'bout it—it makes me feel rale puny when I hears sich largin' words, 'cause I aint got none to jaw back : jest you go 'long an' ress, an' git up a little sperret 'ginst the mornin' ; don't say nothin' mo'," and Jerry, obeying her, shut the door and went upstairs slowly.

He was weary unto death : no aim nor end that could be claimed by man seemed to him worth the exertion that would be necessary to win it. The reaction from a great effort and a great passion was upon him : he had worked to the utmost of his strength, physical and mental, only to find himself thwarted at every point ; only to find himself undermined, and on the brink of ruin.

He turned restlessly on the bed where he had thrown himself.

It was impossible that he should fail : if Eureka did grow equally with Durden's, it would help him, not hurt him. And if the people had found out that he had money, that would not harm him, they could not take it away ; he was sure of this now, for he had heard Mrs. Milton say that Dan Burk's money had come from the same place as Joe's. Dan Burk would keep quiet, and Mrs. Milton was his friend ; beyond this, how could the people have any feeling against him, or harm him because of the money ? he had said publicly how he got it. He was sure it was all safe except the stream, and this last fall of snow would make it rise; he could see it now swirling and foaming on its way. And sleep overtook him as he lay there; the dreamless sleep of exhaustion; and the faint daylight creeping in the window showed him white and haggard, with the bands of silver hair on his temples grown broader, and the lines on his face deepened and drawn.

A worn, weary face that even in sleep had an anxious, eager look on it; and all the youth and hope gone from it.

CHAPTER XIV.

"Something is rotten in the state of Denmark."

A GREAT stillness had fallen over the town: a stillness of disappointment and reaction, and out of the stillness there arose a sound like the whispering of the wind as it creeps by in the summer nights; inarticulate, intangible, and yet a sound caused; a fact that would have an effect.

There was nothing to take hold of; nothing that could be answered; no points that could be fought for and won; no place where a stand could be made.

Day and night Jerry listened and watched: Mrs. Milton fumed and fretted because she could hear nothing: going about among her neighbors more than ever before in her life; condescending even to a conversation with Jim Short, if so be she might gain a little information.

And Greg was uneasy: Paul had been inclined to make a friend of him at first, but after the decided stand Greg had taken at the supper, he had been less effusive. He was pleasant and cordial still; regretted the failure of the excursion and the hasty departure of the ladies; invited Greg to dinner to meet Mr. Henshaw and Mr. Mills, and after dinner read aloud criticisms from the papers on Durden's and Eureka, and on their relative merit as investments; in all of which the danger from the stream was enlarged on to the detriment of Durden's.

"You should write a piece," he said to Mr. Henshaw, "giving your views on the subject."

Mr. Henshaw rubbed his head in a troubled way.

"There is danger in it," he said in his slow, literal

way, "danger I am realizing more and more every day—danger I did not dream of when I wrote my first letter; and perhaps it is my duty to explain the true state of things."

Paul laughed lightly.

"Scarcely your duty to direct the investments of people," he said, "but you should rather build up the credit of Durden's; you must stand up for it."

"And you need not be so anxious about it," Greg added.

Mr. Mills shook his head.

"I should be," he said gravely.

"Well," said Greg, "I am not, and my father is in very heavily."

Paul's face sobered a little. Would the failure of Durden's influence Isabel Greg's fortune materially? he wondered.

"I should advise him to draw out a little," he suggested, "at least until the danger from the spring snow is over."

"I do not admit the danger," Greg answered stiffly; and the next day advised Jerry not to let Henshaw write any more public letters about Durden's.

All was very easy and smooth in the way things were going: the lunch-room in Eureka was gaining favor every day; the *Durden's Banner* had constant notices of people who were negotiating for homes in Eureka, and Jerry was in receipt of many letters as to the leasing of the lots left by the doctor.

From his broker Jerry heard that more Durden's stock had been bought in for him, and that there was no fluctuation about it; the excursion had done good, Mr. Glendale thought, except for a dangerous stream which had of late been brought before the public in connection with the mine; this was a little unfortunate, but when the summer came it would be all right again; and he held all stock according to Mr. Wilkerson's orders, ready to sell at a moment's notice; but if he contemplated selling, now was the time to do it; only telegraph the word "sell," and he would understand.

Only one word, and he would be safe out of all this turmoil and worry, and much benefited by the speculation. And why should not he? Everybody knew the danger now as well as he; why should not he withdraw, and so thwart all Paul's schemes by leaving him no one to scheme against?

The thought of the people had no weight with him now, for day by day he could feel them drawing further and further away from him. There was nothing said or done, but there were no hats lifted now as he passed, and there was always a cessation of talk, and a separating of any group he happened to approach: and he felt that he was free from any responsibility for them. There was no reason why he should not withdraw if he wished; while, on the other hand, one dividend declared and his fortune was made—a great fortune such as he had dreamed of, the gold that was to lie about him like chips. And Edith Henley, could not he win her? He remembered how she had crouched behind him that day when he drove her to the station—and the revenge would be so exquisite.

Fail! He could not fail—he would not fail!

And he would make feverish efforts to push the work on, to have this one saving dividend declared; but Mr. Henshaw would not be hurried. And now another conscientious scruple had entered as a factor to retard things: was it honest to go on spending money in putting works into a mine that was not safe? Would it not be right to wait until the threatened danger was over?

And to this Jerry uttered a point-blank *no;* but somehow the idea crept out among the people, and along with it another idea that a dividend would double Jerry's already suspicious fortune, and that then he could and would sell out, leaving the rest of the shareholders to scramble out as best they could.

And the men who worked in the mine because they were shareholders were sullen, and worked unwillingly; and there was no money to increase the force of day-laborers; and Mr. Henshaw urged nobody, for he thought the work ought to stop—a stolid, passive resistance that made Jerry's blood boil!

And at the end of the forlorn street, standing where Jerry could see it every evening as he came from his work, was the little building known as the telegraph office; every evening when he was weary and harassed the thought would come to him that one word sent from there would free him from all this anxiety. Anxiety? He had worked too hard, he had borne too much, he had fought too long, he had weathered too many storms, to give up now when success was in such close grasp of his hand—to give up and acknowledge himself beaten!

But the murmur swelled as the work in the mine was retarded, and as the snow melted, and each day the miners were more unwilling.

Jerry said no word of remonstrance, urged no haste; he was so eager to win that he saw too many sides of the problem before him. If he urged them on, they would say it was for his own benefit, and so resist; if he did not urge them, they would say he had money enough to carry him over the delay; if he urged Mr. Henshaw, he would stop to argue on the honesty of the proceeding, and so publish their weakness; if he urged the Company, they would instantly lose confidence in the venture. The tension was dreadful; to stand and watch the work diminish day by day in quantity; to watch the people growing more and more restive; to watch the water, that from the dam spread out into a small lake, creep up higher and higher; to watch the days that might each one mean a fortune, slipping by unheeded: how long could he bear it?

If only they would have the sense to realize their own good, and drive forward now, before the snow melted, the declaration of a dividend.

But he could not tell them this: putting it into words made him realize how it went against all the teachings of his life, all the instincts of his nature. To say "work hard while the stream is yet safe, force the declaration of a dividend; then if the danger increases to peril, sell, and so double your investment." He could not say this; he might do it, but he could not look his fellow-man in the face and say it: if it were to be done, it must be accomplished by a side pressure of some kind,—and he said to Dan Burk:

"Mr. Glendale who bought out the half of every Durden's man's share in the mine, when they were pushed in the winter, is willing to buy the other half if they will sell now before a dividend is declared."

"He wants all the profits," and Dan laughed.

"Of course," quietly, "and they will be great."

Dan shook his head.

"Mebbe, an' mebbe not;" slowly, "but I aint got no capital to hold over no longer, an' he kin have all of mine"; then with a smile, 'I hear thet you're agoin' to sell, yourself."

The color crept up into Jerry's face, and he longed to teach the man a lesson with his fists; but it would not be expedient just now, and he answered quietly:

"That is a lie, Burk, and you know it."

"Just so," and Burk smoothed his sleek hair as if in deep thought—"well, it's a lie then; an' Mr. Henley's just done sellin' all of his stock, an' the same Mr. Glendale that wants it so bad," still smoothing his hair, "bought it for you, Mr. Wilkerson," looking up suddenly as if to surprise some tell-tale expression on Jerry's face. Jerry met the look quietly, as he answered:

"Your new master teaches you well, Burk, but not well enough; you will outwit yourselves very soon.

Tell Mr. Henley that there is an old saying 'that a dog that will fetch, will carry'."

"I'll tell him," Burk answered, while his forehead seemed to flatten back with rage, "an' mebbe I don't understand it, an' won't remember it, mebbe. All the same, tell Mr. Glendale he kin have all my shares."

Jerry laughed.

"Very well, when I have occasion to write again I will tell him."

"An' mebbe *when* a dividend is declared, I'll be sorry," Dan said as Jerry turned away, "mebbe."

Reaching his office, Jerry sat down trembling from head to foot: anger was no name for his frame of mind. He had not gained anything by his effort to excite Dan's covetousness in the mention of a dividend, Paul had undermined him too carefully, but he had found out more clearly his own danger, and that it was greater than he thought. And he had found out that Paul had held Durden's stock; of course he had bought it only that he might injure the scheme by selling at a critical moment; and he had sold now!

"I should have killed him long ago," Jerry whispered to himself.

The days crept on; and a sullen, fitful sleet took the place of the snow that had been falling intermittently ever since the excursion. Looking back, and straining his memory, Jerry could not recall any spring like this one; and the only gleam of hope was that it was growing colder.

Mr. Henshaw still hesitated; watching the stream conscientiously, going day after day to stand on the dam—anxious, miserable, ruinously honest!

Longer and longer the days seemed to stretch, until to Jerry they spread into desert-wastes of time. The level sweep of water at the dam was so high that the little film of ice which was gathering along the edges was barely an inch below the top: but this film of ice was a hope!

The silver bands of hair on Jerry's temples grew

wider; the lines in his face grew deeper; the light in his eyes grew into a painful brightness that glittered and flickered restlessly.

More of the stock had been bought in in his name; loan after loan had been negotiated for him that he might buy the shares that now seemed daily on the market; he could not understand it, nor why the people seemed to be returning to their allegiance to him. Hats were lifted now when he passed, and the greetings offered him were more hearty. But Greg grew more and more grave; Mr. Henshaw, more and more uncertain, and Mrs. Milton lifted a warning voice:

"Thar's somethin' wrong sommers," she said, "if only you'd kill a few, Jerry Wilkerson."

The number of shareholders who worked in the mine steadily decreased: every day as Greg called the roll, the answer would come for two or three—"stopped work"; often Jerry stopped them to put them at other work—often they paid money instead of work—but at last when he realized that many had never returned to the mine, it struck him that they must be selling out. None of the directors had sold any stock as far as he could find out from his father and brother, yet it was creeping out in New York that Durden's was selling secretly because unsafe. Something was wrong, and Greg went to see Jerry for the first time in weeks.

"The Durden's people must be selling," he said abruptly, as he took off his hat and coat.

Jerry looked up quickly.

"That solves the problem," he said; "Glendale could not trace the stock."

"I am sure of it," and Greg walked up and down the room impatiently.

"I was afraid the directors were giving in," Jerry went on.

Greg shook his head.

"Father and Van Dusen have bought more; and I came to-day to tell you," and Greg stopped in his walk, "that father urges the declaration of a dividend even if a point is strained to do it."

"Then they must send me another engineer," Jerry answered, "Henshaw will not be hurried."

Greg took another turn up and down the room.

"I have not been able to say this," Jerry went on, "because I have too much at stake: my urging a dividend would only have convinced the shareholders that the investment was not safe, and it would have been a race to see who could sell out first, and the scheme would have collapsed: urging Henshaw and the people, would have caused the same distrust: my only plan was to wait."

"It is all true," Greg said slowly, "but I had not realized it;" then suddenly, "I will say it," and he turned to put on his coat and hat—"I will telegraph this minute," and he left the little office hurriedly.

Jerry listened to his footsteps as they rang on the frozen ground; listened until the sound faded from his hearing, then put his face down in his hands. Was help coming at last? would any response be made to this appeal? were the shareholders anxious enough about the investment to take any steps?

His imagination sprang forward like an unleashed hound: Henshaw would be roused from his lethargy: a dividend would be declared: then—? A shudder as of the parting of soul and body shook him! Then gold would fall into his hands as the stream fell down the mountain side—brimming up—flowing over—slipping through his careless fingers!

And it was growing colder—surely his luck had turned! Ice was lord of water—ice would save him. Colder and colder it grew as the night fell; colder and colder through the long dragging hours that each one found him waiting and watching; colder and colder; bitter, merciless, intense. The pines up on the mountain-side bent down their sturdy heads under their glittering loads of sleet—the beams of the houses creaked, and groaned, and jerked; great masses of rock cracked and fell in the silent night, clanging out sharply as with a protest against their fall. The morning dawned, and no sign of life, save smoke from the chimneys, showed the presence of man in the town; and the old people and the children cried because the cold was killing them.

Twenty-four hours passed, then Greg came with a telegram:

"The board has met: unanimous vote on your proposition: much stock in the market. No one selling here. CHAS. T. GREG."

Jerry read it, then looked up quickly.

"You were right," he said.

"Yes," Greg answered, "the Durden's people are selling; every day as I call the roll one or more shareholders answer 'Stopped work.' I thought you had them at work elsewhere—or that you knew it; Henshaw knew it."

Jerry walked up and down the room restlessly: the race was becoming breathless: the prize was so near!

"This freeze is a godsend," Greg went on, "it makes all safe as long as it lasts, and the order from the board may be for Henshaw to declare a dividend before a thaw comes: I hope they will make it deucedly strong."

Jerry did not answer—he could not, the issue was too vital to him for any discussion; for him life or death was held fast in this freeze.

A dividend while the freeze lasted would put a hundred men to work to save the mine before a thaw came: if Henshaw hesitated, if a warm wind came, his ruin was inevitable; so he could not discuss it.

"And we must not say a word until Henshaw comes to us," Greg went on; "it must seem as if all the anxiety was with the eastern shareholders. If Henshaw should find out that the fears originated here, he would be as cautious and as stolid as ever, confound him! Mills would have saved us long ago."

"I was too anxious to be honest when I described

the engineer I wanted," and Jerry laughed. "Honesty only pays when, as in the copy-books, it is policy."

Greg shook his head.

"I would not say that," he said in a troubled way, "it does not sound well."

"No," Jerry answered, "it does not *sound* well."

Another night had fallen black and cold as death: would not the houses, as well as the rocks, fall in this awful coldness? People were found frozen on the roads: wild creatures came down and sought shelter near humanity; wolves had been found in the mines, and in the nights they were heard wandering up and down the streets and crying, seeking shelter against the outsides of warm chimneys.

Cold such as never had been known in Durden's; and the old people and the little children lay down and died.

It was too late in the year for such a freeze to last forever, Mrs. Milton had said; and much of it had gone when Mr. Henshaw came up to Jerry's office, where Greg and Jerry watched for him with sickening anxiety. He looked drawn and blue with cold, his long, thin nose looked pinched, and behind his spectacles his mild blue eyes were distressed and watery.

"What shall I do?" he asked, before he had taken off his hat or his clumsy woolen gloves that his "Sue" had knit for him; "A telegram from the directors that a dividend *must* be declared; too much stock on the market."

Jerry's eyes gleamed, but for a moment he could not speak, and Greg took the coarse paper from Mr. Henshaw's hands, while he divested himself of his out-door wrappings.

"I had not an idea that it would have such an effect as this," Mr. Henshaw went on, putting his large overshoes carefully aside; "I thought it was right to let the poor who had invested know the danger, and Mr. Henley thought so too; you knew all the danger, Mr. Wilkerson," turning to Jerry, who was looking into the fire steadily, "and you, Mr. Greg; and besides, Mr. Henley said that both of you were well enough off to tide over even a failure," looking anxiously from one to the other, "so he negotiated the sales of the poor people's shares while it was yet time; and he showed me a letter from a broker which said it would not hurt the venture, as Mr. Wilkerson was anxious to buy all the stock he could get, and was rich enough to do it with safety; but," his voice steadying from distress to dignity, "I have not sold my own shares, I have been anxious only about the very poor,"—then a silence fell.

To Jerry many things were explained as Mr. Henshaw went on; Paul's hand was in all his trouble, and Paul might succeed yet. The room seemed to spin round him; it was an agonizing moment; he felt he must realize something in order to steady his mind, and he fastened his eyes on Mr. Henshaw's great overshoes that were ribbed up and down the instep, and turned up a little at the toes that looked as if they might often touch each other; and the heels would fit an African!

Jerry smiled a little, the huge black things looked so ugly, and so narrow-minded, and so honest.

Then Greg said sharply, as he took a turn up and down the room:

"I cannot see why you went to Henley for advice."

"You are mistaken, Mr. Greg," and Mr. Henshaw drew himself up more stiffly in his chair, "Mr. Henley came to me with the advice, and came on behalf of the poor as represented by Daniel Burk. Burk was the first to sell his shares, and said Mr. Wilkerson knew that he was selling."

Jerry shook his head.

"I told Burk only that I was not afraid of the stock," he said; "that selling even then, when I spoke to him, the stock would bring twice as much as he gave for it."

Greg paused in his walk.

"That was unwise," he said; "of course hearing that they would all want to sell."

"It was that, or a strike which would have ruined us," Jerry answered. "As it is, the crisis has come gradually, and we will soon be safe."

Mr. Henshaw shook his head, as he looked mournfully into the fire.

"If we declare a dividend before a thaw comes," he said, "we will save ourselves, but defraud others. I know how many people will be induced to invest in this mine because of this dividend, and how their money will be sunk in the restoration of the mine after the stream has flooded it. I know how all who hold shares now will quadruple the amount they invested, and that many of them will save themselves entirely by selling out the moment the dividend is declared: I know all this, and I know it is not honest—it is not honest!"

"Damnation!" and Greg drove a log into the fire viciously with the heavy heel of his boot.

"It is true, Mr. Greg," Mr. Henshaw went on, "and every hour I live I repent having invested in the mine; if I had not done that, I could have worked with a clear conscience, simply obeying orders; as it is, I am so much interested myself, that I am afraid always of forgetting the cause of the poor, and acting for my own good only: and even if we succeed now before the freeze breaks, I can not bear to think of the poor who may invest, expecting immediate returns; and Mr. Henley says he understands how I feel about it, especially now that I am ordered to send a telegram that will authorize a dividend."

"Have you told Henley that?" Greg asked quickly.

"Yes," mildly; "he was with me when it came, and is such a friend of your family."

Greg stood by the window silent; silence was their only safety now; and into Jerry's mind there came the memory of some words of thanks this simple, honest gentleman had said to him when he had lent him money to invest in the mine: "I thank you, in the name of my wife, and of all my little children," he had said; "you free us from anxiety for the future." He was a simple, honest gentleman, this engineer; and Jerry's face burned as he thought "Too honest for us."

Then Jerry looked up slowly.

"How much did you invest, Mr. Henshaw?" he asked, his voice falling quietly on the silence.

Mr. Henshaw's face grew more mournful still.

"Two thousand dollars," he answered, as if the world must tremble at the amount; it was so much to him—indeed, it was all to him!

Jerry looked into the fire.

"Will you take six thousand for it?" he asked, "and be free to obey orders?"

"Six thousand!" and Mr. Henshaw took off his spectacles to wipe them, and Greg turned from the window quickly.

"Will you take it?" he said.

Mr. Henshaw looked helpless.

"You must remember," Jerry went on, "that you may be worth three times as much as I offer you, if you hold your shares; but if you would rather be out of it, and free of responsibility, I offer you six for two."

"No, no!" Mr. Henshaw faltered, "it is not that; six is too much; but I can not bear to let you risk so much."

Jerry laughed.

"Five or ten thousand more can make very little difference to me," he said, "for if I fail, I am ruined."

The words were said so quietly that Mr. Henshaw scarcely took them in, or believed them: Paul had impressed him so thoroughly with the idea of Jerry's wealth, that ruin in connection with him seemed absurd.

"We will say six," Jerry went on, "and you can make the transfer immediately, and telegraph the same to your man of business," putting a chair near the table, and arranging all necessary materials for Mr. Henshaw, "and I will telegraph Glendale to pay cash."

"Yes," and Mr. Henshaw took the seat prepared for him.

"But write your telegram to the Board first, Mr. Henshaw," Greg interrupted, "so that I can send it; they are anxious."

"Yes, yes," and Mr. Henshaw began to write, and Jerry also.

Greg walked up and down the room; he could not be still; the game he had watched so long, and from which he had held aloof, had drawn him into its vortex at last, and had become painful in its excitement. He looked at Jerry in wonder; with all at stake—his money, his reputation, his whole future—he quietly paused to help a poorer man out of the venture; and betrayed by neither word nor sign any feeling against the enemy who was systematically planning his ruin! This crisis was an awful test of a man's strength and firmness, and yet Jerry did not falter: he must succeed—failure would be too cruel!

"You take this down at once, Greg," Jerry said, reading over the despatch Mr. Henshaw had written to the board, "and telegraph your father to send the news back instantly to the *Banner*," and Greg saw a little shiver run over Jerry as he held out the paper.

"I will," he answered, and went away quickly: his pity, his impatience, and his admiration were too great, he could not bear to watch Jerry now, and hated himself because that once he had turned away from this man.

"And now for the transfer of your shares, Mr. Henshaw," and Jerry turned to the table again.

Presently it was all done, and Mr. Henshaw stood looking into the fire.

"You have put me under great obligations, Mr. Wilkerson," he said at last, "and I can not do anything that will show you ever how deeply I feel your action in this matter, and how much I appreciate your generosity;" then more slowly, "and I can not see what I have done to deserve this kindness."

"Do not speak of it," Jerry answered quickly; "it is no risk for me, and as I persuaded you into the speculation, I could not do less than help you out when it became obnoxious to you."

"It was not in order to persuade me to send the telegram demanded, for I should have had to do that in any case," Mr. Henshaw went on in a preoccupied way, as if hunting for Jerry's motive, "I can see no motive except to relieve my conscientious scruples: I shall never forget it, sir," and Mr. Henshaw wiped his spectacles again—"*never* forget it: will you shake hands, Mr. Wilkerson?" and he wrung Jerry's hand; then putting on his careful wrappings, he went his way, wondering why Jerry's hands were so cold—cold and clammy as death!

CHAPTER XV.

> " And wicked eyes gleamed bright wiih hate—and crowds
> Surged back and forth—and wild hands waved—
> And curses fled from lip to lip, and up
> On the mad wind to where God waited—silent ! "

FORTY-EIGHT hours had come and gone, and Durden's was in a state of silent astonishment.

For the first time in its life, the *Banner* was cried up and down the one street of the town: the people came to their doors and windows as the shrill boy voice broke the dead, frozen stillness—the news was told !

" Dividend declared—great fortunes made—All the world buying Durden's stock—All who had sold, were sold ! "

The son of the editor of the *Banner* who had not sold, cried the news with vicious delight ; absolutely jeering at Dan Burk as he handed him the paper—

" Mr. Wilkerson the richest man in America ! " and the small tormentor danced on the frozen ground to keep his feet warm.

Greg heard it as he dressed, and shouted like a boy at Christmas : Mr. Henshaw heard it as he waked—heard it with a struggle between his longing to have quadrupled his investment, and his consciousness that there was somewhat in this almost bogus dividend that would not be authorized by one's duty to one's neighbor : Jerry heard it as he sat at breakfast, and could not speak nor move ; his heart seemed to stop its beating, and Mrs. Milton's voice, as she greeted the newsboy and paid him for his news, seemed far away. Everything grew red and confused before his eyes, and strange rushing sounds came in his ears as if all the blood in his body had gone to his head. He did not know if he reeled or not, just for a moment, but he knew when Mrs. Milton put the paper into his hand saying:

"Youuns is the riches' man in Ameriky, Jerry Wilkerson;" then more slowly, "an' orl outer 'Lije Milton's mine thet killed him."

"It is all pure luck, Mrs. Milton," Jerry answered huskily, and the sound of his voice seemed to restore his equilibrium. Mrs. Milton shook her head solemnly.

"Thar aint no luck ner no chence in thet mine," she said; "too many sperrets walks roun' in thar fur luck or chence to live thar: it's God or the devil a-helpin' youuns."

Jerry rose from the table, he could sit still no longer.

"Wherever the help comes from," he said, "I am very thankful; but I do not think it is the devil, Mrs. Milton, for Paul Henley is his own child."

"Now you're shoutin'," the old woman cried; then Jerry walked away.

Was he safe? he could have cried aloud in his joy; he felt a foolish desire to mount some high place and shout and shout until he was breathless! All the sickening anxiety was over—his fortune was made—his enemy vanquished. Rapidly he strode up the frozen road toward his office; dismal and cold it looked, but he did not mind that—he had the fire to make, even if he were in Mrs. Milton's eyes the richest man in America! He laughed over the idea—a rich, ringing laugh that seemed to bubble over with joy: and he took Joe's old ax from the corner and went out to where the wood was piled.

Poor old Joe; surely this fortune was his, surely. He had dug it out of the earth through long years; had stored it away day by day for a poor waif he had picked up on the roadside: and there was no luck in it, the old woman had said, no luck; God or the devil had helped him!

Hard and vigorous his blows rang, and the chips flew right and left; so he had struck at life and fortune, and so the gold would lie about him: and when he had enough, would be as worthless as these chips. He remembered when he had said that at the Gregs' table that Fred had laughed; would Fred laugh now? and Isabel, did she know of his fortune? and lovely Edith Henley?

He gathered up his wood and went in: he must have the fire burning and his office in order before any one came: he must not look upset in the turn affairs had taken, nor surprised, not even to Greg. And he must make arrangements to put men to work on the stream below the dam: the mine must be made safe, now that he had time to be honest.

Quickly the fire blazed up: then he opened the windows, and swept and put things in order as old Joe had taught him to do; old Joe asleep up there on the mountain-side, while his fortune had grown colossal!

"Well!" and Greg came in brisk and beaming, though a little hesitating still, "I have come to congratulate you!"

"Thank you," and Jerry shook his hand heartily, "it has been a very near thing."

"Very near, thanks to that blundering Henshaw," Greg answered, drawing a chair near the fire; "I think Henshaw must have been evoluted from a black beetle," laughing, "and if my dear old Dad had not been so prompt, he might have ruined us: but it is safe enough now."

"Or at least we have gained time enough to make it safe," and with the allowing of a doubt that he uttered more to steady his exuberant joy, than because he held it, Jerry felt a nameless fear creep over him.

"Why, man, it is certain!" and Greg slapped his leg emphatically; "your fortune is made, even if you have to spend half on this dividend; and who can hurt us now?"

Jerry laughed.

"I do not know," he said, the joy that he controlled in word and action ringing out in his voice, "but I am afraid to realize it all at once, so try to cool myself off with dismal possibilities."

The door opened and a boy came in.

"For you, Mr. Wilkerson," and he handed Jerry a telegram.

Things seemed to waver before Jerry's eyes as he tore open the envelope: was this a dismal possibility?

"To J. P. WILKERSON—Durden's:
from
J. C. Glendale, New York.
Durden's up,—await orders—three days the limit."

Jerry handed the message to Greg, then turned to the table and wrote:

"To J. C. GLENDALE, No. — Wall Street, New York:
from
J. P. Wilkerson, Durden's.
Wait."

And this was handed to Greg also. Greg read it over.

"Wise," he said, "try the temper of the people on the work first; but why do you sign your name before you send your message?"

Jerry laughed.

"It is one of Glendale's fads," he answered. "He said that as soon as he sees the name of his correspondent, his mind throws itself in position for the message; it does seem more simple.

"Like Glendale, the explanation is thin," and Greg laughed.

Then the paper was put into the boy's hand, the door was shut, and the footsteps of the messenger died away.

"Father will telegraph me some time to-day," Greg went on, "I will bring it up."

"Thank you,"—then Jerry paused in the extraordinary pen-and-ink sketches he was making on his blotting-paper; "I should like to feel Henley's pulse," he said.

The color flashed into Greg's face.

"I should like to punch his head!" he exclaimed, "the miserable sneak! a 'dear friend of my family,' and all the while trying to kill this scheme when he knows my father is in it—"

"Hush!" and Jerry went to the door.

"Hardy, Mr. Wilkerson!" and a body of miners came in; "we've come to shake han's, Mr. Wilkerson, an' to hooray for Durden's, you bet!" and they crowded about him enthusiastically.

"Come in, come in!" and Jerry's voice trembled audibly; "I am glad to welcome those who stood by me, very glad!"

"We brought up a little beer," one man went on modestly, "to warm up our money thet's a-comin'!"

Greg laughed.

"And the money will need warming," he said, "for a freeze brought it to us," taking two tin cups down from a shelf.

"They say that Mr. Henley's sick this mornin'," and the men looked at each other knowingly as the big cup passed from one to the other.

"Are you men the only ones who have held your shares?" and Jerry's voice seemed to settle the company.

"All," was answered.

"Ten men!" and Jerry seemed to be counting them over again to assure himself,

"Ten outside of Titcomb"—the editor of the paper,—"Titcomb aint sold out."

"Eleven men, ten working men," Jerry said. "Well, you must come and have supper with me to-night; we must consult about making the stream safe," and he spread a sheet of paper on the table; "I want you to give Mr. Greg your names."

"All right," and one after another the men gave in their names.

"Come to Mrs. Milton's this evening at seven," Jerry went on, "and we will drink a health to our fortunes."

"We'll sure come, Mr. Wilkerson, plum sure: and to the work too;" then the beer was finished, and the men went away.

"Only eleven men," Jerry said, when the little office was empty once more, "only eleven men to stand by us, Greg."

"Enough to share money with," Greg answered.

"Quite, but an awful minority when you remember all who went in with us."

"Poor fools!" and Greg threw some more wood on the fire, "they are sold enough now."

"If only they will continue 'sold'," Jerry answered slowly.

"What do you mean?"

"I do not trust Henley," Jerry said, "he may hurt us yet: I am sure he will try."

Greg laughed.

"You are worn out, Wilkerson," he said in a more familiar tone than he had used in a long time, "Henley must see that we have won, and will have sense enough to give up the fight."

Jerry shook his head doubtfully—

"I hope so," he said.

Slowly but surely the crowd gathered in the lunch room in Eureka—a glum, silent crowd. There was no laughter; no greeting of each other; no jokes; a sullen, morose crowd, but a crowd. And the seats seemed to have been prepared for them, and also the drink that was distributed free of charge.

All through the cold, slow-falling afternoon men, women, and children were drinking; drinking as if they wanted something to do—as if they wanted the excitement—drinking themselves mad.

As the night fell a dim illumination became visible: "*Free Supper*"; a dim illumination, but an old woman, hovering on the outskirts of the crowd, read it and drew nearer.

It meant something, this gathering, something against Durden's; for all the people she could recognize were people who had sold their shares long ago. Then on the frozen ground was heard the sound of wheels, and through the darkness a wagon rolled down the road: nearer and nearer, then a stop in front of the illuminated sign, and Paul Henley, followed by Dan Burk and Dave Morris, entered the lighted shop. There arose a little murmur from the crowd, a sound that deepened as Paul raised his glass to drink their health, a sound like the turning of the tide.

Then slowly in and out of the crowd Dan Burk and Dave Morris passed, talking first to one and then to another: and the woman out in the darkness drew nearer.

The talk and hum of voices grew louder and louder, until a voice from the back of the building called—

"Three cheers for Mr. Henley, the poor man's friend!" and a disorganized shout followed that dragged along unevenly until Burk cried out—

"Three cheers for Durden's Mine!"

There was a moment's silence, then a howl arose that swept over the assembly like the cry of wild beasts; and a hubbub of voices followed where nothing was distinguishable save the anger that sounded dangerous: a hubbub of voices that was not stilled until Burk sprang on the counter calling out—

"Listen to me!" and the crowd turned in his direction—"I am as mad as you!" he cried, "I've been plum fooled 'cause I b'lieved Jerry Wilkerson was an honest man!" then he paused for the applause that came madly from the half-intoxicated mob—"He's lived in Durden's man an' boy; all his money come outer Durden's Mine; I knows it an' none better," pausing again and looking over the crowd that was now intensely still—"Joe Gilliam was my pardner; an' nobody knows how Joe Gilliam died; an' nobody knows how Jerry Wilkerson got so much money down East; an' nobody knew thet Jerry Wilkerson hed bought most all Durden's Mine; an' nobody knew thet a dividend was a-comin' when Jerry Wilkerson says—says 'ee,"—pausing for greater effect, "'Dan Burk,' says 'ee, 'you kin git back double your money if you'll sell now,' says 'ee; an' Dan Burk trusted him, an' Dan Burk was the fust to sell out!"

"Thet's so—thet's so!" came eagerly from the crowd.

"An' Mr. Henley sold; an' Mr. Henshaw sold; an' every one to Mr. Glendale in New York, for—Jerry Wilkerson!" pausing while a groan went up from his listeners. "An' when our children an' ole folks were a-dyin' from cold, Jerry Wilkerson cussed us into fixin' thet dam!"

There was a dead silence, an unexpected silence that caused Dan to pause for a moment and look at Paul with some doubt.

"You are weary," Paul said kindly, handing him a glass of whisky—"it is hard work talking of the money you have lost."

Burk swallowed the dram eagerly, then again turned to his task.

"Fifty men stood in the water a-freezin', and a-savin' thet damned mine, an' now!" scornfully—"'Leven men gits all the money! Dan Burk fooled you all inter sellin', but Jerry Wilkerson fooled Dan Burk; an' when the freeze come thet would hold the water, an' when all the people have sold out, Jerry Wilkerson orders a dividend; makes the engineer order a dividend,—orders it to run up the stock; an' in two days he'll sell out an' stand free an' rich! yes, an' he'll laugh at us pore folks that has been fooled, an' are as pore as ever! An' the water'll come over the dam all the same, an' all thet buys Jerry Wilkerson's stock'll be fooled, an' be ruined like we have been; an' all because we fixed the dam!" He ceased, and came down from the counter amid a storm of applause and angry oaths that were silenced by Dave Morris, who stood up and asked that the crowd would drink to Mr. Henley. There was an eager rush to the bar where Paul Henley stood thanking the people for their good wishes.

And Mrs. Burk handed out the liquor; strong, crude whisky that burned like fire—that crazed and maddened the people into brute beasts.

"To the health of the dam!" Burk cried out at last.

"Damn it!" was answered by a dozen voices.

"I'd pull it down," Mrs. Burk suggested to one bloated creature whose cup she was filling; and voices all about her took up the words—

"Pull it down—pull it down!"

"One more drink, boys," Dave Morris called, "an' we'll be fit to pull down hell!"

Then through the darkness a woman sped away—an old woman with white hair that, escaping from its fastenings, streamed out on the wind; and her little eyes, set deep in beds of yellow wrinkles, glowed like fire as she ran; and her breath came short and fast, and curses with each breath! On and on, and yet she seemed to go so slowly! on and on over the hard, slippery ground: how often she fell! how often she seemed to slip back! how far Durden's was from Eureka! On and on, worn and almost breathless; panting, while in her ears the wind sounded like the howling of the mob!

Were they coming? Would not she be in time to warn them?

On and on; at last lights gleamed in front of her; they seemed near, but now every step was up-hill! Would she live to reach those lights?

At last!

Almost she fell against the door; the weary old

woman: panting and breathless,—worn and without strength she stood before the thirteen men who were laughing and talking over their quiet supper, secure and at peace.

"Git yer guns!" she cried hoarsely, "an' go to the dam!"

Every man rose to his feet and Jerry sprang to her side. "Mrs. Milton, who told you this?" he cried.

"I hearn 'em a-sayin' it," she panted laboriously, "over in Henley's eatin' house," drinking eagerly some brandy and water which Greg handed her—"I knowed thar were mischief a-cookin' in Henley's free supper, an' the whole crowd is wild alonger whisky, an' is agoin' now to pull down the dam afore any of youuns kin sell out; git yer guns an' go!" then she sank back exhausted. "I runned orl the way," she whispered, seized with an awful shuddering that made Jerry give quick, sharp orders to the servant-girl: then to the men—

"Get what arms and ammunition you can," he said, "and meet me at the dam as quickly as possible;" then he added—"We are few, but we are sober," and almost instantly the room was emptied.

Terribly dark—and the men collected slowly; bitterly cold,—and no fire could be made as it would betray them. Thirteen men crouching on the broad top of the dam, which elevation gave them a murderous descending fire that must destroy whoever approached: and far below them—down the straggling village street, a few lights shone where the women waited and listened.

All was silent save the muffled cry of the stream as it writhed under its fetters of ice—a level sheet of ice from the dam out to where the broadened stream stopped against the cliffs. Still as death, with fingers stiffening about their guns, with the breath freezing on their lips and beards—The time passed slowly—had the old woman made a mistake?

Jerry stood a little apart, thrilling with a terrible

exultation; this night he would meet his enemy face to face—an open, free fight for fortune—if his enemy conquered—if his enemy ruined him:—he gripped his gun tighter—what an exquisite joy of revenge—the stream that ruined him would ruin Paul! And ruin—what did ruin mean? freedom—aye, freedom from the tension and the misery of his present life—his life that almost had crazed him! Almost?—he drew himself together—was not he crazy now?

A murmur arose among the men; and the boys who had come with extra arms and ammunition, were sent home on account of the awful coldness.

The lights were fewer in the street, and the sullen roar of the stream seemed to grow louder.

At last, far off, there came a hum like the hum of swarming bees, and from the Eureka side a few wavering lights were seen. On they came, and the waiting men drew closer together; no sound, only far off the flickering lights like stars: suddenly they paused, then vanished.

"There are some sober men in the party," Jerry said, "and we must be most careful; repulse them once, and they can not reassemble." Calm enough his voice sounded, but his heart seemed to beat in his ears, and the blood surged and tingled in his veins.

Suddenly Greg stood beside him breathless, and caught his arm in a hard grasp.

"Whichever of us is first freed from this crowd," he whispered, "must send the message for both, and the message must be 'sell.'"

The practical words seemed to calm Jerry, and a wild regret came into his mind that he had not sent the message—he uttered a low oath.

"I have been waiting at the office," Greg went on, "trying to send the message, but the man was absent, and I had to come."

"If any disaster threatens, one of us must get there to send it," and Jerry cocked and uncocked his rifle viciously.

"One of us will," Greg answered, then a silence fell between them.

Suppose he should send a message now to Paul about the stream—Paul would not believe it: it could not be proved except by experiment? And of course they could repulse a drunken mob!

"They're jest a-crawlin' by the town," a man whispered to Jerry.

"And perfectly silent," Greg said, looking keenly at the black mass that now could be seen by the wan, dead light of the moon that had risen behind the gray clouds—"the leaders are not drunk."

"Mr. Henley never gits drunk," the man answered, "nor Dan Burk."

"That is true," Jerry commented, and again he cocked and uncocked his rifle; the sound brought him solace: it was better so to win success or death!

Sixteen good cartridges he had, sixteen chances against failure: would Paul fight—would he fasten his longing hands on him this night?

Nearer and nearer the black mass came; they could hear their footsteps ringing on the ice now, and cracking through the frozen crust of the snow.

"Every man pick out his man," Jerry whispered, "take careful aim, and when I give the word, fire as one man," and the order was whispered along the line.

Of course one volley would demoralize the mob completely.

Nearer, and nearer; and the thirteen watchers trembled with excitement in the tense, strained silence that seemed to throb and roar in their ears!

Nearer and nearer: so that the lowered voices could be heard, and a little smothered chuckling; then Dan Burk's voice a little raised:

"Whar's the picks?" There was a pause and a little clatter as of tools being passed from hand to hand, then a voice said—

"Steady now, and move on quickly!"

A shiver ran over Jerry, an irresistible shudder like a death struggle—the voice was Paul's!

Nearer, and nearer they came; making a little more noise now, feeling safe; nearer, and nearer—close under the dam.

"Fire!" one low word, and a belt of light sprang along the dam—a deafening report, and wild cries and confusion!

Then a voice rang clear and high—

"Make for the dam—there are only thirteen men there!"

And the answer came—

"Fire!"

But only four shots answered—there were only four repeating rifles in the party!

Fourteen good bullets left still; and Jerry stood up to his task.

"Fire as fast you can load!" he cried, taking deliberate aim as a white face gleamed more prominently from the black mass: every shot must tell.

More than a hundred men were attacking them: a dense, black mass of maddened, reckless brutes that the unexpected fire had not demoralized: and with every thing in his favor he could kill only sixteen! His pistols! Aye, twelve more shots there; and every shot must kill a fellow-creature; every shot must send an unprepared soul to judgment—and all to save his fortune!

The thought made his hand waver for one shot; did it miss?

The other side were firing now; and Titcomb, kneeling beside Jerry, fell back on the ice, crashing through with a wild cry!

Again Jerry fired, steadily, calmly. He could have cut every throat in that howling mob, wild and mad with drink.

Greg stood close beside him now.

"Four men have been knocked over," he said.

"Make every shot tell," was Jerry's answer in a

voice that was supernaturally calm, "And if you can escape, send a telegram."

"Yes," and they fired simultaneously.

Wilder the confusion grew; cries, mad curses, groans and shrieks from friends and foes; dying sighs going up through the wan dead light.

They were rushing up on the dam now, and only five men left to hold it!

Calmly Jerry waited, his pistols in his hands: twelve more men must die before his fortune should be wrenched from him—twelve men, or he must die.

Steadily his shots told, and Greg, separated from him now, fought desperately.

"Only three men left!" he heard Paul cry out above the din, "and there stands Wilkerson!"

A howl went up from the mob, and Jerry fell on one knee. He was shot!

One moment his senses seemed to leave him; one wild, whirling moment, then he steadied himself: he could crawl away and send a telegram—he could save himself yet!

If Greg were dead, he did not know; if he were fighting yet and depending on him, he did not know; there was but one thought in his mind—the telegram that would save him!

He was out in the darkness now where the flash of the firing could not reveal him: out in the darkness below the dam, crawling over dead and wounded; if he hurt them, if they groaned or pleaded for help, he could not stop; it was a long way and his leg was dragging.

Cold—oh, God, how cold it was! and these wounded creatures, some of them crawling away too, clutched him as he passed—clutched his weary arms and broken leg! He cried aloud in agony: was that his voice? and was it his knife that he stuck deep in the man's warm flesh; aye, and now he had let him go.

How far—how slow—how cold! An hour ago he could have run—could have saved every dollar.

A high, wild cry rent the air, and sharp, ringing blows as of iron on rock.

They were breaking away the dam.

A shudder ran over him, and for a second he stopped: he was in the old bed of the stream and would be swept away. What frantic haste he made; the rocks and the jagged ice tore his hands, and his own blood leaked out now, warm and trickling slowly; and the other man's blood had frozen on him.

How hard they were working, and all the town seemed alive, with lights flashing here and there, and women's voices shrieking and crying aloud!

They were running by him now, and he turned away from the main road. And did they not know that soon the stream would be loosed, and sweep them away? But he would not tell them, they might stop him; they might hold him from his task—and he had killed their husbands and sons, let them be swept away.

Ah, ha! There in front of him he could see the light; the man was in the office!

Another shout.

Was the dam giving way—would he be too late? He listened: there was no rush of water yet, only the foolish cries of the women, who had nothing to lose now.

Another shout; a long, wild shout, then a roar as if the floods of heaven were let loose!

For one instant he lay on his face, powerless.

Nearer, and nearer the rushing came, and wild, flying feet: the women were running. He started up; maybe Paul would remember to send a telegram before he could reach the office!

How long the way was; only now his leg seemed dead—perhaps it was dead. On he crawled, every moment nearer to his goal; if only the mad crowd flying from the stream would not run over him.

How the water rushed: was it in the mine yet—was it pouring down that black abyss, kissing the rocks it had known so long ago,—sweeping away the crumbled white bones of the man who had turned its course? How it would laugh, and sing, and clap its hands down there in its old haunts! Ah, ha! and flow out in Eureka—ha, ha! No one knew that secret but he!

Nearer, and nearer; only the road between him and the open door of the office from which the yellow lamp-light shone, and the operator silhouetted black in the square door-way.

Only the street to cross.

Was that noise the people coming back—that wild shouting and firing: the mad, drunken mob, and the people afraid of them? And up and down the street the quick closing of windows and doors. Would the operator close the door on him.

Great God, he was moving back!

One last supreme effort—his hand was on the sill; the door must crush his fingers if it closed!

His face blanched to a ghastly white; his eyes, strained and burning, fixed the man with astonishment;—a stranger in Durden's, he yet knew this specter to be Jerry Wilkerson!

"A thousand dollars if you send a message!" and the wounded man dragged himself half in the doorway—"A thousand dollars!"

"All right," and the operator stepped to the instrument.

"And no other message to-night."

"All right."

"To J. C. Glendale—" panting heavily.

"J. C. Glendale," the man repeated, while the instrument clicked busily.

"Number —."

"Number —."

"Wall street."

"Wall street—" steadily, although the shouts and shots of the crazy mob were very near.

"New York."

"New York"— the man repeated it after a second's

pause, for the shouts rang all about them, and the wild shots were hitting the house !

Jerry's words seemed to come so slowly,—his breath seemed thick.

"From J. P. Wilkerson, Durden's "—he gasped.

"J. P. Wilkerson, Durden's "—the man said.

"Sell!" Jerry shrieked—

The instrument stopped—there was one shrill cry, and the operator fell dead across the wounded man.

CHAPTER XVI.

" The string o'erstretched breaks, and the music flies."

"HE aint no better, an' kent never get no better," Mrs. Milton said in a voice that was harsh and bitter with anger and grief, and she looked suspiciously at Greg, who, with his arm in a sling and his head bandaged, looked almost as worn and thin as Jerry lying on the bed between them.

Jerry lying still and helpless, with drawn white face and vacant eyes—vacant eyes that made Greg remember his father's warning.

" He's allers a-countin' them chips," Mrs. Milton went on, pointing to a pile of dry chips that lay under the sick man's hand, "or he's a-talkin' to this little passel," drawing from under Jerry's pillow a small package wrapped in old newspaper.

The sick man held out his hands, so white and tremulous, while a wistful look came into his eyes.

" It's Mammy's," he said, " Mammy's."

Greg looked up in surprise ; Mrs. Milton shook her head, catching a sob in her throat.

" He's been atalkin' thet away ever sence he were brunged har," she said ; " he's done gone backer orl his'n larnin', an' orl his'n trouble, to his'n mammy," and she gave Jerry the little bundle.

" It aint wuth nothin'," he said, looking up at Greg wistfully, " it's nothin' as'll do youuns no good—it's Mammy's—Mammy's," his voice falling fainter.

Greg turned away—was it only that he was weakened by wounds and the awful loss and ruin that he had endured, that he leaned against the mantel-piece sobbing so pitifully ?

"The new doctor says thet he kent las' out the night," Mrs. Milton went on, "an' thar aint nary soul to pray alonger him ceppen you, Mr. Greg."

Greg shook his head.

"I can not," he whispered huskily, "I do not know how."

A tired sigh came from the sick man, causing both watchers to turn.

"I can not count them," he said wearily, in the voice and language that Greg was accustomed to hear from his lips, "but what is the use," he went on, "of counting gold that is as common as chips; as chips that I can throw into the water. Ah, the water! how it boils and surges—how it laughs and sings as it goes back to its old home—and it will flash into the sunlight again at Eureka—Eureka!"

Mrs. Milton went hastily to the bedside.

"He'll git wild in a minute," she said, "an thet'll kill 'im," and again she drew the poor little bundle from under the pillow where he had hidden it. "This aller makes him quiet."

"It's Mammy's," and again the weak hand clasped the bundle, "an' mebbe Dad'll forgit them rails, mebbe he'll furgit," the voice sinking gradually, then the tired eyes closed and he seemed asleep.

Greg came back to the bedside now, and the young physician from the railway camp joined him there: he seemed excited.

"They have caught Henley," he whispered, "but the people must not know it,—they would kill him."

Greg's eyes flashed, and he drew a sharp breath between his clenched teeth. Then aloud the physician said:

"Wilkerson can not possibly live," and his hand was on the fluttering pulse, "and it is most fortunate; for his fortune is gone, and his debts are enormous, and he could never recover his mind; it is most fortunate."

"Git away!" and Mrs. Milton pushed the astonished stranger aside roughly—"if Jerry Wilkerson wuz as big a fool as youuns," she said, "Mandy Milton'd be proud to tuck keer of him fur ever—jest you 'member thet; an' pay orl he owes, an' glad to do it too—an' Mr. Greg knows it."

"I beg pardon," and the young man stepped back, "I meant no harm."

"Mebbe not," sharply, raising Jerry's head on her shoulder that the labored breathing might be a little easier—"an' if you kent do nothin' fur him ceppen to be thankful he's a-dyin', jest go 'long; me an' Mr. Greg kin 'ten' to him."

The doctor took up his hat, when suddenly a hand clutched his shoulder, and the old woman drew him to her, looking in his face with burning eyes.

"Kin youuns pray?" she whispered hoarsely.

He shook his head, and the hold on his shoulder relaxed.

"Notter soul to pray fur him," she muttered, smoothing back from the sick man's brow the hair that had grown so white—"notter soul—but God'll know!"

The sick man's eyes opened.

"Mammy's gone to God," he whispered, "the doctor tole me thet."

"Yes, honey," the old woman answered, soothing him as gently as a mother would her little child; then all was still save the fire that whispered and sighed.

The doctor lingered near the door; Greg leaned against the mantel-piece with his hand over his eyes; the old woman stood as if cut in stone, holding in her arms the dying man: the clock told off relentlessly the flying moments, and the solemn hours gathered full and fell.

Slower and slower the breath came; the heart struggled in its beating; the poor hands held close with pitiful faithfulness the little bundle wrapped up so long ago.

He could not last much longer.

The doctor held the failing pulse ; Greg drew a little nearer ; Mrs. Milton bent a little under the growing weight in her arms.

Slower and slower the pulse-beats came ; the eyelids quivered—there was a little sigh, and the tired eyes looked up—wistful, pleading, pitiful !

"I never knowed, Mammy, I never knowed," he said, and the journey begun so long ago among the Southern hills was ended.

THE END.

www.ingramcontent.com/pod-product-compliance
Lightning Source LLC
Chambersburg PA
CBHW031817270326
41932CB00008B/455
9783742892393